Active Knowledge Modeling of Enterprises

Frank Lillehagen · John Krogstie

Active Knowledge Modeling of Enterprises

 Springer

Frank Lillehagen
Active Knowledge Modeling - AKM
P.O. Box 376
1326 Lysaker
Norway
f.lillehagen@akmodeling.com

John Krogstie
NTNU
Sem Sælandsvei 7-9
7030 Trondheim
Norway
John.Krogstie@idi.ntnu.no

ISBN 978-3-642-09831-4   e-ISBN 978-3-540-79416-5

ACM Computing Classification (1998): D.2, H.4, J.1

© 2010 Springer-Verlag Berlin Heidelberg

Cover design: KünkelLopka GmbH, Heidelberg, Germany

Printed on acid-free paper

9 8 7 6 5 4 3 2 1

springer.com

Preamble

This book addresses knowledge processing, product and process design, and systems engineering challenges, and solutions by applying Active Knowledge Modeling (AKM). Examples, directions, methods, and services are given to enable new ways of working, exploiting the AKM approach to enable effective c-Business, enterprise design and development, and life-cycle management.

The purpose of the book is to make industry managers, engineers, and researchers aware of the possibilities that open up with AKM and accompanying execution platforms. Business people will better understand the new value constellations, partners delivering services to other partners, and the stronger dependencies making all actors customers and suppliers. People with different competences and skills will be able to exploit the most recent advances in IT, Knowledge and Communication technologies in industry as well as in research.

The book covers the backgrounds of Enterprise Modeling, including the initial "war-room" thinking, and introduces bounded enterprise knowledge spaces, support for multidimensional thinking and modeling, and references to mental knowledge models. New aspects, such as the importance of capturing pragmatic logic, and the need for new forms of organization are emphasized.

A brief history of modeling approaches and tools is provided including: CASE-tools, design structuring tools, process modeling tools, and diagramming tools to provide a link to existing approaches. The book looks ahead to development of Active Knowledge Architectures for effective collaboration and concurrent design, and to configuring Visual Scenes for proactive collaborative working and learning.

Early efforts in AKM was attempted already in the early 1990s – where early versions of the approach was stretched to its limits through practical applications at manufacturing companies such as Volvo, Ford, Ericsson, and McDonnell-Douglas. The book has practical references to industrial use-cases, specifically from pilots in these sectors and application areas:

- Configurable Product Platforms for Collaborative Product and Process design (CPPD) in the Automotive industry, supporting holistic design, concurrent engineering, adaptable manufacturing, and sales support of mass-customized, multibrand families of car systems

- Use-case pilots from the ATHENA and MAPPER research projects illustrating the use of a model-configured collaboration space for Engineering Change Management. Configured workplaces for product design and supplier collaboration are deployed for commercial testing.

This book is the result from the cooperation of the authors with a number of scientists and industrial practitioners over a long period of time. The core concepts of AKM, such as the knowledge spaces, were conceived at Volvo Cars around 1990, somewhat ahead of its time (and current technology). However, most of the challenges, many ideas, and needs were aggregating in Frank Lillehagen's mental models as early as 1981, when he left his position as Research Manager at the Central Institute in Oslo to join a company he cofounded three years earlier. Frank then founded METIS in 1985, and was invited as tools provider to the Volvo Interactive Graphic Car project in 1989. For many years, he was the general manager responsible for market and product strategy, and business and organizational development.

John Krogstie, with a background both from traditional modeling techniques in information systems and development of business integration solutions in industry, started working on these areas in detail when starting in SINTEF in 2000, working on applied and basic European and national research projects.

Since 2000, the two authors have worked closely together in many national and EU founded R&D projects including:

- EXTERNAL – a STREP on process support environments for dynamic networked organizations
- VOSTER – a clustering project presenting state of the art on virtual enterprises and smart organizations
- UEML – a thematic network on most aspects of enterprise modeling
- IDEAS – a road-mapping project for Enterprise Interoperability
- ATHENA – a large Integrated Project for implementing Enterprise Interoperability
- MAPPER – a STREP, focusing Model-Configured User-Composed Platforms and Services, applied to car system testing, seat-heating design, and hybrid electronics design

Although the book emphasizes certain domains through the cases that are presented, the material is of relevance for all industry sectors, companies in the ICT-sector, and for researchers and people who in the future will want to work closer together and base their working methods on work-centric and situated knowledge, exploiting the Web as a powerful knowledge-sharing medium.

How to Read the Book

The model (which is a view of a METIS model of the book) illustrates the structure of the book, and will be briefly described below (Fig. 1):

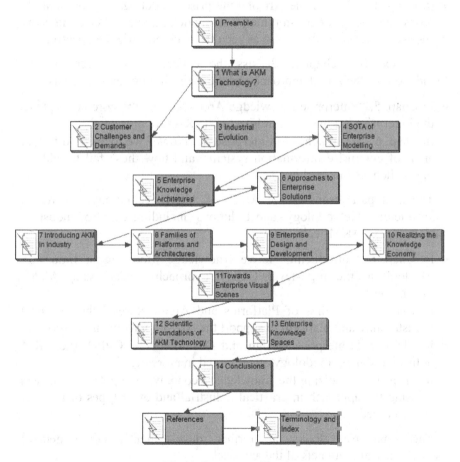

Fig. 1. Structure of book

- In Chap. 1, "What is AKM Technology?," we briefly present the main concepts and approaches of AKM. One of the main case studies that act as an appetizer and motivator for the rest of the book is presented.

The next three chapters describe challenges in industrial computing and past and present approaches to address these. Those who are highly familiar with these areas may want to skip this part.

- In Chap. 2, "Customer Challenges and Demands," we summarize industrial challenges that so far has poor or no IT support.
- In Chap. 3, "Industrial Evolution," we discuss early approaches to AKM that were only partly successful due to limitations in approach and technology at the time.
- In Chap. 4, "State of the Art of Enterprise Modeling," we particularly focus on state of the art in (enterprise) modeling, and indicate the many short-comings that still persist as seen from an industrial perspective.

The next two chapters discuss the conceptual and technological foundations of the AKM approach and the main findings and concepts.

- In Chap. 5, "Enterprise Knowledge Architecture," the core concepts of the Enterprise Knowledge Architecture (EKA) are presented.
- In Chap. 6, "Approaches to Enterprise Solutions," we focus on different areas of enterprise information systems, and how these fail to address the challenges outlined in Chap. 2.

The next part discusses the AIMS of AKM Technology: Approach, Infrastructure, Methodology, and Solutions, including cases of industrial applications of AKM-technology.

- In Chap. 7, "Introducing Active Knowledge Modeling in Industry," we look at the high-level C3S3P approach for applying AKM-Technology.
- In Chap. 8, "Families of Platforms and Architectures," the technical infrastructure and platform to support the AKM-approach are described.
- In Chap. 9, "Enterprise Design and Development," CPPD, the AKM holistic design methodology, is presented in more detail.
- In Chap. 10, "Realizing the Knowledge Economy," the potential impacts of using the approach in practical industrial and other types of projects are discussed.

The final part looks at further developments, complimentary technologies, and impacts of the approach.

- In Chap. 11, "Towards Enterprise Visual Scenes," we discuss how the AKM-approach compliments new computing technologies. In addition to more traditional interfaces, we look at the merger of industrial computing and computer-game technology as found e.g., in Second Life to provide richer model visualization.

- In Chap. 12, "Scientific Foundations of the AKM Technology," scientific foundations are presented, referencing organizational development, psychology, pedagogy, systems engineering, design theory, process engineering, and knowledge management.
- In Chap. 13, "Enterprise Knowledge Spaces," the main categories of enterprise knowledge spaces are presented.
- In Chap. 14, "Conclusion and Outlook," we summarize the contributions of the AKM approach, pointing to future directions and opportunities.

The book also contains references, an overview of the main terminology, and an index.

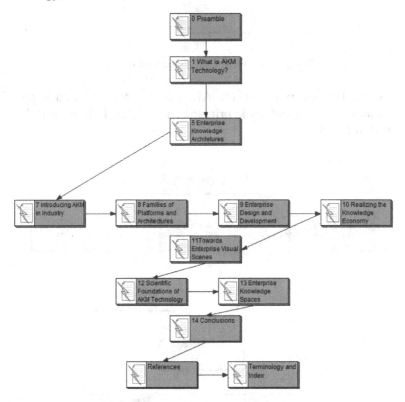

Fig. 2. Possible reading order for those familiar with enterprise systems and modeling

If you are familiar with enterprise modeling, enterprise IT approaches and solutions and current industrial challenges, but not with AKM, you may skip Chaps. 2–4 and 6, as illustrated in Fig. 2.

If you are somewhat familiar with AKM and would like to focus only on the essential contributions, you should focus on Chaps. 7–10 and 14 as illustrated in Fig. 3.

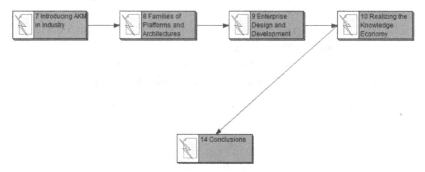

Fig. 3. Core AKM contribution chapters

If you want an overview, where AKM is one Model-based approach among many, you should look primarily in Chaps. 1–4, 6, and 14 as illustrated in Fig. 4.

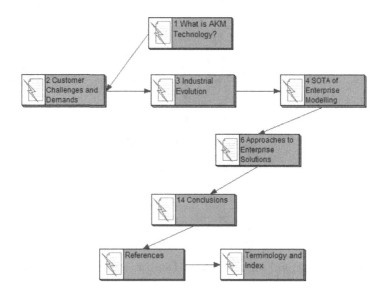

Fig. 4. Overview of enterprise systems and enterprise modeling

Acknowledgments

The AKM technology, its concepts and methods, is the result of a lot of work performed over a number of years in a number of different projects and initiatives. The authors have worked closely with and carry on working with a number of very knowledgeable people, many of whom have also provided feedback to the different parts of the book.

Frank would like to pay tribute to his Autokon ship design team-mates, possibly developing the first parameterized product-structure model ever, his computer graphics pioneers from the Utah vintage years, his many friends and contacts Scandinavian and US industry from the METIS golden years, 1989–1994, including leading scientists and industrial practitioners, and finally his hundreds of friends and foes in international R&D.

We would like to extend special thanks to Frank's AKM cofounders CKO Dag R. Karlsen and CTO Håvard D. Jørgensen. Without their contributions this book would not have contained its use-case and AKM illustrations. Chapters 5, 9, and 13, in particular, are based on methodology handbooks coauthored by the AKM team, where Jørgensen and Karlsen were the prime authors.

In connection to the work leading up to and the preparation of the manuscript, we acknowledge the contributions of Sobah Abbas Petersen, Steinar Carlsen, Helge Grenaker Solheim, Arne Sølvberg, Guttorm Sindre, Csaba Veres, Brian Elvesæter, Arne Jørgen Berre, Oddrun Ohren, Svein Johnsen, Heidi Brovold, Vibeke Dalberg, Siri Moe Jensen, Per Høgberg, Lennart Holmberg, Jan Goosenaerts, Kurt Sandkuhl, Jörg Haake, Adam Pawlak, Thomas Knothe, Kai Mertens, Andreas Opdahl, Birgit Krogstie, Kurt Kosanke, Martin Zelm, Francois Vernadat, Jack Ring, James N. Martin, Christine Legner, Baptiste Lebreton, Hans Johanneson, Christopher Dean, and numerous others.

So, to all of you new readers and followers, we look forward to getting to know you! Remember the advert saying: "You are what you eat!" Well we think: "You are who you meet!" is much closer to the truth!

Thank you all!

Table of Contents

1 What is Active Knowledge Modeling Technology?

Many scientists argue that the main reason why humans have excelled as species is our ability to represent, reuse, and transfer knowledge across time and space. On the basis of mental models, we grow our knowledge and wisdom through experiences and participative learning. Although in most areas of human conduct, primarily standard one-dimensional natural languages are used to express and share knowledge, we see the need for and use of two- and many-dimensional representational forms to be on the rise. One such technique is traditionally termed *enterprise modeling*.

Visual modeling is nowadays used for many purposes in most industrial sectors and application areas. For instance, the automotive industry has used visual process and product modelling since the late 1990s. In 2006 automotive industry started developing visual knowledge models to build configurable product platforms, aiming to realize integrated life-cycle operations. In new approaches to holistic design, product family design, systems engineering (SE), and IT the trend is towards model-based IT solutions using visual languages such as UML, BPMN, and IRTV.

Industry still lack adequate IT support for the early project phases, such as IT support for effective holistic design, involving capabilities for iterations, knowledge sharing, proactive team-learning, visual collaboration, and traceability. The trend is towards configurable product platforms for more effective innovation, for product variants supporting customized product design and manufacture. However, in 2008 idea generation, initial studies and analyses, and conceptual design are still manual work, and documented using tools such as Word, Excel, and PowerPoint. The tasks performed, the data defined, and the issues swirling in designers' minds are lost. This knowledge is part of the logic expressing the design intent, design rationale, and the core product concepts. There will never be support in IT application systems for growing and sharing design data in role-specific reflective views of emerging product structures and process task-patterns. Designers and engineers must be able to take ownership of their data and knowledge by defining data, by giving meaning through reflective views, determining value ranges, and customer-specific values. To perform these tasks, designers and engineers must have access to workplaces and services that evolve with the knowledge created and aggregated. This implies that data and knowledge have to be stored in and reactivated from what we call an *Active Knowledge Architecture (AKA)*. Active implies that its contents of roles, task patterns, information structures, and reflective views will automatically configure the workplaces. Work-centric data created by execution on the workplaces are directly folded back into the architecture, thus closing the learning loop. This behavior is instrumental to collaborative design and engineering.

The AKM company cooperates with industry projects to develop their AKAs and configured workplaces for effectively sharing and refining knowledge, and for defining new design project roles, properties, tasks, and views. Collaboration, concurrent design, and proactive learning are supported by the AKA with services to build knowledge structures, capture contents, build workplaces, and contextualize and configure workplace views. Applying AKM methodologies, industry has started developing new approaches and methods to concurrently design products, work processes, systems, and smart service-team organizations. This is the AKM meaning of holistic design.

The industrial community has not been offered much new in terms of systems engineering approaches, work methodologies, and IT solutions over the last 20 years. The few exceptions that spring to mind are enterprise modeling, industrial information portals, and more recently Web services and service-oriented architecture. This has left industry with a long list of unsolved needs and problems. The situation was analyzed and described in the IDEAS EU project, and elaborated in the ATHENA integrated project (ATHENA 2007). The needs and challenges of these projects are synthesized and described as follows:

1. Aligning business, ICT, and knowledge management
2. Reducing costs for application portfolio management and integration
3. Achieving more effective solutions development, delivery, deploy-ment, and integration
4. Achieving predictability, accountability, interoperability, adaptability, and trust in networked organizations
5. Achieving ease of reengineering, reuse, and management of solutions
6. Supporting concurrency, context-sensitivity, and multiple simultane-ous projects and business processes

7. Supporting multidimensional, collaborative product design and life-cycle innovation and knowledge capture
8. Providing self-organizing, self-managing, and regenerating solutions
9. Semiautomating information and knowledge reuse and management
10. Supporting learning-by-doing, enabling users to acquire and activate new knowledge as work is performed
11. Achieving independence of system and IT experts
12. Designing personal workplaces and harmonizing work environments

Industrial needs and challenges are further discussed in Chap. 2. AKM is developing methodologies and Web platforms to offer solutions to most of these challenges. Dynamic, continuously improving, industrial computing solutions are required to meet the requirements and on-demand business opportunities of the new global networked economy. The customer solutions must be more effective and user-manageable, and must offer capabilities not achievable by current IT systems. A holistic approach is required, involving most key roles of innovation, capturing dependencies and changes in the many enterprise knowledge dimensions. This means developing and aligning the mental models of people involved, and taking multidimensional knowledge spaces and aspects into account. Building a project-specific AKA would allow early prototyping of workplaces, thus involving key users in creating their own work processes, emphasizing collaboration and cooperation.

Enterprise Modeling (EM) grew out of modeling techniques motivated by more effective IT engineering and use. The four IT-inspired modeling origins were the initiatives for CASE tools, modeling processes, product structures, and information structures. Enterprise modeling has been defined as the art of externalizing enterprise knowledge, i.e., representing the core knowledge of the enterprise (Vernadat 1996). Although useful in product design and systems development, for modeling and model-based approaches to have a more profound effect, we propose a shift in modeling approaches and methodologies. Model-based approaches and methods must enable *regular industrial users to be active modelers*, both when performing their work, expressing and sharing their results and values created, and when adapting and composing the services they are using to support their work. Modeling should become as natural as drawing, sketching, and scribbling, and should provide powerful services to capture work-centric, work-supporting, and generative knowledge, for preserving context and ensuring reuse. A solution is the application of what we term active knowledge modeling (AKM). Although AKM has potentially value and usage across a large range of knowledge creation and knowledge representation tasks, our focus is the use of these techniques in providing IT support for performing creative and innovative work.

New SE approaches and IT solutions based on AKAs will emerge, offering capabilities that will reduce lead-times and budgets for developing, deploying, operating, and managing field extendable solutions by units of time and cost.

1.1 Definition of Active Knowledge Modeling

The AKM technology (Lillehagen 2003) is about discovering, externalizing, expressing, representing, sharing, exploring, configuring, activating, growing, and managing enterprise knowledge. An AKM solution is about exploiting the Web as a knowledge-engineering medium, developing knowledge-model-based families of platforms, model-configured workplaces and services. Working in these environments means augmenting the mental models of the human mind.

Coherent and consistent knowledge elements, created by the different kinds of models built, are structured and managed in one or more *AKAs*. Active knowledge architectures will enable the capabilities of what earlier research on "Corporate Memory" failed to achieve and much more. Situated knowledge cannot be managed by traditional software tools on top of a static data model alone.

The AKM approach and integrated methodologies, captured in the AKA, will allow humans to exploit more than the 7% of the capacity of the left hemisphere of the brain, and to express and share internal knowledge resulting from performing work and actions. Most work-centric knowledge would otherwise remain tacit. So AKM enables us to capture, share, and benefit from situated, work-generative knowledge that otherwise would remain tacit in the minds of those involved. Team collaboration in visual scenes amplifies individual knowledge capture and learning.

Active and work-centric knowledge has some very important intrinsic properties found in the mental models of the human mind, such as reflective views, recursive tasks, repetitive roles, and replicable knowledge architecture elements. The best way to benefit from these intrinsic properties is by enabling users to perform knowledge modeling using the AKM platform services to model methods, and execute work using role-specific, model-configured workplaces. So AKM must become as easy as scribbling for designers and engineers in order for them to express their knowledge while performing work, learning, and excelling in their roles. This will also enable users to capture contextual dependencies between roles, tasks, information elements, and the views required for performing work. So modeling roles and tasks in sufficient detail and granularity, as discovered by the CIMOSA project (Vernadat 1998), are crucial for preserving context and the meaning of data for various roles.

The multidimensional evolution from ideas to design concepts and to engineered products and systems must be captured to facilitate iterations and model-driven workplace updating. Designers designing on a model-configured workplace will simultaneously create their product concepts, the languages to express the concepts, and the tasks and views to enhance their workplaces. Each time a designer or an engineer performs a project service a cascaded task structure may be triggered to automatically execute more background routine services, such as change notification.

The AKM technology reforms and extends the roles for enterprise modeling to address important issues, which are as follows:

- Modeling specific roles, tasks, information, and views to capture context, and to configure and generate role-specific workplaces
- Modeling products, organizational resources, processes, and systems to support core industrial design and engineering knowledge
- Modeling properties and parameter trees and their values and value ranges as separate structures, independent of objects
- Managing corporate modeling elements and workplace contents in an AKA
- Managing contextual descriptions of work, and workplace configurations to support extensive reuse of knowledge and data
- Enabling industrial users to build and manage their own working environments, workplaces, and services
- Enabling life-cycle data and knowledge management, capturing and sharing experiences, unresolved issues, and lessons learned
- Expressing knowledge readily reflected as updated menus and views in model-configured workplaces
- Building knowledge models and architectures of methodologies, information libraries, and reference models, currently available only on paper
- Building collaboration spaces and visual scenes for design, engineering, work process experimentation, validation, and proactive learning

To be an *active model*, a visual model must first and foremost be available to the users of the operational information system at execution time. Second, the model must automatically influence the behavior of the computerized work support system or workplace. Third, the model must be dynamically extended and adapted; users must be supported in changing the model to fit their local needs, enabling tailoring of the work environment's behavior. Industrial users should therefore be able to manipulate and use active knowledge models as part of their day-to-day work (Jørgensen 2001, 2004).

Recent platform developments (AKModeling 2007; Intalio 2007) support integrated modeling and execution in one common platform, enabling what in cognitive psychology is denoted as "closing the learning cycle." This implies that knowledge modeling, expressing, and architecting work-centric knowledge will be performed by users executing workplace services and thus allowing the following:

- Discovery of the powers of visual models, visualizing data, and information (e.g., application demands for operative architectures, visible inventory, and visible project management)
- Models to contain actual project knowledge, situated knowledge, and work-generative data, avoiding redundant models
- Viewing of critical data at runtime for monitoring processes and collaborative work, satisfying the cry for so-called dashboards in IT Governance and Collaborative Supplier Management
- The demand from some markets for active or living pragmatic knowledge capture, being able to collaborate on performing complex tasks, and supporting the fulfillment of 4 of the 12 I's – involvement, interaction, integration, and interoperability

Active knowledge modeling is capturing knowledge involved in building workplaces, in supporting work execution, and knowledge generated by work execution. There are many definitions of knowledge, as we will discuss in Chap. 12, dependent on the roles expressing the knowledge and their proximity to the action or the work performed. AKM can accommodate all of them, but the focus is on capturing work-generative and work-supportive data and knowledge, tacit knowledge, and closing the value-cycle integrating the reflective views of these knowledge aspects.

Introducing AKM to support product, process, and system design and development will enable new approaches and ways of working that will have a huge impact on industrial use of IT, on SE, and on many other technologies and sciences.

1.2 State-of-the-art Overview

It is possible to track modeling back to the late 1950s, with the work of Young and Kent (1958). Modeling approaches as we know them today within the information system field were introduced in large scale in connection, around 30 years ago, with developments of such techniques as DFDs (Demarco 1979) and ER diagrams (Chen 1976). In the beginning, focus was on developing conceptual modeling languages that would highlight the important concepts of the world, typically containing a few general concepts, depicted with simple and abstract visual icons. The languages were developed for IT experts to do the model building as a consultancy service, although intended to be used as a communication artifact towards different types of "domain experts." In the 1980s, there were a large number of proposals for the ideal modeling notation. The understanding that language appropriateness depends on the situation and the objectives of modeling grew in the late 1980s. To address this situation, metamodeling approaches started to appear around 1990 (Kelly et al. 1996), making it possible for projects and organizations to extend existing modeling languages and notations, or creating entirely new modeling languages from scratch. Still the main users of these techniques are intermediaries (e.g., analysts, designers), and the models built are meant to document the knowledge as held by different stakeholders for further use, rather than for workers themselves to use as services for knowledge representation, creation, and reuse tailored for their own needs.

Whereas the first modeling approaches were focused on software development, the area of enterprise modeling provided in the 1980s similar techniques to a wider organizational scope than IT systems. On the other hand, after 15 years of industrial enterprise modeling, visual models are still primarily consultancy tools for providing help in understanding and resolving complexity. State-of-practice in EM has progressed furthest in certain manufacturing industries, and in particular, with respect to these four areas:

- Enterprise Architecture (Vernadat 1996) is currently the most vivid and fastest growing market particularly in the USA.
- Business Process Modeling (Havey 2005) looked like a fast-growing market already around 1998, but new requirements for Web-service security and safety have slowed it down. As for Business Process Management, the area appears to be on the rise.
- Business Intelligence or Enterprise Performance Analyses is another promising market that is as yet to really take off.

- Model-based Systems Engineering (Stahl and Völter 2006) is rapidly gaining momentum, but industrial large-scale references are still scarce.

We believe that the major reasons for this slow acceptance and modest market penetration are mainly the fact that EM is still a tool-based effort for experts, lacking scientifically and practically founded methodologies, and dynamic visual languages and services to support pragmatic industrial work. In summary, the characteristics of the EM languages, approaches, and usage of models by industry are as follows:

- Enterprise knowledge can only be represented in predefined, vendor proprietary or prematurely standardized modeling languages.
- The modeling approach, roles to engage, tasks to support, and views to create are predetermined and cannot be adapted to the case in hand.
- Modeling is not an integral part of engineering or product development, but performed in isolation by specialists.
- The user interface is static and systems-engineer-oriented, and supports just one style of modeling.
- There is limited support for knowledge externalization, sharing, reuse, and management.
- Most models are collections of static views and diagrams and give no support for adaptation and extension of metamodels.
- Models and modeling environments are detached from solution execution platforms.
- The leading concepts for modeling languages, view management, and parameter definition are restricted to object-oriented thinking.

A comprehensive source on EM can be found in the ATHENA project (ATHENA 2007), and we will go into some more detail on some of these approaches in Chap. 4. It is fair to state that so far EM is just another technology island in the noninteroperable industrial tools and systems landscape. Current standardization activities have little effect on industry. Although many such activities are going on, present standards (e.g., ENV 12204 or DIS 19439) are rarely used within industry. Now, this situation is about to change. The goal of AKM technology is to make explicit and exploit knowledge that add value to the enterprise and can be shared by business services and users for improving the agility and performance of the enterprise, and for getting much more value from IT and Web technologies.

1.3 Discoveries and Core Concepts

The ten founding discoveries of the AKM technology date back to 1990, when a team, headed by Frank Lillehagen, was engaged in innovative car projects with Volvo Cars, Gothenburg. These discoveries made in the early 1990s are in current language described as follows:

1. Enterprise knowledge exists in *nested multidimensional bounded spaces*, and in delimited layers and domains.
2. The spaces and dimensions involved in enterprising and product design are neither linear nor orthogonal; they reflect *human mental models with perspective views.*
3. Most enterprise *aspects and views are mutually inclusive* – as a consequence of the nested knowledge spaces, ref., the war-room thinking (Zakis 2007).
4. The world is *both perspective view (method) and object-oriented* – we need to integrate mental and object-oriented computer models and views, producing work-sensitive models.
5. *Mental models in the human brain*, with perspective and computed views, content and context contributed by specific roles, are poorly understood and currently not exploited by IT people.
6. Existing models are based on and bounded by diagrams, charts, and mathematical formalisms; there is no capture of situated knowledge, exploiting the intrinsic knowledge properties.
7. Process- and work-flow, and time-dimension phase dependencies must be relaxed or expanded, and minimized by providing intelligent working environments.
8. Present SE approaches will never adequately handle properties, parameter trees, and multiple value sets.
9. Learning, design, and problem-solving are intimately related, use similar methods, and have similar service and viewing needs.
10. Deployed legacy systems are a challenge, but small compared to the prevailing *legacy thinking.* Vaults of information documents describing design rules, materials, reference models, and more should become sharable active knowledge.

The discoveries imply that knowledge exists both as object-oriented IT structures and as perspective method-oriented structures, such as the life-cycle view, where different roles perform tasks to add methods, content, and context in some common views as well as in role-specific views.

These discoveries would not have been possible without the intimate cooperation of industrial practitioners, engineers, and IT experts. The sources and foundations of these discoveries are further described in Chap. 12, and their future outlook as collaborative visual scenes are discussed in Chap. 11.

1.4 State-of-Practice – An Example

The first industrial piloting of visual model-configured workplace solutions were started at Kongsberg Automotive in the Autumn of 2006 as one of three industrial scenarios of the EU project MAPPER, IST 015 627. The objectives at Kongsberg are improved seat heating design, better product quality, less data errors, and improved ways of working. Better work processes for interpreting and fulfilling customer requirements and producing supplier specifications will be developed. The needs of Kongsberg are similar to the needs expressed by companies in other industrial sectors, such as aerospace, construction, and energy systems.

Short-term Kongsberg's needs and goals are as follows:

- Capturing and correctly interpreting customer requirements
- Creating role-specific, simple to use and reconfigurable workplaces
- Creating effective workplace views and services for data handling
- Improving the quality of specifications for customers and suppliers
- Improving communications and coordination among stakeholders
- Finding a sound methodology for product parameterization, automating most of the tasks for product model customized engineering

To fulfill these goals, they are applying the AKM approach, adapting several methodologies and building knowledge-model-based workplaces.

With time, Kongsberg Automotive has focused more on developing an AKA supporting parameterized seat heat product family design. So far, five workplaces have been model-designed, -configured, and -generated:

- The material specification workplace, as illustrated in Fig. 1.1. It shows the workplace for the designer responsible for material specification entering the parameters in the model-generated environment. This case will be further explained at the end of Chap. 9.
- The customer product specification workplace.
- The customer solution configuration workplace.
- Two workplaces for designing configurable product components (See Fig. 1.2).

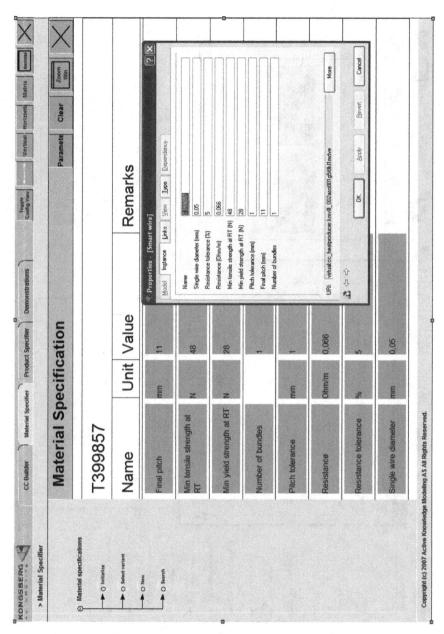

Fig. 1.1. Model-configured workplaces for material specification of heating wire

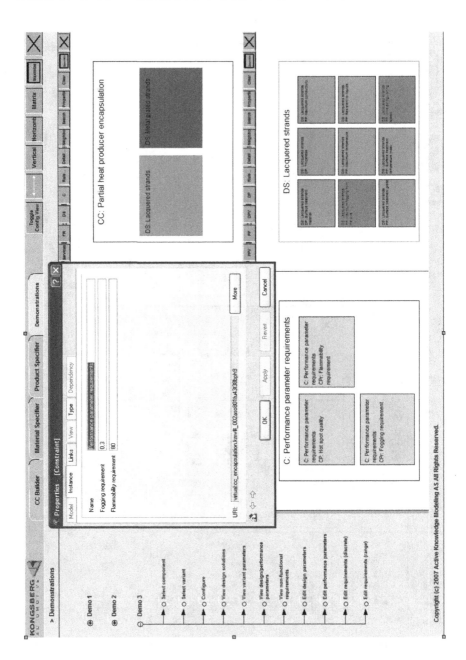

Fig. 1.2. The seat heating design workplace for configurable components

Each workplace is built by configuring knowledge architecture elements captured in three or more different kinds of knowledge models. The different kinds of models used to design and model-configure and model-generate workplaces are explained in Chap. 6 on new approaches to industrial solutions.

The dynamic evolution and adaptation of work-generative content and context, the workplace composition, and the user preferences are impossible to support by programming and compiling the logic. This is simply because any extension or adaptation of contents in one solution model and its views need to be reflected in other models and views that will be used to model-configure other workplaces. The tasks to be executed are totally dependent on the context created by interrelating workplace contents and configuration models. Experiences verify that product and material requirements handling and supplier specifications of the Kongsberg seat comfort product line have been improved in data quality and reliability.

The materials specification workplace is accepted by the users, but will get additional services to manage and communicate design issues among customers and suppliers. The customer product specifications workplace will be further developed and related to three or more role-specific workplaces for product design: the product family responsible, the customer product configuration responsible, and the product portfolio responsible.

In the customer product specifications workplace colors are used to indicate the degree of requirements satisfaction, parameter consistency, and the solution fit to meet the requirements. The more role-specific the workplaces, their tasks, views, and data are modeled, the bigger the potential to further exploit the resulting knowledge architecture elements, and reuse the reflective views and task structures.

The Kongsberg seat heat solution is modeled by a team composed of Kongsberg product designers and engineers, and AKM knowledge architects and model and workplace builders, concurrently developing and adapting the many kinds of models required for the workplace solutions. The first version of the AKM platform and the first prototype components of the collaborative product and process design (CPPD) methodology are developed in this use-case. This produces some extra challenges for the model building team. The CPPD methodology provides the methods, metadata, and services to enhance the AKM platform with configurable components for building customer product architectures.

1.5 The AKM Products

The people behind the AKM company (AKM AS 2007), founded in September 2006, started developing the AKM technology and products as far back as 1998 with the definition of a series of EU-financed projects. AKM has defined four main product lines:

- The AKM Approach providing delivery services to customers
- The core AKM Platform tools, workplaces, and services (described in more detail in Chap. 8)
- The visual solutions development methodology using the C3S3P steps (described in more detail in Chap. 7)
- The CPPD methodology (described in more detail in Chap. 9)

The approach has been refined many times over the last years, and the customer delivery of role-specific workplaces, work processes, services, and views are starting to solidify. The delivery process roles and workplaces development will accelerate with more challenging customer projects. The AKM Platform has proven its capabilities, and will, guided by industrial project experiences, be extended with the necessary systems integration capabilities. The CPPD methodology, targeting the design of product design platforms, collaborative engineering, and systems integration, consists of 12 or more components. Some of the components need more industrial project development and validation, but the configurable product component, the configurable workplace, and four more components have been through solid development and testing in three industrial projects addressing different products and sectors.

1.6 Enterprise Knowledge Spaces

The first enterprise knowledge space, defined by the product, organization, process, and Systems (POPS) dimensions, was discovered as early as 1992. Its integrating capabilities were confirmed in EU projects during the late 1990s, and a uniform modeling language was developed in the ATHENA project in 2005 (Ziemann et al. 2006). A major contribution to the discovery was work performed in the automotive industry on war-room or multidimensional thinking and Doug Engelbart's bootstrap approach. The existence of the other knowledge spaces of enterprises matured from 1998 to 2003, but the exploitation has not been possible until recently because of lack of expressiveness and dynamic extensibility of visual modeling languages by supportive AKAs, tools, and services. The last piece to fall into place was the understanding of how fundamental the personal and role-specific knowledge spaces and workplaces are in being able to execute work, capture context, and access and maintain knowledge architecture content. This understanding has enabled the implementation and operation of Active Knowledge Architectures (AKA)™, enabling industrial users to define and manage their own detailed knowledge elements, local data, views, and model-configured services.

The four categories of generic work-sensitive knowledge spaces we have discovered and modeled are defined and identified by simple names on the four key knowledge dimensions defining each space:

1. The role-specific knowledge space, defined by information, role, task, and view, abbreviated and referenced as IRTV
2. The innovation space, defined by product, organization, process, and system, and abbreviated and referenced as POPS
3. The business space, defined by services, networking assets, projects, and platforms, and abbreviated and referenced as SNPP
4. The community space, defined by values, resources, initiatives, and infrastructures, and abbreviated and referenced as VRII.

These knowledge spaces exist in all enterprises from two people collaborating to global value-chains. The spaces are bounded by identifiable, but fuzzy borders. Now, whether the borders are a result of pragmatic boundaries, such as gateways between project phases and the isolated roles of engineering disciplines, and so forth, or whether they are caused by limitations inherent in the mental models of our brains remains a research issue. Enterprise knowledge spaces are further discussed in Chap. 13.

As we started discovering in 1991 at Volvo, object-oriented thinking is powerful once you have designed an artifact, but it does not provide direct support for design and creative work as object classes represent rule-constrained knowledge.

Product and system design starts with defining conceptual artifacts, concepts of objects, properties and task structures, with no predefined types or flows, and then the concepts undergo functional system design with capabilities to define parameters and rules for embedding properties as parameter trees. One may say that the IT world we have designed and manufactured so far is object-oriented, but what we need to deliver in the future must combine the best of object-oriented and mental-model knowledge representation principles.

1.7 Active Knowledge Architectures

An AKA is a project- or sector-specific "knowledge landscape," built using sector- and project-specific IRTV languages to capture contents from the customer, such as innovative and project knowledge spaces, creating the POPS, SNPP, and VRII languages, for including other customer knowledge dimensions and aspects. The purpose of any AKA is to give product designers, engineers, architects, and other stakeholders involved common languages and workplace contents for building interoperable, collaborative, and reusable customer platforms, enabling reconfigurable workplaces, collaboration spaces, services, and knowledge elements. AKA structures and contents are built and maintained by customer engineers, working in project teams with partners and suppliers. The resulting AKA will therefore have reflective knowledge layers supporting the various enterprise teams.

Building an AKA starts by modeling a customer scenario using what AKM calls the Enterprise Knowledge Architecture (EKA) as a model template. The EKA is a generic knowledge model, able to represent any AKA content as information, roles, tasks, and views (reflecting the IRTV language). This methodology should not to be confused with the goal-information-task approach of the International Society for Performance Improvement. Roles can range from task and work process roles, to personal, team roles, and roles for entire enterprises. The purpose of the EKA is to give knowledge model designers and engineers a common language for building interoperable, collaborative, and agile active knowledge models and architectures, supporting community-wide reusable, reconfigurable knowledge elements.

The EKA is the most abstract and general enterprise model of the entire family of enterprise models, acting as a family reference model for all other kinds and variants of enterprise models. An AKA, built using the EKA template, integrates all other enterprise architectures, such as product architectures and system architectures. An enterprise-specific AKA will support simultaneous modeling, metamodeling, model management, and work execution, using model-configured and -generated workplaces (MGWP; see Sect. 1.7.2). Relationships between AKA, EKA, and ICT infrastructure are depicted in Fig. 1.3.

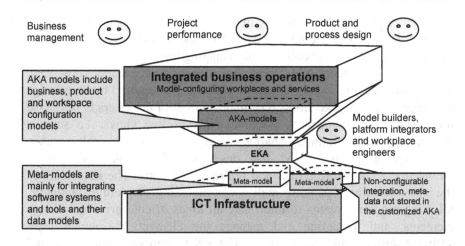

Fig. 1.3. Active Knowledge Architectures integrate enterprises

Intelligence is normally attributed to the associative and creative capacities and capabilities of the human brain, and just as knowledge is externalized and represented in the AKA, so is intelligence. In this context we define intelligence as *"the ability to interactively reuse knowledge to perform actions, and to automatically update knowledge elements and structures when performing actions."* Knowledge elements, structures, and views are adapted, extended, coordinated, and managed by role-specific services, which for quality assurance, should be implemented as recursive and repeatable work processes (what we term task patterns). The task trees, supporting these work processes, are themselves part of the AKA. Any task can be model-configured, invoked, and executed as need arises, supporting unpredictable situations. Execution of most tasks may vary between automatic and highly interactive depending on the context. This means that self-adaptive, self-organizing solutions are possible, whenever situated knowledge models are built, workplaces are model-updated and activated.

1.7.1 How to Represent Enterprise Knowledge

AKAs are sets of role-, task-, and information-specific, interdependent structures of views, both computer- and mentally captured and managed. AKM therefore has a new definition of knowledge: *Knowledge is a continuous flux of reflective views between human minds and external media.* To possess knowledge you must therefore acquire three or more views of any artifact or scene of action. Consequently, knowledge management is best performed by making sure that adequate role-specific views are created and configured, and by associating the views to the task-patterns defining, updating, and managing them.

The AKA contents may come from many sources and knowledge spaces, dimensions, and domains externalized and captured by knowledge modeling and work execution. The main source for designers is of course their own mental model of associative perspective views. To support designing, externalizing, sharing, and representing role-specific knowledge elements, AKM has developed the EKA, the generic knowledge architecture model and reference template. The EKA defines the most abstract, general and accommodating modeling language, allowing modeling teams to interrelate all kinds of enterprise knowledge elements, and to define and manage the elements decoupled from software systems and components. The EKA supports adaptable visual languages by interrelating similar knowledge elements without having to classify them, and automatically yields interoperable AKAs.

The approach to building and representing an AKA involves modeling these knowledge models and storing their elements.

- Use-case scenarios, focused on role- and task-specific data and views
- Integrated and use-case adapted methodologies
- Platform integration, and workplace configuration models
- Workplace set-up and behavior rules

Building and storing these models and their elements transform the EKA or any existing AKA to an operational scenario-specific AKA.

These EKAs are vital for the formation, integration, and operation of intelligent enterprises and smart organizations, and should be visually editable and manageable in a Web environment to harvest the full benefits of visual knowledge architectures. The AKA should also offer metamodeling capabilities to function as an industrial system engineering platform, providing an environment to integrate and perform IT applications and Web services. Application services are work processes, single or cascaded tasks, configured and stored in the AKA for reactivation and repetitive execution. The services that will be provided in workplaces, supported by the AKA, are services to build knowledge models and collaboration spaces, to configure workplaces, to monitor project execution, to do work management, and finally to perform work. Persistent storage of the AKA can be partially hidden from users, by implementing task patterns to automate the communication between the Web-based AKA and any knowledge repository.

Most existing architecture modeling frameworks such as (Zachman 2007), CIMOSA (Vernadat 1998), TOGAF (Open Group 2000), and GERAM (1999) represent useful methodology views, but all of them are lacking in granularity, in reflective views and metaviews, in support for metamodeling languages, and in model activation and management structures. These are crucial knowledge constructs and structures for enterprise integration at all layers, and for linking to execution engines.

No other known technology is aware of the key intrinsic properties of situated knowledge, the nested knowledge spaces, and the integrating properties of a logically consistent, dynamically coherent AKA layer. All AKAs are created from a generic EKA template. The EKA is the base for interoperable families of AKAs. The AKA must be designed for each enterprise, but the design is based on extensive reuse of constructs and structures across sectors and projects, and on reactivation of generic tasks as design services.

1.7.2 Model-Generated Workplaces (MGWP)

A model-generated workplace is a working environment for the business users involved in running the business operations of the enterprise. It is a model-generated user platform that provides the graphical front-end for human users to interact with services, views, data, and knowledge elements, supporting their day-to-day business activities. At Kongsberg Automotive Mullsjø Works three models are concurrently developed and adapted to ensure knowledge and workplace consistency:

- The model of the seat heat design roles, and the information, tasks, and views that Kongsberg designers, assisted by AKM expert model builders, have built to capture future innovative seat heat principles, ideas, and any product family evolution
- The configuration model of each role-specific workplace, capturing its tasks, views, and information elements and data
- The solution and workplace builder workplace model allowing the AKM workplace developer to add new capabilities and contents to the knowledge architecture and the generated workplaces

A workplace can be tailored to meet the specific requirements of different roles or persons within an enterprise, providing customized presentation and operation views. This is achieved through Model-configured and User-comPoSable services (MUPS). These services make use of knowledge models to generate business-oriented and context-aware graphical user interfaces.

Figures 1.1 and 1.2, from the Kongsberg seat heat use-case, depict practical examples of model-generated workplaces. The figures illustrate that persons filling the same general roles, accessing the same IT services and knowledge assets, actually may still prefer and use different views. For project monitoring some people would use Gantt-charts while others might prefer role swim-lanes with assigned tasks. For activity reporting, bar graphs visualizing budget spending, and Web documents reporting on activities are views supporting important methods even though inherited from the paper world. The different views may reflect the same knowledge asset in a different form or manner that best suits the role or person using that asset in a given context. Information represented in the different views is based on contents of the same AKA and models and therefore ensure information consistency. Many MGWPs are implemented on Web portals for security mostly. MUPS services specify and generate the Web elements in the portals.

1.7.3 Model-Based Holistic Design

Design theories and practices exist in abundance, but common to them all is that they are based on distinctly defined project-phased structures and lack layers of abstraction and generalization of common product artifacts. Few industries have common conceptual views or an architecture of their products, and no common integrated product description exists. Product design and engineering disciplines have, since the industrial revolution, developed phased and discipline-oriented product structures, or rather isolated product structure views. This has resulted in many noncohesive and disjoint product structures with predefined object types, parameter sets and values, and phased sequential information flows. Actually, studying most available sources on design theory, you are made to believe that this is pragmatic reality. These disjoint, delimited, product structures are the cause of many of the industrial challenges we will discuss in Chap. 2. To more effectively support design, AKM provides visual language definition services to enable industrial designers to dynamically define evolving product artifacts, combining object instances, properties, and task patterns by capturing the designer actions as an integrating task pattern.

The fact that industry can now develop languages and methods to express conceptual artifacts, capture innovative situated knowledge, and integrate the disjoint product structures into coherent product family model representations will open up for product mass-customization. Integrated product architectures are key structures and contents of the

AKA, capturing new aspects of design, such as experience aggregation. This will support collaborative design, concurrent engineering, and global teambuilding, which is what we call holistic design. It promises to revolutionize industrial product design, engineering, and manufacturing, including SE.

1.7.4 Model-Based Systems Engineering

Systems engineering has not seen much new since the introduction of databases and database schema design using ER techniques and more recently object-oriented modeling methods. Systems Engineering as practiced in many communities is still based on monolithic, strictly sequential, single role and single view waterfall processes. Although new methods, such as agile modeling (Ambler 2002), are trying to attack this differently, the majority of agile approaches are still code-oriented, not AKM-oriented. This is very different from the current industrial approaches to product design, but as stated, product design also has big needs for improvements in how to express and represent product knowledge. The two disciplines could actually both do with a new holistic and common model-based approach and model-designed, integrated methodologies.

Industrial conceptual design is for a large part data-modeling. Design data and the context giving meaning to data and values are captured in the AKA. The database schema could therefore be automatically derived from role-specific elements and data in the AKA. The database schema is today defined by IT people to precisely accommodate and identify data, but could be generalized to accommodate all data definitions and contexts as captured in the AKA. No matter what IT systems offer in terms of services, the layers of compiled code on top of the data-model have made them inaccessible and nonmanageable by industrial users.

1.8 The Core Modeling Languages

In connection to the ATHENA project (Ziemann et al. 2006), we have, based on the innovation space – POPS, developed a first version of a unified enterprise modeling language to enable the exchange of enterprise models independent of tools. The partners have provided new solutions for open, tool-independent visual languages to model enterprise core knowledge aspects. These languages offer consistent and coherent enterprise descriptions, and represent a scientific basis for enterprise modeling, but integrated operations require that the POPS languages are defined and adapted by model-configuring them using the IRTV languages. The core business knowledge of any enterprise is the four inseparable dimensions of product, organization, process, and system (POPS). The POPS dimensions have several intrinsic properties, such as reflective views, recursive work processes, repetitive roles and tasks, and replicable solutions. To create contextual, reconfigurable knowledge model-based solutions, and replicable metamodels and templates, we must add the IRTV methodology for improved language granularity and context preservation.

Business and other aspects and views are derived from these core enterprise knowledge dimensions, enabling us to define, calculate, and manage parameters and balance attributes and value sets across disciplines. Any EM language must be a derivation from this core, otherwise it will not be able to produce quality, manageable models and solutions. Implementing the IRTV and POPS languages has to do with the definition of the "grammar" for descriptiveness and expressiveness, for representation, for extensions and adaptations, and for lifecycle reuse and management.

1.9 Towards Enterprise Visual Scenes

Enterprise visual scenes can provide users with modeling approaches, user environments, and solutions for knowledge creation, sharing, engineering, and management, meeting most of the industrial challenges discussed in Chap. 2.

The most advanced EM approaches and tools contribute to solving interoperability problems by increasing the shared understanding of the enterprise structures, rules, and behavior. EM provides methodologies for the identification of connected roles, objects, and processes between enterprises from different perspectives. Sets of software applications used in the enterprises and their relationships can be identified with EM, and their degree of interoperability can be analyzed. Many languages and tools (more than 350) exist that support some form of EM with partially overlapping approaches. Today, several attempts to combine languages are being pursued. For example, the Unified Enterprise Modeling Language project has prototyped an integrated approach for exchange of enterprise models among EM tools, work that was continued within the EU NoE INTEROP (2007) and in the ATHENA project as described earlier.

As indicated earlier, traditional enterprise modeling shows various inadequacies in many areas: representing enterprise knowledge, combining enterprise models, maintaining enterprise models, developing manageable structures of metamodels, enabling model-generated solutions, supporting dynamic user environments, and creating the link with software execution platforms. The solution of EM tool fallacies is to develop common core languages, services, modeling constructs, models, and metamodel structures based on a common infrastructure (Karlsen et al. 2003). The core components of an AKM-built platform are as follows:

- Its core modeling languages – POPS and IRTV
- Its approach (C3S3P – concept testing, scaffolding, scenario modeling, solutions modeling, platform configuration, platform delivery and practicing, performance improvement and operations)
- Its methodologies (CPPD)
- Its enterprise knowledge spaces and the generic EKA (the enterprise of all enterprises)
- Its customer-specific AKA
- Its reconfigurable user-composable services – MUPS

1.9.1 Visual Scenes and Collaboration Spaces

An enterprise has many knowledge spaces. These spaces can be implemented as enterprise visual scenes, modeled in the AKA. Visual scenes are ensembled views to interrelated active knowledge models supporting archetypical work in an organization.

We see four major enterprise visual scenes required to continuously innovate, operate, evolve and transform, and govern and manage future enterprises. In addition, there will be a multitude of smaller, more project- and task-specific scenes to support situated project work. The four visual scenes for future enterprising are defined as follows:

- *The innovative scene*, where the focus is to invent, reuse, design, and learn. The main concept is the industrial War-room, implemented as application of the POPS modeling methodologies. The innovative scene manages continuous change in product, process, and organizational structures and rules of the AKA.
- *The operations scene*, where the focus is to operate, generate, adapt, extend, manage, and terminate. The main concepts are collaborative business solutions generation and C3S3P delivery approach, supported by multiple life-cycle management (adapting and extending the common infrastructure). Proof of concept has been provided in earlier

projects (EXTERNAL) supporting solutions generation and user deployment (Elvekrok et al. 2003).

- *The governance scene*, where the focus is to govern, plan, decide, assign, measure, and strategize. The main concept is related to aggregation and propagation of parameters, attributes, and values, realizing the "real-time enterprise."
- *The evolutions scene*, where the focus is to analyze, configure, change, transform, align, and manifest. The main concept is continuous collaborative business management. To be supported by continuously adapting and extending the EKA by infrastructure services.

1.9.2 The Powers of Visual Scenes

There is a need to enhance the way people think about computing, and there is a need to extend enterprise modeling from being a tool-based exercise for experts, isolated from operational business solutions, to become visual environments for a new style of computing supported by a common infrastructure. Visual patterns, scenes, and languages, have at least six properties that natural language and current software methods will never acquire. We believe that these properties are fundamental in driving a new approach to SE, and for solving the challenges facing industry and IT provider:

1. Being able to collapse life-cycle stow-piping, i.e., play with abstractions of the time-dimension, removing the phases of material and information flows as documents and files
2. Providing methods for concurrently evolving concepts, content, context, and actions
3. Correlation of conceptual views (metaviews), several content and functional views, and finally contextual views, and all dependencies
4. Defining and applying business and working services and rules that are valid in given contexts and for limited parameter value sets
5. Performing innovative work, and being able to create metamodels by executing tasks
6. Supporting proactive learning in visual scenes by role-playing, dry-runs, and experimentation

When we are able to support these properties then we are closer to truly supporting holistic design, problem-solving, and organizational team learning.

1.10 Implications and Impacts

The demand for AKM technology will explode once western industry faces head on competition from India and China. Global networking will require full integration of enterprise teams across cultures, collaborative design, and global team-composition. The role of learning is enhanced and there will be a need to support on-the-job learning. Active or living knowledge capture, supporting customized working environments, will enable new approaches to industrial computing, exploiting the Web as a knowledge-sharing medium for improved collaboration and coordination.

Involvement of stakeholders in sharing knowledge and data is a key issue. Interrelating all stakeholder perspectives and life-cycle views from requirements, expectations, and constraints on design to maintenance and decommissioning or reengineering. Being able to interrelate and analyze, building the "big picture" and making parts of it active so that it drives execution depend mainly on parallel team-working:

1. Use-case designers and engineers must work with solution model builders on real customer product deliveries, and
2. Product and process methodologies are designed/modeled and applied (executing tasks) in concert with the use-case team.

This implies closing the gap between modeling and execution, supporting the following capabilities:

- Interaction of users in developing common approaches, pragmatic best-practices, and matching solutions
- Integration of systems to create effective, well-balanced solutions
- Interoperability of enterprises in performing networked collaborative business
- The discovery of multidimensional knowledge spaces and views
- The socialization, discovery, and externalization of what would otherwise be tacit human knowledge
- The recognition that software is nothing else but knowledge

A good metaphor is to think of the Web as an intelligent mirror, a mirror "painted" on its back with software components, enabling us to interrelate the mental models of humans and the object-oriented models of computers. This intelligent mirror has memory, and behavior, and can mimic more and more of what humans think and do.

2 Customer Challenges and Demands

In this chapter, we structure and describe the challenges that customers have wanted solutions to for years, but never received adequate IT support to approach. Many challenges have been attempted solved over and over again without success, and that is why many of them became industry slogans. A good example of a challenge never adequately solved is "requirements management and analyses," or in other words being able to turn customer requirements into supplier requirements, specifications, and satisfactory designs. The material presented in this chapter is based on results from the ATHENA project, in particular on (Li et al. 2006).

2.1 Background

Many industrial challenges have survived over a long period, actually as far back as the 1980s. These have now been magnified with the arrival of new technologies, mass customization, and globalization. Some of the challenges were discussed so vividly and often that they became industrial slogans, and examples are "Get it right first time," "Stop the brain–drain," "Avoid reinventing the wheel," "Planners plan and doers do," and "Keep it simple stupid – KISS." Altogether we lived through the 1980s and 1990s with some 15 slogans reflecting unsolved industrial challenges that users expected IT experts and providers to solve. Industrial challenges and road maps are described in nearly all industrial research programs, but no categorization or encyclopedia of industry challenges and demands is currently available.

2.1.1 Structure of Chapter

To be able to relate to the other chapters and in particular Chap. 6 on approaches to industrial solutions, the overall structure is naturally according to Enterprise Knowledge Spaces, their dimensions, key roles, and needs for competences and services. This gives an overall structure as illustrated in Fig. 2.1, starting with ways of categorizing community challenges, then looking at business networking the industry project performance, and finally role and personal workplace challenges. Role and personal spaces produce the architectural structures and contents of workspaces. The enterprise innovation spaces produce the core knowledge of product and service design and delivery, of organizational competences and skills, of process flows and best practice work-processes, and of adaptable agile systems and infrastructures that are easily model-configured. The business networking spaces mainly describe industrial innovation and customer delivery projects covering services, networking teams, project processes, and adaptable platforms. Community spaces describe values, resources, initiatives, and common infrastructures needed to operate a community. The chapter therefore structures challenges and demands into these categories:

1. *Society and Community Cooperation* across industry sectors is discussed. Emphasis is on the vast amount of information not yet digitally available and directly linked to engineering work, and therefore not used or updated by industry. Lack of industrial involvement in developing, using, updating, and managing information contents is another major concern. Finally, we look at the challenges of moving from "blueprint" Enterprise Architectures to *operational* Enterprise Knowledge Architectures.

2. *Collaborative Business Networking* also termed *c-Business*: Emphasis is on the lack of support for shared business models, for digital reference models, business interoperability, and methodologies for inter-enterprise collaboration. Lack of reference models and services for designing interoperable, reusable business platforms are described and discussed. The need for smart cross-organizational service-teams and new knowledge sharing services for simultaneous visual knowledge modeling and execution are discussed and explained.

3. *Interoperable Enterprise Cooperation* models and platforms, supporting project collaboration, providing simpler and safer workplaces, views and services, need urgent solutions. Emphasis is on Web platforms, on personal workspaces, on operational enterprise architectures supporting reuse, and on developing coherent and operational business, project, and engineering methodologies, adapted to specific enterprise projects and tasks. The discovery and existence of Enterprise Knowledge Spaces and the need to develop workplaces and services to support new approaches to holistic design and concurrent engineering, and to provide support for managing work-generative, situated knowledge is discussed.

4. *Innovation and Holistic Design* is possibly the most important business driver in the years to come as PLM systems are failing to deliver vendor promises and meet industry expectations. The major challenges can be found in expressing, representing, and activating knowledge, in integrating the existing PLM systems and in sharing data and knowledge.
5. *Knowledge and Data Representation* is not supporting design, creative work, and engineering. User-defined data and knowledge are currently stored as rigid, predefined data models in legacy databases. Product data are updated, extended, and reengineered through the life-cycles of product development and delivery projects, but this is poorly supported by systems engineering approaches.
6. *Workplace Regeneration and Adaptability* must be supported for designers and creative workers. Workplaces and collaboration spaces must evolve with work progress providing updated services, view contents, and new features, reflecting changes of data and creation of new knowledge.

Finally, we summarize the challenges and discuss the risks that solutions to many challenges and demands related to current practices in systems design and engineering will be sabotaged by the IT system vendors. The challenges to rethink university education and research and innovation are also discussed. Focus is on the time it will take for the educational

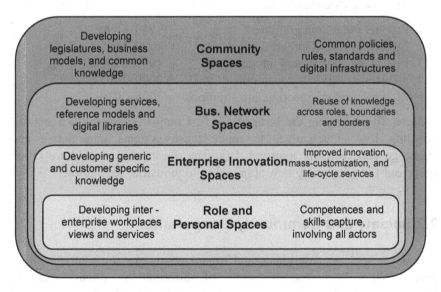

Fig. 2.1. Enterprise knowledge spaces

systems, interest organizations, and industry to acquire the competence and skills and build the confidence and trust to change their approaches.

Only unsolved challenges and challenges with inadequate solutions or where radical improvements are possible are described at any length.

2.1.2 The Evolution of Challenges and Demands

As stated earlier, many challenges date back to the mid 1980s when most actors involved were talking about how to bridge "the islands of automation" caused by application system delivery off the shelf. The evolution of IT systems applied in industry can be categorized in two ways:

1. By Shifts in Market and Business Models
2. By Technology Innovations, Shake-outs, and Exploitation

Looking on this by market and business model shifts, these four stages may be defined:

1. Aggregated industry sector experiences   1980–1990
2. The collapse of vertical markets   1990–2000
3. The push and failure of e-Business   2000–2005
4. The pull and growth of c-Business   2005–2010

Looking on the problem by technology innovation and exploitation, these five stages are identified:

1. Product model integration   1980–1990
2. Business process integration   1990–1995
3. Life-cycle support and integration   1995–2000
4. e-Business services development   2000–2005
5. Model-based engineering and solutions   2005–2010

Now, 30 years after the birth of the first major challenges, we are still devoting lots of resources to make these systems interoperate and exchange and correctly interpret data. The question is: should we rather spend our time designing new approaches to industrial computing?

2.2 Society and Community Cooperation

In today's society, individuals and organizations are confronted with an ever-growing load and diversity of information, causing content management headaches, and with increasing demands for knowledge and skills of turning the information to competence and skills. Coping with these demands requires progress in three closely related areas. First, content must be available as digital libraries providing services for upgrading, accessibility, sharing, usability, and preservation. Second, we need more effective technologies for intelligent content creation and management, and for supporting the capture of human knowledge and its sharing and reuse. Third, individuals and organizations have to find new ways to acquire, contribute, exploit, and manage knowledge, enhancing human learning.

The main challenges, therefore, are to be able to harvest the synergies made possible by linking content, knowledge, and learning; to make content and knowledge abundant, accessible, interactive, and usable over time by humans and machines alike.

Current research is expected to firmly establish digital library services as a key component of digital content infrastructures, allowing content and knowledge to be produced, stored, managed, personalized, transmitted, preserved, and used reliably, efficiently, at low cost, and according to widely accepted standards. The support of more personalized and collaborative services, particularly within self-organizing communities, should lead to more creative approaches to content and knowledge production.

Improvements are also needed in terms of contents accessibility, usability, scalability, and cost-effectiveness of the resulting methods, technologies, and application services with respect to handling large amounts of data and concurrent users. Also, for users to develop confidence and trust in the information sources, the links between content, knowledge management, and permanent learning processes must be improved. Technology should enable us to master content and knowledge exploitation and proactive participative learning from dynamic working environments.

2.2.1 Developing Digital Libraries

Medium term the challenge for most industries is to reengineer manual information sources into global digital libraries with innovative access services that support communities of practice in the creation, interpretation and use of cultural, industrial, and scientific content, including multiformat and multisource digital objects. They should be combined with robust and scalable environments, which include semantic and role-based search capabilities and essential digital preservation features. Particular attention should be given to cost-effective digitization processes and to the use of digital services in multilingual and multidisciplinary contexts.

Longer term the challenge is to develop new approaches to digital preservation, such as those inspired by human capacity to deal with information and knowledge, exploring the potential of new approaches to automatically act on high volumes and dynamic and volatile digital content, guaranteeing its preservation, keeping track of its evolving semantics and usage context and safeguarding its integrity, authenticity, and long term accessibility.

Enriching Today's Information Sources

In most sectors, vast amounts of project information, such as materials specifications, materials and part catalogues, and codes and regulations, is in the form of printed documents. Information collection from these sources implies manually searching and reading documents and often reinputting the same information and data. Efforts to turn this information into active, manageable, and sharable knowledge with stakeholders should be given the highest priority.

Information encoded in natural language, on paper or in preformatted data models, is hard to access, extract, interpret, adapt, change, and manage. Advanced search engines and parsers might be able to figure out what the information is about, but for semantic analyses and knowledge preservation, there is a need for adding more purposeful semantics. As a consequence, a growing number of textual structures are emerging to support semantic Web techniques, for supporting standards, and for developing identification and classification schemes.

Ontologies, taxonomies, thesauri, and other "name–structures" are being developed and applied to add layers of semantics to digital information sources, enabling automatic processing by semantic search engines. Although traditional search engines understand words and word patterns, a semantic search engine will also understand the context in which the word appears. This will be an improvement for retrieving, sharing, and integrating information content, but to understand the true meaning of information and data, role-specific contexts configured by knowledge models should be provided for. Many ontologies are based on the OWL standard (Smith et al. 2004). However, having ontologies based upon OWL does not assure full compatibility between the ontologies, just as having a standard based upon XML does not guarantee compatibility with other XML standards. But it does provide a range of standard tools to choose from and a range of other ontologies to build on. Creating a metaontology capturing all other ontologies is not feasible as each ontology represents a particular perspective view. Perspective views are human knowledge representations, and replacing them by a metaontology destroys their user value. An alternative to metaontologies is mapping ontologies. Either by mapping one ontology to another or as done within the Information Framework for Dictionaries (IFD) published as ISO 12006-3:2007, mapping ontologies to other ontologies or to standards such as IFD by the use of a generic framework structure can be achieved. A more powerful, configurable, and user-driven mapping technique should be developed. More background on semantic Web technologies is found in Chap. 6.

Automating Information Management

Having semantic structures embedded in the information makes it possible to go one step further and identify rules, requirements, and exceptions from the same source of information. This can be done by further tagging of the information or by importing the information to "Reasoning Engines" or to knowledge modeling and execution platforms. The combination of semantic tagging and model-configured approaches, activating rules, exceptions, and requirements should enable effective data extraction directly from the information source to the user workplace. Using mark-up techniques, we should be able to generate "pseudo rules" from textual information. The pseudo rule plays two roles:

- Making the rules language-independent, which means it should be understood across cultural borders, industry sectors, and among stakeholders
- Making possible automatic code generation and execution of pseudo rules to fit different reasoning engines and execution architectures

These techniques are useful for reengineering legacy information sources that are rapidly becoming degraded and obsolete, and then no one will trust or use them. The big challenges are to allow users to do this from their workplaces without having to call on IT experts, and to provide easy to use services to upgrade the contents, define "name–structures," and configure new use services.

2.2.2 Enterprise-Enhanced Learning

On the job training and learning by performing work or role-play will enable industry to engage in more aggressive bidding and contracting, being able to better predict milestones and costs, and thus industry will raise its competitiveness by calculating more predictable margins and lowering risks.

Medium term the failure to meet the challenge for developing responsive workplaces and environments for technology-enhanced learning and learning by doing is rapidly becoming an obstacle to collaborative Business. To motivate, engage, and inspire learners to use learning, services embedded in the business processes and human resource management systems should be provided. This should also involve the transformation of learning outcomes into permanent and valuable knowledge assets. Focus is on the mass individualization of learning experiences, contextualized and adaptable to age, situations, culture, and learning abilities. Learning by doing, performing work, integrating pedagogical and organizational approaches has the advantage of exploiting visual scenes of action, interactivity, collaboration, and context-awareness, all supporting proactive learning.

Longer term adaptive and intuitive learning services, able to support learning through self-configuration from knowledge architecture contents and experiences of the learners' behavior, should be supplied. Cross-disciplinary research on the synergies between learning and cognition in humans and machines should lead to systems able to identify learner's requirements, intelligently monitoring progress, capable of exploiting learners' abilities to let them learn faster. Learning services giving purposeful and meaningful advice to both learners and coaches for self-learning and for learning in collaborative environments should be developed.

2.2.3 Developing Operational Enterprise Architectures

In the current industrial and economic context, enterprises and their systems need to be constantly and smoothly reengineered to respond to changing market demand and technological evolutions. Enterprise architecture (EA), considered as the foundation of enterprise systems, has emerged as a "tool" to help stakeholders manage system engineering and change. EA is not just about IT, it involves strategy, business, knowledge, human factors, and assets. EA is both a challenging and confusing concept. For decades, construction industry uses architecture in the design and construction of all size of buildings. Their "architecture" utilizes standard symbols that can be recognized and understood by all members of their industry for carrying out the construction work. The systems engineering community by comparison has never had the advantage of this type of "time tested" structure. Instead, since the beginning, many heterogeneous architecture proposals have been developed. They are often overlapping approaches, and the underlying concepts are not explicitly defined. Different architecture description languages and model templates are not interoperable, and are consistent in the concepts they support. These languages and templates are proprietary, lack expressive significance to represent specific features, and cannot support operational IT system solutions. Similarities and differences between EA methodologies cannot be perceived by users; and this creates obstacles for its correct understanding in industry and finally its acceptance and use. The lack of a generally agreed terminology and an enriched knowledge corpus in this domain is also a bottleneck for its efficient application.

Enterprise architecture as a "Skeleton"

EA is a conceptual, simplified, and aggregated representation of the basic structures, processes, and organizational structures of an enterprise. As a market for IT systems, it emerged in 1996 with the US Congress passing of the Klinger Cohen Act. EA does not start with technology, but a strategic framework, focusing the vision, goals, priorities, and business activities. An EA is a specific arrangement of business features and functions. The purpose of a "should-be" (target) EA is to maximize a set of business goals and objectives given a set of constraints, conditions, and challenges. The purpose of "as-is" (baseline) architecture is to document the current arrangement such that a transition to the desired target state can be determined.

Independently of business goals or strategies, EA is first and foremost, the foundation of enterprise knowledge structures and IT systems. According to ISO 15704 (2000), an architecture is a description of the basic arrangement and connectivity of parts of a system (either a physical or a conceptual object or entity). The software community also considers that architecture is the fundamental organization of a system embodied in its components, their relationships to each other and to the environment and the principles guiding their design and evolution (IEEE 1471 2000). Specifically, software architecture is "a set of software components, externally visible properties of those components, and relationships among them."

More generally, architecture must possess the following features and functions:

- Have properties that can be verified with respect to user needs (e.g. open or closed architecture, interoperable or not, centralized or decentralized, flexible or rigid language etc.)

- Be communicated as simple views so that business people can easily understand, check, analyze, discuss as a "language" shared at corporate level
- Have a style (by comparison with construction where architecture can represent some particular characteristics of a building such as "gothic" or "romaine"). EA should be able to characterize enterprise systems (e.g. "fractal," "holonic," or knowledge-model configured)

Various Types of Enterprise Architecture

ISO 15704 considers two and only two types of architectures that deal with enterprise integration.

1. *System architectures* (sometimes referred to as "type 1" architectures) that deal with the design of a system, e.g., the system part of an overall enterprise integration
2. *Enterprise-reference projects* (sometimes referred to as "type 2" architectures) that deal with the organization of the development and implementation of a project such as an enterprise integration or other enterprise development program.

In other words, type 1 architecture represents system or subsystem in terms of its structure and behaviors. The type 2 architecture is actually a framework aiming at structuring activities/tasks necessary to design and build a system. For example, Zachman's architecture (Zachman 2007) is regarded as a type 2 architecture. Other works make distinctions between *conceptual* and *technical architectures*. The conceptual architecture is derived from business requirements; and are understood and supported by senior management. The technical architecture provides the technical components that enable the business strategies and functions. Sometimes conceptual architecture is also called *functional* or *business* architecture; and technical architecture, ICT architecture. TOGAF (TOGAF 2000) considers four types of architecture, which are subsets of EA: Business architecture, information technology architecture, data/information architecture; and application (systems) architecture. Lillehagen et al. (2002a) advanced the concept of "knowledge architecture," separating perspective views of business operation, knowledge and ICT architectures as illustrated in Fig. 2.2.

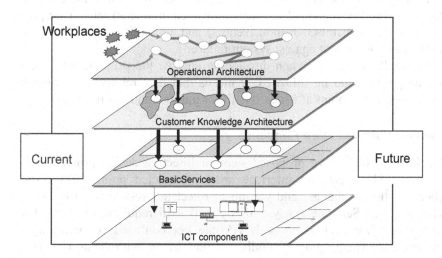

Fig. 2.2. Layers of architecture

To link the four layers of architectures described to one or more of the established EA frameworks is a major challenge, and this will involve new principles of performing visual modeling, linking work environment modeling and work execution, and finally being able to do this and preserve context for the key roles involved, and separating local adaptations and extensions from project and network wide changes. European research projects are attempting to achieve this and more, such as supporting model-configured collaboration spaces, workplaces and services. One of the projects (CoSpaces 2007) is rooted in the TOGAF enterprise architecture model.

General Architecture Principles

General EA principles can be found in the literature such as for example: (a) Business processes drive technical infrastructure; (b) Primary purpose of architecture is to facilitate rapid change; (c) EA must emphasize reusable component building blocks; (d) Architecture must be enterprise-wide; (e) EA must optimize the enterprise system as a whole and many more. Supporting operations is unfortunately not one of the principles.

Another approach can be found in the Government of Canada's Federated Architecture (2001), where these principles are proposed: (1) Reduce integration complexity to reengineer application systems to be "highly modular" and "loosely coupled" to be able to reuse components; (2) Adopt holistic approach with a (whole of enterprise) approach;

(3) Have business event-driven systems; (4) Plan for growth and construct for growth and expansion of services (known requirements) across enterprise; (5) Provide robustness, responsiveness, and reliability with appropriate redundancy to protect against system failure.

Generally speaking, when developing an EA, the principle of fitness-for-purpose should be followed. It means that the architecture should be developed to the point at which it is fit for purpose and not further.

Technical Architecture Principles

Cockburn (2003) have proposed some architecting design principles, for example: (1) Create an interface around predicted points of variation (because things change, and we must protect the system integrity across changes); (2) Separate subsystems by staff skill requirements; (3) Make one owner for each deliverable (People get confused if ownership is unclear); (4) The program is totally program driven, with the user interface just one driving program (because user interface requirements change a lot); (5) Provide a single point of call to volatile inter-team interfaces (Protect developers against rework due to an interface change). Malan and Bredemeyer (2002) also suggested three principles to develop a "Minimalist Architecture": (1) if a decision could be made at a more narrow scope, defer it to the person or team who is responsible for that scope; (2) only address architectural decisions at high-priority architecturally significant requirements; (3) as decisions are added to the architecture, they should be evaluated from the point of view of their impact on the overall ability of the organization to adopt the architecture.

In TOGAF (2000), some principles underlying the design and successful use of specific architectures were proposed, for example: (1) An architecture needs only to specify those services that is required; (2) Elements of an architecture may specify one, more than one, or only part of a service; (3) Elements of an architecture should be defined in terms of standards relevant to the services they specify; (4) Elements of an architecture should be reused from all the categories of the Architecture Continuum and should support reuse of solution elements of the Solution Continuum; (5) Elements of the solution or implementation should be reused from all the categories of the Solutions Continuum; (6) An architecture must be followed, or it is useless: formal IT Governance practices are recommended.

To summarize there is a need to develop commonly accepted architecture representations and specification languages as active knowledge models, enabling architects and key networking roles:

- To describe and represent a common point of departure for families of different enterprise solutions – regional and sector supported operational platforms with EA services to tailor workplaces and services
- To support managers and project leaders in their strategic and business operational decisions to innovate and build new architectures and to pursue new projects and business opportunities
- To answer a key problem: provide architecture service continuity along the whole enterprise and product life cycle (requirements, design, implementation, operation, and replacement)
- To amplify features and functions of various architected platforms so that comparison and choice become easier for users and can be performed upstream, saving time and resources
- To ensure interoperability between enterprises, workspaces, and services, built from various architectures, but with common architectural components and standards
- To effectively support new approaches and methodologies for improving most engineering disciplines in existing and new collaborative networked organizations

The list is by no means meant to be exhaustive.

Community Platform Development and Operation

The major challenge to overcome and develop coherent digital libraries that can be shared by many stakeholders is to provide a generic core platform with some predefined role-specific workplaces and standardized services, supported by generic software components. This should allow members of project teams to build model-driven, role-specific workplaces, and supporting services and views.

For this to happen, model-driven platforms must replace software applications as the means of delivering computing services and capturing industrial knowledge and pragmatic logic. The extreme enterprise knowledge encoding for computer execution support has to seize. Various information libraries, integrated and adapted by modeling, must be made accessible and executable from a range of technology platforms. Future solutions and services to cover growing needs, such as product portfolio management and mass-customized product delivery, must be developed and deployed. This is illustrated in Fig. 2.3. Different categories of knowledge workers will be able to define, share, and manage data, information (documents), and active knowledge models all integrated by a standardized, operational enterprise knowledge architecture.

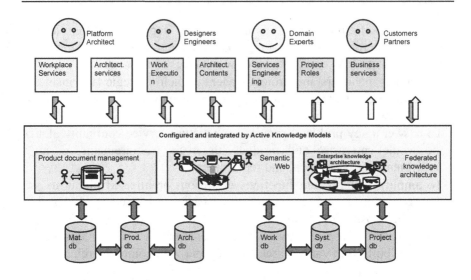

Fig. 2.3. Architecture for role-specific workplaces and services

The enterprise and other knowledge architectures should be implemented and supported by model-composed and configured platform services and methods, implementing an intelligent infrastructure for dynamic solutions engineering. Some of the services must be automatically performed as a consequence of user interaction with natural tasks, but without users being aware of their execution. Otherwise the user dialogue will be much too complex for product designers, industrial engineers, and practitioners to learn how to effectively communicate with the system. Developing the knowledge architectures, the workplaces, the views, the task structures, the basic services, the metamodels binding services to software components, and the overall architecture model are all major interdependent challenges.

2.3 Collaborative Business Networking

Effective collaborative business networking is dependent on industry, research, and system providers solving these major challenges

- Providing services to agree on and renegotiate business models and cooperation rules and issues, even during the execution of a project, including services to share risks and values

- The existence of reference models (reusable sharable knowledge) that can be easily accessed and applied by all stakeholders needing access to their contents
- The development of interoperable systems and established common architectures as models for enterprises and networked organizations to build their own specific models through adaptation to their specific context
- The availability of services to dynamically build collaboration rooms, compose teams and services, and deploy working environments across geographically dispersed enterprises

Services to allow the different actors to share concepts and best practices that make cooperation possible should be part of the core c-Business platform.

2.3.1 Business Models

The theory of network economics is a relatively new topic of research in international economic science. This field of research emerged mainly in the beginning of the 1980s when a growing number of contributions in the field of standards were recognized in the literature. Following Weitzel (2004), it is instrumental that the industry becomes familiar with the basic ideas behind the network economics theory and why businesses should be familiar with the concept. According to Shapiro and Varian (1998), economics of networks are one of the central differences between the old and the new economy: The old industrial economy was driven by the economies of scale; the new knowledge economy is driven by the economics of networks" (Shapiro and Varian 1998). Thus it seems inevitable for survival in the new economy to understand the principles of network economics and their implications for market dynamics.

In Chap. 10, we will take a more detailed look at the many theories of knowledge network economics and what a holistic design approach to business and technical interoperability will involve.

Business Interoperability

In electronic business relationships, interoperability plays a decisive role. Being "interoperable" refers to being able to share information between business partners, understand and process exchanged data, seamlessly integrate it into internal ICT systems, and enable its beneficial use.

Business interoperability is defined as "*the organizational and operational ability of an enterprise to cooperate with its business partners and to efficiently establish, conduct and develop IT-supported business relationships with the objective to create value.*"

On the basis of this definition, business interoperability describes characteristics of a company's external relationships. It extends the more technically focused notion of interoperability to cover strategic, organizational, and operational aspects of setting up and running IT-supported relationships. As such, business interoperability builds on the concept of *networkability* (Wigand et al. 1997; Österle et al. 2001), which is a continuation of coordination theory and sees coordination as the management of relationships of dependence. Among the challenging issues that may arise at the business level are the following issues:

- Defining the business cooperation model and identifying target partners
- Defining consistent business goals and the rules of cooperation
- Formalizing these goals and rules in signed contracts and service level work processes
- Aligning business processes and internal work processes among partners
- Making technology choices and integrating architectures and platforms
- Sharing knowledge and linking information systems across company borders

The breakthrough for networked organizations will occur when companies can cooperate with new partners without any additional cost involved, and even small businesses can easily participate in electronic business relationships. This scalability of electronic relationships is called *m:n capability*.

When comparing different industries, it becomes evident that they are characterized by different levels of business interoperability. In the high-tech industry, the supply chain between original equipment manufacturers (OEM), contractors, and component manufacturers is tightly integrated. In many other areas, e.g., in facility management, the fragmentation and specialization within the value chain is still in progress and has not yet produced stable role models. In addition, the size of the companies makes it more difficult to establish a similar level of inter-organizational integration. These examples illustrate that the achievable level of business interoperability depends on industry structure as well as product functionality and maturity with regard to electronic business and characteristics of the target cooperation scenario.

2.3.2 Reference Models

A reference model (Latin; refere: carry back, reporting) is a *general model* for a class of issues with the following characteristics:

- On the basis of a *general model*, specific models can be developed
- The *general model* can be used as an object for comparison with other models that are describing similar issues

A reference model, therefore, provides an ideal master for a class of issues. A reference model should be relevant for a distinct application domain and describe structures, properties, relationships, and the behavior of objects. A reference model is composed of these main components:

- Basic model building blocks; structures, components, parameters, rules, and services
- Architecture of the entire reference model and its modules with data and examples of practice
- Description language that is used for a uniform display and for exchanging information between different competence centers
- Rules and guidelines for applying the reference model to generate a specific model

Many industries have engaged in developing reference models, but there has all the time been some reasons for industrial reluctance to join, such as giving away core knowledge, costs of community meetings, and time spent on reengineering and deploying the models. However, the major reason for industrial reluctance is the fact that some of the most valuable reference models are developed and deployed as paper documents. Extracting and inputting reference model data is a major expense and source of erroneous data, causing many engineering changes and delays.

Categories of Reference Models

Many reference models are by purpose, scope, and contents already categorized by the organizations behind them. Aligned with the purpose of our approach, we propose to provide these models as platform embedded configurable knowledge models and data. We have identified five major categories, just as there are five major categories of interest organizations:

- Application domain focused, such as the Supply-Chain Corporation (SCC) and the Change Management Institute (CMI)
- Information or Architecture focused like The Open Group (TOGAF) and the Federal Enterprise Architecture Federation (FEAF)

- IT or other technology-specific organizations like OMG and W3C
- Standards or norms for data exchange and information flow like the STEP communities
- Industrial standards, norms and rules like the international initiative in the construction industry and the International Association of Interoperability (IAI)

The industrial platforms of the future will provide workplaces for product and process design, organizational learning and development, and systems design and engineering, where digital reference models can be easily integrated, reengineered, and reused.

Importance of a Reference Models

Reference models represent high-quality knowledge and best practices sharable by all stakeholders involved in community projects and work.

Among the most obvious benefits are:

1. Approaches that provide quality and secure solutions
2. Methodologies that lead to good solutions for all actors
3. Solutions that are repeatable, repairable, and replaceable
4. Norms and components for solutions and information on solutions
5. Norms and components for Infrastructures and platforms
6. Reusability and replication of solutions and parts across a community
7. Enterprise knowledge for global industrial training and education
8. Major areas for further research and development

All these advantages and benefits means great potential savings in not having to reinvent and rediscover knowledge that should be considered noncompetitive, easily accessible and adaptable by qualified stakeholders.

Reference models should be major repeatable knowledge components of the enterprise knowledge architecture (EKA) of networked enterprises. However, today they are mostly used as fragmented information in documents to support disjoint engineering disciplines.

Quality of Reference Models

Experiences from applying EA tells us that any reference model developed by "slide-show" or textual models will not represent a consistent, coherent, and compliant set of reference models for networked modern enterprises. The manual work in developing them is alone becoming too costly, never mind accepting the costs to develop community services to allow users to adapt and apply to business specific solutions. The manual toil and costs of these processes and the lack of services for composing and managing project-specific models are preventing communities from developing models of high quality and value to industry and industrial users. Any model has its own architecture, part of a holistic knowledge domain, and these can be made active or interactive components of operational solution platforms. They should be part of the second layer of EA – the EKA). The groups that develop reference models have little or no contact, so the models will not be compliant or coherent. This is potentially a major source of noninteroperability. These reference models should be integrated in the EKA by standardized metamodels and modeling languages as extensions to the IRTV language.

Reengineering Reference Models

Many reference models need to be reengineered for increased correctness, consistency, compliancy, and cohesion among them, and be developed and delivered as knowledge models accessible from inline repositories. These repositories must provide services to make the reference models easily available and adaptable to changing enterprise solutions for increased user value. In order to support life-cycle stakeholder involvement and user inter-action, one must support knowledge and data service provisioning to users. The projects to develop these reference models with the qualities needed and the services mentioned will have to be performed in industry sector focused projects with competent users to engage in holistic knowledge modeling approaches with industrial users in the driver's seat. The kind of initiative required is best exemplified by the IAI initiative (IAI 2007) in the construction sector. The sector oriented initiatives may take a holistic approach to reference model design and engineering as they can involve and accommodate most industrial perspectives, application models, and standards particular to that sector. Sector initiatives start with their own approaches and methodologies to develop, build, and deliver solutions with increased use of and support for reference models, ranging from design rules and norms for construction details to project approaches and process models for multisite plant management.

Challenges using Reference Models

The way reference models are being developed today, they are a major source of noninteroperability. Some major points are listed below and are further explained in this section. The problems and challenges in using reference models are caused by:

- Mostly textual-based description makes adoption and application difficult
- Too detailed information without layers reduce the applicability of the reference models
- Too high expectations to reference models lead to wrong implementation
- A lot of incompatible standards and de facto standards reduce interoperability
- Reference models are often not aligned with the entire enterprise architecture and goals

Integrity and consistence cannot be ensured on textual descriptions, which makes adaptation difficult and resource consuming. The motivation to fit these reference models to the own enterprise conditions and especially in order to join enterprise networks or force collaboration is low. The consequences are along two dimensions. The reference model will be not adapted, so the effectiveness and unique competitiveness points will be lost. Or the model will be adapted to the own business, but this is connected with costs and risk. Especially a continuous adoption is still a problem. In case of using the reference model of an enterprise application like ERP, an additional risk appears: When the software provider is changing the reference models by providing a new software release, the consequences cannot be foreseen and possibly the specific reference model and the specific customization of the IT System cannot be maintained according to the requirements of the new software release.

Industrial reference models, in particular, the IT-system reference models contain too much detailed information defined inside the reference models. Often only a single layer abstraction with lots of details exist, such as in UML. The adaptation by business people is awkward if not impossible. Another shortcoming is the fact that such models carry a-not-invented-here stamp. In industrial use, very often unrealistic expectations to reference models exist. The fact that a given model is either designed for defining requirements, for providing a high level framework and guidelines, or for providing best practice solutions is often forgotten. Because of various standardization bodies and de facto standards, overlaps exist between reference models to similar business items (e.g., ITIL vs. eTOM). Additional integration effort is clearly needed. By applying both frameworks the user has to integrate not only different terms for the same issue, but has to fight with different level of granularity provided by the reference models. The needed adaptation leads to double effort for development and maintenance. The reason is that most of the reference models do not refer to general enterprise business architectures, which should be independent from the technology and the business aspect of the reference model. Different languages for describing the reference models make merging and synchronization very cost and time intensive.

2.4 Interoperable Enterprise Collaboration

Problems of distributed collaboration are central to the effective management of the product lifecycle, particularly where heterogeneous technologies, tools, and working practices are involved. Many products are developed by means of different technologies on the basis of both hardware and software components. While this is true today for high end and complex products (e.g., cars, aircraft, or mobile phones), this trend is expected to extend to almost all products in the near future (e.g., household appliances).

Three issues are crucial for the proper functioning of product: management, life-cycle support, and reuse, if we are going to succeed in coping with the market trends and meeting the customer demands. The three issues are:

1. The need for virtual work environments and collaboration spaces
2. The need for interoperable knowledge architectures, securing optimal reuse
3. The need for new approaches to Systems Engineering and solutions management

The more multifunctional and complex the product is, the more complicated are the work processes for its design, engineering, customized delivery, and life-cycle support. Industrial knowledge can be flexibly architected and reused, but the manufacturing plants and assembly lines, built with hardware and physical constraints, must also be able to manufacture the customized products. This requires a methodology for modularization of manufacturing and maintenance processes that must be available as design rules to the product designers and engineers. To achieve this support, simultaneously designing for customizable solutions, manufacturing and life-cycle modularity is a challenge that will stay with us for some more years.

2.4.1 Virtual Enterprises: Collaboration Spaces

The period from 2000 to 2005 was dominated by research toward creating the virtual enterprise (VE). A VE was defined as *"a customer solution delivery system created by a temporary and IT enabled integration of core competencies"* (Tølle et al. 2002):

Infrastructure development for virtual enterprises faced three highly intertwined challenges (Jørgensen and Krogstie 2005):

- *Heterogeneity*, incommensurable perspectives, software infrastructures, working practices, etc., among the partner and customer companies
- *Flexibility*, many interdependent knowledge dimensions, the need for learning, design changes and work process alignment, and exception handling
- *Complexity*, the richness and uncertainties of interdependencies among partners, their activities, resources, skills, and products

From some 50 research projects known to the authors, not a single virtual enterprise was made operational. However, some very useful discoveries were made, and some important lessons were learned. Among the important discoveries was the need for building active knowledge architectures, supporting both user-configured and model-configured work environments and role-specific workplaces. In other words, it takes more than software engineering technology to build a real operational VE. The most common and important lesson learned was that industrial product and process knowledge can only be understood and improved when working intimately close with industry. Interpreting specifications written by consultants has for many years been a major challenge for IT people. The VE research drive has now been replaced by the drive for more concrete industrial collaboration spaces, and indeed many projects are recognizing one lesson learned from these VE projects: "No collaboration without contextual roles, views, tasks and industrial data and information!" It is no longer a tools game!

2.4.2 Process Structures: Emergence and Evolution

Unstructured creative activities are often most important for the competitiveness of an enterprise. Even in seemingly routine work, exceptions and uncertainties permeate the environment. Workers reflect upon and manage these problems in a sophisticated manner (Wenger 1998). To some extent, on the one hand, most work can thus be regarded as knowledge intensive. On the other hand, most work processes also have routine parts, which can be structured and automated. Many companies have prescribed quality management procedures for administration, audit, approval, etc. Systems must thus integrate support for ad-hoc and structured work (Haake and Wang 1997; Jørgensen and Carlsen 1999).

Users must be supported in selecting a suitable degree of plan specificity for the current state of their process, balancing plan complexity with the need for guidance and control.

In software engineering, researchers have defined process classification schemes, e.g., to select appropriate methodologies. Reflecting the wide *diversity of processes*, even within a single industry, up to 15 classification dimensions with 37,400 process types have been proposed (Cockburn 2003). This number suggests that predefined ways of working cannot be constructed for all process variants. Instead, process methodologies should be selected and model-configured to the particular circumstances of each project.

2.4.3 Knowledge, Communication and Learning

Inter-organizational and multidisciplinary cooperation requires not only information exchange, but also knowledge sharing. Effective teams must form across local cultures. Common frames of reference, reference models as discussed earlier, are established through working together, so support systems must allow the meaning of terms, plans, and artifacts to evolve. In communities of practice, this learning process is called *negotiation of meaning* (Wenger 1998). Ambiguous models are required because the meaning of formal, well-defined terminologies cannot be negotiated. A VE infrastructure must be intelligent that is it must support the process of creating, negotiating, and reconciling diverging views and interpretations.

Lack of integration into everyday work practices is a reported shortcoming of Knowledge Management (KM), enterprise modeling, and process improvement (Davenport and Prusak 1993). KM too often becomes the domain of outside experts that lack a full understanding of the complications of work and the local language of the work community (Wenger 1998). Work performers become sources of information to KM activities, not active participants. Standardization and codification, rather than local innovation, organizational and social learning, become the focal points of KM. Failure rates above 50% are common (Lawton 2001).

The gap between what people say, observe, and do makes it difficult to use enterprise models and other official accounts of work as input to KM (Argyris and Schön 1978). It must thus be straightforward to modify enterprise information locally. Still some knowledge cannot be articulated and will remain tacit, but visual collaboration spaces supporting proactive behavior will take us a long way. Most descriptions are incomplete while they are used, subject to an ongoing elaboration and interpretation. Change and learning demand that modeling infrastructures be open and be integrated with execution platforms. Knowledge models are completed only when they are no longer in use, and may no longer be elaborated to reflect exceptions and changing circumstances, but then they are most likely obsolete.

2.4.4 Intelligent Infrastructures: Integration and Customization

The unique nature of each VE, and the dynamic set of partners, seldom makes it economically viable to integrate information systems through developing new software interfaces. Standardization (Chen and Vernadat 2003) requires that the domain is static and well understood, and is thus seldom appropriate for knowledge work. Consequently, we need flexible infrastructures that allow shared understanding and semantic interoperability to emerge from the project, rather than being a prerequisite for cooperation and collaboration.

Such flexibility is seldom offered by the tools currently available for virtual enterprise integration, like e-business frameworks, workflow management, enterprise resource planning, etc., (Alonso et al. 1999). Consequently, how to achieve flexibility, configurability, context pre-servation, exception handling, and learning are important research topics in these disciplines.

Simple tools invite use. Software that offers a wide range of functionality often becomes overwhelmingly complex, complicated to use, and incom-prehensible. Consequently, only a small portion of the available services is utilized. This condition is known as *featuritis*. We thus need role and task-specific user interfaces, emphasizing what is needed in the current context. Interfaces and semantics should also adapt to the local needs of each project. Enterprise models, articulating who performs which tasks when and why, are powerful resources for such adaptation.

Workplaces should also adapt to the skills and preferences of each individual. Where experts should be given freedom to exercise skilled judgment, novices need detailed guidance. Personalization fosters a sense of ownership, motivating active participation. Studies have shown that personal templates and configurations spread informally through the organization, improving processes and disseminating knowledge in an emergent manner. We will, however, contend that VE integration is as much a social problem as a technical one. Current modeling infrastructures emphasize technical integration, but the understanding of virtual enterprises as socio-technical systems must be improved. In particular, we seek to replace the common approach of using formal computer languages to control social interaction, with the application of human languages to control and customize computing infrastructures.

2.4.5 Enterprise Interoperability

Interoperability among enterprises wanting to collaborate for stages of or whole life-cycles of processes and products is becoming a competitive lever for industry. The first extended enterprise to build a bidding network involve the stakeholders in negotiating a potential winning bid and interact with partners to assess performance factors will have a tremendous advantage in future c-Business markets. Now, interoperability is as Peter Drucker says not a technology, it is a property of an enterprise or any knowledge space or knowledge dimension, just like scalability, transformability, and similar capabilities that may add up to defining agility.

Enterprise Interoperability can be achieved in at least three ways, and most often by a combination of the three:

1. By reconciliation of business objects and services
2. By reengineering the legacy
3. By enterprise design and development

The three approaches and their supporting technologies are all needed, but the platforms and services offering these capabilities to industry as user services are still at the research stage.

2.4.6 System Engineering Approaches

The trends in systems engineering (SE), aiming to create more agile and better quality systems, are toward more model-architected, model-driven, or model-based solutions, and toward supporting user-driven visual communications among stakeholders and users across communities, projects, and product life-cycles. People with a strong SE background, see INCOSE (INCOSE 2007), believe in either a mathematical foundation or a mix of mathematics, semantics, and pragmatics for progressing systems engineering. The Microsoft Software Factory initiatives have definitely discovered that pragmatic knowledge is the key to any product design, and maybe also holds the key to SE. Some efforts are based on pragmatics and the nature of knowledge modeling and human learning life-cycles.

Research indicates that there are five or more distinct categories of systems and SE approaches emerging and that should be considered, just as there are many approaches to product design and engineering. Ongoing model-based SE efforts will lead to various approaches depending on the specificity of the information and tasks to be supported and the degree of user involvement in the life-cycle stages of the systems. The five major types of IT solutions and systems currently emerging are:

1. Global data collection, analysis, and presentation
2. Process monitoring and control systems
3. Customizable business, trading and transaction systems
4. Technical calculation and analysis systems
5. Product and process design systems

Examples of these five types are under development around the world. The NOSA project (NOSA 2007) in US is a good example of category 1. Category 2 is found in most process industries, in energy producing industries, and wherever human judgment of complex scenes must be assisted in real-time. The seven major IT vendors are employing modern technologies to develop category 3 systems. Also most EU research projects are focusing this system category. Scientists have used category 4 systems for quite some time, but the way they were engineered they could not easily be reconfigured to deal with new artifacts. Category 5 is the most demanding approach as design involves concurrent learning, problem-solving, and collaboration. However, in all five categories, needs for creating and managing local adaptations and configurations, personalized workplaces, and content viewing exist, so model-based approaches and reuse from operational knowledge architectures is the common denominator.

2.4.7 Embedded Systems Engineering

Traditionally, software and hardware development has been performed in separation with little or no interaction. Today, this border between hardware and software products is vanishing. An increasing number of industrial products integrate both hardware and software components, and the decision whether a specific function should be implemented in hardware or software may come late in the project and may even change during the product's life cycle. When the border becomes vague and even emergent, then it is no longer possible to keep the development organizations separate and to use different life cycle processes. So there is a need for unifying traditional product design and engineering with systems development and software engineering. We believe both camps could learn and benefit from each other. However, the requirement for such integration points out a number of problems, such as rethinking and reengineering: work processes, information structures, data management and information flow, infrastructure support, resource management, tool integration, and leveling cultural differences. Finding homogeneous and consistent ways to manage processes, data, and tools have proven to be difficult and challenging, and experiences of quality problems and catastrophic failures are many. Most experiences are associated with the introduction of new electronic systems in automobiles. Several attempts to integrate tools from product and system domains are known, but all report limited success. The main reason for this is that enterprise integration is not achieved by systems and software tool integration. Industrial experiences tell us that four factors play a crucial role for successful integration: role-specific knowledge capture, pragmatic work processes and tasks performed, people's mental models and attitudes, and the overall availability and access to shared information and data. Currently, the functionalities in partially but inadequately integrated system configuration management (SCM) and product data management (PDM) systems are so complex and inconsistent that collaboration across any border is prohibited by usability problems and excessive cognitive load.

The fundamental differences between product and software engineering stem from the fact that, in product engineering, structures and parameters are processed simultaneously by many stakeholders, while in software system engineering, the software components are processed one by one by individual experts. Therefore, product engineering focuses on modeling and sharing knowledge of the total product, while software engineering focuses on building and testing reusable components of the end product. Product engineering emphasizes the creation and management of knowledge as engineering artifacts for roles along the entire product life cycle, while software engineering emphasizes code engineering, individual programming, and debugging of the software components. Clearly, the two approaches have their respective merits and limitations, but being faced with different issues, they end up with different solutions to, apparently, some of the same problems. Therefore, it is not a surprise that the tools provided in one camp cannot fit the needs of the other camp. What makes the problem really difficult is that the existing tools (e.g., SCM and PDM), being based on radically different assumptions, cannot be extended to include the "missing" functionality. For the same reason, combining (integrating or interoperating) one tool from each camp, at best provide a functionally awkward system, too complicated for practitioners to use.

Industrial solutions will require deep rethinking of the very nature of the work processes and product and system knowledge artifacts created and managed, what are the underlying architectures and methods, and how can a common platform be created. Currently, the problem manifests itself at the system level where hardware and software subsystems/components have to be integrated. At least at system level, technology-independent product representations and working processes are essential for achieving a properly functioning product. This is lacking in today's Product Life-cycle Management solutions, and in SCM and PDM systems; it constitutes serious challenges for parties from research to tool vendors and business partners.

Estublier (2000) discusses how to provide a high level view of SCM applications, which is independent from the particular tools. The application's behavior, services, and properties can be described at a high level of abstraction (process control, paradigm control, security, etc). Their experimental system and metamodel shows that advanced state-of-the-art features could be easily included into a federated architecture, where systems can be fed by data, which in turn can be used in an extended enterprise solution focusing product design or other major tasks.

Work at Chalmers University of Technology (Vinnex 2007) has aimed at developing an integrated product lifecycle model framework, connecting information models representing a product through its lifecycle ranging from customer needs to product retirement. To achieve this, product model theories from different domains such as mechanical, electronic, and software engineering were compared. Similarities and differences were found between these models. The Chromosome Model theory tells how to implement information requirements posed by mechanical/electronic products. So some work has been done to find ways of unifying product design and SE, but there are still major challenges with respect to theory and industrial practice, including the achievement of;

- A deeper understanding of the industrial requirements for collaborative development in the area and of the shortcomings of current commercial solutions vs. these requirements
- A shared terminology for interdisciplinary product development enabling engineers from different domains to communicate and collaborate effectively
- A clear understanding of what PLM functions can be generalized across businesses and what function that need to be adapted as services in a business context
- A coherent theoretical basis and concepts that can guide the development of digital product models and of generic work processes, including how to maximize the generic part and how to minimize the business-specific parts of PLM solutions

- Collaborative design, performed by globally dispersed teams, needs to have a holistic approach, considering aspects of technologies, methodologies, and organizational services
- Proof of concept prototypes, meeting concrete requirements, must be validated in industrial settings, including distributed development and multisite installations and applications
- The usability of model-designed knowledge architectures, workplaces, collaboration spaces, task-structures, and tools must be tested in holistic approaches to enterprise engineering

New technologies and services in modeling, such as component-based and model-based development and enterprise integration, building operational knowledge architectures, based on standards, will have to be developed, piloted, and validated in industrial settings. Getting industrial commitment and involvement to start this work is a major challenge.

2.5 Innovation and Holistic Design

Most industrial products are designed as multifunctional systems with complex structures, employing complicated methods. Modern products consist of a growing number of interacting functions, realized by possibly thousands of parts and components. Industrial product models are today poorly integrated as each engineering discipline and major development step has their own disjoint product structure with their local parameters. To support innovation and modern product design, the product model should be integrated with other enterprise knowledge dimensions such as organizational competences and skills, process views and work processes, and systems, tools, and services. The product model development may involve several suppliers, so the product and knowledge integration should happen automatically or by user interaction as design work progresses. Mastering the interactions between product functions and the inter-dependencies between all systems and parts needed to build the product is today a major challenge.

Quickly and safely connecting, communicating with and coordinating customers and suppliers is becoming crucial for the survival of any manufacturing industry. Reducing the time to market by facilitating concurrent engineering, increasing productivity by improved work processes and information quality, and reducing costs by improving work environments are still key operational objectives. Also innovative ideas and concept development must be more tightly integrated with product design and customer delivery, with the value-networks involved and with the entire product life-cycle. Innovation is no longer a threat or the foe of successful customer delivery, on the contrary, without a tight integration between innovating new design principles and concepts and customer delivery, there is no way that the value networks will remain competitive.

2.5.1 Industrial Customer Delivery

The authors have during the last years worked with a dozen Scandinavian companies from diverse sectors of industry, and we interviewed them to understand their short and longer term priorities. Among the questions raised, they were asked to list and prioritize their five most important challenges. This is the dominant priorities from a majority of the responses:

1. Poor connectivity and associations between customer and supplier requirements and expectations, causing many erroneous data entries, interpretation, and use of data
2. Too much unfiltered and erroneous data and information cluttering the user interfaces, working environments, and collaboration spaces
3. Contradicting data definitions and input from users throughout life-cycles
4. Industry keeps repeating mistakes, but has problems repeating their successes
5. Knowledge and insight is lost when key people leave or are unavailable, what is known as the "brain-drain problem."

To solve these urgent high priority challenges, most industries will rely on enhancing their product life-cycle management (PLM) systems with knowledge management tools. Some industries explicitly stated that solutions must become more role-specific and context preserving to ease knowledge capture and reuse. This indicates that industry is becoming aware of the shortcomings of present IT systems. Industry also gave high priority to capabilities that would improve their innovative abilities, their effective collaboration and communication with customers and suppliers, creating proactive collaboration spaces and model-configured, visual working environments.

Some of the key customer requirements for holistic design and concurrent engineering are:

• Designers must be able to model their own concepts and define visual languages to describe their designs to fellow designers and engineers

- Designers should not have to learn to use any IT tools to communicate their designs. Most software tools should be hidden from the designers and engineers
- Suppliers should be able to contribute their ideas, provide specifications, and prepare bids through workplaces generated by purposeful models
- Customers, suppliers, providers, vendors, consultants, and contractors should be able to access the same c-Business networks and collaboration spaces to qualify for work
- Partners, particularly SMEs, must be able to join business opportunities and delivery projects with a minimum of investments in IT competences and systems

Services to help them coordinate work, capture experiences and lessons learned, grow their knowledge and have knowledge integrate, and drive their business projects are at the top of the longer term wish-lists.

Now, a rapidly growing number of them are questioning whether or not current IT systems and SE practices will do the job.

2.5.2 Industrial Innovation

State of practice in most industries is that in which innovation and customer delivery projects are kept strictly apart, just as business process modeling and improvement, and product development or engineering processes are kept apart. This is because today there are no methods or IT systems that support the need to configure the systems according to market and customer demands.

Lack of support for innovation, the creation and articulation of new ideas of product or process, is today hurting mainly because growing and expressing knowledge from human mental models have no or little support from IT. This is not alone to be blamed on the IT community, but also reflects the lack of knowledge cultivation and language to express and share knowledge among industries. Most industrial sectors do not have the concept of architecture, and no layers of abstraction are available to represent product ideas, concepts, and layouts/arrangements as digital artifacts. Most industrial approaches to product design are supported by fairly static drawing and diagramming techniques. The design process, spanning from the most abstracted requirements interpretation to product-end-of-life, is stepwise and supported by disjoint and specific diagrams, drawings and frozen digital models governed by proprietary application systems. This has manifested the belief, even among designers and pragmatic experts, that industry needs a specific product structure for each major step and engineering discipline. Consequently, methods and tools to integrate between the many structures have also been developed and introduced. Now, prototypes exist to prove that this may not necessarily be required and definitely not desired, as it portrays industrial design as a sequential, step-wise process. So developing integrated product structure models, and extending integration across other domains, is one of the most demanding challenges.

Collaborative Product and Process Design (CPPD)

Some digital reference models already exist to support collaborative product development. They address different aspects and viewpoints for design collaboration, including:

- Change and configuration management are key work processes for collaborative product design (CPD) that need to be shared by all the actors of an industrial project
- Information models like STEP Application Protocols that support product data exchange, sharing and retention all along the lifecycle of a product and within the supply chain
- Project management reference models, supporting change and version management, portfolio management and possibly more services
- Sector standards related to the previous aspects, for automotive, aerospace (AECMA), or military (MILS) product specifications

Unfortunately, the models are being used as physical models, but they should be considered as conceptual models. As soon as they become operational, i.e., adapted to specific business and technical ICT contexts, important challenges exist to establish model adaptability, extensibility, and interoperability. Model interoperability cannot be established if no shared business concepts are built to allow high level communication between processes and applications, and extensibility is not possible at all with current IT-systems. These models, as used, address only one particular aspect of what is required to establish effective cooperation and interoperability. The STEP application protocols for instance focus only on product data and information exchange and management issues. Collaborative design for increased customization and life-cycle support are key requirements for dynamic service-oriented industrial communities. As a prerequisite for competitive offerings of products and services, collaborative design is a catalyst for business success, growth, and customer satisfaction.

2.5.3 Service-team Organization

Collaborative holistic design will demand model-composed, configured, and life-cycle managed services operated by teams in a smart organization. The teams with clearly defined roles and responsibilities collaborate as mutually supportive service-teams. Each team owns well-defined basic services, takes on responsibilities for providing, configuring, and adapting project and customer-specific services and service responsibilities. This means industry should own their own project services to be able to recap and reuse any customer delivery process. Figure 2.4 illustrates the interplay between different such teams. We will return with a more detailed description of this concept in the main contribution part of the book.

2.5.4 Concurrent Platform Engineering

Concurrent engineering of layers of project platforms, extending the knowledge architecture with customer models is fundamental to support

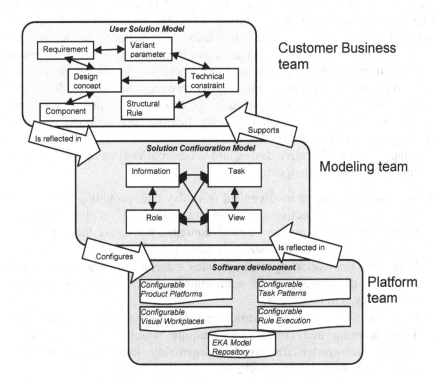

Fig. 2.4. Service-team interaction

holistic design, capturing growing needs, designing new ways of working, cutting lead times, all depend on model-generated shared workspaces and more role-oriented workplaces, separating issues, and supporting simultaneous variants avoiding sequentially forced versioning.

2.6 Knowledge and Data Representation

Information and data exchange between IT systems decides work patterns, and determines work process flows and many tasks that appear in user workplaces. This is evident in all PLM system workplaces where the user is file and content manager for what information is received and sent.

In conceptual and early design, designers must have access to services for defining their own data in their own views, including data formatting views, and associated views to provide context for precise meaning and reuse of the contents by whoever will need access to the data. Conceptual artifacts cannot easily be stored on their own in databases as they do not have any predefined data types. They should be represented as abstract objects combined with their defining tasks. These constructs are what is referred to as artifacts. The knowledge architecture should provide contextual storage allowing designers and engineers to create and recover ideas, concepts and knowledge artifacts. Capturing the sudden good ideas in a form that easily allows industry to recover, interpret, evaluate, and assess their feasibility for realization within an enterprise knowledge architecture and platform that provide flexible and powerful piloting, testing, and learning services.

Supporting collaborative design and concurrent engineering will require solutions to these challenges:

- Securing stakeholder involvement from day one, providing services for role-specific perspectives on and interpretations of the enterprise knowledge dimensions and model domains, managing their particular aspects, methods, and data and parameter values.
- Improving innovation by enabling idea externalization and conceptual design in distributed design environments, enabling robust, dynamic workplaces, and languages.
- Design knowledge externalization and sharing from idea to end-of-life. Team learning and collaboration require simultaneous modeling in *multiple knowledge dimensions*, organizing models into dynamic enterprise knowledge architectures.

- Reducing change and version management by closing the gap between evolving business operations, alternative knowledge structures, and model-configured software support.
- Generating effective role-specific workplaces as well as services and views for portfolio management and agile collaborative decision-making.
- Configuring services for enterprise knowledge capture and architecting, building and adapting *modeling templates, workplaces, and services*, partly automating knowledge management and organizational learning.
- Runtime extensions and adaptations, effectively including SME's in design projects by model-generating simple to use workplaces without demanding IT investments and extensive, time-demanding training.
- Flexible, interoperable, and reusable platform building workplaces on the core platform, isolating software changes. Model execution services should be loosely coupled by *event notification*, making the platforms robust, extensible, and configurable.

Defining, calculating, and balancing design parameters and their valid value-ranges, deciding design bandwidth for product families is an extra challenge to meet customized product design and delivery that will imply more role-specific views of parameters and their acceptable values.

2.7 Personal Workplaces and Interaction

Industrial innovation is dependent on information being collected, harnessed, and shared as knowledge (reflective information views) in context, and converted to operational knowledge that can be activated to contribute to new and improved workplaces and dynamic work environments, if possible avoiding any in-between interpreters of information and data, thus being able to close the learning loop of participative learners. Learning-by-doing or by performing work is a must in order to support distributed design and engineering team-work, as is supporting automatic workplace enhancement from work performance, experiences, and lessons learned.

Successful model-based platforms should have extendable modeling and execution capabilities to support and be supported by these role-specific workplaces:

- *The designers and engineers* deal with evolving and dynamic multidimensional data, such as product structures, properties, and rules. Their workplaces must be knowledge-driven and model-configured with user-composed services and views, and adaptive to changing contexts. The more design and local customization the more need for services to extend and adapt the knowledge architectures and platforms.

- *The knowledge manager* has a very demanding job, having to deal with dynamically created data-models, services, views and workplaces and to support them all in enterprise knowledge architectures. Platform services, views, tasks, and workplaces will change from project to project, and must be coordinated locally as well as across enterprises. User-driven model-based service orchestration must be supported by the basic knowledge engineering platform, which should provide support for tailoring these model-configured workplaces.
- *The model builder* must perform metadata definitions concurrently with product design, and must provide services enabling users to change and extend the data model and its supporting services. New workplaces, tasks, and views will have to be model-designed and configured.
- *The platform manager* must perform platform extensions and adaptations to integrate new IT systems and tools, to support data exchange and data definition and sharing services, and implement protocols to support data collection from various external sources.
- *The workplace designer* must build workplace design models for new roles with tasks, views, and sources of content, and perform workplace configuration modeling, and workplace generation with the preconfigured contents and behavior.
- *The knowledge architect* defines new metaviews, metadata, and methods, and performs the analysis, classification, and standardization of the data and knowledge content of models and the operational enterprise knowledge architecture.
- *The support engineer* needs services to translate and extend EKA structures, services to define and adapt new view types, and also services to integrate data and parameters from partner sources, representing project and business data and knowledge.

2.7.1 Innovation and Knowledge Repositories

Repository services to support the knowledge architectures must be role, task, and view accessible, so services to access the repository following any of the three dimensions must be supported. This would be like navigating a visual map. The more classical identification schemes based on characteristics properties and categorization structures, reflecting user perspectives, should also be supported for those that do not relate to any roles defined.

Common design artifact expression, language definition, and extension and task-structure navigation must be supported. This will change the way we perceive of, engineer, use and manage repositories, enhancing the services on top of relational and object-oriented databases.

2.8 Summary

Summarizing we have defined the major industrial challenges to be:

1. Building searchable digital information libraries of present common information sources, to improve data and knowledge sharing and use
2. Developing consistent reference models that are easily integrated with Web-platforms, to allow more effective community and project extensions and adaptations
3. Developing knowledge engineering platforms and services that can add value to and integrate present IT application systems, "the islands of automation"
4. Developing operational enterprise knowledge architectures and platforms to concretize and make operational current blueprint architectural frameworks
5. Develop methodologies as descriptive templates to support the building of industry platforms, for example the CPD methods to build collaborative design platforms
6. To model reference models that can be reused and drive knowledge standardization initiatives across projects and sectors
7. To support holistic design implying that multidimensional modeling capabilities to express mental models of designers and engineers must be supported
8. To provide modeling team services and role-specific workplaces and views to support concurrent knowledge engineering for collaborative product design
9. To provide model or knowledge architecture configured workplaces to enable new approaches to model-based systems engineering and solutions deployment
10. To provide services to enable data definition and sharing without being dependent on IT-defined data-models, thus supporting idea capture and conceptual design

In addition to these mostly technical challenges, there are educational, organizational, and managerial challenges that must also be dealt with. However, with the Web transforming into a knowledge-sharing medium, "a knowledge reflector and amplifier," we believe the technology will serve to augment the human mental models and help us use more than 7% of our left hemisphere of the brain; the visual part.

The definition of what is an IT-system may have to be rethought and systems engineering will need to align with product engineering and take advantage of knowledge architectures and holistic design approaches. Another consequence is that many architecture and systems standards will have to be reengineered and put into their correct context.

3 Industrial Evolutions

This chapter presents a number of cases representing early approaches to Active Knowledge Modeling (AKM) solutions in precommercial EU projects, specifically the EXTERNAL (2003) and ATHENA (2004) EU projects. Although the current AKM approach is described in more detail in Chaps. 5 and 7–10, it is important to look back briefly at the developments that have brought us to where we are. The AKM technology is the result of a long ongoing learning process that we expect to go on for a number of years.

3.1 History of AKM Development

The industrial needs and thinking that sparked the initial development of the AKM technology, in the late 1980s, was inspired and influenced by so-called *Industrial War Rooms*. War rooms, see Fig. 3.1, were created in most aircraft and automotive industries. The industrial war rooms have four dimensions of core innovative knowledge. In early industrial war rooms, each wall was covered with engineering drawings, plots, and familiar paper images depicting traditional aspects and views of enterprise knowledge, described in Chap. 1 as the POPS dimensions:

- Product and Services: depicting the many disjoint product structures, designs, engineering methods, parts, and classes
- Organization and People Development: organizational structures, positions, teams and roles, and their competence and skill profiles
- Process Modeling and Work Management: process and task models, work execution, and management views
- System and Tool Development: use, solutions and maintenance architectures, components and constructs

War rooms were meeting places to discuss the many known, but not all described and considered, and often forgotten, dependencies and relationships between objects, structures, views, and responsible people. Attempts to model holistic life-cycle views of product data were performed, revealing some interesting information. In these models, more relation-ships had to be drawn between relationships than between objects, simply because the abstract objects defining the relationship were not known and could not be represented. This identified a lack of language for expressing product concepts, systems, and life-cycle evolution, representing layers of abstraction of product knowledge.

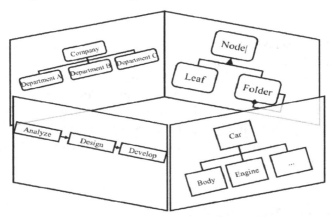

Fig. 3.1. The industrial war room-inspired AKM thinking

The foundations of the AKM technology were discovered in industrial innovation projects, attempting to build digital product models according to war room thinking. Here is an excerpt from a business report from one of these projects, written in 1993:

"Coherent and logically consistent representations of work-centric enterprise knowledge automatically yield reflective views, recursive processes, repetitive working solutions and replicable structures of meta-data. Knowledge from other layers and representations on other media does not possess these properties. Implementing the war room concepts, applying visual modeling languages, automatically give us these intrinsic properties. This in turn yields powerful development, integration, management and reuse capabilities. Most other knowledge domains needed for business operations, such as abstracted process flows, or single views or diagrams of any domain, do not exhibit these properties. Any aspect and view must be derived from the core operational POPS knowledge, to be coherent, consistent and compliant".

On the basis of 15 years of enterprise modeling experience from leading industries, we conclude as follows: *"The variations in knowledge from one enterprise to another are mostly changes in semantics and complexity of structures, in methods and in property embodiment as parameter structures and values. Complexity of structural layers, visual representations, and type hierarchies of the four main enterprise knowledge dimensions, in particular of process and product aspects, contribute to the modeling confusions".*

Therefore, to model agile enterprises with support for coherence, consistency, and reuse, we must be able to separate business, knowledge, and IT architectures and models for designing and configuring these layered knowledge architectures.

These early attempts produced important lessons to learn and helped categorize and describe the challenges. Innovation projects such as Volvo IGP, FORD PW60, the Ericsson A project, and McDonnell-Douglas MD12X made significant contributions to bring forward visual knowledge modeling. In recent years, as the underlying web infrastructure has matured, we have come closer to fulfilling the promises of the AKM approach, including configuring workplaces for executing practical work.

3.2 Experiences from EXTERNAL

An early attempt to realize the AKM approach was made in the EXTERNAL project (Krogstie et al. 2002a). One focus in EXTERNAL was to support the formation and running of smart networked organizations, also known as extended enterprises, by combining the resources from a number of existing organizations in forming a common enterprise. The infrastructure to support smart networked organizations, developed in EXTERNAL, consists of three layers (Karlsen et al. 2001; Krogstie et al. 2002a; Krogstie and Jørgensen 2004). These layers are identified as follows:

- Layer 1, the *information and communication technology* (ICT) layer: defining and describing the execution platform, software architectures, tools, software components, connectivity, and communication
- Layer 2, the *knowledge representation* layer: defining and describing constructs and mechanisms for modeling
- Layer 3, the *work performance and management* layer: modeling and implementing customer solutions, generating work environments as personalized and context-sensitive user interfaces available through portals, and performing work

3.2.1 The ICT Layer

The ICT infrastructure is an integration of the enterprise and process modeling tools brought into the EXTERNAL project by the partners:

- METIS (Lillehagen 1999): a general purpose enterprise modeling and visualization tool, allowing model builders to define tailored metamodels and views
- XCHIPS (Haake and Wang 1997): a cooperative hypermedia tool integrated with process support and synchronous collaboration
- SimVision (Kuntz et al. 1998): a project simulator used to analyze resource allocation, highlighting potential sources of delay and backlogs
- WORKWARE (Jørgensen 2001, 2004): a web-based emergent workflow management system with to-do-lists, document sharing, process enactment, and awareness mechanisms
- FrameSolutions (Kallåk et al. 1998): a commercially available framework for building automated workflow applications

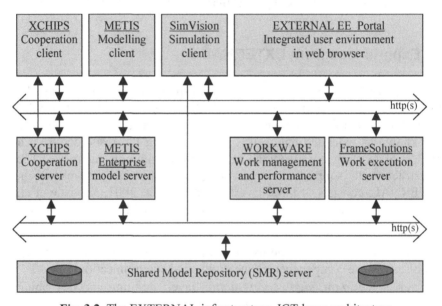

Fig. 3.2. The EXTERNAL infrastructure, ICT layer architecture

The ICT layer is depicted in Fig. 3.2 indicating the clients, servers, and database layers. In addition to the tools described earlier, we have included a portal as a common front-end to automated processes governed by FrameSolutions and to emergent processes supported in WORKWARE.

3.2.2 The Knowledge Representation Layer

The knowledge representation layer defines how models, metamodels, and metadata are represented, used, and managed. A version of Action Port Modeling (APM) (Carlsen 1998; Jørgensen 2004) constitutes the core of EXTERNAL's modeling language (EEML). The kernel concepts are shown in Fig. 3.3 as a simplified logical metamodel. The process logic is mainly expressed through nested structures of *tasks* and *decision points*. The sequencing of the tasks is expressed by the *flow* relation. *Roles* are used to connect resources of various kinds (people, organizations, information, and tools) to the tasks. Modeling smart networked organizations in EEML thus results in models that capture extensive sets of relationships between the organizations, people, processes, and resources. This is particularly useful considering the dynamic nature of networked organizations. For new partners joining the network, the rich enterprise models provide a valuable source of knowledge on how to *behave* in the network.

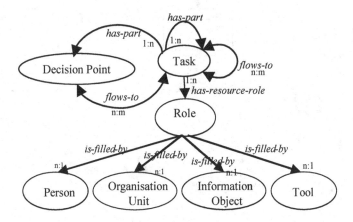

Fig. 3.3. Simplified logical metamodel of EEML

Moreover, the interactive nature of the models, meaning that the users are free to refine them during execution, increases their potential as sources of experience and knowledge. As such, they can be used to *document* details on how the work was actually done and not only on how it was once planned.

From a knowledge management perspective, process models are carriers of work-centric knowledge, that is, knowledge of how to do things, but through the possibility in EEML of attaching information resources to the tasks at any level, such a model also imposes a structure upon the set of information resources relevant for the work described by the process model. To a large extent, the process models themselves form the basis for information management.

The notation of the main concepts within the language is illustrated in Fig. 3.4, which shows a conceptual metamodel of EEML. In addition to the core concepts of tasks, decision points (including milestones), roles, and resources, it illustrates support of goal and competency modeling.

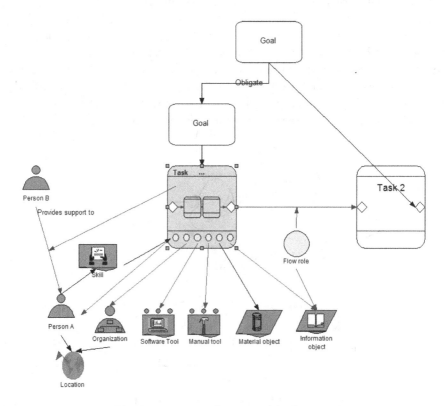

Fig. 3.4. Conceptual metamodel of EEML

3.2.3 The Work Performance and Management Layer

Users access their solutions through portals. A project portal for a networked organization must have support for methodology adaptation and for communication, coordination, and collaboration in teams. Project work management, reporting, and other services must be offered, and finally project work must be performed with possibilities for repetition, providing security and privacy to knowledge workers.

In the EXTERNAL infrastructure, the web-based portal registers and qualifies users, and invokes other tools through the WORKWARE tool set. Modeled tasks are executed through the invocation of tools and applications from the web-based user environment comprising the portal and WORKWARE. WORKWARE sets up the context for each task, giving access to the knowledge and resources needed to perform the task. The actual work performance is done by invoking appropriate services. The task performers may access desktop tools, organizational information systems, web services, or automated processes (in FrameSolutions) through this user environment.

User environments are generated dynamically based on the definition of tasks using EEML. Forms and components for interacting with different model objects are selected and composed based on user interface policies. These policies are also modeled objects. This enables user interface customization and personalization.

The dynamically generated work management interface includes services for work performance, and also for process modeling and metamodeling. The *worktop* (what is later renamed MGWP – Model Generated Work Place) is the main component in this interface. Each task has its own worktop. In addition to the services for performing and managing the task, it contains links to all knowledge in the process models that is relevant for the task. Since the worktop is dynamically generated, subject to personal preferences, the skill levels of task performers can be taken into account, e.g., to provide more detailed guidelines for people who have not previously worked on such tasks. Similarly, customized worktops for project management can support the project management team. The contents may include an overview of the project, adopted management principles, applicable methodologies, project work breakdown structure, results, plans and tasks, technologies and resources, status reporting, and calculations.

The EXTERNAL infrastructure was applied in a number of projects as reported earlier in Jørgensen (2004). These cases constitute a representative selection of knowledge-intensive virtual enterprises. One was a business-consulting firm interacting with its customers. The second was a network of small software companies. The third was an international research project (EXTERNAL itself). Interaction between users and developers ensured an ongoing practical validation. This process started already during the development of WORKWARE in the AIS project (Jørgensen and Carlsen 1999), which was a predecessor to EXTERNAL.

3.2.4 Case 1: The EXTERNAL Project

EXTERNAL took its own medicine as an early experimentation arena for the AKM technology. Experiences were fed back into the development process for the benefit of the industrial cases. The project plan was articulated in early prototype versions of EEML, and later imported to the work execution environments (WORKWARE and XCHIPS). Because of resource limitations and the instability of an evolving infrastructure, it was decided to put particular emphasis on supporting two typical process examples rather than the whole project:

- *Periodic progress reporting*: A mandatory, routine administrative procedure, where reports are written for each work package each quarter, and then collected and sent to the customer (in this case the EU Commission) twice a year.
- *Joint project planning*: A knowledge-intensive activity, elaborating work package plans. Often, planning takes place after reporting to accommodate deviations and provide more detailed plans for the next period.

In addition to these planned case studies, which were carefully evaluated, ad hoc utilization of EXTERNAL tools also took place in the project. The following subsections summarize lessons learned from these cases, focusing on the aspects most relevant for evaluating the interactive modeling approach, the language, and tool support from WORKWARE. More details are available in Haake et al. (2002).

Periodic Progress Reporting

The main activity in this case is quarterly progress reporting (QPR). For each of the nine work packages (WP), the WP manager writes a separate report. The report template and actual report are modeled as information resources to these work items. The project manager is responsible for coordinating and following up the reporting process. In the model, an optional meeting is included for coordination purposes. Though this process is quite simple, it shows that the interaction perspective helps to limit the complexity of the model. For instance, we need no flows from the start of the main process to the concurrent subitems. The lack of input flows means that no constraints prevent the items from starting. Another simplification is evident in the location of the task *Evaluate need for meeting*. This is something that all nine WP managers must do. In systems that only allow one person per task, you would thus need nine items. Here, all WP managers are allocated to one collaborative item. This allocation is made indirectly through the actor roles on each of the *Write WP progress report* items, so if one of the managers delegates the task to someone else, that person is automatically involved in the meeting as well. (In this example, indirect resource allocation does not follow the work breakdown structure.) There are more examples where resource allocation captures dependencies that need not be duplicated to the process dimension. One is the use of information resources to represent the report document parts produced by each WP manager. The architecture of multiple model interactions between the document manager and the workflow engine thus simplifies the models.

The tasks of the project manager (PM) are supported by the services of the infrastructure, and thus need not be articulated in detail. Work lists provide overviews of the current state of the process, helping the PM to see which WP managers have not yet written their report. Through the *Mail to all* service on the worktop, the project manager sends reminders to the WP managers when it is time to write a new report, and again when the deadline approaches. The PM role was reassigned five times throughout the project, so there was a need for explicit coordination routines that the new manager could reuse.

Progress reporting is a routine, administrative procedure that recurs throughout the project at regular time intervals. This model was thus reused a number of times. When the process was first articulated, the support for reuse was limited to copy-and-paste in METIS. A lot of the initial learning and alignment of reporting practices across organizations and countries was already captured in the first version. However, an updated procedure was implemented 1 year later, taking into account experiences with working together as well as increased understanding of the capabilities of the model-driven infrastructure. The new version improvements included the following:

- Changed work breakdown structure to make individual responsibilities clearer.
- Resource allocation was made more explicit to handle reassignment better.
- Added output flows so that *Write QPR* automatically finishes when all of its subitems have been completed.
- Added previous reports for each WP as resource and template for the *Write WP progress report* work items.

Another occasion of end user innovation in the reporting case involved metamodeling. The process in general and the management work in particular are time-driven. The participants decided to model *timers*, a decision connector subclass not part of the EEML at that time, but one that they needed to handle exceptions (delays) and coordination. As WORKWARE did not support timers, the project manager had to remember to do these things, but she was reminded by the presence of the objects in the model. The timers were thus manually activated. For process knowledge management and IS evolution, this information was highly relevant, as it pointed to requirements that were not expressed in the specification documents (Strømseng et al. 2000) but emerged during use. An AKM active knowledge arena has improved such process knowledge management in a number of ways, including the following:

- Incorporating local modifications and metamodeling (adding a trigger-time property to the decisions) supported by the instance-oriented meta-metamodel
- Allowing propagation of dynamic changes so that updated definitions are used in all instances
- Implementing parameterization of model properties. Most of these tasks' names refer to WPs or the current time period, and could easily be generated from parameterization rules
- A specialized, semiautomated reuse metaprocess called *Create new periodic progress report* could be included as a service in WORKWARE. Based on some property values from the user, e.g., the name and deadline of the current period, as well as the current project plan, the reporting process model was automatically generated

Joint Project Planning

Project planning was selected as the second case from the EXTERNAL project because its characteristics complemented the reporting case. Planning is a more knowledge-intensive ad hoc activity, and it utilizes modeling tools for work performance. While the emphasis of reporting was activation and reuse, planning primarily concerns model articulation. It was also expected that the need for coordination between different work packages would require the collaborative modeling services of XCHIPS. The first implementation included the *plan* (a process model) as well as the *planning process* (metaprocess), but not the operation of the plans.

The planning process was modeled in EEML and enacted in XCHIPS. XCHIPS supports closer (in time) collaboration than WORKWARE. When two people work on the same item, they immediately see the effects of each other's actions. The interface provides real-time awareness of who is currently working, and shows the current status of the tasks by color coding. The use case report contains an example of how these features were utilized for defining a template (Haake et al. 2002):

"Once the joint planning (JPL) process model was finished, one designer created a work package model template in the METIS modeling environment and made the template available by using the shared repository[...] Subsequently, she put a link to the template into the JPL process model. Now, another designer used that template to create a sample work package model, by using modeling services. This model was reviewed by the first designer and improved in a number of iterations. The final example model was made available in the shared repository and linked to from the JPL process model. This mixture of largely asynchronous work and some synchronous discussions was greatly facilitated by the shared repository, collaboration, and modeling."

The template produced here is typical. It includes a basic structure for objects, with separate folders for tasks, inputs, outputs, organizations and people, as well as a project document archive. Some elements, e.g., parts of the archive and the organizational structure, are shared among the work packages. The inputs to one WP in many cases are the outputs of another.

This example shows how (meta)process support can facilitate knowledge management. XCHIPS was also used for enacting the process of *defining new projects* in this version of the infrastructure, invoking METIS to let users define the first plan of the project and then forwarding it to WORKWARE. However, real-time collaboration met technical difficulties with firewalls and limited bandwidth across the Internet. Consequently, for version 2 of the infrastructure, a web-based solution replaced XCHIPS for project definition.

Evaluation Results

The QPR and JPL cases were subject to a formal evaluation where 10 people answered a questionnaire (Chrysostalis et al. 2003; Krogstie et al. 2002b; Lillehagen et al. 2002b; Scagno 2002). The same questions were asked after the first period, when none of the EXTERNAL tools had been used, and then again after the second period, during which the infrastructure had been in use. For the reporting case, the time spent, perceived quality of results, and the need for outside help or documents showed great improvement (Scagno 2002). Part of this improvement could be due to learning that would occur anyway from the first to the second cycle. However, a baseline survey of the similar process of *Summary Cost Statements* showed less improvement than QPR.

For the planning case, opinions were more mixed. Some of the respondents felt that quality and effectiveness had improved, while others claimed the opposite. A clear majority however thought that the plans had become more accurate. When asked what the most important problem was in planning, half of the respondents originally said lack of collaboration. After having tried the tools, however, all but one chose *identifying dangerous delays*. It was also reported that initial experience shows that the current infrastructure and tools are too rigid (Haake et al. 2002). While the numbers from this survey clearly are too small to draw statistically significant conclusions, the relative results of the two cases, and also for different criteria, are interesting. The opinions by the participants were more clearly articulated (both positive and negative) after tools were applied. Apparently, real-time cooperation was not as important as we thought, while simple enactment support seemed more useful. For the further experimentation, it was thus decided to add more work performance orientation to the planning case as well. Experiences from this are reported later.

Action Lists – Emergent Project Planning

The first implementation of the JPL process took a top-down perspective, where managers were responsible for planning the work inside their work package. Such plans, however, seldom are detailed enough to cover all the tasks that are to be performed. Consequently, the EXTERNAL project also had a web-based action list located at the project web server. This solution had a number of limitations, typical of publish-oriented web environments:

- Only the project manager could change the list, update status, add new actions, etc.
- The actions lacked context and were often hard to comprehend.
- The actions were not explicitly connected to project plans.
- Actions were not linked to a work environment, documents, or tools.
- Although the list could be sorted on different attributes and filtered according to certain criteria (e.g., one list for each person), it was not possible to add new criteria.

Consequently, the action lists were not actively used by many of the project participants. During the spring of 2002, it was thus decided to replace them with the EXTERNAL infrastructure. WORKWARE had the central role in this application, managing the actions as tasks. It took just a few hours of work to customize a WORKWARE installation for action lists. It organized actions according to these criteria:

- Status, e.g., most lists contain only ready and/or ongoing actions
- Delay

- Work packages
- Teams that are responsible for coordinating interrelated tasks across work packages
- Persons and roles, separating the actions which the current user is responsible for from the ones where she is just a participant
- Follow-up lists, containing all tasks that the current user is customer of.

The increased access to edit actions should make the list more up-to-date. Although the structure for the actions was not connected to a full project plan, teams and work packages provided increased context for the work. Explicit assignment of follow-up responsibility and the ability to look in the event log to see who created the action made each item easier to understand. The old, static action lists contained 288 actions after 2½ years of operation, while WORKWARE contained 131 after just 2 months, even though it was installed during the summer holidays. It thus seems safe to claim that the second application was experienced as an improvement. After the action lists had been available in WORKWARE for a while, however, usage frequency dropped significantly. This happened although consensus was articulated that the application was useful and should be used. A number of factors may have contributed to this decline:

- Lack of project management commitment and contractual obligations to use the system.
- No clearly defined roles were modeled with a consistent set of user-composed coordination services and views.
- Since WORKWARE allows everyone to define new tasks and themselves mark them as finished, the project manager no longer had to perform these tasks. Although this relieved him of some duties, it also gave him less responsibility for following up all actions. For instance, at project meetings, nobody was assigned responsibility of recording new actions.
- A number of major deliverables were completed, e.g., final versions of the tools, infrastructure, and methodology. Several of the most eager users thus no longer participated actively in the project.
- There were technological limitations, e.g., cumbersome document upload. User interfaces and enactment policies for tasks, in general, were perhaps too complicated for simple actions.
- Instability and poor performance of servers may also have discouraged some users. Performance suffered when the action model grew large.
- For a number of situations, e-mails remained the simplest and most used coordination tool.
- In spite of its web and e-mail integration, some users saw WORKWARE as yet another tool added to an already complex user environment.

During the main period of use, however, it was noted on a number of occasions that people sent out e-mails referring to tasks, and pointing to documents uploaded to WORKWARE. This did not occur with the previous application.

This case shows how quickly and easily WORKWARE could be customized to a particular usage need by defining an overall process model (in this case, the WP structure), a menu structure, and some specialized work lists and services. After people started to use the application, further customization was made based on their experiences. The case also shows how bottom-up emergent process articulation can complement top-down project planning and give the organization a more accurate picture of what is really going on in the project.

3.2.5 Case 2: The Business Consulting Project Cycle

The business consulting case involved primary users outside of the EXTERNAL project. The company in question was supported by process modeling experts from one of the EXTERNAL partners. The company had already defined a procedure for how their projects should be executed. This procedure was available on the corporate Intranet, in the form of textual descriptions and informal visualizations. One of the first tasks for the EXTERNAL consultants was thus to model this procedure, known as the *project cycle*, in the EEML language. Local requirements were then collected, and a customized version of the EXTERNAL infrastructure was installed. The users in this case were novices with respect to process modeling and groupware systems, so they selected WORKWARE as their primary tool.

Reuse of Project Templates

In addition to the process model, the template also includes an organizational model with typical project roles, as well as the firm's tools, information repositories, and document templates. The template contains optional items, which are only needed for certain types of projects, e.g., those with a budget larger than a certain amount. These options are currently modeled as normal decisions. However, since many decisions can be made at project startup, modeling them as reuse decisions would simplify the local models. Many of these decisions are controlled by properties of the project, so the potential for automated reuse decisions is substantial.

It is interesting to note that the project cycle mainly defines the administrative work. The actual performance of the project is to be included inside the item *project work*, a subitem of *project execution* at level 3 in the work breakdown structure. This pattern can be expected in a model that represents management perspectives rather than work perspectives, a typical bias in process modeling. It also reflects the fact that administrative procedures are easy to define and reuse without change across all projects, while the core work is dependent on the situated work environment. Therefore, if knowledge management and process improvement are truly to create a competitive advantage, bottom-up core work must be modeled as well.

Security and Access Control

Improved security and multilevel access control was an absolute requirement from the business consulting company. This was the main reason why access control was prioritized for implementation in WORKWARE. A typical project in this company requires these default access rights:

- Only internal participants should be allowed to read and update all documents.
- Employees not working on a project may not have access to project information.
- Only the project manager should be allowed to grant access rights.
- Participants and customers from other organizations should be allowed to read and change documents and plans within their part of the project, but not the others. In some cases, different customers in the same project should not even know about each other. Different customers may have partially conflicting agendas, leading to less than full disclosure of information.

The access and interaction controller of WORKWARE allowed these policies to be articulated at the general level and reused across projects.

Experiences and Evaluation Results

On the basis of his previous experience with Internet tools, the pilot user in this case regarded WORKWARE primarily as a document repository. The concepts of enactment, work management, and status reporting were not useful to him because in the first project, he was the only participant. Consequently, the system was regarded as too complex and cumbersome to use. This initial reaction indicates that simpler user interface components and enactment policies should be the default for novice users. Though some simplifications were made as part of the customization process for this case, they were insufficient. The EXTERNAL process modelers were able to reconstruct the project cycle template using the available constructs in EEML. In some cases, however, limitations of the tools and errors in the documentation prevented them from achieving what they wanted. One example was the modeling of template actor roles. The documentation, for the version at that time based on atomic semantics, stated that resource roles could only be modeled inside tasks, whereas they wanted to model the roles independently. When this confusion was cleared and the semantic holism of the modeling language was described, the template was adjusted.

3.2.6 Case 3: IT Consulting in an SME Network

The final case study in EXTERNAL aimed to support a network of small- and medium-sized IT companies located in different countries, mainly in eastern and southern Europe. Many of these companies are owned by the same group and have cooperated in a number of projects. Three cases with different characteristics were selected (Giotopoulos et al. 2001):

1. Proposal submission for government funding based on a simple and well-defined procedure
2. Software development subcontracting based on a case of medium complexity
3. Management of a Leonardo DaVinci project based on creative and unstructured activities

An overview of the characteristics of these scenarios is presented in Table 3.1.

Table 3.1. Characteristics of different SME network scenarios

Property	Proposal submission	Software subcontracting	Project management
Main objective	Flexibility	Maintainability, reliability	Reliability, adaptability
Duration	Single unit	Long-term alliance	Temporal
Topology	Fixed structure	Dynamic	Mixed
Participation	Single alliance	Multiple alliances	Multiple alliances
Coordination	Tree structure	Tree structure	Star structure
Visibility	Single level	Multiple levels	Multiple levels
Collaboration	Activity coordination	Distributed process management	Joint resource management, cosupervision

Process and Model Diversity

It is interesting to see how these differences manifest themselves in the process models. Table 3.2 shows the number of primary objects of each category in the models of the three cases in this study. For the first two cases, we clearly see that the increased complexity of the cases is reflected in the size of the models. The project management case, however, has a rather simple model. The reason for this is partly that more work has been devoted to studying the two simpler cases, but it may also reflect that project management is harder to articulate than administrative work. For case 3, just the management activities were articulated and not the core work.

Following the history of these cases, it was interesting to note that software subcontracting, the most elaborate case, was originally modeled as a copy of the project cycle from the business consulting use case described earlier. This template was generic enough to be transported to another country and application domain. The fact that the participants in the SME networks had limited previous experience with process modeling also helps to explain why they would rather start with a template than from scratch. Over a couple of months, however, the software subcontracting model evolved, and new items were added to all levels of the work breakdown structure, and existing items were renamed to fit the local terminology. Here, we saw the process of template *appropriation* in practice.

The project management case was modeled as two separate processes, one for the work before the project actually started, and another for the management activities to be carried out during the project work. This modularization makes it easier to reuse the latter process, as management is an ongoing activity that recurs many times throughout the lifecycle of the project.

Table 3.2. Statistics for models of different SME network scenarios

Property	Funding proposal	Software subcontracting	Project management
Number of work items	25	80	10
Depth of work breakdown	3	4	1
Number of actor roles	4	25	9
Number of object/tool roles	0	19	18

3.2.7 Final Evaluation Results

One year after the survey discussed earlier, all the three EXTERNAL cases were subjected to a joint evaluation (Chrysostalis et al. 2003). A questionnaire was sent by e-mail to 19 users, including managers and project participants. They were asked to rate how much they agreed to statements (both positive and negative) on a 7-point Likert scale, and in-depth interviews of some of the participants were carried out. Frequency of use, user-friendliness, and the usefulness of provided functionality were assessed. In general, inexperienced users responded neutrally to all categories of questions. People who had used the tools were typically slightly positive, giving average ratings between 4.8 and 5.6, where 4 is neutral and 7 is maximum.

The major innovative contributions created by these use cases are as follows:

- Developing the active knowledge model-configured infrastructure, work arenas, and workplaces.
- Developing executable emergent work processes as task patterns, and supporting continuously improving work processes.
- Developing the understanding of the importance of capturing work-centric knowledge elements by inventing common visual solutions modeling language and approach.

3.3 Experiences from ATHENA

In the ATHENA Integrated Project, subproject B5 (ATHENA 2007), interoperability in industry and collaborative business, c-Business, was assessed and validated using six concrete business use case pilots. All six pilots were designed using various infrastructures, knowledge architectures, and methodologies as developed in the project.

The pilots were quite different with respect to approaches, infrastructures and methodologies applied, and service platforms configured and operated. The services therefore do not constitute a homogeneous set of services from one approach for developing and configuring and using Service-Oriented Architectures to build and operate the pilots. There are at least three distinctly different approaches to developing the pilots.

The pilots built to prototype ATHENA components and services were as follows:

- The automotive pilot at CRF, focusing on the testing of car systems

- The aerospace pilot at EADS, focusing on engineering change management of aircraft landing gear
- The furniture pilot at Aidima, focusing on the exchange of information and data among the key stakeholders and the decision support given
- The telecom pilot built at Intracom, focusing on model-configured workplaces for product managers, supporting Product Portfolio Management (PPM) services
- The IV&I pilot, focusing on Inventory Visibility, built by a group of partners coordinated by AIAG/NIST in the United States
- The Outbound Logistics pilot, focusing on part identification scheme interpretation, built by a group of partners coordinated by CAS AG

We have selected to present the telecom pilot at Intracom as a generic use case prototype illustrating the approach, architectures, and methodologies that contributed the most to realize the AKM approach and the visual solutions modeling methodology.

3.3.1 Telecom Pilot

The telecom pilot is about PPM where support for selecting the right product to produce and deliver is in focus. The pilot was developed at Intracom in close cooperation among partners developing model-configured solutions.

The pilot focused on PPM and product data sharing among key actors inside a telecom company. Charged with the task of selecting the right products and product variants to produce products for a dynamic market and customer base, the company must find new ways of managing product design and engineering and supporting customer communications. The pilot was implemented using a model-configured, user-composed platform and services (MUPS) architecture to design a service layer with roles, views, and model-generated workplaces and services, focusing on the needs of the product manager.

The technicalities and architectural details of these technologies and how they are applied to ATHENA results are described in more detail in ATHENA deliverable DB5.3. Here, we limit our discussion of what these technologies contribute to, stating that CBP (Collaborative Business Processes) is a top-down approach to put more coordination into work processes. MDA is a middle-out approach to provide mapping and transformation services to data, messages, and work processes. SOA is a bottom-up technology to reengineer legacy systems and provide generic components. Finally, the MUPS approach combines all the three, and adds role-specific services, reflective views, and collaborative context.

Pilot Purpose and Architecture

The telecom pilot was intended to test the applicability and usefulness of the ATHENA interoperability solutions in a typical industrial scenario, developing and maintaining a variety of high-technology product lines in a sector characterized by highly competitive and rapidly changing market conditions. The use case scenario is based on the process of PPM. Starting from enterprise modeling constructs, web-based workplaces are created, offering navigation and work views supporting all operational tasks as depicted in the enterprise model. Interaction with enterprise information repositories is facilitated via an underlying service-oriented architecture.

PPM is a process involving decisions made at different levels, where the company's active products list is constantly updated and revised. New products are evaluated, selected, and prioritized, and existing ones may be accelerated, killed, or reprioritized. The objective is to allocate resources in a way to maximize sales and profits and minimize risks.

PPM is of significant importance especially to a large enterprise with many business units and complex products. Product design typically requires the collaboration of many different engineering teams inside the same corporate environment, as well as within a business network of collaborative enterprise. PPM involves many business processes (new product development, product management, supply chain management). Many actors in different roles from strategic level (e.g., business unit manager, sector manager) and tactical level (product manager, project manager) to operational level (team leader, engineer) will be involved.

The focus of the pilot was on product management and on supporting the role of the *product manager*. The product manager is assigned to a product or product family and is responsible for developing or overseeing all aspects of the product including product definition, product development, product launch, current product management, and product phase-out.

It is apparent from Fig. 3.5 that PPM and particularly the role of product manager (PM) entails access to information of varying nature, stored in various systems and diverse platforms and implementations. The evolution of such systems in any typical medium-size enterprise has been typically outside a planned framework of interoperable systems, a situation that is changing lately with the introduction of service-oriented platforms and architectures. It is therefore currently difficult for the PM to access those disparate systems and retrieve the information needed in a comprehensive and user-friendly presentation mode.

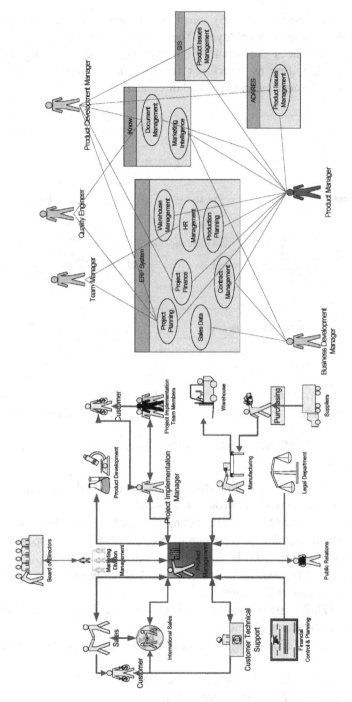

Fig. 3.5. A high-level overview of the as-is situation in the telecom pilot

In the architecture (Fig. 3.6), most of the enterprise modeling takes place in the *business* level/layer. The *process* layer represents model-generated workplaces that result from the enterprise modeling and are presented to the user as interfaces for their tasks. The *services* layer encompasses all services that are used or created to support the workplaces.

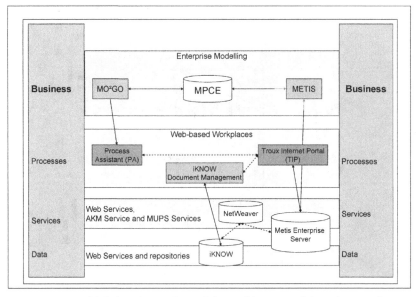

Fig. 3.6. A high-level overview of the architecture of the telecom pilot

The following ATHENA results and tools have been used to support the telecom pilot:

- *POP** – for modeling the different aspects of the enterprise and generating the workplace through the models
- *Import/export of POP** – for modeling different aspects of the enterprise
- *MPCE* for supporting interchange of models of different aspects of the enterprise in different tools
- *Transform ITM and BPM models to MEAF models* for modeling different aspects of the enterprise
- *MEAF ATHENA extensions* to facilitate web services, task management, and user interface modeling
- *MGWP (PA + TIP)* during the generation of the workplaces through the models
- *MOOGO* for process assistant (PA) generation
- *Metis* for Troux Information Portal (TIP)

- *MGWP TIP Services for Web* Services for discovery of web services and linking them to the models
- *Johnson* (+ Lyndon) for design, testing, and deployment of services

How to Use the Services

The services and tools used in the ATHENA telecom pilot are organized as shown before in the architecture figure and are generally presented along the six steps that are shown in Fig. 3.7.

- Model reference model in MO²GO
- Generate a Process Assistant
- Use MPCE to exchange reference model with Metis
- Create and make available Web Services
- Model Workplace models in Metis
- Generate Workplaces in TIP

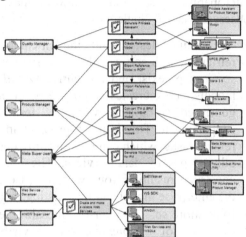

Fig. 3.7. Steps of using ATHENA services in the telecom pilot

Step 1, modeling the Reference Model in MO²GO is a preliminary modeling step that results in the enterprise reference model in MPCE. The Process Assistant Workplace can be automatically generated in step 2.

MPCE is used to exchange the reference model with the Metis tool where additional modeling is performed to instantiate constructs of the Instance Model relevant to a user role. In the telecom pilot, this role is the product manager. Before the TIP workplace can be generated with any meaningful usability, web services that interact with the data layer and retrieve information from enterprise repositories must be designed, tested, and made available through metamodels built in Metis. When the web services are created, they are deployed in a service infrastructure accessible by Metis. Metis is used to import the available web services, instantiate MUPS services, and finally generate the TIP workplace, which is the actual GUI the PM uses to perform his work.

Guidelines and Experiences

Present experience with the development of Model-Generated Workplaces in the PPM scenario strongly supports the effectiveness of the approach for creating *role-specific application spaces* that can support day-to-day tasks while adhering to the corporate standards captured in the enterprise model. It has been clearly shown that the generated workplaces can go far beyond a traditional application development approach. Future directions for extending the MGWP concept so that it can evolve into an end-to-end interoperability solution framework may be inspired by the following observations and challenges:

- The actual design and implementation of underlying-information-retrieving web services does not stem from the enterprise models. The services preexist and are currently *linked* to appropriate tasks in the models. This creates a *boundary* or *mismatch* between the model-generated workplace, which is formally created, and the services supporting it. This is not a problem in services supporting document-related tasks, which can be uniformly designed, but it *is* a problem in all other types of data services. The main issue is the need to *match* constructs resulting from two very different processes at the boundary of the enterprise model and the existing (legacy) systems.

- Even more so, TIP User-Composable Services (MUPS) presuppose the existence of a *complete* set of visible services or the ability to transparently combine and orchestrate existing services to support all tasks modeled and supported by TIP. This is not a workplace task, but is a barrier in the effective utilization of such a workplace. Further efforts should identify ways of formally creating a description of this *complete* set of services needed and expected by the workplace.

- Deriving views for each role, which is the last step in the modeling procedure, is roughly defined in ATHENA. There is no current best practice, guideline, or mechanism that identifies how to derive the role-specific view from a model *automatically*. A preferred approach is probably the customization of appropriated services (e.g., web services) based on the enterprise model on demand. Subsequently, the model has to contain all necessary information to customize the right service. This means a high level of granularity and increased model complexity. Some solution to manage this issue has to be developed.

- Model-configured solutions can facilitate tangible knowledge sharing across roles and disciplines involved in PPM, only if actual product structures are captured in the models, so that workplaces can be adapted to them. Recent extensions to the Metis/TIP web service plug-in are intended to support importing of large data structures from XML business documents (e.g., Web service results) so that they can be mapped to model concepts and imported automatically. The workplaces can also update legacy system data by replicating the tasks that invoke updating web services for each component, element, or parameter in the product models.

3.3.2 Conclusions

As a general conclusion of the usefulness of the ATHENA results, one pilot builder stated as follows: "The functionality provided by the services often is not comprehensive enough. In future work, the prototyping services should be enhanced step by step to provide a full set of functionality for practical applications."

Another pilot builder stated: "What you do not design for you will never get, implying that interoperability must be designed for."

However, the conclusion from all six use cases was that the approaches to interoperability developed in ATHENA have proven to be good approaches and working methods to reengineer the systems that are deployed and operational. The challenge is rather to use the AKM and SOA approaches to find new ways for designing future systems.

There will always be a demand for reengineering services, as demonstrated by these pilots, to extend and adapt operational platforms and services. The IT system providers will produce new approaches and methodologies to allow a wide variety of adaptable and extendable customer services for industrial users and partners to build their own operational workplaces. However, for markets and application areas where stakeholders and users are not easily involved in operations or maybe not even available we will have other approaches and methodologies for developing systems and operational solutions.

The pilots belong to three distinct types of operational industrial solutions:

1. Global horizontal peer-to-peer systems: characterized by repeatable business objects and clusters of services, where interoperability can be achieved by *bottom-up* resolution, model-configured services, model-mapped semantics, standards, and logistics alignment, prototyping and supported by the results of the ATHENA project
2. Collaborative business process systems: characterized by a service-oriented architecture middle layer, integrating services across various legacy systems, where interoperability is achieved by *top-down* model-driven architectures (MDA), standards, and services

3. Collaborative product and process design (CPPD): characterized by process flows being designed as task patterns, and related to add intelligence to product structures, where interoperability is achieved middle-out, through model-configured, user-composed layered service architectures

Most global, multinational corporations have a need for all of the three approaches. The common glue is a set of web services for project portfolio management, services management, and document management, all integrated in an Active Knowledge Architecture (AKA) and made accessible through a service-oriented architecture.

Future systems will be designed by employing more services to involve stakeholders and support user interaction, so we will be *designing for interoperability*, supporting continuous team learning, and life-cycle knowledge harnessing for reuse. Active business knowledge will drive system development and configuration of workplaces and services.

Certainly trying to implement interoperability in deployed traditional IT systems that have been in use for some time is not easy and will not give agile solutions or support design and services evolution. Current operational IT systems, sold off the shelf, suffer from a dramatic loss of stakeholder contextual knowledge in their life cycle from specifications to delivery and to reengineering or demolition. Service provisioning is a step in the right direction, but support for users to configure, adapt, and manage their own services and workplaces is needed. As seen from the experiences from EXTERNAL, the user interface to support such service must be highly usable.

3.4 Summary

In this chapter, we have recapped experiences and lessons learned, particularly from 1998 to 2006, through the application of early versions of the AKM technology in the EXTERNAL and ATHENA projects. The intent has been to shed light on the evolution from off-line modeling of smart infrastructures, including MDA to inline modeling for building AKAs, automatically configuring workplaces and visual arenas for work execution.

With the introduction of the IRTV visual modeling language, refinements of the AKA structures and contents, and implementation of design methodology components the first AKM arena for AKA-configured workplaces was ready for delivery.

4 State of the Art of Enterprise Modeling

This chapter gives an overview of the state of the art and the state of industrial practice within enterprise modeling, reflecting the current market situation and industrial use of enterprise modeling technologies. The chapter is partly based on the material originally presented in ATHENA (2004).

4.1 Industrial Diversity of Meaning and Usage

Although the term enterprise modeling (EM) is widespread in industrial usage, there are many different meanings and understandings about what EM is and what it is good for. Mostly, the meanings derive from the application purpose in different projects of each enterprise. Even in the same enterprise, when the participants in a project come from different organizational units, they will by their different experiences and expertise have different understanding and different views of what EM means in their daily business.

For some people, modeling the enterprise means defining the business strategy and plans, for others it means defining the quality procedures for the enterprise, and yet for some others it means modeling and designing the enterprise systems.

In general, five main categories for EM can be distinguished (Nysetvold and Krogstie 2006):

- Human sense-making and communication: To make sense of aspects of an enterprise and communicate this to other people
- Computer-assisted analysis: To gain knowledge about the enterprise through simulation or deduction
- Business process management (BPM) and quality assurance
- Model deployment and activation: To integrate the model in an information system and thereby make it actively take part in the work performed by the organization. Models can be activated in three ways:
  - Through people guided by process "maps," where the system offers no active support

- Automatically, where the system plays an active role, as in most workflow systems
- Interactively, where the computer and the users co-operate in interpreting the model. The computer makes decisions about prescribed parts of the model, while the users resolve ambiguities
- To give the context for a traditional system development project, without being directly implemented

As soon as we introduce specific business areas, aspects, disciplines, and roles, we have many diversified views to inter-relate, interpret, and adjust. At the early stages of the product design projects there are many noncoordinated views of the new product enterprise, and so consistency, coherency, completeness, and compliance are temporarily sacrificed for creative innovation.

From a knowledge externalization, expressiveness, representation, and architecture point-of-view, the present state of EM can be divided into seven categories of solutions being provided and used:

1. EM tools with proprietary templates, notations, meta-models, and models. Modeling is driven by a set of predefined views and diagrams
2. EM tools with user-modifiable templates, extendable meta-models, and languages. Again dominated by frameworks of predefined views and meta-views limited to object-oriented analysis and design (OOAD)
3. EM tools and platforms with modifiable templates, offline modeling and meta-modeling languages, and model-management services. Platforms are needed to support true holistic approaches working in knowledge spaces with reflective views and recursive work patterns
4. EM platforms including the offerings of category 3 and with services for template, model, and meta-model development and management, and offering interfacing to legacy systems and other platforms
5. Modeling and execution platforms with customizable workplaces and services for concurrent multi-project modeling, solutions development, and business execution and governance
6. Point 5 adding self-generating, self-adapting, and eventually self-adjusting (executing) services
7. Points 5 and 6 adding services for developing, composing, executing, and remotely monitoring business and engineering services

Today, most vendors belong to categories 2 and 3, and to our knowledge only two providers are in transition between categories 3 and 4. Most models are replications of fixed templates and the others are mostly developed and even primarily applied by consultants or internal modeling experts. Modeling is in most organizations not an integrated service adapted for and by the users.

Most current EM offerings have a weak holistic knowledge perception and support, because EM is used to help solve isolated local problems in the enterprise. Therefore, different methodologies and tools are often used. This provokes that reusing elder results and handling many tools become necessary capabilities and activities. This also results in high costs for training and a low initial acceptance among the employees for improving methodologies and adapting tools for each new project.

4.2 International EM Markets

The market penetration of EM is about 8% in US market and 7% in Europe according to Gartner Group, and the EM markets are still perceived and measured as separate markets with approaches, methodologies, tools, and solutions separate from the operational enterprise systems and solutions. Most EM projects are performed disjoint from the operational environment and solutions being modeled. So the purpose of EM is mostly for human sense-making and communication, creating improved insight, overview, and common understanding across disciplines and processes.

The dominant market in US is the enterprise architecture (EA) market, while in Europe the EA market is developing rather slowly, but for a few exceptions. In Europe, the BPM market has been dominant so far.

4.2.1 The Enterprise Architecture Market

The objectives of the offerings in this market are to get an overview of the IT systems and operational solutions in the enterprise, aligning new information technology (IT) initiatives and strategic investments, and to get maximum value from vested resources. The EA market can further be split into a military segment, a bank and finance segment, a public services segment, and an industrial segment. The most active segment in US is the military segment, with many interest and market analysis organizations doing educational and promotional work. The second most active segment in US is the government departments. In Europe, the most active segments have so far been the bank and finance segment and the industrial telecom segment.

In the EA military segment, the Federal Enterprise Architecture Framework (FEAF) organization with its Department of Defense Architecture

Framework (DoDAF) standard is very active. FEAF coordinates the efforts in all branches of the military market, and also has links in Europe and other areas through NATO in the Bank and Finance segment. The Open Group is an interest organization specializing on EA methodology and services, such as training, certification, and standardization.

The trends for the future in the EA market are for architectures to become more operational, making architecture models the foundational description for enterprise design and development, much like product architectures in certain industries, and covering most enterprise knowledge element and life-cycle services.

4.2.2 The Business Process Management Market

The BPM market will evolve from single business process modeling and management to multiple concurrent business processes, and BPM will eventually require the same kind of knowledge and business architectures, capabilities, and services as do single networked enterprises. Also the span of business processes will include more and more service provisioning.

The EM methods and tools used to date support mostly the organizational and IT departments. But these are only 3% of the overall staff in the enterprise. So there is an insufficient use of EM by the other employees, especially the operational employees.

4.3 Application Domains

To get a better overview, four main application domains for EM are analyzed:

- Enterprise engineering and reengineering
- Product life cycle management
- Choice and implementation of IT systems and solution
- General enterprise architecture and operations support

In Fig. 4.1, the product, organization, process, and system (POPS) dimensions and the application domains are related to show how frequently EM is applied to each type of domain. As described, there are several overlaps between the main application domains from having common subdomains.

Application Domain	Enterprise Modelling Dimension			
	Product	Organization	Process	System
Enterprise Engineering and Reengineering	Manage Product variants, Phase management (from Idea to replacement)	Virtual Organization/ Extended Enterprises	Performance Analysis	Development/ Choice and Implementation of IT Systems and Solutions
		Visual Enterprise Integration	Continuous Process Improvement	
		Organizational Change Management	Workflow Management	
Product Life Cycle Management		Qualification for new products	e.g., Synchronization of product development and manufacturing engineering	
Choice and implementation of IT Systems and solution				
General Enterprise Architecture and operations support	Quality Management			
	Knowledge Management			
	Strategy Definition			
	Decision Making			

Activity type	Shading
Continuous	
Periodic	
On demand	

Fig. 4.1. Main application domains for EM

4.3.1 Enterprise Engineering and Reengineering Activities

BPM can be regarded as a kind of overall strategy. Continuous process improvement (CPI) is part of this strategy, and performance analysis and change management are steps of the CPI-cycle. The linkage between them is shown in Fig. 4.2.

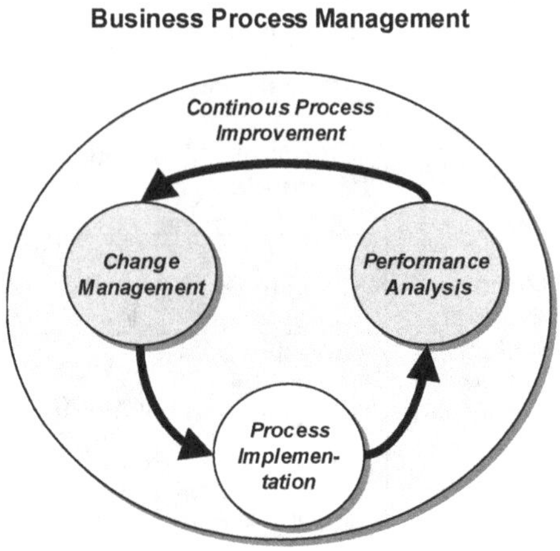

Business Process Management

Fig. 4.2. CPI-cycle

The step "process implementation" has been added in the figure to accomplish the CPI-cycle. In the following, the connection between the different parts is explained.

Business Process Management (BPM)

BPM includes not only the design of the business processes, but also the control and operation of common functioning procedures and services. This applies to common views of shared risks, pooled resources, values, and intellectual property rights (IPR) issues, as well as work management of distributed business tasks execution.

BPM implies that for each logical enterprise there will be many concurrent business processes. The involvement in many business processes has created a demand for providers to support and supply replicable services, allowing business partners to compose, orchestrate, and perform governance, manifestation, and monitoring of business process execution.

This means that the cycles in Fig. 4.2 are replicated for each partner each time they pursue and enter a new business opportunity. The fact that each enterprise will be engaging in many and diverse business processes has some very important implications:

- Top–down BPM must be complemented by bottom–up service-oriented architecture and middle-out knowledge architecture modeling, and be supported by a BPM model and a governance and portfolio management model

- BPM modeling is a layer of collaborative EM on top of each partner Enterprise, which is operated and managed by an internal, continuously evolving enterprise knowledge model
- The business architectural layer of each partners' enterprise model will have to be partly replicated and adapted to each collaborative business process they are engaged in
- There will be a need for monitoring, management, governance, and business process portfolio management services and shared views

Collaborative business process networks will be a kind of super-enterprise, where concerns for concurrency and for the core enterprise logic, knowledge, and competence of each partner will require model-driven solutions and systems engineering.

Continuous Process Improvement (CPI)

The main objective of CPI is to adapt the business processes and, by this, adapt the enterprise to new market requirements in order to keep on being competitive. CPI has been described using a number of models. Here CPI is described by a three-step procedure. After the process has been designed, the actual CPI-process starts by implementing the designed process. To get information about the as-is-situation of the processes, the next step has to be done.

Performance Analysis (PA)

Performance analysis delivers information about the business situation to the company. This information can be separated into different time horizons. Indicators such as the trend in sales revenues, cash flow, profit, contribution-based accounting, sales volume figures, etc. are relying on information that is rooted in the past. Therefore, real time information like the following are needed:

- Are some customer orders completed late, or even lost?
- How cost- and time-effective are individual procurement and distribution channels?
- Where are the weak points and bottlenecks in the procedures?
- How good was deadline reliability for a certain product line in July?
- What was the average throughput time for this product line and what were the outliers?
- How successfully have improvement actions been implemented? Have the processes improved since the last quarter?

When the relevant information is collected and analyzed, the necessary steps to improve the current situation have to be defined and implemented.

To better support performance analysis and monitoring, modeling and execution platforms must be integrated, so that models can import and base the model-supported analysis on operations and data that are as close to real-time as possible. This is also important for achieving trust and confidence in the analysis.

Change Management (CM)

The goal of change management is to ensure that the necessary changes of a business process fulfill the following conditions:

- Necessary actions are initiated with an acceptable delay after the change has happened (or has been decided to happen, if proactive change management is needed)
- Necessary actions are executed in a fast and effective way
- All reactions and actions are initiated and executed in a controlled manner

An effective management of the permanent change becomes a key success factor for an enterprise. It is of fundamental importance that the people involved in changing processes are able to understand and accept those changes and make them finally happen. Therefore, the most appropriate characterization of change management is as follows:

- Information
- Communication
- Training

The content of the relevant information, communication, and training concerning specific business processes has to be structured. The major questions that have to be addressed in change management activities are the following:

- Who (people, departments, different enterprises…) is involved in the change (Organization view)?
- What are the new or modified activities (functional view)?
- What new or modified information is needed or produced (data view)?
- Which new or modified deliverables are expected (deliverable view)?
- How do the changes fit together and how do they influence the process logic (control view)?

EM can deliver the models for enterprise engineering and reengineering activities in order to have a common language that is understandable by all participants. Besides that, if the models are sufficiently formalized, it would be possible to map the enterprise engineering and reengineering activities directly onto the business process execution.

Extensive change management is also dependent on creating an integrated modeling and execution platform, and on being able to analyze impacts and consequences of the proposed change.

Change management in design and engineering today follow very tedious procedures, and the tasks to complete these procedures are mostly paper-based and of administrative character. Simple proposed changes can take months to be evaluated and performed. With a holistic enterprise model, which provides views on the impact and involved elements of a change proposal, change management effort can be drastically reduced by removing the administrative paper work.

4.3.2 Product Life Cycle Management

The product life cycle (PLC) is a proven concept that delivers information about the competitive dynamics of products. It illustrates the sales process of a product and separates this process into five steps:

1. New product development stage. Ch aracteristics: very expensive, sales revenue low, and losses
2. Market introduction stage. Characteristics: cost high, sales volume low, and losses
3. Growth stage. Characteristics: costs reduced due to economies of scale, sales volume increases significantly, and profitability
4. Mature stage. Characteristics: costs are very low, sales volume peaks, prices tend to drop due to the proliferation of competing products, and very profitable
5. Decline stage. Characteristics: sales decline, prices drop, and profits decline

The progression of a product through these stages is by no means certain. The objective of the product life cycle management is, simply speaking, to take care that a product reaches the mature stage as fast as possible and stays there as long as possible.

EM could be a basis for decisions that have to be made concerning the enterprises that work together along the product life cycle (in one or several of the stages). The modeling language could be a common language between the participants. Additionally, EM allows the specification and sharing of new and emerging approaches for product development and delivery. The flexibility in the relationships with the customers in the product production and delivery stages should be also managed by the new EM approaches, which allow fast adaptation with the proper impact analysis.

4.3.3 Choice and Implementation of IT Systems and Solution

In today's business, the IT support is one of the key success factors. To find the suitable IT system, several steps must be performed. Traditionally, this transformation process has consisted of four phases:

1. Phase 1: the IS-oriented initial strategic situation is established. "IS-oriented" means that basic IT effects on the new enterprise concepts are already taken into account. Strategic corporate planning determines long-term corporate goals, general corporate activities, and resources.
2. Phase 2: the requirements are defined. Individual views of the application system are modeled in detail. Here as well, business and organizational content is focused. Because of the fact that the descriptions for the requirements definition are the starting point for IT implementation, it is important that more conceptual description languages are used. The used description languages have to be understandable from a business point of view as well as sufficiently conceptual in order to be a starting point for a consistent IT implementation.
3. Phase 3: focuses on design specification. The business models are adapted to the requirements of the implementation tool interfaces (database, network architectures, or programming languages, etc.), but at this time, specific IT products are not taken into account yet.
4. Phase 4: the implementation description. It deals with the implementation in physical data structures, hardware components, and real-world IT products.

These four phases describe the creation of an IT system and are therefore in traditional approaches called "build time." Afterwards, the operations phase which is known as "run time" follows. The requirements definition is closely linked with the strategic planning level. However, it is generally independent of the implementation. Implementation description and operations, on the other hand, are closely connected with the "IT equipment and product level." If any changes were made on this level, they would have an immediate effect on the kind of implementation and operation.

EM could support the different steps for choosing and implementing IT systems by delivering suitable models. The enterprise models provide a good view of the requirements that the IT systems will have for collaborating with external entities. On the other hand, the EM also defines the desired functionality of enterprise systems and solutions with respect to enterprise operations when interoperating with others. Finally, in the holistic approach for EM, the links and traceability between the enterprise model and the IT systems architecture are part of the model. This ensures that the enterprise is using the right systems for its operations. Additionally, it facilitates a consistent change and evolution of IT systems when the enterprise makes a business decision that has impacts on the enterprise model.

4.3.4 General Enterprise Architecture and Operations Support

This application domain includes disciplines such as strategy definition and decision making, virtual organizations/extended enterprises definition, visual enterprise integration, planning and controlling, collaborative work management, knowledge management, quality management, and environmental management.

The EM could support general enterprise architecture and operations support by delivering suitable models for the different disciplines. The holistic approach to EM provides different views over the same model, allowing the enterprise to specify and analyze each discipline independently while automatically reflecting the impact of decisions in the other views.

4.4 Enterprise Modeling Frameworks and Architectures

This section describes the main EM approaches. They typically build on and extend existing modeling notations, particularly in process modeling. A systematic typology of approaches to process modeling is provided in Chap. 12.

We define a framework as a fundamental structure that allows defining the main sets of concepts to model and to build an enterprise. This section describes two main types of frameworks: those for integrating EM (such as Zachman, CIMOSA, etc.), frameworks for integrating enterprise applications (such as ISO 15745, the MISSION approach, etc.).

The dominant EM frameworks and architectures (in addition to AKM technology) that are being pursued by industry and interest organizations are the following:

1. The Zachman Framework from the Zachman Institute for Architecture (Sowa and Zachman 1992; Zachman 1987)
2. The GERAM Framework from The University of Brisbane (Bernus and Nemes 1996)
3. The GRAI Framework from GRAI Lab and Graisoft (Chen and Doumeingts 1996; Doumeingts et al. 1998)
4. ARIS (Architecture of Integrated Information Systems) from IDS Scheer (Scheer 1999).
5. The CIMOSA Framework from CIMOSA GmbH (ESPRIT Consortium AMICE 1993; Zelm 1995).
6. The DoDAF Architecture Methodology from the FEAC Institute (DoD 2003a,b)
7. TOGAF Architecture Methodology from the Open Group (TOGAF 2000)
8. The TEAF Methodology from the US Department of Commerce (TEAF 2007)

These and others such as ISO 15745 (ISO 2003) and the MISSION (2003) approach will be briefly described in the following subsections, with emphasis on their potential contribution towards future layered operational enterprise architectures.

Common to all of these is that they are descriptive frameworks, defining enterprise domains and their views and contents, but they are all today architecting methodologies for producing descriptive architectures detached from the operational platforms and systems out there.

4.4.1 The Zachman Framework for Enterprise Architecture

The framework as it applies to enterprises is simply a logical structure for classifying and organizing the descriptive representations of an enterprise that are significant to the management of the enterprise as well as to the development of the enterprise's systems.

The framework graphic in its most simplistic form depicts the design artifacts that constitute the intersection between the roles in the design process, that is, owner, designer, and builder; and the product abstractions, that is, What (material) it is made of, How (process) it works, and Where (geometry) the components are relative to one another. These roles are somewhat arbitrarily labeled as planner and sub-contractor and are included in the framework graphic that is commonly exhibited.

From the very inception of the framework, some other product abstractions were known to exist, because it was obvious that in addition to What, How, and Where, a complete description would necessarily have to include the remaining primitive interrogatives: Who, When, and Why. These three additional interrogatives would be manifest as three additional columns of models that, in the case of enterprises, would depict the following:

- Who does what work
- When do things happen
- Why are various choices made

A balance between the holistic contextual view and the pragmatic implementation view can be facilitated by a framework that has the characteristics of any good classification scheme, that is, it allows for abstractions intended to

- simplify for understanding and communication, and
- clearly focus on independent variables for analytical purposes, but at the same time,
- maintain a disciplined awareness of contextual relationships that are significant to preserve the integrity of the object.

In summary, the framework is meant to be the following:

- *Simple*: it is easy to understand. It is not technical, but purely logical. Anybody (technical or non-technical) can understand it.
- *Comprehensive*: it addresses the enterprise in its entirety. Any issues can be mapped against it to understand where they fit within the context of the enterprise as a whole.
- *A language*: it helps you think about complex concepts and communicate them precisely with few, non-technical words.
- *A planning tool*: it helps you make better choices as you are never making choices in a vacuum. You can position issues in the context of the Enterprise and see a total range of alternatives.
- *A problem solving tool*: it enables you to work with abstractions, to simplify, and to isolate simple variables without losing sense of the complexity of the enterprise as a whole.
- *Neutral*: it is defined independently of tools or methodologies, and therefore, any tool or any methodology can be mapped against it to understand their implicit trade-offs, that is, what they are doing and what they are NOT doing.

4.4.2 GERAM

GERAM (generalized enterprise reference architecture and methodology) encompasses knowledge needed for enterprise engineering/integration. Thus, GERAM is defined through a pragmatic approach, providing a generalized framework for describing the components needed in enterprise engineering/enterprise integration processes, such as the following:

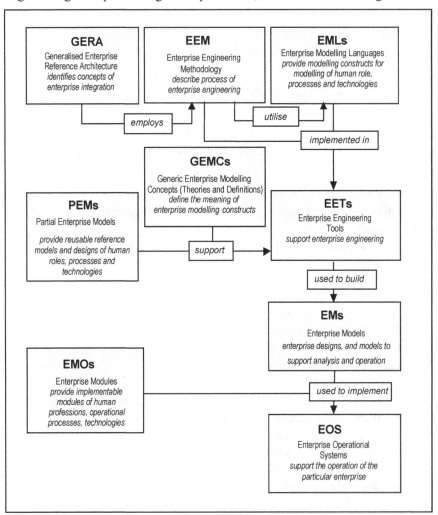

Fig. 4.3. GERAM (generalized enterprise reference architecture and methodology) framework components

- Major enterprise engineering/enterprise integration efforts (green field installation, complete reengineering, merger, reorganization, formation

of virtual enterprise or consortium, value chain or supply chain integration, etc.)
• Incremental changes of various sorts for continuous improvement and adaptation

GERAM is intended to facilitate the unification of methods of several disciplines used in the change process, such as methods of industrial engineering, management science, control engineering, communication and information technology, that is to allow their combined use, as opposed to segregated application.

Previous research carried out by the AMICE Consortium on CIMOSA, by the GRAI Laboratory on GRAI and GIM, and by the Purdue Consortium on PERA (as well as similar methodologies by others) has produced reference architectures, which were meant to be organizing all enterprise integration knowledge and serve as a guide in enterprise integration programs.

Starting from the evaluation of existing enterprise integration architectures (CIMOSA, GRAI/GIM, and PERA), the IFAC/IFIP Task Force on Architectures for Enterprise Integration has developed an overall definition of a generalized architecture. The proposed framework was entitled "GERAM." GERAM is about those methods, models, and tools that are needed to build and maintain the integrated enterprise, be it a part of an enterprise, a single enterprise, or a network of enterprises (virtual enterprise or extended enterprise).

Figure 4.3 depicts the components of GERAM. GERA (generalized enterprise reference architecture) defines the generic concepts recommended for use in enterprise engineering and integration projects. These concepts can be classified as follows:

1. *Human oriented concepts*: They cover human aspects such as capabilities, skills, know-how and competencies as well as roles of humans in the enterprise. The organization related aspects have to do with decision level, responsibilities, and authorities, and the operational ones relate to the capabilities and qualities of humans as enterprise resource elements. In addition, the communication aspects of humans have to be recognized to cover interoperation with other humans and with technology elements when realizing enterprise operations. Modeling constructs will be required to facilitate the description of human roles as an integral part of the organization and operation of an enterprise. The constructs should facilitate the capture of enterprise models that describe human roles, the way in which human roles are organized so that they interoperate with other human and technology elements when realizing enterprise operations, and

the capabilities and qualities of humans as enterprise resource elements. An appropriate methodology will also be required that promotes the retention and reuse of models that encapsulate knowledge (i.e., know-how possessed by humans expressed as an enterprise asset) during the various life phases of enterprise engineering projects.

2. *Process oriented concepts*: They deal with enterprise operations (functionality and behavior) and cover enterprise entity life-cycle and activities in various life-cycle phases: life history, enterprise entity types, EM with integrated model representation, and model views.

3. *Technology oriented concepts*: They deal with various infrastructures used to support processes and include for instance resource models (information technology, manufacturing technology, office automation, and others), facility layout models, information system models, communication system models, and logistics models.

Modeling Framework of GERA

GERA provides an analysis and modeling framework, which is based on the life-cycle concept and identifies three dimensions for defining the scope and content of EM.

1. *Life-cycle dimension*: Providing for the controlled modeling process of enterprise entities according to the life-cycle activities

2. *Genericity dimension*: Providing for the controlled particularization (instantiation) process from generic and partial to particular

3. V*iew dimension*: Providing for the controlled visualization of specific views of the enterprise entity

Figure 4.4 shows the three-dimensional structure identified above, which represents the modeling framework. The reference part of the modeling framework consists of the generic and the partial levels only. These two levels organize into a structure the definitions of concepts, basic and macro level constructs (the modeling languages), defined and used for the description of the given area. The particular level represents the results of the modeling process, which is the model or description of the enterprise entity at the state of the modeling process corresponding to the particular set of life-cycle activities. However, it is intended that the modeling languages should support the two-way relationship between models of adjacent life-cycle phases, that is, the derivation of models from an upper to a lower state or the abstraction of lower models to an upper state, rather than having to create different models for the different sets of life-cycle activities.

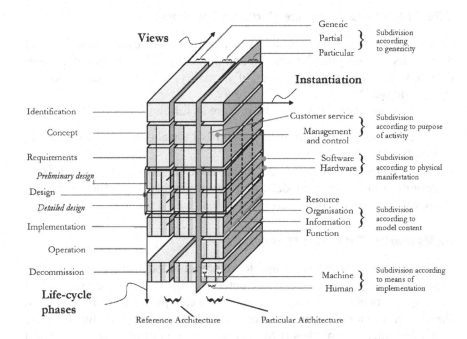

Fig. 4.4. GERA modeling framework with modeling views

EEMs (Enterprise Engineering Methodology)

Enterprise engineering methodologies describe the processes of enterprise integration. A generalized methodology like generalized architectures is applicable to any enterprise regardless of the industry involved. An EEM will help the user in the process of enterprise engineering of integration projects whether the overall integration of a new or revitalized enterprise or in management of on-going change. It provides methods of progression for every type of life-cycle activity. The upper two sets of these activities (identification and concept) are partly management and partly engineering analysis and description (modeling) tasks.

EMLs (Enterprise Modeling Languages)

Enterprise modeling languages define the generic modeling constructs for EM adapted to the needs of people creating and using enterprise models. In particular, EMLs provide constructs to describe and model human roles, operational processes, and their functional contents as well as the supporting information, office and production technologies.

GEMCs (Generic Enterprise Modeling Concepts)

Generic EM concepts are the most generically used concepts and definitions of enterprise integration and modeling. Three forms of concept definition are, in increasing order of formality, Glossaries, meta-models, and ontological theories.

Some requirements that must be met are as follows:

- Concepts defined in more than one form of the above must be defined in a mutually consistent way
- Those concepts that are used in an EML must also have at least a definition in the meta-model form, but preferably the definition should appear in an ontological theory

PEMs (Partial Enterprise Models)

Partial enterprise models (reusable reference models) are models that capture concepts common to many enterprises. PEMs will be used in EM to increase modeling process efficiency. In the enterprise engineering process, these partial models can be used as tested components for building particular enterprise models (EMs). However, in general, such models still need to be adapted (completed) to the particular enterprise entity.

Partial models may be expressed as follows:

- Models that capture some common part of a class of enterprises
- Paradigmatic (reference or prototypical) models that describe a typical enterprise of a certain class. Prototype models can be subsequently modified to fit a particular case
- Abstract models of a part or whole of a class of enterprises that capture the commonalities but leave out specific details. This type of model is of the "fill-in-the-blank" type

EETs (Enterprise Engineering Tools)

Enterprise engineering tools support the processes of enterprise engineering and integration by implementing an enterprise engineering methodology and supporting modeling languages. Engineering tools should provide for analysis, design, and use of enterprise models.

EMOs (Enterprise Modules)

Enterprise modules are implemented building blocks or systems (products, or families of products), which can be utilized as common resources in enterprise engineering and enterprise integration. As physical entities (systems, subsystems, software, hardware, and available human resources/professions) such modules are accessible in the enterprise, or can be made easily available from the market place. In general, EMOs are implementations of partial models identified in the field as the basis of commonly required products for which there is a market.

EMs (Enterprise Models)

The goal of EM is to create and continuously maintain a model of a particular enterprise entity. A model should represent the reality of the enterprise operation according to the requirements of the user and his application. This means the granularity of the model has to be adapted to the particular needs, but still allows interoperability with models of other enterprises. Enterprise models include all those descriptions, designs, and formal models of the enterprise that are prepared in the course of the enterprise's life history.

EOSs (Enterprise Operational Systems)

Enterprise operational systems support the operation of a particular enterprise. They consist of all the hardware and software needed to fulfill the enterprise objective and goals. Their contents are derived from enterprise requirements and their implementation is guided by the design models that provide the system specifications and identify the enterprise modules used in the system implementation.

4.4.3 GRAI Framework

The GRAI methodology includes GIM, which is composed of three parts:

- A reference model of an enterprise system (GRAI model)
- Several modeling formalisms organized by a modeling framework
- A structured approach

The Modeling Framework

The GIM modeling framework has two dimensions: functional abstraction and decomposition levels.

Abstraction levels: The modeling activity implies a simplification of a too complex reality. So, a model keeps only concepts and elements that will be necessary at the time of the model use. The introduction of the abstraction levels allows a "stratified description" in the sense that the GIM framework is in fact constituted of several levels that integrate specific concepts. Practically, the GIM framework provides three abstraction levels:

- *Conceptual level*: Made up without any organizational or technical consideration, it is the most stable level and aims at asking the question "What?"
- *Structural level*: It integrates an organizational point of view and aims at asking the questions "Who?", "When?", and "Where?"
- *Realization level*: It is the most specific level because it integrates the technical constraints and enables the choice of real components.

Domain decomposition: A *domain* can be defined as a selective perception of a manufacturing system, which concentrates on some particular aspect and disregards others. According to the GRAI model, any production system may be split up into three systems: the physical system, the decision system, and the information system. These three systems lead to three domains. According to the needs of the enterprise, these domains are extended by a functional, process, and resource views. The functional view allows to easily build a model that depicts the main functions of the enterprise system and the flows (of any nature) between them, while exactly defining the boundary of the domain. The process view allows one to describe the processes across the various functions of the enterprise.

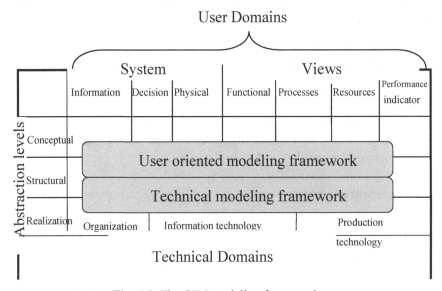

Fig. 4.5. The GIM modeling framework

Crossing the functional and process view results in the GIM modeling framework described in Fig. 4.5, of which the upper part is user oriented and the lower part is oriented towards the technical realization.

Modeling Languages

The three domains referring to a technical representation call upon knowledge of the experts concerned with these domains:

- The *organization* refers mainly to human resources, concerning the definition of both their roles and their structuring.
- *Information technologies* include the hardware (computers, networks, etc.) and software (operating system, database management system, application software, etc.) specifications.
- The *production technology* specifies the physical equipment (machines, means of transport, stores, etc.).

This allows to distinguish two different levels in the overall representation: a user level and a technical level.

We focus on the upper levels of the modeling framework, because only the user domains levels have GRAI languages. This includes the following:

- *Conceptual information model (CIM)*: The CIM is a description of all stable and "natural" data of the organization, of their attributes, and of the links between them. The language used here is UML class diagram.
- *Structural information model (SIM)*: The SIM describes the data structure in relation to the distribution of data and the computerization. The language used here is also UML class diagram.
- *Conceptual decision model (CDM)*: The CDM is a description of the decision making structure, links between decision levels, analysis of links between objectives, analysis of constraints, and description of decision variables. The language used here is the GRAI grid at the global level and the GRAI nets at the detailed level.
- *Structural decision model (SDM)*: The SDM mainly enables the identification of decision makers, responsibility, and authority. It links decision makers and decision making. The language used here is the GRAI grid at the global level and the GRAI nets at the detailed level.
- *Conceptual physical model (CPM)*: The CPM is a description of process and routes with physical flows between operations. The language is the extended actigram (a language of the IDEF0-type).
- *Structural physical model (SPM)*: The SPM gives information about time, work centers and operators, elements about linking and synchronization, and indicates who does what. The language used is the extended actigram.

4.4.4 ARIS (Architecture of Integrated Information Systems)

The EM approach of ARIS is based on a view concept. The objective is to reduce the complexity by dividing the enterprise into individual views.

To model the different views, different modeling languages are allocated to them:

- Organizational charts, network diagram, or shift calendars to model the organizational view.
- Function trees, objective diagram, or application system diagram to model the function view.
- Entity relationship diagrams (ER) attribute allocation diagram or class diagrams to model the data view.
- Product tree to the product view.

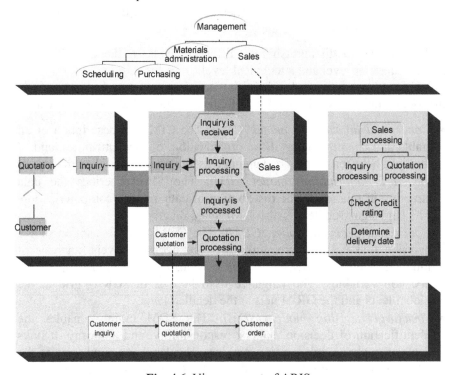

Fig. 4.6. View concept of ARIS

The integration of the different languages is done by the control view (see Fig. 4.6). This combination process is done for two reasons. First, the structural relationships between the views are described, and second, status modifications are explained, which show the dynamic behavior of the system. Languages used there are, for example, event-driven process chain

(EPC), function allocation diagrams, or value-added chain diagram. All languages assigned to the control view include constructs of at least two of the external views.

The advantage of this procedure is on the one hand the extensibility of the actual object and method list, and so new requirements to existing methods can easily be realized. On the other hand, the disadvantage is the huge amount of already existing methods and objects in ARIS. In the future, extensions will be done only if this would benefit either the usability of the technique or the customer. At the moment, it is possible to reduce the amount of methods by setting up filters to fade out unneeded methods or objects.

Description of the Framework

ARIS has been developed by Prof. Scheer at the University of Saarbruecken in Germany. The conceptual design of the ARIS is based on an integration concept that is derived from an analysis of business processes. The first step in creating the architecture calls for the development of a model of business processes that contains all basic features. The result is a highly complex model, which is divided into individual views in order to reduce its complexity (see Fig. 4.7):

- *Function view*: The processes transforming input into output are grouped in the function view. The terms "function," "process," and "activity" are used synonymously. Because of the fact that functions support objectives, yet are controlled by them as well, objectives are also allocated to the function view. In application software, computer-aided processing rules of a function are defined. Thus, application software is closely aligned with "functions," and is also allocated to the function view.
- *Organization view*: The organization view presents the hierarchical organization structure. It is created to group responsible entities or devices executing the same work object. This is why the responsible entities "human output," responsible devices, "financial resources," and "computer hardware" are allocated to the organization view.
- *Data view*: The data view comprises the data processing environment as well as the messages triggering functions or being triggered by functions. Preliminary details on the function of information systems as data media can be allocated to data names. Information services objects are also implicitly captured in the data view. However, they are primarily defined in the output view.

- *Output view*: The output view contains all physical and nonphysical input and output, including fund flows.
- *Control view/process view*: This view displays the respective classes with their view-internal relationships. Relationships among the views as well as the entire business processes are documented in the control or process view, creating a framework for the systematic inspection of all bilateral relationships of the views and the complete process description.

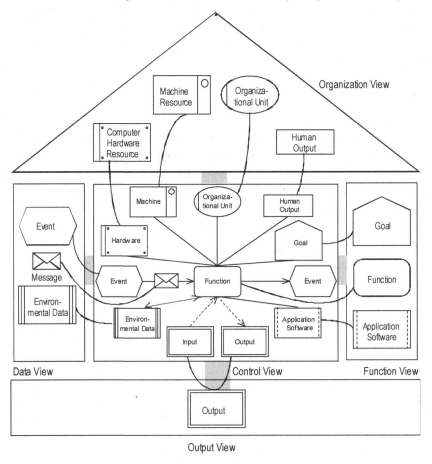

Fig. 4.7. Views of the ARIS house (Scheer 1999)

Because of this division, the contents of the individual views can be described by special methods, which are suitable for this view, without having to pay attention to the numerous relationships and interrelationships with the other views. Afterwards, the relationships between the views are incorporated and combined to form an overall analysis of process chains without any redundancies. A second approach that also reduces the complexity is the analysis of different descriptive levels:

- Requirements definition
- Design specification
- Implementation

Following the concept of a lifecycle model, the various description methods for information systems are differentiated according to their proximity to the information technology. This ensures a consistent description from business management-related problems all the way down to their technical implementation. Thus, the ARIS architecture forms the framework for the development and optimization of integrated information systems as well as a description of their implementation. In this context, stressing the subject-related descriptive levels results in the ARIS concept being used as a model for creating, analyzing, and evaluating business management related process chains.

Within the ARIS Toolset™ many different modeling languages are supported:

- Event-driven process chains (EPC)
- Value added chains
- Different UML-diagrams
- Entity relationship model (ER)

Overall, there are 114 different model types and 207 different object types in the ARIS Toolset™. In addition to traditional modeling functionality, the system includes support for web publishing and simulation techniques.

4.4.5 CIMOSA

CIMOSA was developed under the framework of the European Union ESPRIT research program. It results from the consortium AMICE (European CIM Architecture). The first objective of CIMOSA is to provide a framework to analyze the evolving requirements of an enterprise and translating these into a system that enables and integrates the functions that match the requirements.

The CIMOSA framework (Fig. 4.8) outlines three dimensions as follows:

- A dimension of genericity (three architectural levels) composed of the following:

- A generic level, which is a catalogue of basic building blocks
- A partial level, which is a library of partial models applicable to particular purposes
- A particular level, which is a model of a particular enterprise built from building blocks of partial models
• A dimension of model (three modeling levels) composed of the following:
  - A requirements model for gathering business requirements
  - A design model for specifying optimized and system-oriented representation of the business requirements
  - An implementation model for describing a complete CIM system and all its implemented components

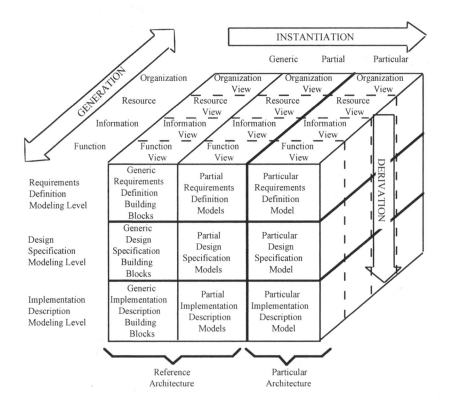

Fig. 4.8. The CIMOSA framework for modeling

• A dimension of view (to describe the model according to its four integrated aspects) composed of the following:

- A function view for describing the expected behavior and functionality of the enterprise
- An information view for describing the integrated information objects of the enterprise
- A resource view for describing the resource objects of the enterprise
- An organization view for describing the organization of the enterprise

CIMOSA is only a framework for structuring EM related issues. It addresses concepts and models that are necessary to model integrated enterprise systems focusing on process model-based enterprise activity control.

A number of tools support the approach. Interfacing Technologies Corporation provides collaborative software tools that enable business users to model, map, and manage business processes and related knowledge with easy-to-use and intuitive single-user desk-top products and multi-user enterprise solutions.

The FirstSTEP Model schema used by all members of the FirstSTEP Tool Suite originates in the ISO-model of the manufacturing enterprise and have a very close relationship with CIMOSA. Its application areas of business process design, simulation of what-if scenarios, and even its more recent applications of monitoring and management corresponds well to the upper levels of the CIMOSA system life cycle oriented process model. Therefore, the schema also conforms to the relevant European and international standards of enterprise engineering and integration.

The enterprise process center (EPC) is a multi-user BPM software product. It delivers collaborative process modeling and content management to every employee desktop.

Charter is a desktop BPM modeling software, which integrates directly within the Microsoft® Visio® interface

Designer is a desktop BPM modeling and simulation software. It allows business users to map and model business processes and run what-if scenarios on any aspect of their model for better business results.

4.4.6 The DoDAF Architecture Methodology

DoDAF (Department of Defense Architecture Framework) was formerly called C4ISR and the name reflects its original target customer-group and market. C4 refers to systems for military operations, and ISR to Information System Resources. DoDAF is being further developed by the FEAC Institute of Washington DC in close cooperation with the Air Force, The Navy, The Army, and Pentagon. Training is offered in cooperation with the California State University at Hayward. This professional Practitioner's

Enterprise Architecture Certificate program covers enterprise architecture as mandated, used, and applied in the US Federal Government.

There is cooperation with Zachman (ZIFA) and naturally with the US Government and Department of Defense.

DODAF is a requirement in all US military agencies and institutions, and is supported by the leading enterprise architecture vendors.

Constructs and Syntax Definition

Many universities and research institutes in US give courses on DoDAF, such as CMU. The METIS DoDAF model of the meta-model allows visual navigation of all core domains and their constructs and relationships to other constructs and domains, such as strategies, proposed initiatives, present IT portfolio, present systems and their use, users and vendors, all systems, their capabilities and use, and support for searching, view-generation, reporting, "what-if" analysis.

Most leading enterprise architecture vendors are supporting DoDAF, such as Metis from Troux, System Architect from Popkin, and Mega.

4.4.7 TOGAF Architecture Methodology

TOGAF (The Open Group Architecture Framework) has from its early days, 1997, been developed and owned by the Open Group, an international interest organization. It now has a strong position with private industry in US, Britain, and Japan.

The present version of TOGAF being offered is version 8 and work on version 9 is underway. TOGAF has a good certification and training services in place since version 7. Most EA tool vendors are members and have access to these versions and to services, helping them to qualify as authorized and certified TOGAF compliant providers of the methodology, and to get access to other services like training, consulting, and events participation.

TOGAF has itself an interesting architecture. It offers an architecture development methodology (ADM) as a separate model; the current model is built in Metis from Troux.

Constructs and Syntax Definition

Popkin System Architect has the most comprehensive model of the TOGAF methodology, allowing visual navigation of all core domains and their constructs and relationships to other constructs and domains, such as strategies, proposed initiatives, present IT portfolio, present systems and their use, users and vendors, all systems, their capabilities and use, and support for searching, view-generation, reporting, and "what-if" analysis.

Most leading enterprise architecture vendors are supporting TOGAF, such as Metis from Troux, System Architect from Popkin, and Mega.

4.4.8 The TEAF Methodology from US Department of Commerce

TEAF (Treasury Enterprise Architecture Framework) is derived from an earlier treasury model, TISAF (Treasury Information Systems Architecture Framework) and the FEAF (Federal Enterprise Architecture Framework). Additional direction was provided by the Information Technology Management Reform Act, also known as the Clinger-Cohen Act of 1996, and the Government Performance and Results Act of 1993.

As stated in TEAF Version 1.0, July 2000, the purpose of this architecture framework is the following:

- Provide guidance for treasury enterprise architecture development and management
- Support treasury bureaus and offices with the implementation of their architectures based on strategic planning
- Show the benefits of incorporating enterprise architecture disciplines and tools into normal business operations
- Provide a structure for producing an EA and managing EA assets

TEAF is to guide the planning and development of enterprise architectures in all bureaus and offices of the treasury department. There are more than 300 agencies and bureaus around the US. The responsibility for ensuring this action falls on the office of the Treasury CIO.

Constructs and Syntax Definition

A TEAF model developed in Metis Enterprise of the meta-model allows visual navigation of all core domains and their constructs and relationships to other constructs and domains, such as strategies, proposed initiatives, present IT portfolio, present systems and their use, users and vendors, all systems, their capabilities and use, and support for searching, view-generation, reporting, and "what-if" analysis. Four of the leading enterprise architecture vendors, amongst which is Metis from Troux, are supporting TEAF.

4.4.9 ISO 15745: Framework for Application Integration

ISO 15745 – Open System Application Integration Framework is elaborated by ISO TC184 SC5/WG5. It consists of four parts:

- Part 1: Generic reference description
- Part 2: Reference description for ISO 11898 based control systems
- Part 3: Reference description for EN 50170 and EN 50254 based control systems
- Part 4: Reference description for Ethernet based control systems

The Application Integration Framework (AIF) defines elements and rules that facilitate the following:

- The systematic organization and representation of the application integration requirements using integration models
- The development of interface specifications in the form of application interoperability profiles (AIPs) that enable both the selection of suitable resources and the documentation of the "as built" application.

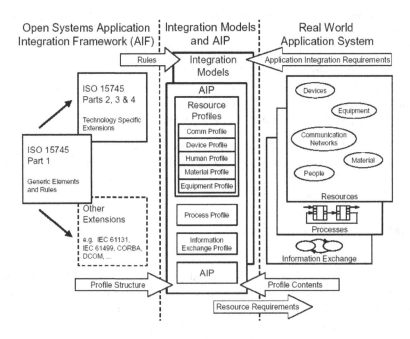

Fig. 4.9. ISO 15745 content (ISO 2003)

ISO 15745-3:2003 defines the technology specific elements and rules for describing both communication network profiles and the communication related aspects of device profiles specific to IEC 61158-based control systems. In particular, ISO 15745-3:2003 describes technology specific profile templates for the device profile and the communication network profile. Profiles for ISO/IEC 8802-3-based control systems are outside the scope of ISO 15745-3:2003.

ISO 15745-3:2003 is to be used in conjunction with ISO 15745-1:2003 to describe an AIF. Generic elements and rules for describing integration models and application interoperability profiles, together with their component profiles (process profiles, information exchange profiles, and resource profiles) are specified in ISO 15745-1:2003.

Figure 4.9 gives an overview of ISO 15745 content and relationships between various parts of the standard.

Constructs and Syntax Definition

To achieve application interoperability, a key condition to be satisfied is that interfaces of the resources used to perform the function are configured to work with the corresponding resource interfaces of the other functions involved in a target manufacturing application (DelaHostria 2002). The three basic integration models are the process integration model, resource integration model and information exchange integration model.

The AIF focuses on the integration aspects of an application system, and provides elements and rules for the development of integration models and profiles based on the process, information exchange, and resource views of the application. Integration models represent the application requirements, and profiles are interface specifications that enable both the selection of suitable resources and the documentation of the "as built" application. Integration models are in the form of UML diagrams while profiles are XML documents (ISO 15745-1, 2002).

More specifically, scheme for describing an integrated view of an industrial application based on a set of visualization elements and composition rules elements include reusable, object-based representations of an application's processes, resources, and information exchanges. Rules include relationship, interaction, and deployment diagrams to capture the roles of the elements throughout an application's life cycle.

- Integration models expressed in UM-diagrams, which provide extensible methods for integration of new functionality
- Scheme for creating a concise statement of an application's interoperability requirements
- Identifies and organizes the elements' service interfaces as interoperability profiles

- Standardizes an extensible method to describe a profile and exchange it among the stakeholders of an application
- Interoperability profiles are denoted in XML

4.4.10 MISSION

The MISSION approach focuses on distributed, decentralized simulation and, furthermore, on the supply chain process. The global concept is originally based on the results of the European MISSION Module and on an extension of the EM tool MO^2GO.

The approach includes the modeling aspects, which describe how a user can collect the necessary data for the distributed simulation. Furthermore, it describes how the different simulation models can be connected: starting from a template library, via an enterprise model, to the automatic generation of the required interface files. A brief description of a framework for distributed enterprise simulation including configuration will be presented. The approach extends the High Level Architecture (HLA) (Mertins et al. 2000, IEEE 2000) approach to support the industrial use of distributed simulation. This can be seen as an application-specific enrichment of the HLA standard.

A simulation manager (realized as extension of MO^2GO) supports the definition and the interoperability of simulation templates by exchanging objects (Rabe and Jäkel 2000). It delivers a graphical approach for the design of simulation scenarios by process chains. The simulation manager secures the consistency between the federate configuration files (FCF) for a distributed simulation scenario by the generation of all FCFs for the federates and the Federate Execution Definition (FED) file for the HLA RTI, automatically.

Constructs and Syntax Definition

Distributed simulation between different simulation tools (e.g., Arena, Enterprise Dynamics, eMPlant) as well as including different software components (MS Excel, 3D Visualization, etc.) into such simulation process is still a new technology. Despite the existence of proprietary solutions for individual simulators (e.g., AutoMod, eMPlant, Enterprise Dynamics, etc.), a standard "plug and play" mechanism is still missing.

However, big companies invest in the digital enterprise concepts and within the next few years they will force their suppliers to be more integrated. That will also require new concepts of distributed, decentralized, but synchronized analysis and simulation methodologies and platforms.

Years ago, the situation at US Department of Defense (DoD) was similar to this situation regarding modeling and simulation. Many simulation models already existed. The necessary effort for developing new simulation models increased. At the same time, the available amount of money for the development decreased. So, it became more and more important to use or to reuse existing systems and existing information in a distributed decentralized environment. Moreover, the possibility to substitute systems within a runtime environment (e.g., to substitute an old jet fighter by its new version in different scenarios) was required. The DoD initiated a research program to develop architecture for distributed simulation. One result of this approach is the high level architecture (HLA) and its runtime infrastructure (RTI). Until 2002, the DoD provided a free version of this RTI to support the dissemination of that technology. Now some vendors of RTIs are available. HLA has become an IEEE and OMG standard.

The HLA satisfies many requirements for distributed simulations, for example, time synchronization, communication between independent simulation models, etc. Within military applications of the HLA, for each new model a new simulator will be usually need to be programed. Therefore, a flexible interface for simulation models is not required for military applications. This is completely different within civil domains where the total effort spent on one simulation study is extremely low in comparison with defense applications. The dependency of the interface description to the HLA-RTI from the specific simulation model is a critical disadvantage for regular civil applications of HLA.

Based on the HLA approach different groups work to extend the technology and to bring the distributed simulation into the civil domain. Examples are the Extensible Modeling and Simulation Framework (XMSF) and The High Level Architecture – COTS Simulation Package Interoperation Forum (HLA-CSPIF). The Simulation Interoperability Standards Organization (SISO) is also interested in such a standard. The XMSF group works on a new generation of web-based modeling and simulation, for example, using XML and web-services. HLA-CSPIF established an international group to support the interoperation of discrete event models created in commercial-off-the-shelf simulation packages by HLA.

Needs for distributed simulation are the following:

- *Reusability*: available simulation models are implemented in different tools (off-the-shelf simulation packages) and have to be remodeled in a single tool before they can form an executable model

- *Selection of information*: need to hide internals of simulation models, especially when simulation is executed cross-enterprise or organizational, for example, for supply chains
- *Simulation for SMEs*: for SMEs quite often it is too expensive to support the different tools of their customers within the supply chain, especially if for each tool special training or consulting is necessary
- *Modular structures*: call for efficient maintenance of very large simulation models
- *Flexible test environment*: specific components, like shop floor control, have to be modeled within the simulation system again or with high effort linked to the specific simulation model and tool

The framework proposed here illustrates an approach for the use of HLA in the civil, industrial domain. The starting point for this framework was the European Module of the IMS MISSION project (EP 29 656). It is based on a configuration mechanism on the top of HLA, which allows a user oriented configuration of decentralized, distributed simulation by enterprise models.

A template library allows the definition of different application templates. Concerning the simulation process, each application template refers to simulation models. The simulation model implements the content of the application template. Each model has to be able to execute this partial simulation process standalone. Further, the notation "application template" will be used for templates that are directly applicable within a simulation scenario, in opposite to templates supporting a clear search structure within the template library.

Furthermore, the definition of input and output segments of the simulation models as well as of the exchange objects between the simulation models is necessary. For example, an output segment of a processing line could be the output buffer. Within a simulation scenario, this output segment will be associated with an input segment of another simulation model, for example, a transportation system. The data exchange is done by objects. These objects are called exchange objects within the framework. They have to be described for each application template. Exchanged objects are those objects that are necessary to define a communication between simulation models. They are not directly sent to a receiving federate. They just get a mark which indicates the receiver. A possible receiver checks the mark and identifies if the object has its address. Afterwards the object will be processed by the receiver.

The application templates are used within an enterprise process model as operational resources. The graphical process model defines the general order of the different processes within a distributed simulation scenario.

Each process is related to an instance of an application template. During the instantiation a setting of parameters provided by the template is possible.

Based on the process model a building block structure is generated. Each operational resource represented in the process model is included as a building block within the building block structure. A building block has input and output segments related to the used application template. By this, it is possible to define the connection between the segments of the different building blocks. The connection includes the definition of the used exchange object classes.

After this step the distributed, decentralized simulation scenario is designed.

Within the simulation scenario each building block will be a federate. A federate is a running simulation model in a group of running simulation models (federation) connected to other simulation models of the group via HLA-RTI. The HLA-RTI is configured by a federation execution definition file (FED-File). This file includes general information of object classes and attributes managed by the HLA-RTI. As extension, the presented framework includes the definition of a configuration file for each federate: The Federate Configuration File (FCF) includes information of object classes and attributes used by the federate as well as information about connections with other federates.

Each used off-the-shelf simulation package requires an interface to the generic HLA adapter. This interface has to be configurable by the FCF. The generic adapter is used to simplify the connection to the RTI and to hide proprietary features of the RTI implementation.

4.5 Conclusions on Enterprise Architecture Frameworks

The architectural frameworks mentioned in the previous section are descriptive frameworks designed to define views on the contents of specific enterprise domains. However, most of the frameworks and technologies supporting them lack capabilities and services for meta-data management, role-driven viewing, and integration with operational platforms and systems. These are the main short-comings that have to be resolved by the approaches, methodologies, and solutions. A tighter integration of descriptive model views with operational and execution views, supported by model-configured platforms integrating systems, tools, and new services, will achieve full support for model-driven and model-generated business process and work execution at all levels.

An analysis of the frameworks concerning their appropriateness and usability for designing and developing architectural enterprise interoperability solutions leads to the following conclusions:

The architecture of the Zachman framework provides the set of concepts and principles to model, describe, and categorize existing enterprise artifacts in a holistic way. It supports the integrated interoperability paradigm. Research has been reported to map Zachman's framework to the GERAM framework, which is now an ISO standard (ISO 15704). The Zachman framework has with some success been used by the Ontario Government in Canada to design their EA approach, and has been used as a reference categorization structure for enterprise knowledge repositories.

GERAM gives a very good overview of the different EM aspects and domains, but lacks some very important aspects such as meta-modeling capabilities, knowledge spaces, and the importance of supporting modeling and execution by integrated platforms with repositories.

The GIM modeling framework introduces the decision views, which are not explicitly taken into account in other modeling frameworks. The decisional aspect is essential for establishing interoperability in the context of collaborative enterprises. To interoperate in such an environment, decision-making structures, procedures, rules, and constraints need to be explicitly defined and modeled, so that decentralized and distributed decision-making can be performed and managed. The decisional model is now a European TS (technical specification) elaborated by CEN TC310 WG1. However, while providing a strong support for performance indicator management and decision making, the GIM framework has limited expressiveness and platform integration.

ARIS has strong top–down process modeling and integration capabilities, but lacks expressiveness for other aspects and the "big picture" created by a holistic approach. The different views of the ARIS-concept include different modeling languages, for example, EPC for illustrating the collaborative business processes. But there are extensions needed concerning the requirements of modeling collaborative enterprises like new role-concepts or the problem of depicting internal and external views of the same business process. At the moment there is a close cooperation with SAP concerning interoperability of modeling methodologies and software systems.

The CIMOSA framework is a comprehensive reference framework at the conceptual layer, but lacks expressiveness for multiple dependencies of types and kinds of views, for evolving concepts, contents, and capabilities, and for capturing context. It is the basis to establish the European Pre-standard ENV 40003 now published as a joint European and ISO standard known as EN/ISO 19439: Framework for EM. Although the CIMOSA framework does not explicitly consider interoperability issues, it can be a contribution to an integrated paradigm at the conceptual layer to establish interoperability.

The DoDAF Architecture Methodology from the FEAC Institute is a comprehensive framework and methodology targeted specifically at systems engineering in the military forces, and covers all kinds of technical systems and not just software systems. It has a strong categorization of enterprise knowledge contents. The DoDAF is along with TOGAF, one of the most comprehensive enterprise architecture frameworks, and provides a good understanding of the stakeholders and users and the minimum of information they must receive to align business and IT and get value out of their business and IT initiatives. However, as all the other enterprise architecture frameworks it contributes little to integrated platforms, to model-driven design and to generation of interoperable solutions.

TOGAF from the Open Group has a good methodology for developing an approach (the Architecture Development Methodology; ADM), but again TOGAF is just a framework of descriptive and fairly abstract views. The Open Group is now cooperating with OMG (Object Management Group) to investigate synergies by integrating the OODA, SOAD (Service Oriented Analysis and Design) approaches, and the ADM methodology.

The TEAF Methodology from the US Department of Commerce is specifically tuned to deliver a methodology to the US Government agencies and all administrative, legislative, and financial systems, and so this architecture is very rich for those application domains. A TEAF model developed in, for example, METIS Enterprise allows visual navigation of all core domains and their constructs and relationships to other constructs and domains, such as strategies, proposed initiatives, present IT portfolio, present systems and their use, users and vendors, all systems, their capabilities and use, and support for searching, view-generation, reporting, and performing analysis, from simple "what-if" to network and impact analysis.

The ISO 15745 standard allows to deal with interoperability of applications early in the stages of system requirements and design and through the lifecycle by using the AIF. It provides a clear definition of manufacturing (enterprise) application as a set of processes, resources, and information exchanges. The desired or as-built interface configurations can be described in a set of XML files using the XML schemas defined in the standard. This approach can work only if various standards used to specify interfaces are interoperable between them.

The MISSION approach is mainly concerned with establishing a framework for distributed simulation scenarios, but at the same time lacks standardization in various aspects, which hinders interchange of simulation object structures, configurations, and parameters.

5 Enterprise Knowledge Architecture (EKA)

As mentioned in Chaps. 1 and 3, the Active Knowledge Modeling (AKM) technology was originally invented/discovered in industrial attempts to build digital "industrial war rooms," around 1990, and through studies and discussions with leading scientists. The inventor recognized that core enterprise innovation is within the four inter-dependable core knowledge dimensions of any industrial enterprise. Holistic, multilayered knowledge models can be used to capture aspects of these dimensions. Holistic models create coherent knowledge representations that are logically consistent and have reflective views, recursive processes, repetitive working solutions, and replicable structures of metadata. These intrinsic properties of participative and active knowledge, called the 4R's, give us powerful development, integration, management, and reuse capabilities.

In this chapter, we describe the main principles and parts of AKM and EKA.

5.1 Knowledge Architectures

Knowledge architectures consist of knowledge explicitly represented in structured models, and of the mental views of the people involved in creating and using these models. Knowledge is explicitly represented as information and data structures. Data consist of symbols used for conveying information and knowledge. Data become information when its meaning is interpreted by some actor. We thus see data as a one-dimensional representation: a stream of symbols. Information adds a second dimension that reflects the meaning of the original data. Knowledge implies a justification of the information or that the information guides action. Knowledge representations must thus possess at least three dimensions: data, its meaning, and the justifications and actions that the knowledge results in. To support reflection on knowledge, a fourth dimension is needed. Reflection on knowledge is required to support, for example, learning, knowledge management, design, innovation, collaboration, creation of shared understanding, and other creative tasks. We refer to representations that contain four reflective dimensions as knowledge spaces. These concepts are illustrated in Fig. 5.1.

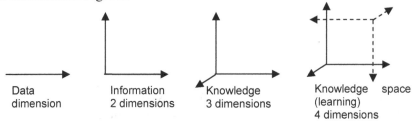

Data
dimension

Information
2 dimensions

Knowledge
3 dimensions

Knowledge   space
(learning)
4 dimensions

Fig. 5.1. From data to knowledge spaces

In a computerized system, the information dimension is typically represented as software program code that defines how the data is manipulated, stored, and presented to the user. Among humans, the second dimension can be illustrated by the capability to understand a certain language, such as English. If you do not understand the language, speech becomes incomprehensible data.

Few computerized systems are really knowledge based. Their data structures and program code are fixed. By using the system, humans can bring in the extra dimensions of reflection needed for knowledge and even learning. However, these additional dimensions cannot be reflected back into the computerized system as updated languages or logic. Reflection, knowledge, and learning can thus not be shared among the people using the system. What a user can learn from the system is limited to the two dimensions that were coded into the system from the start.

The practice of software development involves two explicit dimensions (data, code) and two mental views possessed by different roles (programmers, users). These dimensions and their typical relationships are depicted in Fig. 5.2.

Representing three or four randomly related dimensions is insufficient. The dimensions must as well be *mutually reflective*, capable of changing each other the way software code manipulates data structures, a programmer can change the software code, and users can change the way they work and how they want the support system to operate. Today, this learning cycle is decoupled, demanding a lot of resources, and taking far too long time. AKM methodologies aim to fix these problems.

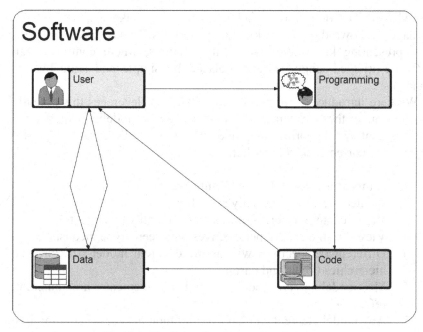

Fig. 5.2. Traditional software development

Some current approaches go beyond these limitations, for example,

- Metamodeling tools such as Metis, which allow the data formats and application rules to be updated during use
- Knowledge based engineering (KBE), where the application logic is captured as formal rules that may be altered during the use of the system

However, KBE tools use formal languages that are alien to ordinary users, relying on expert knowledge engineers to elicit and represent the user's knowledge. This is a small improvement from the conventional approach, where programmers perform the task of encoding the user's knowledge. True knowledge-based systems should thus enable the users to represent their knowledge themselves. For learning and innovation, we need knowledge spaces that facilitate lifecycle management and operation of the knowledge representations.

5.2 Principles for Active Knowledge Modeling (AKM)

AKM regards business knowledge to be the main innovative and integrating force. In order for IT to facilitate harvesting and cultivation of business knowledge, it must be driven by pragmatic representations of people's knowledge. The only way to achieve this is to make end users define, manage, and own their active knowledge models. This requires a new way of representing knowledge as visual structures, where complex, rigid, software-oriented languages are replaced by simple and agile business concepts.

We here introduce 31 principles for AKM that leverages this potential. While some of these principles are known to a few modeling experts, none are adequately supported by modeling tools, PLM, BPM, or EAI approaches currently on the market.

1. A model is a constellation of multiple views.
2. Related views are mutually reflective.
3. Views capture different dimensions of reality (as aspects).
4. Views from different perspectives may seem to be inconsistent.
5. Different perspectives will define different model structures and hierarchies (types and parts).
6. Metamodeling is modeling, and all elements are inherently reflective.
7. Any model element can have a multitude of types (including basic types such as object, relationship, property, etc. in different views).
8. Explicit classification should be complemented by implicit and derived classes.
9. *Property* is a fundamental modeling construct.
10. Properties anchor evolving parameter trees and value sets.
11. *Relationship* is a fundamental modeling construct.
12. Relationships represent complex task patterns.
13. *Value* is a fundamental modeling construct. Values can be related to other elements, have properties, etc.
14. Identification of individual elements happens through many nontrivial identification schemes, utilizing any model hierarchy or relationship.
15. Reuse is better supported by templates (prototype and stereotype instances) than by class instantiation.
16. The essence of an element is its context, not the element by itself. The meaning of any model element may depend on the meaning of any other element (semantic holism).
17. Every model/view is an open system; the meaning of any model fragment may depend on factors yet unknown, implicit or tacit.
18. During design, all dependencies are bidirectional.

19. A model/view is always in flux. Evolution must be managed as versions, variants, and configurations.
20. Access rights should be explicitly managed through modeled privileges. Role restrictions should not be hard-wired into the modeling services.
21. Models represent reality with different and evolving degrees of formality and ambiguity.
22. Models should be interpreted pragmatically.
23. Models should be executed interactively.
24. Inheritance is meaningful through any model structure, and so detailed inheritance semantics must be model-configured.
25. Parameters and values are propagated according to modeled inheritance and execution rules.
26. Models can be viewed through multiple presentation formats.
27. Models can be edited through multiple media interfaces.
28. Modeling user interfaces should be customized to role, task, and user preferences.
29. Model and view translation and transformation is best facilitated through interaction, identification, and propagation.
30. Any modeled relationship can be viewed as an annotation, adding semantic content to the elements it connects.
31. Like stories, templates should be connotations, conveying meaning by describing parallel realities that users can identify as overlapping their own in some way.

A consequence of these principles is that scientific research, with formal languages and reductionist hypothesis formulations, is almost irrelevant for further improving modeling technologies and design methodologies. How these principles are supported in the general architecture (the EKA) is described below. How these principles can be supported in practice in a modeling infrastructure based on the EKA is described in further detail in the next chapters.

5.3 EKA (Enterprise Knowledge Architecture)

Figure 5.3 defines the core constructs used for representing models on the technical layer. All constructs are regarded as *Elements*. *Models* contain elements, but one element may be found in multiple models. Models can thus capture partial, overlapping, and incomplete views.

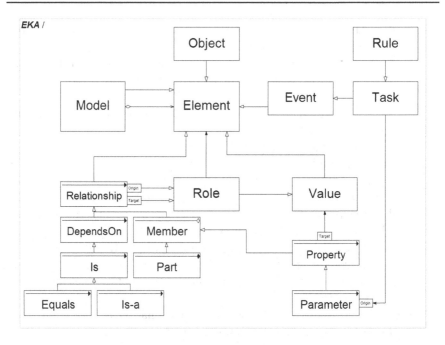

Fig. 5.3. Core EKA elements

Conventionally, most model elements will be *Objects*. All kinds of elements may have *Properties*, and *Relationships* link two elements through *Origin* and *Target Roles*. Relationships, roles, and properties are also elements, so they may possess properties and have relationships to other element.

The EKA does not separate between meta-classes, classes, and instances because of the following:

- One person's roof is another one's floor, thus an instance in one view may be a class in another.
- AKM models represent mutually reflective views.

Instead, a special relationship called *Is* between two objects (or relationships or properties) denote that the origin is defined by the target, and can thus express both specialization (Student is Person) and instantiation (George is-a Person). The instantiation relationship *Is-a* has similar meaning as Is, but it is used to separate meta-levels (for the modeling contexts where this is required). Finally, *Equals* is a bidirectional Is-relationship, which implies that the two elements represent the same concept, phenomenon, or entity. *Equals* is typically used for representing mappings between models that represent different perspectives on the same domain.

Other relationship types include general links and associations, and decomposition with (*Part*) and without (*Member*) ownership. Relationships and properties have *cardinality*. Note that this approach enables classification, decomposition and states of properties, relationships and views just like objects.

Values are also represented as first class model elements. This implies that values can be related to other values (e.g., "derived-from" or "in-conflict-with"), that values may be shared between multiple elements, that value sets may be defined (using member relationships), etc. *Roles* are values that reference other elements. *Properties* are modeled as relationships from an element to a value. A *Parameter* is a relationship between a task and a value, signifying that the task processes are influenced by the value.

The right column of the EKA core concepts model define basic constructs for representing the dynamic execution aspects of model elements. As a core concept, *Task* represents any unit of behavior or action. *Events* represent the statement that something has happened, and may trigger tasks. A *Rule* is a special kind of task that defines constraints, laws, or intentions that should be enforced.

5.3.1 Aspects and Multiple Dimensions

The above classification of core modeling concepts is no taxonomy. The same element may be represented in different ways in different models, for instance, as an object in one view, a relationship in another, and a property in the third. Many language constructs will also be defined as member of multiple core concept classes. As an example, take the language concept "state transition" found in a state diagram or statechart in UML (Booch et al. 2005), which can be a task, a relationship, and possibly an event or a rule at the same time. The core concepts can thus be seen as aspects or facets that any element may include as part of their definition.

Multidimensional meta-views are captured as multiple Is or Is-a relationships from an element. This approach can also be applied to mix in new *aspects* locally. For instance, if a group wants to add a cost dimension to a process model, they simply add an Is relationship from "Object" to "CostComponent" in their model. All objects within the model will then inherit the properties and behavior of cost components. Such extensions are local to each view.

5.3.2 Reflection and Metamodeling

The EKA is inherently *reflective*; it makes no separation between meta-levels. Objects, relationships, and property elements can be applied at any level. Inherent reflection also makes the EKA *coherent*, in that users apply the same modeling constructs and operations on any meta-level. They may perform "metamodeling" operations such as adding a property in the same way on instances and classes, or for that matter relationship and property instances and classes. This facilitates *instance level exceptions and evolution*. Similarly, users may perform modeling operations on objects representing classes, e.g., adding default parts and property values.

5.3.3 Inheritance

Multiple inheritance is controlled by Is and Is-a links between the properties of objects. These links articulate which properties are inherited from which superclass. This also opens up for reuse along other structures than classification and specialization, for example, to have property hierarchies cross-cutting the class hierarchy. Through reflection, we may define, for example, that a "Part," "Member," or ordinary relationship is Is relationship as well, enabling reuse along these dimensions. In previous work, we have discovered a number of scenarios where such inheritance is valuable for and intuitive to business users (Jørgensen 2004). We thus define inheritance as "reuse along relationships," extending the conventional definition "reuse along classification relationships" (Jørgensen 2004).

As a consequence, inheritance is not treated as a part of the core concepts with hard-wired semantics. Instead, the inheritance services can be adapted through the *value and change propagation and derivation engine*.

5.3.4 Expressiveness

The *expressiveness* of the EKA satisfies AKM principles outlined in Sect. 5.2. Basic elements such as objects, properties, and relationships can be described uniformly on any level. Aspects or facets can be represented as objects, and reused through local Is links. Multiple inheritance allows not only aspects, but also interoperability between overlapping classification schemes. Because properties and relationships are first class elements, they may be defined and managed just like objects, specialized and decomposed. Properties can have an extensible set of properties themselves (meta-properties) that define, for example, how they are to be managed (e.g., "readonly," "derived," "priority level"). The tasks and decisions involved in creating/selecting and maintaining a relationship may, for example, be defined as a process meta-view on the relationship.

5.3.5 Simplicity

Even though the EKA is this expressive, its core is still quite simple compared to most other frameworks. This, together with coherent modeling constructs and techniques across meta-levels, implies that it should be usable for business people, given some training, and a suitable set of metamodeling services integrated in the modeling user interface. Our previous experiences described in Chap. 3 indicate that users are capable of both modeling and metamodeling, *provided* customized views are available for such tasks (Jørgensen 2004). The design and derivation of such views for different contexts will be a key challenge in our further work. We need to design general frameworks for typical view types, integrated in suitable methodology processes, in a manner which can be adapted to each customer's organizational maturity and individual skill levels.

5.3.6 Degrees of Ambiguity, Formality and Uncertainty

While some of the statements a model contains will represent precise and certain facts, innovative design requires as well the capability to communicate and reason about more vague and evolving ideas. In general, AKM models will tolerate that every aspect of an element can be unknown. We may for instance encounter the following:

- Elements whose identifiers are not completely known (*anonymous elements*)
- Elements whose basic types are not known (e.g. object or property)

*Implicit and derived s*tatements constitute another important feature for enabling learning, emergent use, and reinterpretation of informal and semi-formal models. The EKA supports the following:

- *Implicit types*, such as "all objects of type T1 that have property X" or "all objects that are the targets of at least one relationship of type Y"
- *Implicit states*, defined by all or a set of the elements related to the element we are describing the state of, for example, its property values or connected relationships
- *Implicit versions and variants*, derived by selecting a set of features and values for a set of elements, suppressing others

5.3.7 Complex Relationships, Roles and Boundary Management

Through practical modeling of business processes, products, organizations, and IT systems, we have experienced several problems with common approaches to modeling relationships and roles. In early phases and general models, roles are used as placeholders for concrete elements to be specified (filled in) later. Roles thus denote a relationship where one of the participating elements is unknown. In this capacity, roles also act as *connectors* when model fragments are put together in a concrete context. The EKA modeling framework above supports this approach well.

At the same time, after roles have been filled with concrete objects, the existence of the relationship between the elements are paramount, and roles serve less of a purpose, except for capturing requirements and other information about the elements' participation in the relationship. This implies that view management should enable us to switch between views with and without roles, with and without the elements in the other side, roles shown on opposite sides or the same side of the relationship, etc.

When we look at an element such as an object, we see that the roles capture the interface of this element. Roles are thus crucial for interface or boundary management. When we are dealing with composite structures, this becomes apparent. A relationship between two elements that are part of larger elements also constitute a relationship between these parent elements. Taking a lifecycle perspective, relationships may be created between high-level elements first, and then connected to concrete parts later, for example, in process or product modeling. In a module- or component-oriented approach, the interface to a component should include all relationships that go into or out of it or to or from any of its parts. This implies that each relationship can be viewed on any level or decomposition above the one where it is defined. Similarly, during the design process, roles can be defined at any level, that is, at any place where the relationship arrow crosses an object box border.

These concepts are illustrated in the model in Fig. 5.4. Here one high-level relationship between the IT department and the process "Write progress report" has been concretized into three lower-level relationships between people within the department and subtasks within the process. There are roles connected to each subtasks, but also to the boundary on the top level where the relationships between people and subtasks cross the overall process boundary. The mapping at this boundary is not always trivial and automatable, as illustrated by the fact that three internal roles are mapped to two boundary ones, and two people are connected to the same role. The fragment also shows unfilled roles (input and output) shown on the opposite side of the relationship (the role of the *origin* element Plan is shown on the *target* end of the input flow relationship).

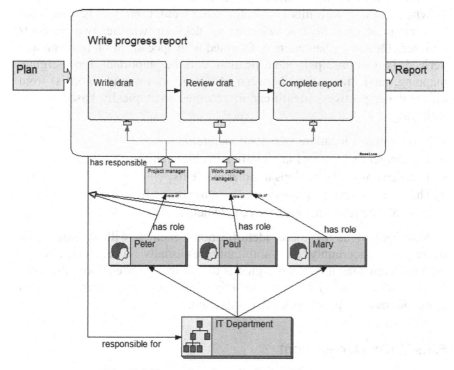

Fig. 5.4. Example role and relationship structure

To support this life-cycle process, the EKA proposes the following:

- Automatically establish Is-links from low-level to high-level relationship representations (as illustrated above).
- Automatically establish Is-links from low-level to high-level roles on both sides (e.g., links between roles on different decomposition levels above).
- Provide modeling services for abstracting and concretizing relationships (creating new representations one level up or down in the decomposition hierarchy). In some views, these services may be automatically invoked.

5.3.8 Identification Schemes and Resolution

Identification is a crucial service for modeling and model analysis. Most elements will have globally unique identifiers (GUID) on the technical level. This GUID has no meaning or semantics. Technical IDs should, however, not be confused with the interactive process of identifying which entity or phenomenon a model element represents.

When working with models, on the other hand, users will be supported by a range of *identification schemes* for deciding whether two elements represent the same phenomenon. Coupled with specialization (explicit and derived Is-relationships), identification will be important for merging, mapping, and translating between different views and models from different perspectives. Identification schemes are typically based on the following:

- The element's locations in part-of hierarchies
- The element's locations in classification hierarchies
- The element's relationships to other elements
- The element's name, number, and/or other properties
- Equivalence relationships between elements

Note that some of these identification schemes will include some degrees of uncertainty and ambiguity, especially in evolving design models. View mapping and merging is therefore supported, like other core EKA modeling services, as interactive task patterns, where different assumptions and opportunities may be tested.

5.3.9 Model Management

As mentioned above, multiple models may contain some of the same elements, and there may be relationships between elements in different models. One model may also include another as a *submodel*. We will for the moment base our solution of managing these dependencies on the existing submodeling and relationship bundling services of Metis.

5.3.10 Versioning, Variants and Configurations

All elements should be versioned. The repository must record all previous versions of elements. Variant configurations should be defined as separate models with overlapping element sets. More details will be elaborated based on pilot requirements.

5.4 AKM Execution: Interactive Behavior

The AKM modeling platform must include a number of basic services for concurrently accessing, updating, and executing models. The AKM execution platform provides four main services:

- Basic modeling
- Value propagation and derivation
- Task execution
- Rule execution

This section describes how these services are implemented and utilized in AKM platforms and solutions.

5.4.1 Interactive Execution and Evolution

To recap, models are defined as explicit representations of some portions of reality as perceived by some actor. A model is *active* when it directly influences the reality it reflects. *Model activation* or execution involves actors interpreting the model and adjusting their behavior accordingly. This process can be

- *Automated*, where a software component interprets the model,
- *Manual*, where the model guides the actions of human actors, or
- *Interactive*, where prescribed aspects of the model are automatically interpreted and ambiguous parts are left to the users to resolve.

The AKM platform is constructed to support interactive execution. By updating an active model, users adapt the system to fit their local work, preferences, and terminology. This concurrent process of modeling and execution is depicted in Fig. 5.5.

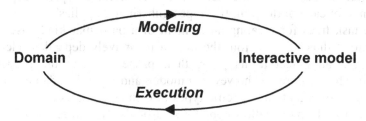

Fig. 5.5. The interplay of articulation and activation

The four core services of the AKM platform complement each other to achieve an agile and flexible execution platform. All services are modeled and executed as tasks, often as composite task patterns. Dependencies between model elements are managed through derivation and propagation of values, while rules control the triggering of tasks as well as the propagation of values. Like other models, tasks and rules are defined through the basic modeling services.

5.4.2 Basic Modeling Services

The basic modeling services allow you to access and edit the information captured in models. These services are accessed through visual and textual user interfaces components, described later. Modeling services allow you to create, read, update, and delete (CRUD) elements from a model:

- Create: Assign id and name, create and link all dependent elements (properties, parts etc.) that the template have
- Read: Return id, name, and dependent elements (recursively)
- Update: Update name and dependent elements only if changed
- Delete: Remove this element and dependent elements from the model

These atomic operations are combined to form *object-structure-driven recursive task trees* in order to create complete services that are simple for users to apply. When you access or manipulate an element, you are almost always as well dealing with some other elements that depend on the primary element. For instance, an object is described by its properties, and relationships need its origin and target roles to be meaningful. This implies that you are never interacting with one element at a time, but rather with a structured set of elements that are created, read, updated, and deleted together. The CRUD services are thus composed of a set of tasks that work on different objects in the set. Table 5.1 defines typical dependent elements for each of the primitive types. Inheritance applies.

The task trees for creating an element of a particular kind based on a template is thus derived from the tree of recursively dependent elements (e.g. from an object to its parts, their properties, and the properties' values). This task tree is, however, a model, and it can be adapted to meet specific requirements for specific types of elements, for example, in order to customize deep or shallow copy for a particular type of relationships.

Table 5.1. Dependent elements for CRUD operations

	Create	Read	Update	Delete
Element	Properties, Roles, Parts, Member relationships; Update: Relationships	Properties, and other elements according to configuration	Properties, Roles, Parts, Relationships	Properties, Parts; Update: Roles and relationships
Model	Parts and member relationships (recursively)	Parts and members (recursively)	Parts and members (recursively)	Parts (recursively), unless the element is member of other models
Object	Same as element			
Relationship	Same as element, in particular Roles			
Role	Same as element, in particular reference values			
Property	Same as element, in particular values			
Value	Primarily the actual value, potentially other elements			
State	Same as element			
Task	Same as element, particularly the parameters			
Rule	Same as task			
Parameter	Same as property			

Object-Structure-Driven Recursive Task Trees

Let us look at an example. The process template depicted in Fig. 5.6 is to be created in the context of a particular project, where it will become one of the tasks to be performed as part of the project plan.

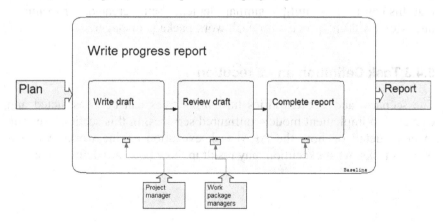

Fig. 5.6. Process template example

The object structure of the template model controls the task structure of the creation. In addition to creating a new process, you also create new properties, roles, parts, and values, recursively. The basic task tree would look something like this:

- Create a new object
  - Create a property called name and assign it to the object
    - Create a value "Write progress report" and assign it to the property
  - Create other properties and values that the process should have
  - Create all roles on the object (Plan, Report, Project manager, Work package managers)
    - Create their properties
      - Create the property value(s)
  - Create all parts of the object (three processes)
    - Create their properties
      - Create the property value(s)
    - Create their roles
      - Create their properties
        - Create the property value(s)
  - Create relationships between the parts (and their parts/roles)
    - Create their properties
      - Create the property value(s)

Additional dependencies may also be defined and executed, either by the propagation services or as tasks (triggered by event of creating an element). Below, we discuss how this task tree can be extended with rules that automatically connect roles of the template to elements in the context where the new model fragment is placed (the actual project). We also see that this can lead to multiple similar elements being created, for example, one "Review draft" process for each work package manager.

5.4.3 Task Definition and Execution

The scenario above exemplifies how tasks trees can be constructed and executed to implement model-configured services. In this section, we look in more detail on how the AKM task execution engine works, when it triggers tasks, what execution may result in, how tasks are defined, etc.

Definition of Tasks

A task is defined just like any other model element by its properties and the context where it is placed. Tasks typically have some of these properties:

- Name
- Description
- Planned start time
- Planned completion time
- Actual start time
- Actual completions time
- State (for automatic tasks, this is often a derived property)

Often, tasks will have the following roles (to be connected to other elements):

- Trigger (Event that starts the task or makes)
- Condition (Rules that prevent the task from starting)
- Responsible (e.g., a person)
- Service (software support for performing the work)
- Content (documents, model elements, etc.)
- Context (the object that the task works on)

Tasks that have a trigger will be automatically started. Tasks that have a service are partially automated (they may be manually or automatically triggered).

Triggering of Task

In general, there are three ways of starting a task:

- When the triggering event occurs and the condition is fulfilled
  - When the condition becomes fulfilled (trigger=when)
  - Whenever the condition is fulfilled (trigger=anytime)
  - When tasks that this task depends on have completed (enacting task pattern or process models)
- When a user explicitly starts the task as a service from the user interface

Task Execution States and Transitions

To handle both manual and automatic tasks in an integrated framework that allows evolution of the task models, we define these basic states for tasks:

- *Blocked*: The condition is not fulfilled, or the event has not occurred
- *Available*: The condition is fulfilled, but the task is defined to be triggered by a user (trigger=manual).
- *Ongoing*: The task is being worked on (manually or automatically), that is, the property "Actual start time" has a value
- *Completed*: The task has been performed (the property "Actual finish time" has a value)
- *Terminated*: The task failed or was cancelled during execution, and will not be completed ("Actual start time" has a value, "Actual finish time" has no value, Condition=Terminated/False)

The transitions between these states are depicted in Fig. 5.7. Completed tasks form the core log of events on the AKM platform. For manual tasks, a more elaborate state system can be encoded by additional properties, for example, to capture suspension of tasks. We decline from defining *State* as an explicit concepts in our core model, because as the above discussion shows, states can be adequately captured as rules over the set of primary model element properties.

Task

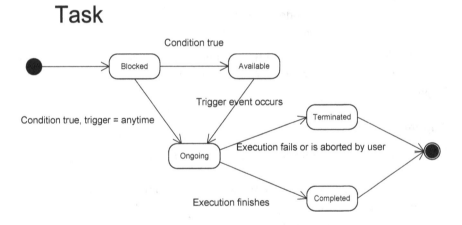

Fig. 5.7. Task state transition diagram

For automatic tasks that are invoked by an event, it makes sense to delay creation of individual tasks until they are started, simply because defining all allowed and potential services as separate model elements would greatly increase the size of the model. For such tasks, blocked and available tasks are templates that may be instantiated, for example, if the user decides to invoke the service. For manual tasks that, for example, are part of a project plan, blocked and available tasks should on the contrary be instantiated as soon as they are planned to be performed, in order to get a complete overview of the project plan. Luckily, since project plans are explicit models managed by the users, the task execution engine need not worry about instantiation, because it occurs when the users perform instance modeling.

5.4.4 The Execution Context of a Task

The execution of an individual task always occurs in a given context. Generic and potential tasks may be defined with a wider scope, for example, to be triggered whenever an object of a given type is created or updated. A generic task thus becomes instantiated and bound to the actual context when it is triggered. We define the context of a task to be a single model element, connecting to the task using a *Context* relationship. The context is used for retrieving input parameters and storing the results of tasks. Sometimes, as in the creation example described above, the structure of elements related to the Context-object may also define the structure of subtasks to be executed as part of this task.

In the user interface, the set of available tasks for each element represents services that the user may invoke on the element. The set of ongoing tasks capture collaboration dependencies that need to be coordinated. The set of completed tasks constitute the history or log of the element.

Parameter Binding

The binding of task parameters to context values is potentially a complex process. For most tasks/services, clear rules should be defined for how to identify parameter values, as described below. If, however, the rules cannot determine which value to use for a mandatory parameter, users must be involved in selecting the right values. The provision of such inputs will itself be represented as a subtask of the main task. If the task provides output values as results, they are automatically stored in the parameter elements related to the task. Further use and processing of these results will take place through subsequent tasks in the same context, or in contexts that are related to this one. Rules may of course also be defined for populating object and property structures from task result values, for example, importing data from a web service result into model elements.

In the EKA model, parameters are properties and therefore relationships from tasks to values. Like other relationships, they will appear as roles when no element has been connected to the other end. The process of binding values to parameters is thus facilitated by the same services that allow you to connect relationships. Similarly, the binding of values can be seen as a process of identifying the right element to apply. Parameter binding is thus able to utilize some of the same principles and rules that we apply for identification of objects.

Artifacts: Reflective Objects and Task Structures

In the example described above (creation of a composite task from a template pattern), the roles represent connection points between the new task and the instance model where it is placed. The task of connecting this object to its surroundings thus has the roles of the object as its parameters. Here we see the duality if object and task structures come into play. The task of connecting the object to its surroundings becomes a reflection of the object and its roles into the task dimension, a "typecasting" of the object as task. To capture, for example, repetition, undo and redo of the connecting task, we do, however, need to represent the task reflection of the object explicitly as tasks (as separate elements for the object context) as well.

Relationship is another kind of element that often will be interpreted as a task. Typically, it will have subtasks for creation, connection, sustenance, disconnection, and deletion of the relationship. Often, the effect that the relationship has on the elements it connects will as well be represented as sets of potential and available tasks/services.

In general, all elements will have a set of tasks associated with it. To manage, control, coordinate, learn, and perform your work supported by active models, task views will be available that for each model, model fragment, or element shows you the past, current, and/or future tasks related to each element, and as well how the object structures have created reflective task structures.

Process Execution and Sequencing of Tasks

Process model constitute a particular kind of active knowledge models. Processes are modeled using several different notations, including transformational, conversational, role-based, system-dynamic, etc. Details on the different types of process modeling languages are discussed further in Chap. 12. Process enactment should be facilitated by the task execution semantics defined here. Each process step will then be interpreted as an object that is both a task and a context for a task, in order to capture parameter values in the process structures. In addition, process execution must be controlled by (reusable) triggering rules that let process flow relationships control the sequencing of the steps.

Composition of Tasks

Above we have come across different kinds of task composition trees:

- Explicitly modeled task trees
- Explicitly modeled processes or task patterns
- Object-driven task structures (*recursive method* tasks)
- Relationships interpreted as tasks

We thus need well-defined rules for how task decomposition trees are to be executed. In most cases, the starting of tasks should be conditioned by the general criteria that if it has a parent task, then this task should also be triggered, or at least available, before the subtask can be triggered. There may, however, be situations where this rule is relaxed, and task composition is merely used for organizing tasks by human users. This implies that the decomposition guard rule stated above must be made explicit and part of the default conditions for tasks, so that it may also be deleted when necessary.

In general, all rules that control task execution should be made explicit. This may, on the other hand, generate quite a lot of overhead, increasing the size of (task) models. Though we need not store the rule multiple times, the Condition relationship from the task to the rule must in some way be represented for all tasks. Whether this and similar features is to be implemented by derivation/lookup or propagation will depend on detailed performance studies. This implementation level problem should, however, not affect users.

Task Patterns, Order and Dependencies

As mentioned above, we may use the task execution system to support more conventional process execution with explicit sequencing of tasks defined by process flows and routing objects such as gateways, joins, and forks as found in, for example, BPMN and UML activity diagrams. Because of the many different kinds of processes and the multiple process modeling languages that users may want to apply, we will, however, not code any specific process enactment scheme into the software. The AKM platform must be configurable in this area.

In general, however, when multiple automatic tasks are triggered by the same event, the execution engine is faced with the problem of deciding which task should be triggered first. For this problem, we define these rules:

- All triggered tasks are placed in a queue.
- When one task is taken out of the front of the queue and performed, it may cause new events that trigger new tasks. If so, these tasks are put at the end of the queue.
- When a task is to be performed, but lack values for a mandatory parameter, it is removed from the queue and put into another queue for tasks that lack parameters.
- After a task is performed, the tasks in the parameter queue are validated once more, and executed if they now have all the necessary values.
- When the execution queue is empty, a manual task to provide parameter values is created for each of the tasks still in the parameter queue.

In general, however, models should contain enough information to control the sequencing of tasks by triggering events and conditions, if and when this is important.

Rule Definition and Execution

In the EKA, a rule is a kind of task. This is because we are interested in the active nature of the rule, the effect it has upon the model and platform, and how these effects are achieved in a model-configured way by the software code. By representing rules as tasks, we also capture the rules' effects in the history of the models, and allow users to override rules when they see that they are no longer valid, or perhaps just to explore what opportunities were to arise if we are able to find a way to work around this rule in our design. After all, rules, like all other model elements, have different degrees of certainty and precision throughout their lifecycles.

As we have seen above, rules are applied in three elements:

- To define events that trigger a task
- To define conditions for starting a task
- To define actions that carry out automatic operations on the platform

The language should be suitable for textual as well as visual rule definition. We have used elements and notations from industrially applied rule languages such as OCL (Object Constrain Language) or SRL wherever that makes sense.

5.5 Summary

We have in this chapter described the main principles for AKM. With this as a basis we have described the EKA, including both structural and dynamic aspects. The EKA is the most abstract and general enterprise model of the entire family of enterprise models, acting as a family reference model for all other kinds and variants of enterprise models. An AKA, Active Knowledge Architecture, built using the EKA template, integrates all other enterprise architectures, such as product architectures and system architectures. An enterprise specific AKA will support simultaneous modeling, metamodeling, model management, and work execution, using MGWP. Relationships between AKA, EKA, and ICT infrastructure was previously depicted in Fig. 1.3. Before delving into how to use these architectures in practice to support integrated business operations in Chaps. 7–9, we in the next chapter survey relevant standards for ICT infrastructure for enterprise solutions used as a basis for developing generic ICT services.

6 Approaches to Enterprise Solutions

Business analysts recognize that innovative design is the most important competitive factor for western manufacturing industries. In more and more industries, product platforms with dynamic modularization and configurable components are introduced to meet evolving diverse and contradicting customer, technology, and business requirements. Conventional IT applications are built to support routine information processing, rather than creative design work. Analysts claim that "IT doesn't matter," because IT does not extend the capabilities of the core of the business.

In this context, interoperability should remove barriers to the following:

- Interdisciplinary *knowledge* sharing and cooperative problem solving
- *Information* logistics and quality management
- *Data* exchange between companies and targeted applications for different disciplines

We aim to bring together three distinct forces currently not well coordinated in the product life cycle:

- *Voice of the customer*: expressing the needs and requirements of the market
- *Voice of business*: ensuring that the company is profitable, managing its resources and competences in the best way, following clear visions and strategies
- *Voice of technology*: representing the various disciplines that design and manufacture the products, and technological constraints and opportunities

Current product life cycle management (PLM) systems tend to favor one of these forces at the expense of the others, leading to multiple *islands of automation*, as each function or discipline selects the tools that fit best their needs.

In Fig. 6.1, product-oriented collaboration is broken down into three distinct focus areas – one that addresses the *access to the knowledge sources*, and one that addresses *how the users*, through their workplaces, *get concurrent access to knowledge sources and applications/services*, and finally one that addresses how the users, *through a collaborative environment, can work together on the same product.*

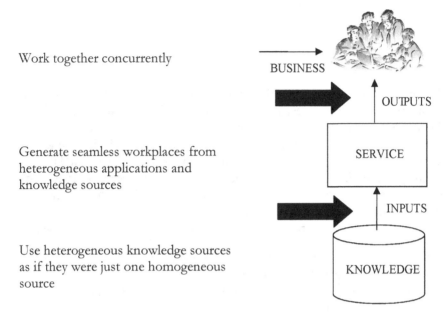

Work together concurrently

Generate seamless workplaces from heterogeneous applications and knowledge sources

Use heterogeneous knowledge sources as if they were just one homogeneous source

Fig. 6.1. Product-based collaboration

This simple scenario description points to three important requirements to the product-based interoperability infrastructure:

- The users must be able to work together in a collaborative environment.
- The user's workplace must be able to seamlessly integrate content and results from applications/services and knowledge sources.
- The access to heterogeneous knowledge sources must appear as an access to one homogeneous source.

6.1 Product-Oriented Business Interoperability Profiles

In ATHENA (Athena 2007; Jørgensen et al. 2007), we have identified typical, recurring business interoperability issues and systemized them into a set of Business Interoperability Profiles (BIP). Here, we outline five different profiles from a product-oriented perspective. The product-oriented profiles are differentiated by how data, information, and knowledge about the content of work is shared and exchanged between partners, internally in a company or cross-organizationally.

6.1.1 Product Document Exchange and Management

The most basic level of product-based interoperability relies completely on manual interpretation and processing of the product information. It is captured in documents, including drawings and spreadsheets, and exchanged in a rather ad hoc manner. Fig. 6.2 illustrates this profile. There are two variants of the profile:

- Document exchange, using, e.g., e-mail to send documents
- Document sharing, using a repository that multiple partners can access

Fig. 6.2. Product document exchange and management

This business interoperability scenario is dominant among SMEs. For larger corporations, it is still widely used, though most often in combination with more sophisticated automated information systems. Situations with a rapid pace of change or a high degree of uncertainty typically must be handled manually.

6.1.2 Product Data Exchange through Mapping

In this profile, product data is stored in a structured format in different application systems used by the partners. Most applications offer generic or specific import/export mechanisms toward other major players in the same or related application markets, and toward standard formats such as XML, or higher level standards such as STEP EXPRESS. Application programming interfaces (API) such as Web services are also common-place. Through Enterprise Application Integration (EAI), these interfaces are typically mapped directly, linking data elements and services in one tool to corresponding elements and services in another tool, as illustrated in Fig. 6.3. The figure shows that each partner or application has its own internal database, with its own execution rules implemented in the application (as indicated by the lightning symbol).

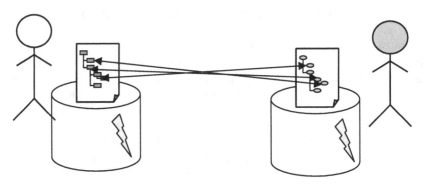

Fig. 6.3. Product data exchange through data mapping

In this profile, you typically end up making a new integration solution for each pair of applications or companies involved.

6.1.3 Product Data Exchange Based on Reference Models and Semantic Mediation

The data level mapping approach outlined in the earlier section is straightforward and direct. However, the large number of bidirectional links needed for each application pair makes it less scalable when a large number of companies and engineering disciplines are involved in the supply network, such as in the automotive or aerospace industries. The bidirectional links between data elements also become hard to maintain consistently when many different systems are involved in the life cycle. Consequently, *global reference models* such as thesauri, taxonomies, ontologies, and product data dictionaries have been introduced. As shown in Fig. 6.4, multiple local models, e.g., from different companies or applications, are linked to a central reference structure, and the links to this structure are used for automatically identifying the best semantic mapping between two concepts.

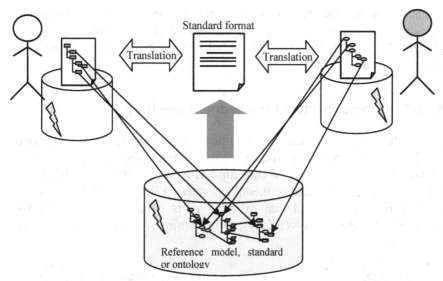

Fig. 6.4. Product data exchange through semantic technologies

6.1.4 Shared Product Information Repository

For close collaboration, e.g., in concurrent design projects, the classification and generic part structure provided by an ontology or reference
model is insufficient as a shared product architecture. Instead, the concrete
product information being worked on must be available to all participants
and stakeholders. This single global product data model is found, e.g., in
Product Data Management (PDM) systems. As illustrated in Fig. 6.5, the
global data model now contains a lot of instance data, in addition to the
categorization information included also in Fig. 6.4.

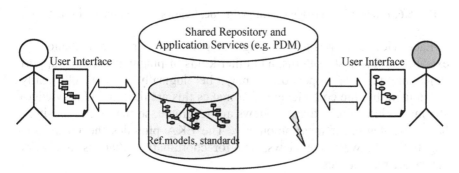

Fig. 6.5. Product data management with a shared repository

The figure also illustrates some important features of shared information repositories. Execution semantics is maintained at the global level, with a global rules engine, and typically global process management around the product information base.

6.1.5 Federated Product Knowledge Repository

The fifth product-oriented BIP is illustrated in Fig. 6.6. Like the two previous profiles, a shared product representation is the main coordination artifact. However, the later architecture is based on the recognition that different participants and stakeholders have different perspectives on product information, and that different parts of the overall enterprise knowledge architecture (EKA) will require different management approaches.

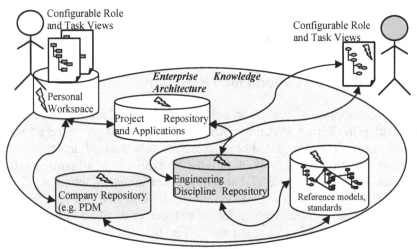

Fig. 6.6. Product knowledge sharing with local views and pragmatic execution

Each view or repository in Fig. 6.6 may have its own metamodels, execution rules, task patterns, and other kinds of pragmatic design support functionality. The repositories may be logically and/or physically distributed, but the core element that makes this architecture a knowledge-sharing architecture is that the views are federated, so that each repository has some degree of local autonomy. The EKA provides the means for negotiating between the views, and for coordinating changes and work across the repositories.

Local ownership to a view is crucial, because maintenance of single global models such as that of PDM systems in Fig. 6.5 quickly becomes too complex and bureaucratic especially when done across organizational borders. In PDM systems, autonomous local views typically are constructed ad hoc by someone taking data out of the system to perform some analysis, and then inputting the results (hopefully).

6.2 State of the Art and Requirements for Enterprise Solutions

This section gives a brief summary of the state of the art in product-based infrastructures, highlighting the need for configurable solutions that can integrate and mediate between heterogeneous views on product data, held by different stakeholders and disciplines.

6.2.1 Product Design and Life Cycle Management

Separating product-oriented work from process-oriented work as done earlier is of course artificial. Product design, while focused on the product information, does of course involve processes and emergent task patterns. Understanding the deep nature of the relationships between product and process structures does however require a thorough understanding of new approaches to holistic design.

Initial or early design work, creating new products, covering idea expression, conceptual design, and architectural compliance design focus on creating a precise definition of the product family logic and logistics. This is innovating new products by realizing new ideas and applying new principles and product materials, functions, and technologies to define agile configurable product platforms.

Product design to deliver to specific customer requirements is maybe better denoted as *product development*. This implies taking an already validated design solution, designed in a holistic approach, and using configurable product platform services to customize the product, making it ready for manufacturing and delivery.

If the product delivery design or construction is based on a configurable product platform, then that platform may also offer sophisticated process support, combining the following:

- A generic *top-down* process hierarchy with logic and logistics
- *Bottom-up* emerging work processes as task patterns to handle unforeseen problems and allow a space of freedom and creative chaos for innovation

- *Middle-out* business processes providing property and parameter balancing, supporting collaborative business management and coordination among roles and disciplines.

This implies that most of the process design is indeed performed in the early design stage. Process knowledge is created by capturing the pragmatic logic (natural sequence of events) and the task patterns and structures, and implementing intelligent design to meet design constraints and requirements. The main future challenge is therefore to support early design, enabling us to concurrently perform holistic design of products, organizations, processes, systems, and services.

In current markets, many people confuse the knowledge required to do early design with the knowledge to support construction for customer delivery. A product-based infrastructure is, or rather will be, characterized by these properties and capabilities:

- Concurrent access to shared data, knowledge, and working methods
- Role, task, discipline, and service-specific contextual views of product data, design logic, and rules
- Common structures and views for coordination and decision support
- Capturing the evolution of product data and structures
- Capabilities to calculate, compare, balance, and change properties and their distributed parameters
- Capabilities to define and integrate the many product structures required to support the many engineering disciplines and their methods

6.2.2 Life Cycle Knowledge Integration

A key dimension of product-based interoperability has to do with interoperability within and between life cycle phases of the product, such as design, engineering, and manufacturing. The corresponding interoperability issues are related to the diverse effects of changes along the life cycle; these issues will have impacts upon all detailed phases and processes and their relationships between, as well to, all other enterprise areas of concern, e.g., IT infrastructure, manufacturing tools, and organizational development.

In such situations, multiple actors collaborate in doing a variety of activities (such as product development, product engineering, product manufacturing, PDM), but the focus is on the product and the knowledge about the product rather than the processes used to develop and manufacture the product.

Within each area, there are multiple disciplines involved (such as electronics, hydraulics, mechanical, IT hardware, and software).

The actors involved may be different people (electrical engineers, mechanical engineers, CAD engineers, product data managers, etc.), with different backgrounds.

Different disciplines often refer to the same bulk of information, but with different degrees of precision and/or detail. As a matter of fact, the information does not simply record the status of a process (i.e., if a process has been completed and with what results it has been completed), but it is the substrate that supports the evolving knowledge about the product. Interoperability must support the sharing of knowledge rather than just the transfer of information as documents in business processes.

6.2.3 State of the Art in Product Design

Information about products and their design and production is the key source of knowledge for most companies. As indicated in Fig. 6.7, this information reflects three main forces that shape product design:

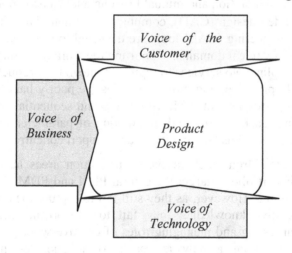

Fig. 6.7. Forces shaping product design

Different technologies have emerged to support each of these forces:

- Voice of the Customer (VoC): representing the needs and requirements of the market

- Voice of Business (VoB): ensuring that the company is profitable, managing its resources and competences in the best way by following clear visions and strategies
- Voice of Technology (VoT): representing the various disciplines of design and manufacture of products, technological constraints, and opportunities.
- Customer Relationship Management (CRM) and requirements management systems aim to capture the VoC, but lack services for product design engineers to capture life-cycle experiences, for manufacturing engineers to adapt to the design, and for life-cycle management engineers to influence both design and manufacturing.
- Enterprise Resource Planning (ERP) and Business Process Management (BPM) are applied to ensure that the voice of business managers is heard, that work is performed with maximum efficiency and according to established procedures, but these processes do not currently embrace any product engineering, customization, or design activity. Conventional approaches to IT systems development enforce sequential peer-to-peer work processes and unidirectional information flows with poor support for collaboration and mutual learning and decision making.
- Computer-aided design (CAD), computer-aided manufacturing (CAM), and other engineering (CAE) tools are designed to represent general or specific technological domains, supporting the work of engineers from a specific discipline. No services to represent integrated product structures are currently provided, and most properties are poorly handled, forcing users to revert to parameter file versioning and sequential computation with personal backups to avoid overwriting of parameter values. Data management must thus be reengineered to support concurrency.

System vendors from each of these application areas have naturally extended their portfolio to target the central PLM and PDM challenge, as depicted in Fig. 6.8. However, as they still fail to capture the core situated or work-generative knowledge, they fail to support the most critical knowledge harvesting and managing roles of creative work processes. To resolve this situation, a new approach to holistic design must be introduced. This is the focus of AKM.

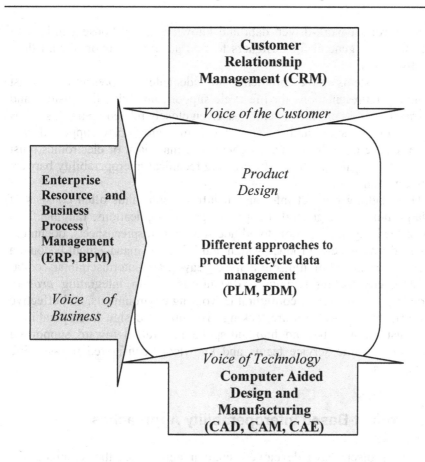

Fig. 6.8. Inroads toward product life cycle data management

All the approaches in Fig. 6.8 share one important shortcoming: They favor one perspective over the others. This is evident in the following:

- The focus on business processes and document management in ERP-based PLM offerings
- The focus on predefined structures and Cartesian geometry calculations and geometric data structures in CAD-based PDM

Such perspective bias often leads to a lack of support for other voices and disciplines. If product information is mainly captured in documents, then the main design work occurs outside of the PLM system. The result is that the core information about knowledge discoveries and innovation is not structured so that it may be processed automatically or transformed into new views suitable for other perspectives. The knowledge architecture is predefined and the content is generic and static. Nor do the application services reflect work-driven data and knowledge, and consequently they are much too general for designers to find adequate support for all their creative tasks.

CAD systems have problems in adequately representing robust geometry representations for life cycle support, involving dimensions and tolerances across product assemblies. Even closely related domains such as calculations of static and dynamic mechanics are poorly supported, and more remote disciplines such as chemistry, materials, or electronics must be handled by disjoint tool sets, creating technical interoperability barriers between engineers.

The resulting product information infrastructure thus often consists of a large number of general, poorly integrated applications, ranging from established engineering tools to ad hoc solutions in spreadsheets, document tables, drawings, etc. Product design and life cycle management become a poorly coordinated multidisciplinary endeavor, and interdisciplinary collaborative engineering remains a distant vision. An integrating *product knowledge architecture*, configurable working environments, and effective role-oriented workplaces are lacking. To support design interoperability, we must go way beyond hub-and-spoke integration toward supporting roles of dynamic service teams and knowledge-configured role-specific workplaces.

6.3 Product-Based Interoperability Approaches

Various projects have developed singular approaches that embrace and extend established research strategies toward solving problems in product-based interoperability. Though many of these approaches show promising early results, they do not represent a holistic approach for capturing and nurturing enterprise knowledge:

- *Enterprise modeling* as discussed in Chap. 4 provides generic and user-oriented means for capturing information about most aspects of the product life cycle, but primarily from the business perspective. Customer input and market analysis is also commonly represented, but the messy technological details of product design, such as property embodiment and parameter handling, are typically outside the scope of enterprise modeling. However, with its focus on capturing multiple views of business knowledge, enterprise modeling is a promising starting point for a more powerful and configurable product interoperability infrastructure.

- *Cross-organizational business processes* deal with the automation of routine procedures, supporting some of the tasks in the product life cycle, but not the most innovative and important ones, e.g., in the early phases of design. Product information is typically treated as black box artifacts and business documents being manipulated and exchanged during the business process. The content and structure of product information is outside of the BPM scope. To support design, a more configurable and user-controlled process enactment approach is needed, working in concert with a business rule engine capable of capturing and managing product design rationale.

- *Ontology and semantic web research* is concerned with capturing and reasoning about product information. Ontology captures essential established facts about the product domains, and applies a global logic for reasoning about these facts, for transforming between different data representations, etc. Ontology languages such as OWL and RDF (see later) are better equipped for representing, e.g., product property structures than conventional software engineering approaches such as UML. However, by demanding a formal, precise, and global representation, ontologies are not well equipped to capture local, heterogeneous product views from different disciplines, or unfolding incomplete and incoherent models reflecting the current state of product information during, e.g., the early phases of design. Semantic approaches are designed to simplify automatic reasoning, but the critical problems of pragmatic information capture from users, interdisciplinary sense making, and interpretation of product information demand more interpretive flexibility and situated, user-controlled analysis and reasoning.

- *Service-oriented architectures (SOA)* aim to break up monolithic applications into reusable component services that can be put together in new ways to support emerging business needs. To be useful, this foundation does however require business and user-level, product-oriented configuration and composition tools, and an integrating product knowledge architecture.

- *Model-driven architectures (MDA)* utilize modeling languages and approaches derived from object-oriented programming (e.g., UML and MOF) to build new software applications and to integrate existing applications. As a relatively young discipline, software engineering has not yet developed as sophisticated modeling approaches as other engineering disciplines. In particular, MDA has inadequate support for reflective models, instance modeling, multiperspective, aspect-oriented, and multidimensional modeling. Some recent software engineering advances, e.g., Microsoft's approach to software factories, have started to learn from the experience of the manufacturing industries, advocating more configurable and domain-specific visual languages (DSL), but at the moment, mainstream MDA offers little support for product-based interoperability.

- *Industry standards and reference models* exist in multitude. Typically, they are designed to support a concrete interoperability need to bridge two particular application islands. The number of different combinations of disciplines, roles, applications, and processes in each industry sector implies that the number of particular standardization needs is insurmountable. The standardization process, often ending up in consensus compromises that allow most competing approaches to coexist, further contributes to the ever-increasing complexity of industry standards. A simple, well-designed core product knowledge architecture would be needed to ensure that a single family of standards, such as STEP or ebXML, does not become unmanageable. However, if there is such a core, it is generally based on ill-suited approaches such as MDA or semantic web. The result is unnecessarily complex giving large standards that are too expensive for most companies to apply more that a small fraction. These standards only support data exchange, and not interdisciplinary knowledge sharing and mediation.

6.3.1 XML

XML will receive the least coverage in this review. It is the most general and widespread of the technologies we consider, and is therefore likely to be familiar to the majority of readers. Basically, XML defines a set of syntax rules that can be used to create semantically rich markup languages for particular domains. Once a markup language is defined and the semantics of the tags known, the document content can be annotated. The XML language thus defined can include specification of formatting, semantics, document metadata (author, title, etc.), and so on. XML allows for the creation of *elements*, which are XML containers consisting of a start tag, content, and an end tag.

Because of the flexibility of XML in defining domain-specific, meaningful markups, it has been widely adapted as a standard for application-independent data exchange. These properties combine to make XML the foundational technology for the semantic web, providing a common syntax for authoring web content. On one hand, XML provides means for syntactic interoperability, as well as ways to ensure the validity of a document, and most importantly the necessary syntax to define the meaning of elements in a domain-specific application. On the other hand, providing the syntax for defining meaning is only a necessary, but not sufficient condition for the specification of semantics that allows interoperability.

Building on the XML specification also becomes necessary because the hierarchical structure of XML documents makes them difficult to use for extensible, distributed data definitions. Much of the information about relationships in the data is implicit in the structure of the document, making it difficult to use and update this information in a flexible and application-independent way.

6.3.2 Web Services

There is a great deal of interest about Web services (Alonso et al. 2004) and SOA in general. A useful definition can be found in Daconta et al. (2003): "Web services are software applications that can be *discovered, described,* and *accessed* based on XML and standard Web protocols over intranets, extranets, and the Internet." This definition exposes the main technical aspects of Web services, to do with discovery and description, as well as the role of WWW (e.g., XML) technologies for data exchange and communication. Also, the definition is abstract enough to exclude low-level protocols like RPC as Web services. These core concepts along with the associated technologies are shown in Fig. 6.9.

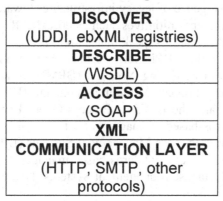

Fig. 6.9. The basic layers of Web services

It is important to situate the role of Web services in the real world. Daconta et al. (2003) argue that the most important factor for determining the future of a new technology is not "... how well it works or how 'cool' it is ..." but on business adoption. Along this line, they see a bright future for Web services, which is being promoted by Microsoft, IBM, Sun, as well as the open source community. But why such widespread support? One reason is the promise of interoperable systems. Once businesses adopt standardized Web service descriptions, the possibility of exchanging data and sharing the cost of services increases. In addition, the open standards prevent monopolization of applications, preventing the dreaded *vendor lock-in* associated with proprietary solutions. Finally, a widespread adoption of Web service protocols means that existing applications can be leveraged by turning them into Web services. As an example, it is possible for .NET clients and servers to talk to J2EE servers using SOAP.

The point of all this is that Web services enable interoperability at the level of business processes without having to worry about interoperating between different applications, data formats, communication protocols, and so on.

6.3.3 BPMI

The Business Process Management Initiative (BPMI.org) is an independent organization devoted to the development of open specifications for the management of e-business processes that span multiple applications, corporate departments, and business partners, behind the firewall and over the Internet. BPMI.org complements initiatives such as J2EE and SOAP that enable the convergence of legacy infrastructures toward process-oriented enterprise computing and initiatives such as ebXML, RosettaNet, BizTalk, WSDL, UDDI, tpaML, and E-Speak that support process-oriented business-to-business collaboration. BPMI.org defines open specifications such as the Business Process Modeling Notation (BPMN, now taken further by OMG), the Business Process Modeling Language (BPML, although not further supported), and the Business Process Query Language (BPQL) to enable the standards-based management of e-business processes with forthcoming Business Process Management Systems (BPMS), in much the same way SQL enabled the standards-based management of business data with off-the-shelf Database Management Systems (DBMS).

6.3.4 WfMC

WfMC (Workflow Management Coalition) was founded in 1993 to develop and promote workflow integration capability. It is a nonprofit, international organization of workflow vendors, users, analysts, and university/research groups.

According to WfMC, a workflow can be defined by three definitions:

- The automation of a business process, in whole or part.
- Information or tasks are passed from one participant to another for action, according to a set of procedural rules.
- A number of logical steps, each of which is known as an activity.
  We can see the workflow overview in Fig. 6.10.

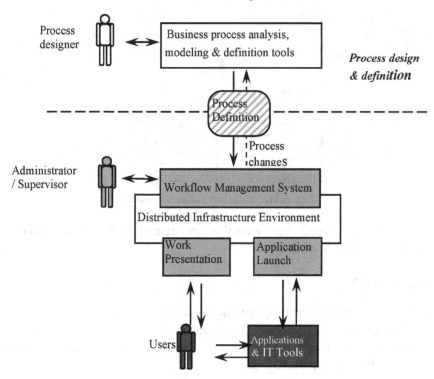

Fig. 6.10. Workflow overview

A Workflow Management System is a system that defines, manages, and executes *workflows* through the execution of software whose order of execution is driven by a computer representation of the workflow logic.

Three functional areas are supported by WfMC:

- The build-time functions concerned with defining, and possibly modeling, the workflow process and its constituent activities
- The run-time control functions concerned with managing the workflow processes in an operational environment and sequencing the various activities to be handled as part of each process

- The run-time interactions with human users and IT application tools for processing the various activity steps

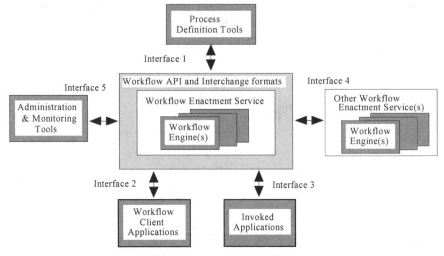

Fig. 6.11. Workflow reference model

Fig. 6.11 represents the workflow reference model. The different elements are described later.

Workflow API

- Workflow application programming interface
- The interface around the workflow enactment
- A service interface that is to support workflow management functions across the five functional areas

Workflow Enactment Service

A software service that consists of one or more workflow engines to create, manage, and execute workflow instances. Applications may interface to this service via the WAPI.

Workflow Engine

- A workflow enactment service consists of multiple workflow engines
- A software service or *engine*
- Execution environment for a workflow instance

Process and Activity State Transitions

- The workflow enactment service may be considered as a state transition machine
- Individual processes or activity instances change states in response to external events (e.g., completion of an activity)
- Specific control decisions taken by a workflow engine (e.g., navigation to the next activity step within a process)

6.3.5 OAGIS GIS

The Open Applications Group, Inc. (OAGi) is a nonprofit consortium focusing on best practices and process-based XML content for e-business and application integration. OAGi has extensive experience in building an industry consensus-based framework for business software application interoperability and has developed a repeatable process for quickly developing high-quality business content and XML representations of that content.

OAGIS (Open Application Group Integration Specification) is an Integration Specification: A technology-neutral means of integrating enterprise applications and of engaging in e-business transactions. In a world where integration is a necessity – enterprises face EAI scenarios daily – having a technology-neutral reference specification provides the clear benefit of minimizing pairwise integrations. For OAGIS, Integration Scenarios are the basis for integration message design, establishing the context of messages that accomplish the integration, whether B2B or EAI. These scenarios are reusable designs that can be modified to meet specific business process needs.

The Business Object Document (BOD), OAGIS's atomic transactional interchange message, is the structured XML message interchanged between applications, either intraenterprise or interenterprise. BODs (e.g., ProcessInvoice, ChangePurchaseOrder) represent applications' integration APIs and/or the enterprise's e-business service interactions. The BOD defines, among other things, a Noun, the business object (Invoice, PurchaseOrder,...) that is the subject of the interchange and a Verb, the operation (Add, Change, Process, Cancel,...) to be applied to the Noun. Benefits of using the BOD message architecture include consistency of architecture, message, and dictionary; high levels of reuse across messages; rapid development; and a smaller learning curve for users and developers.

6.3.6 OASIS BPEL

The Business Process Execution Language (BPEL), also sometimes identified as BPEL4WS (BPEL for Web Services), provides a language to specify business processes that are composed of Web services as well as exposed as Web services. The specification states that the language specifies *business process behavior based on Web services*, i.e., the language can be seen as a (business) extension to the Web services paradigm. It can be used for composing solutions from processes and other components in the realm of a Service Oriented Architecture. The language supports specification of business protocols by defining partner relationships and their external visible behavior through abstract business processes.

Business processes in BPEL represent stateful, long-running interactions. Process instances are created implicitly through initial activities receiving messages. Correlation of incoming messages to process instances is supported based on business tokens – significant data carried with the message, such as surname together with birthplace and date.

Process behavior is described using a single model with both hierarchical structure of specialized control constructs and graph structure. Handlers specify further behavior for compensating activities, acting on unsolicited events, and error recovery and alternatives.

The OASIS Web Services Business Process Execution Language Technical Committee (WSBPEL TC) continues the work on BPEL. The WSBPEL TC scope is to support process mechanisms in the following areas:

- Sequencing of process activities, especially Web service interactions
- Correlation of messages and process instances
- Recovery behavior in case of failures and exceptional conditions
- Bilateral Web service-based relationships between process roles

6.3.7 UN/CEFACT BCF

UN/CEFACT is the United Nations Centre for Trade Facilitation and Electronic Business. It is open to participation from Member States, intergovernmental organizations, and sectorial and industry associations recognized by the Economic and Social Council of the United Nations (ECOSOC). The Centre's objective is to be *inclusive* and it actively encourages organizations to contribute and help develop its recommendations and standards.

UN/CEFACT was established in 1996 in response to new technological developments, a desire to officially recognize the contributions made by experts, and the need to make better use of available resources. UN/CEFACT supports activities dedicated to improving the ability of business, trade, and administrative organizations, from developed, developing, and transitional economies, to exchange products and relevant services effectively. Its principal focus is on facilitating international transactions through the simplification and harmonization of processes, procedures, and information flows, and so on contributing to the growth of global commerce.

UN/CEFACT's vision is to provide *simple, transparent and effective business processes for global commerce.*

At the centre of this vision (e-business strategy) are three fundamental elements:

- Cross industry and government sector analysis (to promote business level interoperability and synchronicity for all parties in the value chain)
- Business process and information modeling (to formally describe business requirements in Business Collaboration Models)
- Leverage existing and new technologies (e.g., extensible markup language (XML), Web Services, etc.)

By combining these elements of the vision, UN/CEFACT developed the UN/CEFACT Business Collaboration Framework (BCF) to enable business process and information models to be specified in a technology and implementation neutral manner that can then be implemented in software using the information exchange syntax and structures of choice. The primary goal of the BCF is to systematically capture business and administrative process knowledge that will enable the development of low-cost software components for use by small and medium-size companies adopting e-business practices. By first focusing on defining the business process and information models, the BCF itself is technology-neutral. However, it facilitates e-business implementations based on the technology of choice, whether it is EDI (Electronic Data Interchange), XML, or some future information exchange technology.

6.3.8 RosettaNet

RosettaNet is a nonprofit consortium of more than 400 of the world's leading Information Technology (IT), Electronic Components (EC), Semiconductor Manufacturing (SM), and Solution Provider (SP) companies working to create, implement, and promote open e-business process standards. By establishing a common language – or standard processes for the electronic sharing of business information – RosettaNet attempts to open the lines of communication for everyone involved in the supplying and buying of today's technologies.

Developed with the collaboration and expertise of leading high-tech companies worldwide, RosettaNet standards offer a robust nonproprietary solution, encompassing data dictionaries, implementation framework, and XML-based business message schemas and process specifications, for e-business standardization. These standards are free to the public on the RosettaNet Web site. They are dedicating to e-business. RosettaNet offers everyone involved in the supplying and buying of today's technologies an opportunity to profit: Businesses that offer the tools and services to help implement RosettaNet standards gain exposure and business relationships. RosettaNet-adopting companies realize global, dynamic, and flexible trading networks, time- and money-saving operational efficiencies, and new business. End users enjoy speed and uniformity in purchasing practices.

Leaders from elected partner companies comprise RosettaNet's global Supply Chain Boards. Representing a cross section of RosettaNet Partner companies in terms of core competencies and regional involvement, Supply Chain Board Members drive development and priorities, serve as examples of implementation success, and actively promote RosettaNet. RosettaNet has a Supply Chain Board for each vertical industry in its current scope: The global EC Supply Chain Board consists of representatives of the EC trading network, including semiconductor suppliers, passive suppliers, connector suppliers, distributors, and customers. The global IT Supply Chain Board consists of representatives of the IT trading network, including manufacturers, software publishers, distributors, resellers, end users, shippers, and e-technologists.

Content of the RosettaNet Standards

RosettaNet Business Dictionary and RosettaNet Technical Dictionary provide a common vocabulary for conducting e-business, and reduce confusion in the procurement process due to each company's uniquely defined terminology. The RosettaNet Business Dictionary designates the properties for defining business transactions between trading partners. These Business Data Entities and Fundamental Business Data Entities are described in PIP Message Guidelines. The RosettaNet Technical Dictionary provides properties for defining products and services.

The RosettaNet Implementation Framework (RNIF) Core Specification provides exchange protocols for quick and efficient implementation of RosettaNet standards. The RNIF specifies information exchange between trading partner servers using XML, covering the transport, routing, and packaging; security; signals; and trading partner agreement.

RosettaNet Partner Interface Processes™ (PIPs™) are specialized system-to-system XML-based dialogs that define business processes between trading partners. Each PIP specification includes a business document with the vocabulary, and a business process with the choreography of the message dialog. PIPs apply to the following core processes: administration; partner, product and service review; product introduction; order management; inventory Management; Marketing Information Management; Service and Support; and Manufacturing.

The validation program, a foundational program, is RosettaNet's formal process for driving partner implementation of newly published standards to ensure a high level of quality. Under the validation program, a group of RosettaNet Partners commit to implementing a standard upon publication. The Partners run the standard in production for a period of time, providing and reviewing feedback to enhance the standard, and ultimately attesting that the standard meets predefined requirements and has been successfully implemented in production. The validation program encourages rapid evolution of new standards to improve robustness and lower the frequency of change in the future.

6.3.9 OMG

The OMG was formed to create a component-based software marketplace by accelerating the introduction of standardized object software. The organization's charter includes the establishment of industry guidelines and detailed object management specifications to provide a common framework for application development. Conformance to these specifications will make it possible to develop a heterogeneous computing environment across all major hardware platforms and operating systems. Implementation of OMG specifications can be found on many operating systems across the world today.

The OMG's series of specifications detail the necessary standard interfaces for Distributed Object Computing. Its widely popular Internet protocol IIOP (Internet Inter-ORB Protocol) is being used as the infrastructure for hundreds of technology companies. OMG specifications are used worldwide to develop and deploy distributed applications for vertical markets, including manufacturing, finance, telecom, electronic commerce, real-time systems, and healthcare.

The Model Driven Architecture® (MDA®) initiative aims to raise the abstraction level and separate business logic from the underlying platform technology. MDA can be seen as OMG's MBSE approach where you specify a system independent of specific target platforms, specify and choose platforms, transform the system specification to a platform-specific specification, and most likely generate the platform artifacts.

MBSE, also often termed MDSD (Model-Driven Software Development; Stahl and Völter 2006) is in fact a broader concept, including also such approaches as Microsoft Software Factory (DSL), and Eclipse. According to Stahl and Völter (2006), the goals of MDSD are as follows:

- Increased development speed through automated code generation
- Improved software quality through the use of automated transformations and formally defined modeling languages
- Possibility to change crosscutting implementation in one place
- Higher level of reusability of SE expert knowledge
- Improved manageability of complexity through abstraction
- Interoperability and portability of software systems

The Business Process Definition Metamodel (BPDM) that is currently standardized by the OMG applies MDA to business process modeling to provide it a consistent end-to-end approach. BPDM acknowledges that business process definitions are frequently used for purposes that do not require automation (e.g., simulation and optimization of manual processes). In cases where a business process is to be (partially) automated, the BPDM enables sufficient detail to be added to a process definition to completely specify the process to the level of detail that is required to generate executable run-time artifacts.

SysML customizes UML for systems engineering applications. It supports the specification, analysis, design, verification, and validation of a broad range of systems and systems of systems. These systems may include hardware, software, information, processes, personnel, and facilities. The SysML Partners completed their SysML v. 1.0a open source specification draft and submitted it to the Object Management Group (OMG) in November 2005. A series of competing specification proposals was followed by a *SysML Merge Team* proposal submission to the OMG in April 2006, which was adopted by the OMG as OMG SysML in July 2006 (SysML 2007).

In connection to rule-base system, there are a number of initiatives particularly within OMG and W3C (other W3C initiatives are described later)

- OMG's PRR – Production Rule Representation (OMG 2003) – This group is working toward a proposal for a standard since early 2007. The standard is focused on the management of production rule sets, e.g., the kinds of rules that execute in Blaze Advisor, JRules, etc.
- W3C's RIF – Rule Interchange Format (RIF 2003) – This standard has a very large number of companies involved and is trying to decide how much detail about the rules to manage in the interchange format. This is being coordinated with PRR. This would allow the interchange format for PRR to be RIF.
- OMG's SBVR – Semantics of Business Vocabularies and Rules (OMG 2006) – This standard is supposedly closing in on a final specification, but it is struggling to resolve large numbers of open issues. It is a standard designed to manage source rules and is a very thorough/complex standard. The linkage from SBVR to PRR has yet to be defined, but both teams are working on the assumption that traceability will be the key, rather than transformation.

6.3.10 ISO/IEC 15414: Open Distributed Processing – Reference Model – Enterprise Language

ISO/IEC 15414: ODP Enterprise Language is elaborated by the joint working group ISO/IEC JTC 1/SC 7/WG 17. This standard provides the following:

1. A language comprising concepts, structures, and rules for developing, representing, and reasoning about a specification of an ODP system from the enterprise viewpoint
2. Rules that establish correspondences between the enterprise language and the other viewpoint languages (defined in ITU-T Recommendation X.903 ISO/IEC 10746-3) to ensure the overall consistency of a specification

Previously ISO/IEC 10746-3 – ODP – architecture has proposed to model an enterprise from five viewpoints: enterprise, information, computational, engineering, and technology. In this standard, enterprise concepts and rules of structure are defined as a Reference Model. A metamodel in UML is also provided to define the structure of an enterprise specification.

The ODP-RM standard creates an architecture within which support of distribution, interworking, and portability can be integrated. It is concerned with the integrated and federated interoperability paradigm rather than a unified approach. The standards support enterprise interoperability at the application and software levels rather than enterprise modeling level as it is in EN/ISO 19440 and ISO 18629 (PSL).

ODP-RM supports the modeling of distributed processing entities. The modeling concepts defined in this standard focus on high-level enterprise concepts such as Purpose, Scope, Role, and Policies of a computerized system. Distributed Processing capability is an important functionality of Collaborative enterprises; most of the concepts are relevant to described virtual enterprise and extended enterprise. The role concept, which is absent in EN/ISO 19440, is defined in the ODP Enterprise Language standard. Role is defined with respect to a community. Four kinds of role are proposed: Actor role, Artifact role, Resource role, and Interface role.

6.3.11 W3C

The World Wide Web Consortium (W3C) creates Web standards. W3C's mission is to lead the Web to its full potential, which it does by developing technologies (specifications, guidelines, software, and tools) that will create a forum for information, commerce, inspiration, independent thought, and collective understanding. This summary in seven points explains W3C's goals and operating principles:

1. Universal Access: W3C defines the Web as the universe of network-accessible information (available through your computer, phone, television, or networked refrigerator...). One of W3C's primary goals is to make these benefits available to all people, whatever their hardware, software, network infrastructure, native language, culture, geographical location, or physical or mental ability. W3C's Internationalization Activity, Device Independence Activity, Voice Browser Activity, and Web Accessibility Initiative (WAI) all illustrate commitment to universal access.

2. Semantic Web: People currently share their knowledge on the Web in language intended for other people. On the Semantic Web, one envisages that one will be able to express oneself in terms that computers can interpret and exchange. Doing so will enable people to solve problems that they find tedious and help them find qickly what they are looking for: medical information, a movie review, a book purchase order, etc. The W3C languages RDF, XML, XML Schema,

and XML signatures are the building   blocks of the Semantic Web. These are further described later.

3. Trust: The Web is a collaborative medium, not read-only like a magazine. In fact, the first Web browser was also an editor, though most people today think of browsing as primarily viewing, not interacting. To promote a more collaborative environment, we must build a *Web of Trust* that offers confidentiality, instills confidence, and makes it possible for people to take responsibility for (or be accountable for) what they publish on the Web. These goals drive much of W3C's work around XML signatures, annotation mechanisms, group authoring, versioning, etc.

4. Interoperability: Twenty years ago, people bought software that only worked with other software from the same vendor. Today, people have more freedom to choose, and they rightly expect software components to be interchangeable. They also expect to be able to view Web content with their preferred software (graphical desktop browser, speech synthesizer, Braille display, car phone...). W3C promotes interoperability by designing and promoting open (nonproprietary) computer languages and protocols that avoid the market fragmentation of the past. This is achieved through industry consensus and encouraging an open forum for discussion.

5 Eolvability: W3C aims for technical excellence but is well aware that what we know and need today may be insufficient to solve tomorrow's problems. They therefor e strive to build a Web that can easily evolve into an even better Web, without disrupting what already works. The principles of simplicity, modularity, compatibility, and extensibility guide all W3C designs.

6. Decentralization: Decentralization is   a principle of modern distributed systems. In a centralized system, every message or action has to pass through a central authority, causing bottlenecks when the traffic increases. In design, W3C therefore limits the number of central Web facilities to reduce the vulnerability of the Web as a whole.

7 Cooler Multimedia: Who would not li ke more interactivity and richer media on the Web, including resi able images, qality sound, video, 3D effects, and animation? W3C' s consensus process does not limit content provider creativity or mean boring browsing. Through its membership, W3C listens to end users and works toward providing a solid framework for the development of the cooler web through languages such as the Scalable Vector Graphics (SVG and the Synchronized Multimedia Inte gration Language (SMIL).

An important area here is semantic web technologies, which we will look at in more detail in the next section.

6.3.12 Base Ontology Technologies

Here, we briefly describe core technologies within the area, including RDF, RDF Schema, and ontologies including an overview of OWL. This overview is based on Krogstie et al. (2007).

RDF

The first level at which a concrete data model is defined on XML is the Resource Description Framework (RDF). Actually, RDF as a data model is independent of XML, but we consider it as a layer extending the XML because of the widely practiced XML *serialization* of RDF in semantic web applications (RDF/XML).

The basic structure of RDF is a triple consisting of two nodes and a connecting edge. These basic elements are all kinds of *RDF resources*, and can be variously described as <things> <properties> <values> (Manola and Miller 2004), <object> <attribute> <value> (Broekstra et al. 2003), or <subject> <predicate> <object> (Powers 2003). There are alternative serializations of RDF, including N3, N-Triples, and Turtle. Each of these professes some advantages, for example, human readability, but RDF/XML is the normative syntax for writing RDF.

This relatively simple basic model has several features that make it a powerful data model for integrating data in dispersed locations (Butler 2002).

1. RDF is based on triples, in contrast to simple attribute–value pairs. The advantage of using triples is that this makes the subject of the attribute–value pair explicit.
2. RDF distinguishes between resources and properties that are globally qualified, i.e., are associated with a URI, and those that are locally qualified. The advantage of a globally qualified resource or property is that it can be distinguished from other resources or properties in different vocabularies that share the same fragment name, in a fashion that is analogous to XML namespaces.
3. As a result of the first two properties, RDF can be used to make statements about Web resources, by relating one URI to another.
4. It is easy to encode graphs using RDF as it is based on triples, whereas XML documents are trees, so encoding graphs is more complicated and can be done in several different ways.

5. RDF has an explicit interpretation or model theory; there is an explicit formal, application-independent interpretation of an RDF model (Hayes 2004). XML documents also have interpretations but they are often implicit in the processor or parser associated with that particular type of XML document.

But in spite of the apparent usefulness of RDF, there is relatively slow adoption of RDF compared with XML (Batzarov 2004). There are many possible reasons for this slow adoption. Daconta et al. (2003) take an optimistic position and attribute the long lead-in time to poor tutorials, minimal tool support, and poor demonstration applications, arguing that once the practical limitations have been overcome, adoption will grow rapidly. However, we must not ignore the presence of dissatisfaction with RDF in both practitioner and research communities. Some of the challenges for RDF in light of this dissatisfaction are as follows:

- RDF/XML (or XHTML) integration needs improvement. The W3C RDF Working Group is working on solutions for successfully embedding RDF within XHTML (RDF/A), and tools such as SMORE purport to making HTML markup easier. But so far, there are no high profile, compelling applications to showcase the advantages of RDF. For example, microformats, which can be seen as a very simple version of RDF/A but are *designed for humans first and machines second*, have enjoyed a rapid uptake. For example, both Yahoo! and Google can run specialized searches on microformats.
- The RDF data model can be complex and confusing because it mixes metaphors and introduces new concepts that can be tricky to model. For instance, the standard notion of RDF as composed of subject-predicate-object is linguistically derived, but its relationship to concepts in other representations is somewhat unclear, e.g., class–property–value (object-oriented), node–edge–node (graph theory), source–link–destination (web link), entity–relation–entity (database), and can cause confusion. One of the particularly tricky constructs is reification, which introduces an unproven modeling construct that is foreign to most data modeling communities. Reification can cause confusion because it can be used to arbitrarily nest statements, possibly negating the stated truth value of statements (Daconta et al. 2003).
- The RDF/XML serialization is confusing and difficult to work with, especially in the absence of proper tool support. The striped syntax (Brickley 2001) can make it difficult to understand the proper interpretation of statements. For instance, it is often impossible to tell whether an XML element in the RDF serialization represents an edge or a node. The complexity of the syntax is partially responsible for a

relative support of the RSS1.0 specification. RSS1.0 is an RDF-based variant of the popular RSS format, and is probably the most high profile use of RDF on the Internet. However, it is losing ground in terms of popularity to the non-RDF-based and syntactically much simpler RSS 2.0.

Clearly, there is a great deal of work to be done in establishing RDF as a core technology that adds value to the widely adopted XML syntax alone. There are some fledging ventures launched in 2007, backed by high profile investors, which attempt to bring the advantages of RDF to mainstream social networking applications. Should they become successful, then RDF will become more prominent in the public eye.

But RDF is also important as a foundation layer for *Ontologies,* making it relatively simple to express higher level ontological constructs. Implementing ontologies in XML and XML Schema without RDF is tricky for several reasons. In describing a procedure for translating an ontology into an XML Schema, Klein et al. (2003) note several important problems. First, superclass/subclass inheritance is problematic and has to be overcome with artificial workarounds in the XML specification, and defining multiple inheritance is not possible at all in XML/S. Second, the possibility of fully automating the translation process is questionable, limiting its use for large ontologies.

To use RDF as a means of representing knowledge, it is necessary to enrich the language in ways that fix the interpretation of parts of the language. As described thus far, RDF does not impose any interpretation on the kinds of resources involved in a statement beyond the roles of subject, predicate, and object. It has no way of imposing some sort of agreed meaning on the roles or the relationships between them. The RDF schema is a way of imposing a simple ontology on the RDF framework by introducing a system of simple types.

RDF Schema

We have seen that RDF provides a means to relate resources to one another in a graph-based formalism connecting subjects to objects via predicates. The RDF schema (RDF/S) provides modeling primitives that can be used to capture basic semantics in a domain neutral way. That is, RDF/S specifies metadata that is applicable to the entities and their properties in all domains. The metadata then serves as a standard model by which RDF tools can operate on specific domain models, since the RDF/S metamodel elements will have a fixed semantics in all domain models. The RDF/S elements are shown in the following Tables 6.1 and 6.2:

Table 6.1. RDF/S classes

Class name	Comment
rdfs:Resource	The class resource, everything
rdfs:Literal	The class of literal values, e.g., textual strings and integers
rdfs:Class	The class of classes
rdfs:Datatype	The class of RDF datatypes
rdfs:Container	The class of RDF containers
rdfs:ContainerMembershipProperty	The class of container membership properties, rdf:_1, rdf:_2, ..., all of which are subproperties of *member*

Table 6.2. RDF/S properties

Property name	Comment	Domain	Range
Rdfs:subClassOf	The subject is a subclass of a class	rdfs:Class	rdfs:Class
rdfs:subPropertyOf	The subject is a subproperty of a property	rdf:Property	rdf:Property
rdfs:domain	A domain of the subject property	rdf:Property	rdfs:Class
rdfs:range	A range of the subject property	rdf:Property	rdfs:Class
rdfs:label	A human-readable name for the subject	rdfs:Resource	rdfs:Literal
rdfs:comment	A description of the subject resource	rdfs:Resource	rdfs:Literal
rdfs:member	A member of the subject container	rdfs:Resource	rdfs:Resource
rdfs:seeAlso	Further information about the subject resource	rdfs:Resource	rdfs:Resource
rdfs:isDefinedBy	The definition of the subject resource	rdfs:Resource	rdfs:Resource

RDF/S provides simple, but powerful modeling primitives for structuring domain knowledge into classes and subclasses, properties and subproperties, and can impose restrictions on the domain and range of properties, and defines the semantics of containers.

The simple metamodeling elements can limit the expressiveness of RDF/S. Some of the main limiting deficiencies are identified in Antoniou and van Harmelen (2004):

- *Local scope of properties*: In RDF/S, it is possible to define a range on properties, but not so that they apply to some classes only. For instance, the property *eats* can have a range restriction of food that applies to all classes in the domain of the property, but it is not possible to restrict the range to plants for some classes and meat for others.
- *Disjointness* of classes cannot be defined in RDF/S.
- *Boolean combinations of classes* are not possible. For example, *Person* cannot be defined as the union of the classes *Male* and *Female*.

- *Cardinality restrictions* cannot be expressed.
- *Special characteristics of properties* like transitivity cannot be expressed.

Ontologies

A good starting point for understanding what ontology entails is to consider Fig. 6.12, adopted from Daconta et al. (2003), which places a number of knowledge models on a continuum. As you go from the lower left corner to the upper right, the richness of the expressible semantics increases. This is shown on the right side of the arrow with some typical expressions that have some sort of defined semantics for the particular model. The names for the knowledge models are given on the left of the arrow. It is important to note that all of the terms on the left-hand side have been called *ontology* by at least some authors, which is part of the source for confusion about the word.

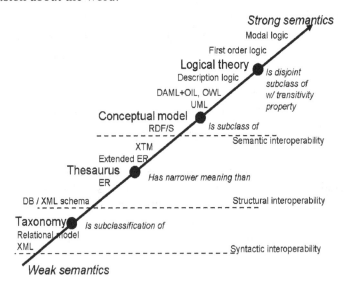

Fig. 6.12. The ontology spectrum

Models based on the various points along the ontology spectrum have different uses (McGuinness 2003). In the simplest case, a group of users can agree to use a controlled vocabulary for their domain. This of course does not guarantee that they will use the terms in the same way all the time, but if all the users including database designers chose their terms from an accepted set, then the chances of mutual understanding are greatly enhanced.

Perhaps, the most publicly visible use for simple ontologies is the taxonomies used for site organization on the World Wide Web. This allows designers to structure information and users to browse and search. Taxonomies can also help with sense disambiguation since the context of a term is given by the more general terms in the taxonomy.

Structured ontologies provide more sophisticated usage scenarios. For instance, they can provide simple consistency and completeness checks. If all *products* must have a *price*, then web sites can automatically be checked for missing or conflicting information. Such ontologies can also provide completion where partially specified information can be expanded automatically by reference to the terms in the ontology. This expanded information could also be used for refining search, for instance. Ontologies can also facilitate interoperability by aligning different terms that might be used in different applications (McGuinness 2003).

Now we are in a position to see why the ontologies on the most formal end of the spectrum are often taken as the default interpretation in the context of the semantic web, providing the conceptual underpinning for "... making the semantics of metadata machine interpretable (Staab and Stuber 2004). But for the semantics of a domain model to be machine interpretable in any interesting way, it must be in a format that allows automated reasoning in a flexible manner. Obviously, taxonomies can specify little in this sense. Database schemas are more powerful, but limit the interpretation to a single model in terms of reasoning over the knowledge base. The only automated reasoning that can be performed is what is allowed by the relational model, i.e., retrieval of tuples actually represented in the database. Formal logic-based reasoning about ontologies can consider multiple possible models (Bordiga and Brachman 2003). They are at the same time more formally constrained and more semantically flexible than database schemas. Ontologies based on different logical models can support different kinds of inference, but a minimal set of services should include reasoning about class membership, class equivalence, consistency, and classification (Antoniou and van Harmelen 2004).

The ontology representation language adopted by the Web Ontology Working Group of the W3C is the Web Ontology Language (OWL). OWL is a response to a number of requirements (Smith et al. 2004) including the need for a language with formal semantics that enables automated reasoning, and to address the inherent limitations of RDF/S as described earlier.

OWL

According to the original design goal, OWL was to be a straightforward extension of RDF/S, guaranteeing downward compatibility such that an OWL-aware processor could also understand RDF/S documents without modification. Unfortunately, this did not succeed because the generality of some RDF/S elements (e.g., the semantics of *class* as *the class of all classes*) does not make RDF/S expressions tractable in the general case. To maintain computational tractability, OWL processors include restrictions that prevent the interpretation of some RDF/S expressions. The OWL specification defines three sublanguages: OWL Full, OWL DL, and OWL Lite. OWL Full is upward and downward compatible with RDF, but OWL DL and OWL Lite are not.

The names of the three sublanguages of OWL describe their expressiveness, keeping in mind a fundamental tradeoff between expressiveness, efficiency of reasoning, and support for human understanding. OWL Full has constructs that make the language undecidable. Developers should therefore only use OWL Full if the other two sublanguages are inadequate for modeling the relevant domain, or if they wish to maintain full compatibility with RDF. Similarly, OWL DL should be used if OWL Lite is not sufficient. Details of the syntax and semantics can easily be obtained from the technical documentation web site of the W3C (W3C 2007).

6.3.13 Semantic Web Services: OWL-S and WSMO

As described earlier, Web services must be discovered, described, and appropriately connected in an implementation-independent way. Berardi et al. (2005) outline three different approaches for Web service discovery, on a tradeoff between ease of provision and accuracy: (1) natural language keyword matching, (2) ontology-based keyword matching (increasing precision through a controlled vocabulary), and (3) semantic matchmaking, based on precise semantic descriptions of services and service needs. Currently, service descriptions in registries such as UDDI, for example, are primarily text descriptions with no semantic markup, requiring a lot of manual input and not facilitating the more advanced approaches to discovery. But there are several emerging approaches to facilitate machine-processable semantic markup for Web service descriptions: Two of these are Web Service Modeling Ontology (WSMO 2005) and OWL-S (OWL-S Coalition 2004).

WSMO consists of three main components: a modeling framework of core elements for semantic Web services, a formal description language

(Web Service Modeling Language – WSML), and an execution environment (WSMX). The WSMO core elements are as follows:

1. Ontologies – provide the formally specified terminology of the information used by all other components
2. Goals – objectives that a client wants to achieve by using Web services
3. Web Services – Semantic description of Web services including functional capability and usage interface
4. Mediators – Connectors between components with mediation facilities for handling heterogeneities

Each of these elements is further described by nonfunctional properties including the Dublin Core Metadata Set, versioning information, quality of service information, and other relevant annotations.

Together, these components are able to define the terminology of the domain and how it relates to applications, and to describe the service in terms of its preconditions, postconditions, effects, and mediators required during the discovery and execution of the service.

OWL-S is a W3C initiative to provide an ontology and language to describe Web services. It is less revolutionary than WSMO, as is evidenced by its closer ties to current standards like WSDL and UDDI. Its primary role is to assist discovery, which it fulfils by specifying three key components of a service:

- *What does the service provide for prospective clients?* The answer to this question is given in the *profile*, which is used to advertise the service.
- *How is it used?* The answer to this question is given in the *process model*. This perspective is captured by the ServiceModel class.
- *How does one interact with it?* The answer to this question is given in the *grounding*. A grounding provides the needed details about transport protocols.

Thus, each service presents a ServiceProfile (what it does), is described by a Service Model (how it works), and supports a ServiceGrounding (how to access it).

While OWL-S is a less comprehensive approach, there are certain similarities between the two approaches:

- OWL-S Service Profile ≈ WSMO capability + goal + nonfunctional properties. WSMO separates provider (capabilities) and requester points of view (goals) while OWL-S Profiles combine existing capabilities (advertisements) and desired capabilities (requests).

- OWL-S process model ≈ WSMO Service Interfaces. The process model in the OWL-S ServiceModel roughly corresponds to the interfaces in the WSMO Web Services descriptions of WSMO.
- OWL-S Grounding ≈ WSMO Grounding. Both provide a mapping to WSDL.

Nevertheless, clear differences exist in the overall architecture as well as the reliance of WSMO on explicitly defined mediators. A key objective of the WSMO is to define a taxonomy of mediators to translate between message produced by one Web service and those expected by another. In the OWL-S vision, this is a step that can detract from the primary purpose of discovery. To be sure, the translation problems still need to be solved, but OWL-S assumes that this will be possible through some form of composition (Ankolekar et al. 2004). But this has some implications for the use of each system in a specific context, such as the system described in subsequent sections.

Service Composition

As for service composition, Berardi et al. (2005) distinguishes between *synthesis*, which means building the specification of the composite service from its subservices, and *orchestration*, which is the run-time management of the composite service (scheduling, invoking subservices, etc.). Synthesis can be done either manually or automatically, the latter requiring that services have been specified formally. The orchestration problem for Web services has a lot in common with similar issues in workflow management. Dijkman and Dumas (2004) identify four different viewpoints from which the control flow aspects of Web services can be described, distinguishing between *choreography*, which is a collaboration between service providers and user to achieve a certain goal, and *orchestration,* which is what a service provider performs internally to realize a service it provides. (The other two viewpoints are *behavior interface* and *provider interface.*)

There are two ongoing standardization efforts related to service composition (Barros et al. 2005): the Web Service Business Process Execution Language (WS-BPEL), described in Sect. 6.3.4 earlier) and the Web Service Choreography Description Language (WS-CDL). WS-BPEL (Arkin et al. 2005) is meant to specify both abstract and executable business processes, and the language contains one section of core concepts (needed for both kinds of specifications) as well as sections with extensions for executable processes and abstract processes (a.k.a. business protocols), respectively. The main viewpoint taken in WS-BPEL is that of orchestration, requiring centralized control of the business process. WS-CDL (Cavantzas et al. 2005) takes the alternative viewpoint of choreography, meaning that this language is better suited for describing interplay between several independent parties in a shared control domain.

6.3.14 WEB 2.0

In contrast to the *Semantic Web*, another interesting development is what is termed Web 2.0. Each has a separate vision for transforming the relatively static Internet driven by focused content providers into a dynamic and largely self-managing entity enabled by large volumes of metadata. But while the general vision is shared, the details of the two approaches appear to be opposites. While Web 2.0 is focused on free-form, user-generated ad hoc metadata provision and opportunistic social organization, the Semantic Web is a vision containing strict and enforced data structures suitable for automated machine processing. While Web 2.0 has proven advantages in the ease of data creation and a correspondingly lower threshold for user adoption, the lack of predefined structure may inhibit effective retrieval as the amount of unstructured metadata grows in volume. The Semantic Web relying on the precise definition of structured metadata would have an advantage in this regard. A major problem with this approach is the lack of widespread consensual metadata.

An obvious idea is to combine the two sets of technologies so that the users can have systems that behave as Web 2.0 at the point of insertion yet as Semantic Web at the point of retrieval. The major obstacle is that user-generated metadata from folksonomies, the emergent systems of classification based on user tags, appear to display none of the requisite properties of ontologies: there is no obvious hierarchical organization among tags; distinctions between concepts and properties are not made; and there are no other sorts of associations between tags. As a consequence, the current state of the art in making sense of tags involves probabilistic and statistical methods to find semantically interpretable correlations. But we argue that the lack of structure in user tags is only apparent. Since tags are the product of classification processes performed within the minds of individuals, they should display ordered patterns that result from the cognitive activities involved in classification.

We will look briefly at the relative strengths and weaknesses of the two paradigms to see why emergent patterns of folk classification have become useful, and why it is reasonable to suppose that some meaningful patterns will emerge.

Web 2.0 Versus Semantic Web: Strengths and Weaknesses

The conception of *Web 2.0* can be traced to a conference brainstorming session between the O'Reilly group and MediaLive International, where it became evident that many successful services on the Internet had certain qualities in common. A major hallmark is that they leverage collective intelligence through simple applications that grow more feature-rich as more people use them (e.g., http://del.icio.us/). The Semantic Web is a much more architected view of the future in which revolutionary new technologies play a big part.

In spite of radically more haphazard beginnings, the Web 2.0 approach appears to be gaining prominence much faster than the Semantic Web. Not only is it difficult to keep track of the growing number of services on the internet, but Web 2.0-inspired technologies are making rapid inroads into corporate intranets. A corresponding uptake of high-profile Semantic Web applications is so far dramatically nonexistent. Yet each technology prominently features metadata applications, *tagging* applications such as Flickr and del.icio.us for Web 2.0, and the Dublin Core and exif vocabularies in RDF. Web 2.0 seems to be winning the metadata war. As R. McCool argues, Flickr (photo-sharing service) has succeeded in establishing a Web community on the strength of simplicity and, ironically, by eliminating explicit semantics he is able to implement a solution for indexing photographs that currently has no equal in the more formalized approaches!

Yet social tagging is not a panacea to information management either, and its limitations are starting to be recognized. A recent article points out that even the simple task of exploring URLs on the basis of *related tags* may not be very useful because those tags often form a loosely affiliated set in which the interrelationships are not clear.

6.4 Summary

As we have seen in this chapter (and in Chap. 4), on one hand there are a number of proposals and standards for parts of what is needed for enterprise and cross-enterprise solutions. On the other hand, there is not yet a consistent or comprehensive standard for enterprise interoperability in the large.

The RosettaNet Interoperability Program improves software and implementation interoperability within the RosettaNet trading network through collateral education and testing activities. Its business and technical dictionary are a useful help in orienting the work to be done concerning ontology solutions. The RosettaNet Partner Interface Process is an example of the standardization of practices and business processes that should be taken into account.

The holistic approach of EN/ISO 19439 (CIMOSA, described in Chap. 4) is very useful to identify already existing concepts. System design phases are integrated completely. The definitions are clear. However, the approach is not applicable in practice. Enterprise knowledge views do not fit into a cube of linear and orthogonal axis of views, granularity, and phases. EN/ISO 19439 describes only a partial framework for modeling. It strives to support enterprise interoperability adopting the integrated paradigm and to provide a standard framework to describe and model enterprise systems in a consistent and complete way. In our opinion, it does not enable us to consistently and coherently describe enterprise knowledge spaces, spatial dimensions, aspects, types of views supporting logical operations, and kinds of views supporting numeric operations. However, two different enterprises modeled using this standard framework can easily be compared and mapped one to another in support of collaborative work between enterprises.

Business network knowledge spaces would require configuration management service that would need to support the following:

1. Dimension of model stages (requirement definition, design specification, implementation description, and operational contexts).
2. Dimension of model views, but the definition of views would need to be changed to separately define types and kinds of views.
3. Dimension of model genericity (metamodel, model, enterprise assets). This is a mapping of OMG-layered model to the ISO 19439 genericity dimension.

The EN/ISO 19440 approach supports enterprise interoperability at the enterprise model level, i.e., interoperability between enterprise models and tools. The standard can be used in two ways. It would support the integrated interoperability paradigm if two enterprise models are built using the (same) set of constructs provided by the standard. This standard also supports the Unified Interoperability Paradigm in the case where the set of constructs are used at a metalevel to allow mapping between enterprise models/tools built using different formalisms and constructs, for example, the UEML initiative. This approach focuses on the business process and user-oriented modeling. This is particularly relevant for the modeling of collaborative enterprises in business networks, as most of the interactions between two collaborative enterprises are activity flows at the business process level.

The EN/ISO 19440 standard is considered to be quite relevant due to its focus on the process aspect. Most of the proposed constructs such as domain, business process, activity, event, product, order, resource, capability, decision, and organization-related constructs can be defined by POPS metamodels. When developing an enterprise model, these object types and their classified kinds are represented as recurring objects and will be defined and managed by their respective type hierarchies built and serviced by the EKA.

The ISO CD 18629 Process Specification Language adopts a unified paradigm to establish interoperability between various process models and tools. It consists in defining a mapping mechanism via a neutral format. The approach is similar to the UEML approach with the difference that PSL includes an ontology while UEML (1.0) does not. This standard can provide some semantic definitions relative to processes involved in collaborative enterprises.

The ISO 15704 standard is developed at a higher level of abstraction. It supports the integrated interoperability paradigm and provides a framework to name and link various enterprise engineering and integration components. The GERA architecture (as described in Chap. 4) can be used to support enterprise modeling of collaborative enterprises. The GERAM framework can be used to categorize research results and better structure solution components.

The ISO/IEC 15414 standard ODP-RM creates an architecture within which support of distribution, interworking, and portability can be integrated. It is concerned with integrated and federated interoperability paradigms rather than with the unified approach. The standard supports enterprise interoperability at the application and software levels rather than at the enterprise modeling level as it is the case in EN/ISO 19440 and ISO 18629. ODP-RM supports the modeling of distributed processing entities. The modeling concepts defined in this standard focus on high-level enterprise concepts such as Purpose, Scope, Role, and Policies of a computerized system. Distributed processing capability is an important functionality of collaborative enterprises and most of the ODP-RM concepts are relevant for describing virtual and extended enterprises. The role concept, which is absent in EN/ISO 19440, is defined in the ODP Enterprise Language standard. The role concept is defined with respect to a community. Four kinds of roles are proposed: Actor role, Artifact role, Resource role, Interface role.

7 Introducing Active Knowledge Modeling in Industry

The Active Knowledge Modeling (AKM) approach was described briefly in Chap. 1. We describe in this chapter the overall approach of applying AKM in an enterprise or business network setting. The business networking knowledge space is generally denoted by four dimensions: Services, Networks, Projects, and Platforms (abbreviated SNPP). When employed in a customer delivery project, the four knowledge dimensions contributed by AKM will be customized through the target-specific modeling activities of the solutions modeling step. The AKM models of the approach, the methodology, and the platform change as customer solution models and operational solutions are scoped, used, and analyzed for validity. Purpose, guidelines, principles, language, and techniques for performing solutions modeling is therefore the prime purpose of this chapter

7.1 Major Industrial Computing Challenges Revisited

As described in Chap. 2, the major enterprise computing challenge is to find an approach, methods, and a web-platform that consistently and persistently support innovative design approaches and methods by using the knowledge of those involved. Model-configured and managed services are created and supported to dynamically develop visual design language, role-specific workplaces with powerful viewing and execution services, and more. The services are delivered as customizable product platforms or integrated operation platforms, all depending on which industrial sector. This would enable industry to remove many and minimize other challenges, such as change and version management, and to find good solutions for needs (not even attempted) solved by traditional IT systems, such as handling information flows in supply chains and implementing visual inventory management.

The AKM approach and the Collaborative Product and Process Design (CPPD) methodology support collaborative Business networking (c-Business), as illustrated and explained in Fig. 7.1, in the setting of the Kongsberg Automotive seat heating case. Current information flow is unidirectional and peer-to-peer, and the knowledge and data created by partners is not shared or developed for common values and reuse. Too much pragmatic knowledge and working methods are either encoded in software or kept hidden in the heads of experts. These are all causes for bad designs, risky faults, last minute changes, loss of expertise and experiences, and loss of market opportunities and customer satisfaction. c-Business is supported by model-designed and model-generated workplaces, configurable collaboration spaces, enterprise knowledge architectures and services, dynamic visual language composition, and powerful view handling and task execution, allowing new ways for project managers, designers, engineers, and business people to interact and learn by proactive collaboration.

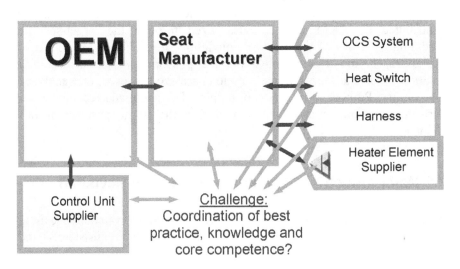

Fig. 7.1. Needs for collaborative business networking

7.2 The Customer Delivery Process

The AKM approach has at its core a customer delivery process with seven distinct steps. The first time an enterprise applies the AKM technology, we recommend that these steps are closely followed in the sequence indicated. However, second and third time around work processes and tasks from the last five steps can be reiterated and executed in any order necessary to achieve the desired goals.

Not abiding by these steps and the recommended ways of working, modeling, and executing could have highly negative consequences for model, solutions, and result quality. This is all about how to best capture and represent work-generative enterprise knowledge.

The AKM approach is also about mutual learning, discovering, externalizing, and sharing new knowledge with partners and colleagues; knowledge that neither you nor they knew they possessed. Tacit knowledge is most vividly externalized by letting people who contribute to the same end product actually work together, all the time exchanging, capturing, and synthesizing their views, methods, properties, parameter trees and values, and validating their solutions. Common views of critical resources and performance parameters provide a sense of holism and are important instruments in achieving consensus in working towards common goals. The seven steps are defined as shown in Fig. 7.2. The steps are denoted C3S3P. Concept testing, performing a proof-of-concept at the customer site, is not included in the figure. The solutions modeling stage is vital for creating holistic, multiple role-views supporting work across multidimensional knowledge spaces, which in turn yield high-quality solution models.

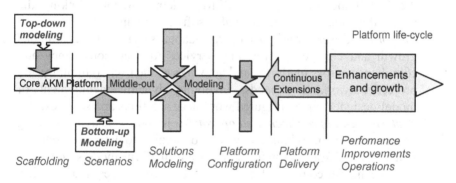

Fig. 7.2. The steps of the customer delivery process

7.2.1 Description of Methodology Steps

1. *Concept testing* is about creating customer interest and motivation for applying the AKM technology. This is done by running pilots and by assessing value propositions and benefits from applying the AKM approach.
2. *Scaffolding* is purely about expressing stakeholder information structures and views, and relating them to roles, activities and systems to provide a model to raise the customer's understanding for

modeling and inspire motivation and belief in the benefits and values of the AKM approach.

3. *Scenario modeling* is about modeling "best-practice" work processes. Capturing the steps and routines that are or should be adhered to when performing the work they describe. This is the core competence of the enterprise, and capturing these work-processes is vital to perform work, support execution, and perform several kinds of analyses in the solutions modeling step.

4. *Solutions modeling* is about cross-disciplinary and cross-functional teams working together to proactively learn and improve quality in most enterprise life-cycle aspects. The purpose is creating a coherent and consistent holistic model or rather structures of models and submodels meeting a well-articulated purpose. Solutions modeling involves top–down, bottom–up, and middle-out multidimensional modeling for reflective behavior and execution.

5. *Platform configuration* is about integrating other systems and tools by modeling other systems data models and other aspects often found as UML models. These are created as integral submodels of the customized AKM platform, and their functionality will complement the CPPD methodology with PLM system functions, linking the required web-services with available software components.

6. *Platform delivery and practicing* adapts services to continuous growth and change by providing services to keep consistency and compliance across platforms and networks as the user community and project networking expands, involving dynamic deployment of model-designed and configured workplace solutions and services.

7. *Performance improvement and operations* is continuously performing adaptations or providing services to semi-automatically reiterate structures and solution models, adjusting platform models and regenerating model-configured and -generated workplaces and services, and tuning solutions to produce the desired effects and results.

7.3 Each C3S3P Step

In the following, each step will be described in more detail from a customer value perspective. Each step will be described by the following:

- Purpose: Why is this step important?
- Approach: How do we work to achieve values?
- Methodology: What CPPD language and components are used? The CPPD components will be described in detail in Chap. 9.

- Platform services: Which services should and will be available?
- People involved: What are the customer and partner roles, and what AKM roles are necessary?
- Results: Active models driving new ways of computing and working.

The descriptions will reflect the capabilities of the current version of the CPPD methodology and of the AKM platform.

7.3.1 Concept Testing

Purpose

Concept testing, performing proof-of-concept tests, is creating customer interest and motivation by assessing value propositions and benefits from applying the AKM approach.

Approach

Work processes are being developed to deliver, customize, and support industrial pilots covering a rapidly growing range of application service.

Methodology

Depending on the customer purpose and scope, one can select from some seven of the twelve configurable CPPD components and supporting platform services when defining customer test pilots. Also deliver services to validate the results should exist.

Platform Services

- Piloting preconfigured product platform development and customization
- Piloting preconfigured collaboration spaces and visual client-based workplaces
- Piloting configurable web workplaces and model repository structures and contents
- Piloting configurable work processes and enabling web services integration

People Involved

All modeling tools, languages, and techniques should be performed and delivered by certified personnel. Normally a business or project manager is in charge of the test at the customer site. Piloting engineers with relevant competence and skills will also be trained to adapt and perform the test.

Results

Piloting performed as a proof-of-concept with the goal of launching a customer project to implement a platform solution.

7.3.2 Scaffolding

Scaffolding has as main purpose to acquaint industrial users with AKM technology and visual enterprise modeling, and AKM people with customer challenges, information structures and practices. In this way it has a lot of similarities to what we, in Chap. 4, termed enterprise modeling for sense-making and communication. Scaffolding can imply building models for use to widen internal understanding between departments and disciplines. Models are often laid out as a mosaic of views of existing information structures and as a description of their sources. Scaffolding models are rarely used for other purposes than agreeing on descriptions of present operations and enhancing stakeholder and employee insights. Figure 7.3 is an example on one such model, a knowledge map of which processes exist and how they are composed. Most scaffolding models do not meet the requirements nor follow the principles of solutions modeling.

Purpose

Scaffolding is about raising the customer's understanding of modeling and to achieve consensus and understanding of customer needs and preconditions; thus raising the customer motivation and belief among stakeholders and helping all to select the right scope of work for the solutions modeling step.

Approach

Select the business area of most concern and gather the most competent people holding key roles in the disciplines involved. The work is performed by conducting workshops to perform information collection, modeling, and deliberation.

The scope of modeling is the entire enterprise, but the modeling should stop at a comfortable level of generalization as no execution is intended. Only the most obvious and important relationships will normally be modeled, and so model coherence is low. Professional model builders handle the modeling tools, but customer engineers may be trained for participation in the solutions modeling step.

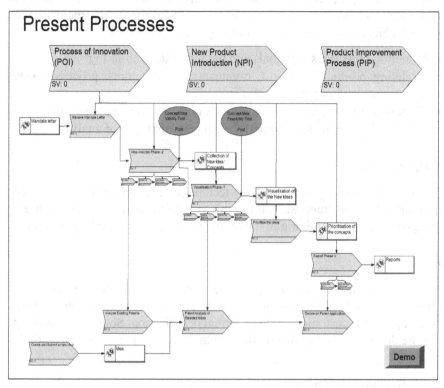

Fig. 7.3. Example on scaffolding model

Methodology

The CPPD methodology components and supporting templates need not be used, but they would provide a good basis for modeling and training, and so we recommend using them if they are available.

Otherwise select any modeling language capable of expressing enterprise information, as views and information structures, relating them to roles, products, information carriers, processes and tasks, and systems that can be integrated to support this step. Meta-models need not be modified to reflect precise types. Any part of the model can be transferred to other meta-models in a later step if appropriate.

Platform Services

The mandatory services are those for performing modeling of the selected customer business area and scope in terms of information structures and contents. Here are the most used modeling services:

- Modeling objectives and goals and the views defined in Fig. 7.4
- Modeling product structures, organizational structures, process flows, and system landscapes
- Modeling roles, people, competences and skills, and responsibilities
- Services for supporting and performing relevant types of analysis

People Involved

All modeling tools, languages, and techniques are delivered by certified personnel, but customers should use this step to involve their leading users and give them basic training in modeling and model-designed techniques.

Results

The resulting model and any submodels created is a potential source of reference for solutions modeling. This is particularly true for the system landscape of the customer and their formal organization. Some of the aspects may be done to a level of quality that it may be reused in a solutions model.

7.3.3 Scenarios Modeling

Scenarios modeling is targeted on modeling work processes as repeatable task-patterns (Fig. 7.5). They represent enterprise core competence and "best-practice." A task-pattern may be used in several processes. This is typical of task-patterns defining core data and knowledge management services.

Purpose

Scenario modeling is about modeling the core competence of the enterprise, integrating methods on product and system structures, and capturing the core competence and skills as work-processes for execution as task-patterns.

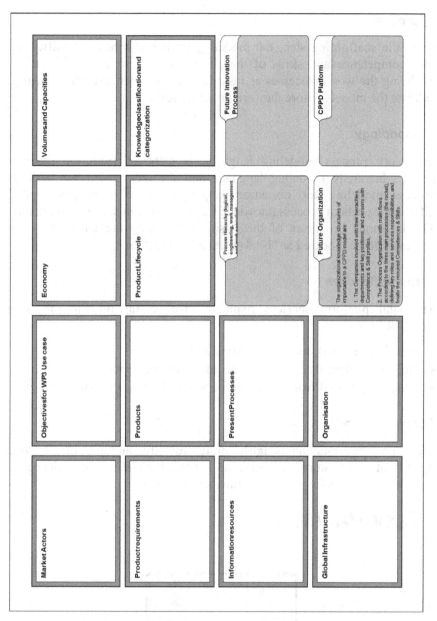

Fig. 7.4. Model views often used in scaffolding

Approach

From the scaffolding step, the modeling team might have identified the core competence and skills of the enterprise, and so the major task is modeling the work processes as task-patterns and then executing them to validate the models before they are saved for reuse.

Methodology

The work process modeling language is different from the business process hierarchy modeling language and the cross-enterprise business process modeling for execution language. These languages capture different aspects of process knowledge as explained in solutions modeling. The leaf-node processes of the business hierarchy are candidate work processes to be modeled as "best-practice" task-patterns.

Platform Services

The vital platform services required have to support the following capabilities:

- Work process task-pattern modeling and execution
- Input and output data management and repository operation
- Generating visual workplaces on the web and invoking task execution

People Involved

Work process modeling is fairly straightforward, and provides a good opportunity for customer engineers to get training and gain experiences in work process modeling and executing task-patterns.

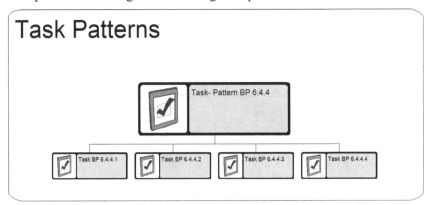

Fig. 7.5. Task patterns as reusable process fragments used in several processes

Results

A selection of work processes representing enterprise core competence and skills are modeled and represented as validated sustainable task-patterns for reuse and repeated execution.

7.3.4 Solutions Modeling

Purpose

The main purpose of solutions modeling is to externalize holistic and pragmatic enterprise knowledge, and to represent it in an enterprise knowledge architecture that can support work process and method engineering and execution. This is the first step towards delivering model-designed computing solutions to users of enterprise knowledge and data.

Creating holistic knowledge models implies capturing knowledge across many multidimensional knowledge spaces and representing multiple roles, their reflective views, and recursive task-patterns, striving for coherency and consistency. The objectives, goals, and scope of solutions may shift and relate to new products, new or improved processes, better team-working, competence and skills management, more effective innovation, or better control with business margins. Also the ambitions of customers may vary. Some may want to go for new advanced computing solutions, while others are content with integrating the legacy as web services. To decide on the goals and levels of ambition will always require that some kinds of analyses involving customer management are performed on the models. Project purpose, goals, and scope may therefore shift as model building and analyses progresses.

Approach

Solutions modeling is performed in all industrial innovation and application projects where the ambition is to model for method and process execution. Solutions modeling requires dedicated teams of people with competences ranging from leadership in AKM, customer business management, and organizational development to product design. Teams must be able to work intimately close together and be willing to try new approaches and techniques to perform and manage work. Which aspects of enterprise knowledge to model would depend on the objectives, goals, and the scope of the customer project, and not least on the ambitions of management.

Typical of solutions modeling are these characteristic concepts, work processes, and capabilities:

- The knowledge dimensions of the innovation space with product, organization, process, and system aspects (POPS), with their many relationships through shared and tied parameter-sets, will always be the core knowledge to model, improve, and innovate.
- Many modeling languages may be involved, depending on scope and ambition, and some of them will be designed and created just for the given project. An example is developing a language for creating new artifacts representing new product concepts or new design principles. Such specific languages might be developed as an adaptation of existing languages or as totally new languages all together.
- Innovation and improvements of business processes will, with increasing globalization and customization of products, involve multidimensional holistic modeling for innovative design of product, organization, processor system structures, and services.
- Services for system integration modeling will be central, as project platforms will need to dynamically and readily integrate functionality from the existing customer network PLM systems.
- To create quality, performance, predictability, and values in solutions, customers would expect to find a rich set of services for different analysis and services testing. Among them are root cause and cause effect, affinity, gap, impact, network, overlap, cluster, integrity, validity, comparative, risk, association, and services to perform simulation or test runs.

Solutions modeling will involve modeling the following aspects:

- The business process hierarchy is modeled top–down, starting with the business process, and then modeling the required subprocesses all the way down to leaf-nodes corresponding to work processes actually found in real practice. The process hierarchy gives rise to unique identities of data, identification schemes and logistics, as well as being the core for achieving holistic coherence and consistency.
- The work-processes are modeled, what we term bottom–up modeling, and already modeled task-patterns are adapted. The task-patterns are related to process-hierarchy leaf-nodes and to competence and skill profiles of roles and people involved, as illustrated in Fig. 7.6. This is the fundamental, if competence and skill management are among the services desired.

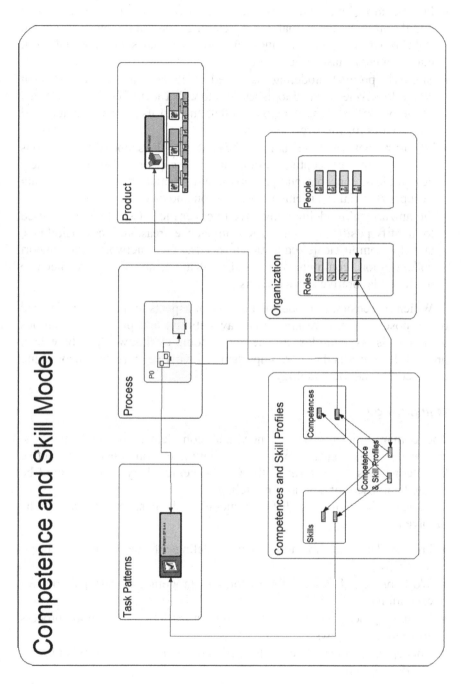

Fig. 7.6. The fundament for semi-automating competence and skill management

- Process modeling finally also has to be performed as what is termed middle-out modeling, that is, developing common views among all stakeholders to govern business performance and support visual work management as task assignment.
- Similarly product modeling also need to cover many aspects, starting with a life-cycle oriented logistics structure that identifies the subsystems of the product and the components that support its implementation, and the services for life-cycle support.
- Other product structures that may be central to the scope of the solutions are a dynamic conceptual design language capable of expressing new design ideas, concepts, and principles, and function-means tree modeling to support initial requirements registration and categorization.
- Organizational modeling may have to cover the classical hierarchy used to identify positions, labor costs, competence areas, and responsibilities, and to communicate educational needs, then networks to support collaboration, communication, and messaging, and finally we need to model collaborative service teams.

Which dimension to model first and what aspects to include are decided by purpose, scope, core knowledge availability, and priorities. Solutions modeling is as complex as the most complex knowledge dimension product design; it is therefore important to involve experienced people and to select a sound methodology.

Methodology

The demand for a series of new and complementary methodologies, supporting and using powerful configurable components of active knowledge, has given birth to the CPPD methodology, which should be adapted and used for solutions modeling.

At least the following different modeling languages will have to be involved:

- Process language for top–down modeling of the business process hierarchy
- Work process language for bottom–up modeling of task-patterns for execution
- Business process language for middle-out modeling of common process and parameter views
- Conceptual product structure for early conceptual product artifact layout and description

- Product structure modeling for topological definition and geometry and tolerance calculations
- Technical product modeling languages, defining a multitude of variant structures for calculating many different properties, for defining parameter-trees, and for handling multiple parameter-sets
- Modeling for production and assembly and for life-cycle services development and provision

Depending on purpose and scope, most of the aspects identified in Fig. 7.7 will have to be modeled, and most of the CPPD methodology components may be involved. The core of a solutions model will always be the POPS dimensions of the innovation space, driven by the knowledge dimensions of the customer business network.

Platform Services

- Developing configurable product platforms with services to handle customization and multibrand design and manufacturing
- Adapting preconfigured collaboration spaces and visual client-based workplaces
- Adapting configurable web workplaces and model repository structures and contents
- Adapting configurable work processes and web services integration
- Adapting modeling languages

People Involved

All modeling tools, languages, and techniques are performed and delivered by certified modeling personnel. These people will be modeling advisers and facilitators in project service teams (see description of service teams below). To overcome trust and confidence barriers, stakeholders must be willing to share knowledge and IPR. This is not a problem if the users see clear benefits and values to be shared.

Results

The solution model or models and submodels will eventually require a well-structured enterprise knowledge repository for sustainable use and management. The solutions modeling will produce the models required for whatever goals and ambitions are decided by the customer business network, and store the models and workplaces in platform repositories.

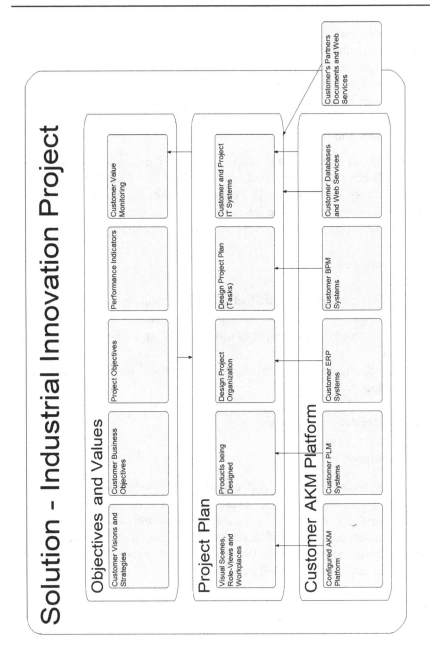

Fig. 7.7. Example of concepts in a holistic solutions model

7.3.5 Platform Configuration

Purpose

Platform configuration is about integrating other systems and tools by modeling other systems data-models and other aspects, often expressed as UML models, using the CPPD CWI methodology (see Chap. 9 for more details).

Approach

Work processes are being developed to deliver, customize, and support industrial pilots, covering a rapidly growing range of application services.

Methodology

Integration models are created as submodels of the customized solution models, and their functionality will be available to complement the CPPD methodology with PLM system components, linking the required web-services with available software components.

Platform Services

- Integrating configurable work processes and legacy systems as web services
- Integrating preconfigured solutions and systems, involving development and customization
- Integrating any preconfigured collaboration spaces and visual client-based workplaces
- Integrating configurable web workplaces and model repository structures and contents

People Involved

Services and system integration is performed by a separate system integration team of experts from modeling environments and system vendors.

Results

The resulting models are referred to as integration models, and they are typically submodels of the solutions model.

7.3.6 Platform Delivery and Practicing

Purpose

Platform delivery and practicing adapts services to continuous growth and change by providing services to perform extensions and still keep consistency and compliance across platforms and networks. As the user community and project networking expands, the knowledge models must be sustainable, and so services for semi-automatic maintenance and validation are important.

Approach

Work processes will be developed to deliver, customize, and support industrial pilots and solutions with sustaining services, covering a rapidly growing range of monitoring and management services.

Methodology

Depending on the customer purpose and scope, AKM will develop and deliver sound methods for performance testing, adaptation, and eventually also deliver services for upgrading and replicating platforms and their workspaces.

Platform Services

As user communities grow and change, the platforms must expand and adapt, and so the following services are needed:

- Extending active models with new aspects to incorporate extensions
- Adapting model-designed and generated visual modeling workplaces with new modeling and execution services
- Adapting model-designed and generated web workplaces with new services

As we gain delivery experiences, needs for new life-cycle services, not yet known, will emerge.

People Involved

These services, languages, and techniques will be developed and delivered by certified personnel. Delivery will to a large extent be performed automatically over the web.

Results

Model-designed and -configured solutions open up the possibility to automatically adapt operational solutions to customer needs and the working environments involved. This will be balanced with services to monitor and govern these changes, creating a self-adapting project platform and workplaces.

7.3.7 Performance Improvement and Operations

Purpose

Performance improvement and operations is continuously performing improvements and adaptations, and providing services to semi-automatically adjust models and regenerating model-configured and -generated workplaces and services, tuning solutions to produce the desired effects and results.

Approach

Customer network stakeholders and actors will need to know if they are working at required levels of performance and quality, controlling margins, and so services to perform and share results of performance monitoring and bench marking should be made available.

Methodology

Again we start work to develop or find and integrate a solid methodology for configurable project platform monitoring and benchmarking.

Platform Services

Services to improve work performance and monitor operations involve the following:

- Measuring, comparing and reporting workplace performance deviations
- Performing service and test pilot bench marks
- Preparing performance reports

People Involved

All services and techniques will be performed and delivered by certified personnel.

Results

Performance measurements and reports will be saved for history records, benchmarking, and comparisons.

7.4 Service Teams

The customer delivery process may also be seen as seven major teams, developing and providing mutually complimentary services (Fig. 7.8). Each team provides and has life-cycle responsibilities for maintaining a well-defined set of services to each of the other teams. Each team also has a set of roles with clear responsibilities and competence and skill profiles. The profiles of roles are then matched with the profiles of available staff to find who best fits each individual roles as well as team roles. The services mix communicating data, static information carriers, knowledge views, and workplace designs with work-generative services and data.

The scope of the solutions model, solutions to be executed, decides the amount of work at each stage and the number of cycles and iterations between stages that must be performed.

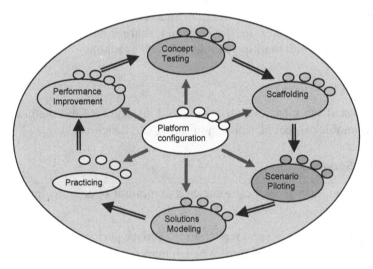

Fig. 7.8. The seven C3S3P steps as seven collaborating service teams

So this is a view of the AKM delivery process of the service-team organization, of the customer solutions platform delivery services, and of the product competences and skills being created. The delivery process has task-patterns for execution, which are reflective and recursive to customer solution task-patterns, it has role views for delivery, which are reflective to role views of the customer solution, and so on. This is so because the solutions modeling implies top–down modeling of logical structures and flows, bottom–up modeling of living complex relationships and task-structures to capture evolutionary dependencies (patterns are the process perspective), and middle-out modeling to capture the business and technology management views of requirements, constraints, interactions, design rules, properties with multiple parameter sets and values.

In other words, this is an intelligent behavioral representation of enterprise knowledge.

7.5 Integrated Product and Services Platforms

For instance, the automotive industry is targeting configurable product platforms. Projects to develop and deploy platforms are underway, for example, in Sweden. Figure 7.9 below is taken from one of these projects and illustrates very well how the AKM technology will add configurability, interoperability, flexibility, sustainability, and openness to industrial platforms and systems integration and use. The AKM set of configurable models and components will be applied to develop a visual Active Knowledge Architecture (AKA). This will have great impact on industrial networking and collaboration, and will simplify and change industrial computing and IT systems development and engineering. New approaches for solutions to support creative work will emerge and compliment existing systems engineering methods.

The AKM platform and the CPPD methodology will sit on top of existing PLM systems, integrate them as web-services through business configurable visual models. Interacting with model views users build, adapt, and execute model-configured services and methods.

Requirements management (RM) must become a repetitive work process because as the design solution evolves so will the interpretation of requirements. The platform configuration system will integrate and enhance the RM and PLM applications systems.

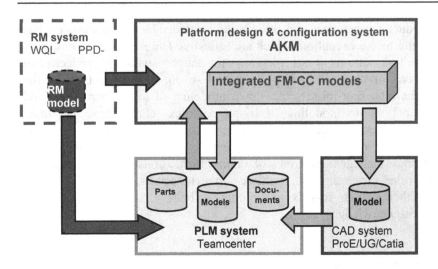

Fig. 7.9. Example of integrated product and service platform

Other industries, like the offshore oil and gas industry, have similar needs. As offshore operations move underwater, the offshore projects cry for integrated operation platforms is becoming louder and louder each day.

The construction industry program called building smart expresses similar needs. Now, there are many commonalities, such as engineering methods, across these sectors, but the semantics of natural language and the information carriers and flows, and the data formats are today very different.

7.6 AKM Approach to Customer Projects

During the first phase of the innovation project, work will concentrate on three parallel activities:

1. Solutions modeling by the customer (supported by AKM)
2. Platform configuration
3. Platform delivery

The solutions modeling deals with applying AKM to support concrete work tasks performed by people in the customer's organization. In an innovation project, solutions modeling starts using the existing AKM technology, and then new solutions are phased in as they are developed. The objective is to train users in modeling and to provide input to how the final solution should be designed and configured in activities 2 and 3.

The core aspect we are trying to capture in solutions modeling is the content of the users' work. In CPPD they are most often related to product models. In the current project, we propose to start modeling requirements, design alternatives, modularization, and configurable components, using the existing CFD (Configurable Function Deployment) and CPC (Configurable Product Components) template in the Metis client. Further details on CPPD-components are described in Chap. 9. This approach must be applied in a real project in order to get realistic input and provide values to the users. AKM will provide training, support, and modeling facilitation services during the solutions modeling. An AKM expert should sit in with the users in a joint modeling session at least once every second week during this phase.

Parallel to the pilot solutions modeling by the customer, AKM works on the solution configuration models for the solution to be delivered. This model defines the workspaces and workplaces of the solution, capturing the following aspects:

- Information (I), which information is needed to perform the work, which information is produced, etc.
- Roles (R), who are involved in the project, what is their responsibilities, which tasks do they perform, which information do they use, which views should their workplace consist of, etc.
- Tasks (T), which task are performed, which services are used to achieve the results.
- Views (V), which views should be available in different users' workplaces, which information and services should they give access to, what should it look like, which tasks should be available for triggering, which tasks should each view support, etc.

The IRTV solution configuration model is related to the user solution model in a reflective way. The object, relationships, properties, values, and types applied by the users constitute the information model, the roles and tasks capture a reflection about how the work is and should be performed, etc., as illustrated in Fig. 7.10.

The platform implementation deals with designing and implementing the software components and services needed to support the new solution. It should support all the information content, roles, tasks, and views reflected in the solution configuration model. Once the platform is ready, the IRTV model contains all the information needed for configuring the solution, which the users can then continue using in the next projects. By adapting the IRTV structures of the configuration model, refined or variant platform solutions, for example, for different product families, can be implemented by the customer. All the three activities thus come together in the end to produce the workable solution. The figure below gives an overview of the activities, listing example content in each area.

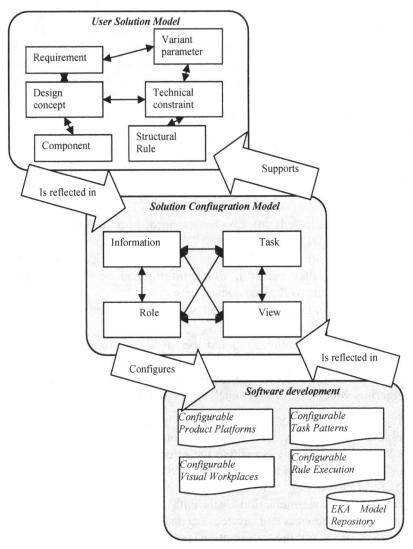

Fig. 7.10. Overview of the AKM approach to customer development projects

7.6.1 IRTV in Action

The IRTV approach is supported by the AKM template in Metis. By default, the template organizes the IRTV specification as illustrated in Fig. 7.11.

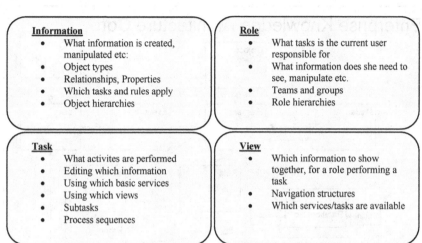

Fig. 7.11. Typical contents of IRTV areas

In each of these areas, the AKM platform comes with an initial model that specifies the core, most generic elements in each dimension. The standard visual workplace likewise contains generic views and services that activate these generic structures, for example, generic views for editing the information about a product element. These workplace components can be extended and customized by providing more detailed specifications in any of the four dimensions:

- If the customer defines more specific types of information objects, relationships, properties, etc., the modeling and visualization services automatically adapt to include the new features. No view model extension is needed to achieve this, but if the customer wants to override the default specifications and customize how the new elements are to be displayed and manipulated, the view model must be updated as well.
- If the customer adds new and more specific roles, new workplaces for the roles are automatically available. The services and configuration defined on the generic level apply to the new roles according to the role specialization hierarchy. The role models themselves contain little information that can be activated in the following:

Information Modeling

The information elements that are used in the system are modeled using the EKA core concepts. At the high level, we find the core EKA concepts as illustrated in Fig. 7.12 (refer back to Chap. 5 for additional explanation).

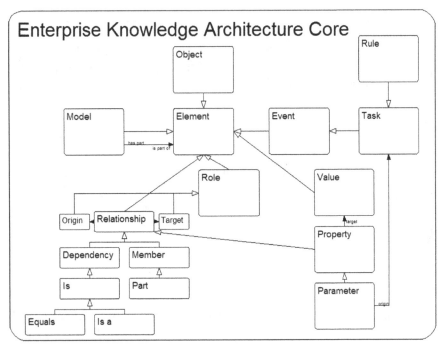

Fig. 7.12. Enterprise Knowledge Architecture, the core of information models

Role Modeling

Top level role hierarchy:
- Participant
  - Manager
  - Responsible
  - Reviewer
- Customer

Task Modeling

Top level task hierarchy:

- Create
  - New object
  - New relationship
  - New property
- View
  - View object (context, description)
- Update
  - Update object
  - Update relationship
  - Update property value
- Delete
  - Delete object
  - Delete relationship
  - Delete property
- Select

Decomposition of these tasks and sequences, for example, from create to update, must also be modeled. Each task is bound to an object which it works on. This object may be a set of objects, for example, expressed by query selected by the user (see the view model below). The generic tasks, as defined above, work on very generic information elements. One important way of specializing tasks is thus according to the object they work on, for example, from "Update object" to "Update product component." Another dimension to specialized tasks is of course the roles. It is more common that specialization of roles affect the view (which parts of the information to include) rather than the task specification. The view also controls which of the available subtasks (services) to make available to which user in a work area context; thus influencing (filtering) the potential task structure.

We call this duality/composition of task and object an *artifact*.

View Modeling

A view component such as a work area or a navigation menu item most commonly represents a task. A menu item often reflect a "Select task," while a work area might represent a view or update task. The services available in a view for a task reflect the possible subtasks of that task, filtered according to the role of the user. Tasks are filtered according to the same principles as information. Which tasks and information (model) elements to include in a view is defined through multidimensional inheritance according to the IRTV dimensions.

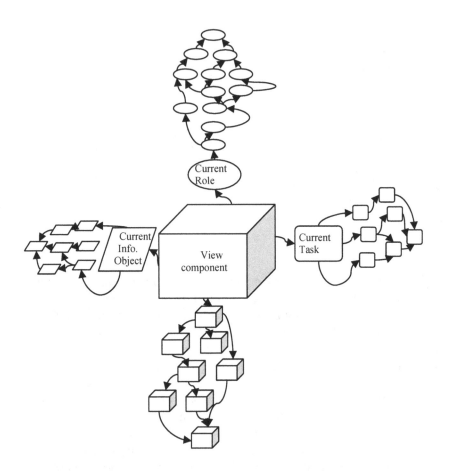

Fig. 7.13. Multidimensional, multilevel specification inheritance

The view specification might bring in some tasks (e.g., close view, maximize, navigate to other object), the task specification certainly will bring in optional and mandatory subtasks, and the information object might as well bring in new tasks, for example, a subtask for editing each property of the element. In each of these dimensions, multiple inheritance is the rule of the game, and so each element will inherit from a range of ancestors.

Which information and tasks/services are available in a view component such as a work area is illustrated above. It shows the inheritance graphs within each of the four dimensions. Furthest away from the "scene of action" in the middle, we find the generic concepts "Element," "Role," "Task," and "View," where the most generic specifications are found.

This model implies that there is not one configuration model for a workplace, but an architecture of different component specifications inherited according to the modeled structures. Each specification should be able to add, refine, or remove features defined in the more generic specifications to achieve maximum agility. This is called "cancellation inheritance."

While we so far have mainly discussed specialization and instantiation as structures for inheritance, we will also deal with inheritance along composition, membership, and indeed also ordinary relationships, in both directions. For instance, depending on which task the current task is part of, we may have different rules. Project specific extensions may propagate down through the task decomposition hierarchy from the top level task that represents the projects. Likewise, elements in the electrical subsystem of a car might have different properties or behavior compared to hydraulics components, inherited down from one of the product part hierarchies. In the Role dimensions, groups may define specifications for all their members.

One important topic is the relationship between view and task. Each view component at a certain level represents a task. When, for example, a work area is opened, we create a new work area object and fill it with content, but we also create a new task. Everything the user does inside the work area should by default be regarded as subtasks of the work area task.

We also need merging rules to combine specifications from different sources and dimensions. For instance, a rule might be to repeat subtask X for all information elements part of or related to the element that the main task works on, for example, "add a field for each property of the object," "invite all participants of this work package to the meeting."

Rules for resolving conflicts between overlapping specifications constitute another challenge. They should be kept as simple as possible. We should here utilize the four dimensions, and the fact that the current context (elaborated below) always includes all the IRTV dimensions. We propose the following rules:

- A specification (value, property, relationship, symbol, task, etc.) can be defined for any element in any of the IRTV dimensions, at any level of specificity.
- A specification can also be defined for any combination of elements from two or more dimensions, for example,
  - For project managers in development projects (role, task)
  - For editing product component relationship in a matrix view (information, view)

- For project managers in a development project editing product component relationship in a matrix view (R, T, I, V)
- A specification can be inherited along any relationship. If a given relationship is a specialization or instantiation of the generic "Dependency" relationship (type), it does by default cause inheritance (so Is and Is-a are included).
- When two or more specifications conflict (set different values for the same specification item), the one closest to the scene of action wins. This can be resolved in any of the four dimensions:
  - If the information object of candidate A depends on the object of candidate B, A overrides B.
  - If the role of candidate A depends on the role of candidate B, A overrides B.
  - If the task of candidate A depends on the task of candidate B, A overrides B.
  - If the view component of candidate A depends on the task of candidate B, A overrides B.
  - In this framework, specifications that are not relative to all the dimensions are regarded as being related to the most generic concept in the dimensions for which it is not specific, (element, role, task, view). Global specifications (not associated with any specific IRTV object) thus apply to all contexts, but are also overridden by all other contexts.
  - In the case where A depends on B in one or more dimensions and B depends on A in one of more other dimensions, we first decide the winner by the number of dimensions each is dependent on. If the number is equal, View takes precedence over Task, Task takes precedence over Role, and Role takes precedence over Information.

7.6.2 Current Context

The usage context contains specifications and parameters, values, etc., which can be used by different services (tasks) in the workplaces. The usage context consist of the following:

- The view component itself and all its subcomponents (multiple levels)
- The current task performed in the view and all available subtasks (multiple levels)
- The information object or set (query or user defined) that is being worked on

- The roles that the current user performs in the context, and as well values from the user interaction history (e.g., if the user has already provided a username and password for connecting to external system X, we should reuse that, rather than ask again).

7.6.3 The IRTV Methodology

Fig. 7.14. provides another version of Fig. 7.13.

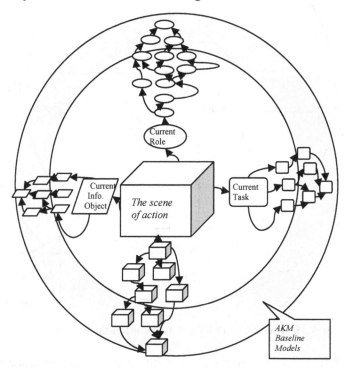

Fig. 7.14. Multidimensional, multilevel specification inheritance

Here we have highlighted the baseline generic structures, the prepackaged information elements, roles, tasks, and views that an empty AKM solution comes with. This is what the users start applying in their initial solutions modeling. We find these reusable elements on the other periphery of the figure, further away from the scene of action, where the users model to perform their work.

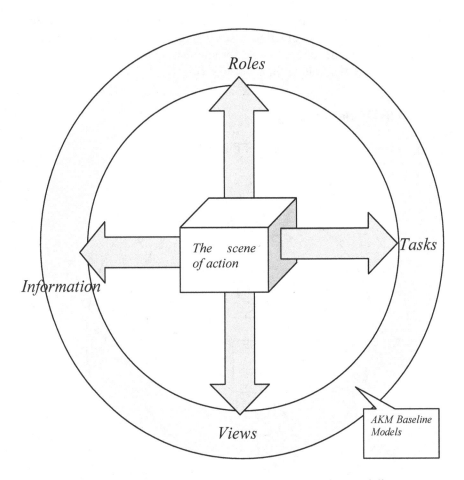

Fig. 7.15. The role of IRTV solution configuration modeling

Figure 7.15 shows the approach of solution configuration modeling in the AKM approach. Here we start with the early models that constitute the users' scene of action, and capture which information, roles, tasks, and views are needed to support the work. These are then defined, and more sophisticated services can be configured for each of the various contexts by specializing and composing the basic elements. Solution configuration modeling thus fill the gap between the scene of action and the peripheral generic application services with increasingly customized solutions for the role specific knowledge architectures and workplaces.

7.7 Summary

We have in this chapter given an overview of the AKM customer delivery process which have been termed C3S3P based on the seven steps:

1. *Concept testing* is about creating customer interest and motivation for applying the AKM technology. This is done by running pilots and by assessing value propositions and benefits from applying the AKM approach.
2. *Scaffolding* is purely about expressing stakeholder information structures and views and relating them to roles, activities, and systems to provide a model to raise the customer's understanding for modeling and inspire motivation and belief in the benefits and values of the AKM approach.
3. *Scenario modeling* is about modeling "best-practice" work processes, capturing the steps and routines that are or should be adhered to when performing the work they describe. This is the core competence of the enterprise, and capturing these work-processes is vital to perform work, support execution, and perform several kinds of analyses in the solutions modeling step.
4. *Solutions modeling* is about cross-disciplinary and cross-functional teams working together to pro-actively learn and improve quality in most enterprise life-cycle aspects. The purpose is creating a coherent and consistent holistic model or rather structures of models and submodels meeting a well-articulated purpose. Solutions modeling involves top–down, bottom–up, and middle-out multidimensional modeling for reflective behavior and execution.
5. *Platform configuration* is about integrating other systems and tools by modeling other systems data models and other aspects often found as UML models. These are created as integral submodels of the customized AKM platform, and their functionality will complement the CPPD methodology with PLM system functions, linking the required web-services with available software components.
6. *Platform delivery and practicing* adapts services to continuous growth and change by providing services to keep consistency and compliance across platforms and networks as the user community and project networking expands, involving dynamic deployment of model-designed and configured workplace solutions and services.
7. *Performance improvement and operations* is continuously performing adaptations or providing services to semi-automatically reiterate structures and solution models, adjusting platform models and regenerating model-configured and -generated workplaces and

services, and tuning solutions to produce the desired effects and results.

For all phases we have described the following:

- Purpose: Why is this step important?
- Approach: How do we work to achieve values?
- Methodology: What CPPD language and components are used? The CPPD components will be described in detail in Chap. 9.
- Platform services: Which services should and will be available?
- People involved: What are the customer and partner roles, and what AKM roles is necessary?
- Results: Active models driving new ways of computing and working

We have also described more concretely how parts of the EKA described in Chap. 5 fits into a project, covering the main steps of this methodology. In the next chapter we look in more detail how different parts of an ICT infrastructure can be packaged and included in the AKM approach.

8 Families of Platforms and Architectures

This chapter presents the underlying Active Knowledge Modeling (AKM) technical platform, exemplified in particular with the instantiation of this platform developed in the MAPPER project.

A specific focus in on how we have layered different types of services. The term *service* is used today for denoting a wide range of concepts, from a hard-coded software function wrapped inside a SOAP/XML interface (a Web service) to the products and services a company sells and delivers.

The ambiguity of the term is further amplified by software professionals often using the term *business* to denote low-level technical elements such as *business documents*, *business processes*, *business objects*, and even *business services*. In connection to AKM technology, we have developed an ICT infrastructure for model-configured, user-composed services. These services span different layers:

- *Infrastructure services* whose interfaces may be as follows:

  - Application programming APIs on different layers depending on the generation of the programming language, e.g., the Metis Client COM API
  - Socket-based services such as notification services using various communication protocols (e.g., JMS)
  - Web services, with explicit XML interfaces and interface definitions (WSDL), accessible over SOAP

- *User services*, for example, the following:

  - Interactive portal services and portlets, accessible, e.g., as URLs with parameters, pluggable inside HTML frames.
  - Application services, consisting of a number of related software functions, often used by a specific role to perform an interdependent set of activities. Today most applications are hard-coded, noninteroperable software *islands*. With AKM technology, we aim to replace this with model-configured application services, which can be more easily linked with other role views, and reconfigured to local variation and evolution in organization and ways of working.

- Business processes and task patterns, containing a set of activities that together lead to the accomplishment of a business goal, often involving multiple roles performing and using different fine-grained services.
- *Business services*: services that are offered, sold, and delivered by a company, like products, including the following:
  - Generic application-type oriented services (ERP, PLM, application service provisioning, etc.)
  - Industry sector-specific services (e.g., VLSI design)
  - Company-specific services, utilizing the core, differentiating competence of the company

The IT industry delivers services across all of these layers. One of the long-term contributions of AKM technology is a new way of organizing the IT service delivery value chain. Enabled by a model-configured infrastructure, higher level user and business services can be more easily adapted and composed. Since the models are enterprise models, reflecting active business knowledge and not just IT structures, AKM facilitates business-driven solution engineering. The AKM approach thus contributes to raising the abstraction level of computing, enabling people to set up services that previously required programming by using visual modeling.

Although infrastructure level services such as developing Web service interfaces to existing tools are important, our main emphasis is on moving up one layer by discussing how user services can be model-configured and composed from lower level infrastructure services to support generic, technical use cases.

Fig. 8.1 illustrates this approach in more detail. On top of the three infrastructure layers (here based on the infrastructure developed in the MAPPER project), more complex functionality can be model-configured for individuals, groups, projects, companies, business networks, and communities. In particular, generic solutions for methodologies (layer 4) should be operationalized by configuring lower level user and infrastructure services into coherent task patterns.

Each layer filters, combines, and contextualizes services from the layers below to construct increasingly customized services for business users. In the service teams that perform this customization, ordinary users and superusers are supported by solution and platform modeling experts. Partners and customers thus extend the platforms on different levels, filling different roles in the service team organization, forming a software supply chain.

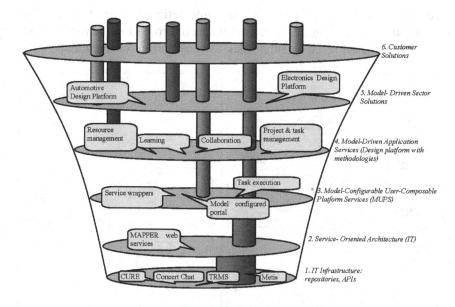

Fig. 8.1. Layers of services

8.1 The MAPPER Architecture

The architecture of MAPPER is based on the idea of loosely interacting Web services. This means that the individual components stay as independent as possible while still allowing the users to experience a coherent usage experience.

An overview diagram of the architecture is shown in Fig. 8.2, and the details are explained in the following sections. The most important part is the Metis Enterprise Portal that provides the model enactment engine. This engine remote-controls the configuration of the other collaboration support tools. It reads an input from a METIS model describing the workflow between different participants. The METIS model also includes information on the required documents and the expected results of each step in the modeled organization's processes.

At each step, the workflow engine detects the required tools, the interacting users, and the input documents. On the basis of this information, the workflow engine can configure the tools in order to create a collaboration environment that is tailored to the current step and provide this environment to the interacting users. In steps where collaboration support is required, the workflow engine will configure TRMS (secure tool invocation), CURE (for asynchronous interaction), Concert Chat (for synchronous discussions), and other services referred to in the model. The configuration is achieved by submitting a set of Web service requests.

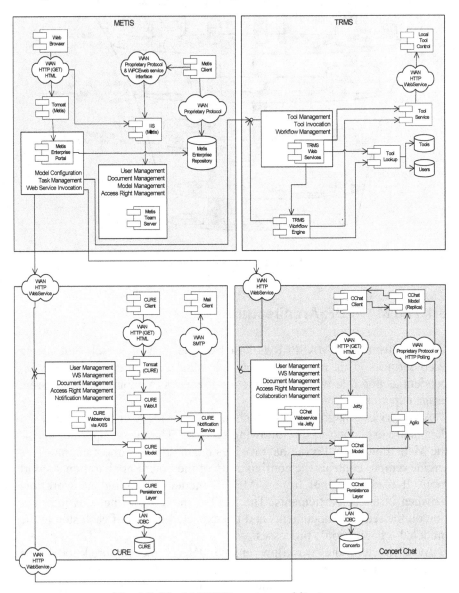

Fig. 8.2. The MAPPER system architecture

8.2 Component Descriptions

This section describes the components that constitute the MAPPER services. The tools used in order to implement the services are also described briefly.

8.2.1 Metis Enterprise Portal and Repository

The Metis Enterprise (ME) platform provides data collection, management, administration, and delivery services required to build any enterprise modeling application.

In addition to hosting Troux's products, ME can be used by customers to build their own applications. Metis Enterprise Repository (MER) is the only platform on the market that provides an automated, enterprise-scalable information foundation for IT governance.

The technical architecture of MER is depicted in Fig. 8.3.

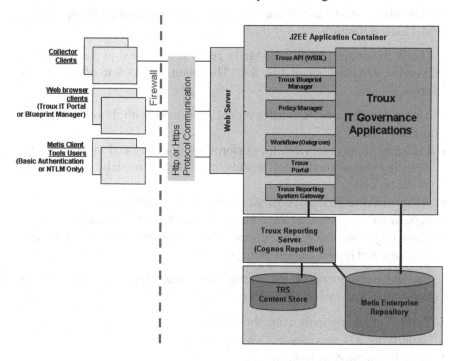

Fig. 8.3. Metis enterprise architecture

Extended with MAPPER services, this portal provides functionality for the following:

- Model configuration
- Task management
- Web service invocation

On the basis of Web service invocation functionality, the security (TRMS, see Sect. 8.2.2) and collaboration services (CURE, see Sect. 8.2.3; Concert Chat, see Sect. 8.2.4) can be invoked by users.

Metis Team

Metis Team is a file repository used for storing Metis models (views and data) as files. It may also be used for document management. In addition to the Web interface used in the MAPPER project portal, Metis Team content can be accessed and managed directly through the repository browser of Metis modeling clients. In addition to basic file access, user management, and access control, the Team server supports the following:

- Versioning and locking
- Dependency management and simple transactions through change lists
- Metadata definition

The Web service interface of Metis Team is described in the ATHENA deliverable DA1.5.1 as in Fig. 8.4. The main services it offers are as follows:

- An enterprise model and meta model *repository* with its content stored as XML files
- *Modeling* support services for performing modeling and metamodeling, including transformation of models, changing of models, and working on the models
- *Administration* services, e.g., security and access control
- *Repository* services, e.g., versioning and configuration management
- *Knowledge management* services for language extensibility, and language and model change management

The main components interfacing with the Modeling Platform for Collaborative Enterprises (MPCE) are as follows:

- Various modeling tools using the MPCE
- Underlying ICT services, e.g., Web services or agents
- Model-generated workplaces
- Execution services, such as business process management systems and rule engines

Specialized interfaces are defined for each kind of tool, in addition to generic model and metamodel access services.

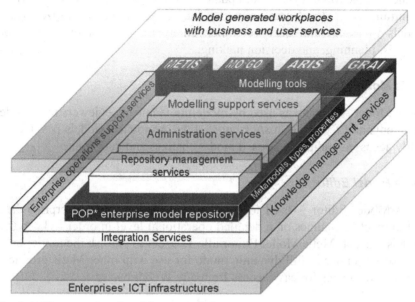

Fig. 8.4. The conceptual architecture of the Modeling Platform for Collaborative Enterprises (MPCE)

Metis Client

Metis brings the world of advanced visualization, modeling, and analysis to independent commercial enterprises and government users. This tool enables organizations to support the needs of additional users to enhance their existing enterprise architecture (EA) activities.

Metis Desktop is a single tool that can be easily tailored to meet the needs of the following five roles:

- Metis Model Browser
- Metis Model Annotator
- Metis Model Editor
- Metis Model Designer
- Metis Metamodel Developer

Collectively, these products are known as Metis client tools. Each higher level of the product includes the functionality of the preceding level. For example, Designer consists of the features of Editor, Annotator, and Browser. The following are the product levels, starting with the lowest level.

Metis Model Browser

Metis Model Browser is primarily an end user tool for employees who should be able to view – but not update – models published on the Internet, an intranet, or a local area network. These users typically utilize visual models to assess and query complex enterprise information as part of analysis, planning, and decision making.

Metis Model Annotator

Metis Model Annotator is used by modeling teams or reviewers to provide comments and feedback in *sticky note* style. Annotated models provide an easily accessed audit of proposed model changes and decisions.

Metis Model Editor

Metis Model Editor is used to create visual models from enterprise data and to react to changes on a detailed operational level in order to keep the models current. Metis Model Editor allows users to publish the model on a Web server either in full dynamic mode for use with other Metis products or as HTML pages for easy access from any Web browser.

Metis Model Designer

Metis Model Designer is used by the more advanced modelers responsible for the visual display and dynamic behavior of the models, objects, and relationships. Metis Model Designer can be used for creating search paths through the model to produce valid answers for key business and IT-related questions.

Metis Metamodel Developer

Metis Metamodel Developer is used by advanced modelers who want to create, adapt, or extend object types, relationship types, search criteria, etc., within a metamodel template. Users have the ability to augment an existing template or to create an entirely new template.

8.2.2 Workflow Engine – TRMS Client

Tool Registration and Management System (TRMS) is an innovative solution that constitutes a kernel of the collaborative infrastructure, as it enables distance-spanning tool integration. The architecture of Tool Registration and Management Services system comprises three main components: the Global Tool Lookup Services (GTLS) server with data bases, the Tool Servers, and the Client application. For the purposes of the MAPPER project, an applet version of TRMS Client was developed. The TRMS workflow engine is extended to allow more flexible enactment of models. Fig. 8.5 presents a general architecture of the TRMS environment.

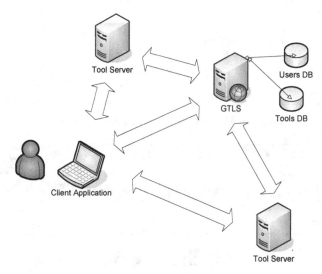

Fig. 8.5. The TRMS architecture

In the general case, all the three TRMS environment components are run on separate machines connected to the Internet. Thus, there is a need for communication between them. Security reasons motivated the use of HTTP/SOAP communication protocol. In this case, it was natural to use XML as a data transfer format. All sensitive data is encrypted (ciphered) and digitally signed by a sender.

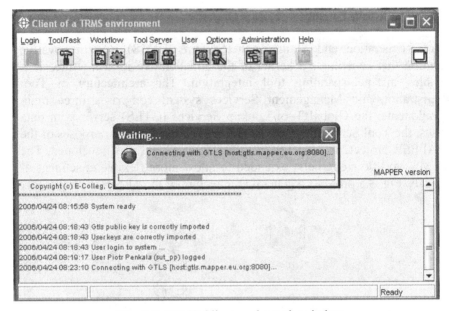

Fig. 8.6. TRMS Client applet main window

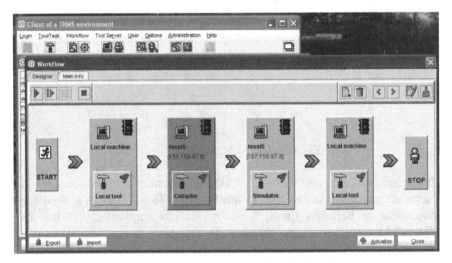

Fig. 8.7. Example of workflow in TRMS

The Client applet (cf. Figs. 8.6 and 8.7) has a simple GUI that allows for log-in to the system and its administration and usage of available tools. The sequence of tasks to be performed is represented visually in the TRMS Client as a simple workflow. This workflow can be executed by the TRMS Client.

Tool Registration and Lookup – GTLS

The main component of TRMS constitutes the GTLS server. It is responsible for registration and modification of data on users and their privileges, elements of the system as well as information on accessible tools and machines that make them available. GTLS is also responsible for the security policy of the whole system, registration of user activities, and registration of access to tools, maintaining statistics and identification of an intruder attack. Furthermore, GTLS is responsible for generation of keys used for encryption of a transmission and generation of digital signatures.

All the aforementioned data are stored in the databases. Current TRMS implementation uses two databases. The first one is the XML native database that comprises tool descriptions. The second one is the HSQL relational database that is used for storage of information on users and their complex privileges.

Fig. 8.8. Results of the tool search

Once registered, tools provide their services to distributed engineers. Advanced service discovery methods are used to connect to the most appropriate service with respect to optimal availability within the current configuration of the virtual engineering network. Fig. 8.8 provides an example of how tools can be discovered using search queries.

Remote Tool Execution – TS

The Tool Server (TS) is responsible for controlling users' access to tools and their execution. A client invoking a tool does it through the Tool Server (Fig. 8.9). Its additional task constitutes of brokerage in user authentication. The Tool Server queries GTLS whether a user who invokes a tool has sufficient privileges.

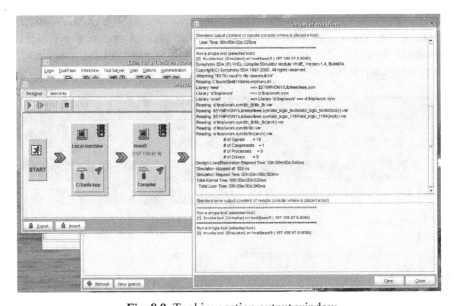

Fig. 8.9. Tool invocation output window

TRMS enables secure data transfer with authentication and authorization of users, as well as it includes security management mechanisms that allow an administrator to monitor users' activity and to execute a proper security policy.

8.2.3 CURE

CURE is a Web-based system that facilitates collaboration in distributed teams using standard browsers over the Internet. The server is based on standard Web technology including the Tomcat Web server engine, servlets, electronic mail using the James open-source mail server, and the Axis Web service technology. The persistence is based on a MySQL database. These main components of the architecture are shown in the lower left part of Fig. 8.2.

From a user's perspective, CURE is based on the room metaphor combined with WIKI ideas, and communication tools. To use CURE, the users need a CURE client, which can be any major Web browser that is capable of JavaScript and Java applets.

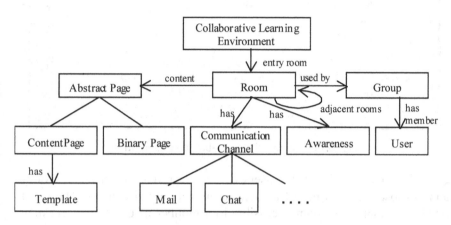

Fig. 8.10. Conceptual design of CURE

Fig. 8.10 illustrates the conceptual design of CURE. To build up structured collaboration environments, a room may be connected to adjacent rooms, thus forming a virtual collaboration infrastructure represented as an acyclic directed graph of rooms. Every collaboration infrastructure is represented by a designated entry room and all rooms recursively connected to it. In fact, a whole virtual organization can be constructed by creating an entry room of the network of partners, which links to collaboration spaces for each participating partner and teams formed by representatives of the partners. The following will explain these main concepts from a user's perspective.

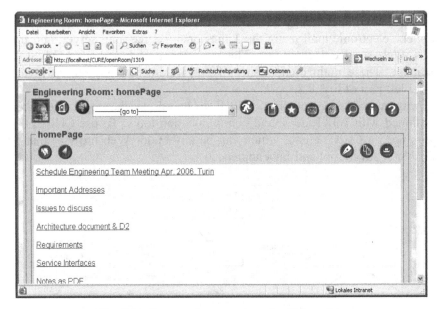

Fig. 8.11. Support for room-based collaboration

As illustrated in Fig. 8.11, users can create rooms for specific groups and purposes. The owner of a room defines its initial content. The room owner can make the room accessible to a number of users, or users may request access from room owners. Room owners can restrict access rights.

A room contains pages, resources, and communication tools, which are created, manipulated, navigated, and read by users of the room. Users can add/remove/view resources associated with the room (e.g., to open a binary file or to start a binary tool). A simple WIKI syntax is used to write the content of pages including formatted text, images, and TEX for expressing mathematical formulas. Changing a page results in a new version; thus, multiple parallel write accesses result in alternative versions that can be merged later.

Rooms can be connected, and thus dedicated environments with special rooms for specific purposes can be constructed. Easy navigation in the so-constructed virtual environment is supported via maps.

Users have their personal home page providing options for personalizing CURE. They can, for instance, subscribe to change notifications of rooms that can be delivered via e-mail. Each room may have its own mailbox that is kept persistent. All users in a room can view and send mails to the discussion threads in the room's mailbox. Chat and mail messages can use the WIKI syntax, and thus may be used to communicate mathematical formulas, etc. Users can control the access to the rooms in CURE by passing on a key to another user.

From a service perspective, most of the aforementioned functions can be accessed using a Web service. The current version of the Web services does not yet address the room-based communication and community building aspects.

User Notification Service

The user notification service allows informing users on events using e-mail or daily reports.

The user notification service is part of the CURE infrastructure and available as a prototypical implementation. Users are notified whenever their collaboration context (their access rights to a specific room) changes. They are frequently updated with respect to changes of the content managed by the CURE system. Other tools can add their notifications to these two notification channels using the notification Web service. However, up to now, this service is not yet connected to model-based processes or tool-based interaction (provided by TRMS or Concert Chat).

8.2.4 Concert Chat

Concert Chat consists of a client and a server component.

Concert Chat Client

The Concert Chat client provides synchronous collaboration services to the users. It offers user awareness, text-based synchronous communication support, a shared whiteboard, and referencing functionality using a virtual *room* as the metaphor to realize a shared workspace.

On the left side in Fig. 8.12, the shared whiteboard is shown. It provides a *content space* that can be used to share material among all collaborating users providing a spatial layout. The top right of the figure shows the users who are currently participating in this session. At the lower side is the *interaction space* that offers text-based communication. To be able to directly refer to shared material (as a virtual substitute of the pointing by hand gesture in face-to-face meetings), chat messages can refer to regions of the shared whiteboard but also to previous messages or parts of previous messages. By using references between chat messages, it is much easier for users to understand the context of this message.

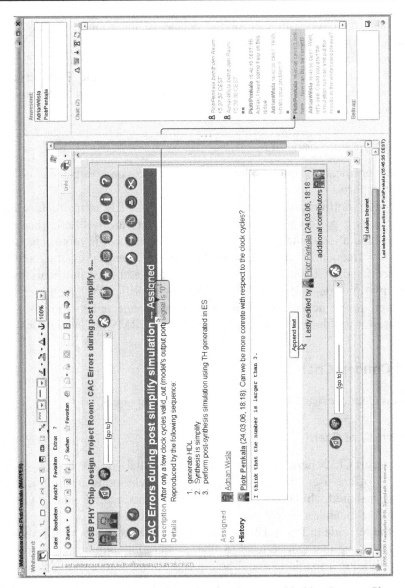

Fig. 8.12. Synchronous collaboration services provided by Concert Chat

The Concert Chat client is implemented in Java. It can be started by users clicking a Java Web Start link (or by JavaScript, etc., that uses such a link) that is provided by the contextualized MAPPER Portal. This way, all users engaged in a common task can quickly start a synchronous collaboration session, e.g., to discuss an important issue, while all necessary material is easily available.

Concert Chat Server

The Concert Chat server hosts persistent rooms for collaborative sessions. It is implemented in Java and runs as a servlet that can be used in a Tomcat or Jetty server engine. For synchronous communication with the clients, it uses the Agilo groupware framework (developed at Fraunhofer IPSI) that offers reliable messaging, and it is designed for flexibility to easily adapt messaging protocols or marshalling algorithms. The persistency of whiteboard content and transcripts uses a MySQL database.

The Concert Chat server can be configured by the Metis Enterprise model enactment engine to set up collaboration structures for the tasks defined in the current project model. The Web service interface that is provided by the server is implemented using the Axis Web service technology.

8.3 Task Patterns

Task patterns have been defined as a primarily educative means for capturing best practices. More precisely, a task pattern has been defined as *a self-contained model template with well-defined connectors to application environments capturing knowledge about best practices for a clearly defined task*, where

- *Self-contained* means that a task pattern includes all perspectives, model elements, and relationships between the model elements required for capturing the knowledge reflecting a best practice
- *Model template* means that the task pattern has to be expressed in a defined modeling language (preferably a (visual) enterprise modeling language) and that no instances are contained in the task patterns, i.e., no real actors, documents, or IT systems
- *Connectors* are model elements facilitating the adaptation of the task pattern to target application environments, i.e., only the connectors may be adapted
- *Application environments* currently are limited to enterprise models. It should be investigated whether this can be extended to process models

Note that this definition of task patterns differs from the understanding of patterns in architectural construction and in the software development community (when speaking of design patterns). In summary, a task pattern combines parts of these two definitions. It borrows from the term *design patterns* the idea of reusable best practices that can be partially reflected in organizational interaction structures. However, the representation is closer to that of a component that is a unit (self-contained), expressed in a language (a modeling language in the case of the task pattern), and carries explicit context dependencies that need to be connected (by means of connectors) to a composition context (the application environment in our case).

8.3.1 Modeling Task Patterns

This section describes which modeling constructs to use in order to represent task patterns that can be executed by the AKM infrastructure. This description emphasizes how to transform abstract process models into executable task patterns.

Adding Execution Details

On the basis of traditional process models, one needs to add execution detail using the AKM task management template, selecting precise services that should be invoked for each task. Sometimes you will find a service that does most of the job; other tasks may be completely manual, and you will perform some tasks interactively through a Web portal. Experience shows that often tasks have to be split into two or three subtasks, because different services are to be used in sequence. In other cases, you may be able to remove a very technical task, because the work was already done automatically by the infrastructure.

Connecting AKM Infrastructure Portal Services

Portal services are connected by including the portal service model as a submodel in your task pattern solution model. This submodel is shown later.

Connecting Services to Tasks in Task Patterns

Portal services (and other services as well) are linked to task through the *works on* relationship type (Fig. 8.13). The portal services linked in using this relationship will appear in the user interface when it is time to perform the task. The example in Fig. 8.14 shows the CURE service *Create new mail thread* being invoked from the task *Notify person ordering the material specification*. The left-hand explorer menu of the user interface includes the services that are put into the Portal container in the earlier model.

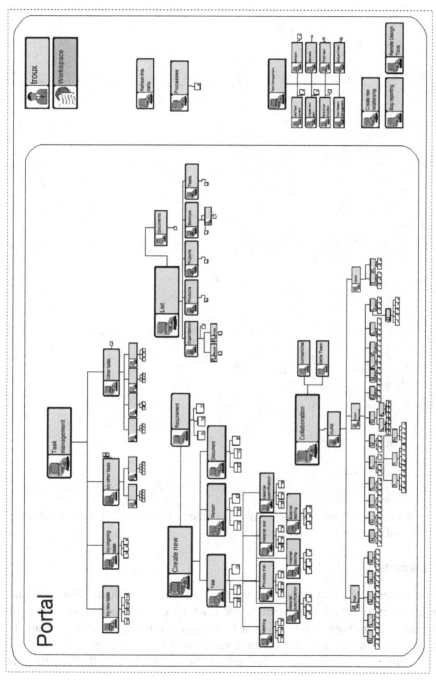

Fig. 8.13. Portal navigation structure model

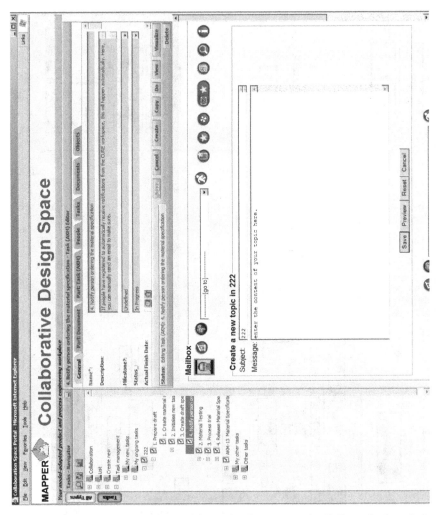

Fig. 8.14. Portal user interface with navigation structure (*left*), task description (*top*), and plugged-in service frames (*bottom*)

Parameters

Some services will have parameters attached to them that tell the infrastructure which document to open, which user is working on it, etc. In addition to linking a service to a task, you should make sure that all its mandatory parameters are given a value in the task context. The service from the earlier example is defined in the model in Fig. 8.15, with four parameters:

- *sessionId*: identifying an already logged-in user
- *roomId*: identifying the collaboration workspace to start the mail thread in
- *subject*: the header of the mail thread
- *method*: the operation to invoke in the room

As you can see, the method parameter already has a fixed value (*createMailPage*).

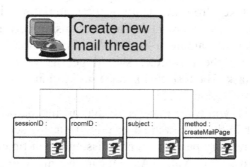

Fig. 8.15. Example of portal service with parameters

SessionId is mandatory if the user has not previously logged into CURE.

Here you find an excerpt of the task pattern model, which shows how the other parameters get their values from the task pattern context (Fig. 8.16).

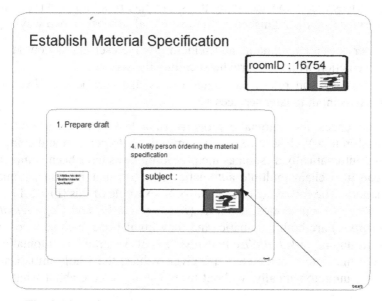

Fig. 8.16. Task pattern fragment with instance parameter values

The *roomId* parameter should be given a separate value for each concrete material specification instance. The correct level for specifying this parameter is thus at the top-level task in the pattern (*Establish material specification*). Parameter values are inherited down to all the subtasks, so a parameter attached at this level will be valid for the whole process. Later, we will see how this parameter value is given by a Web service that performs a previous task in the pattern.

The *subject* can be set interactively by users, but in this case, we provide a default value taken from the name of the material specification. This is illustrated in the model view later. The relationship between the top-level task and the subject parameter is a *Value for* relationship, which has a property that says the parameter should get its value from the *Name* property of the task. The resulting service invocation was shown earlier for the material specification "222."

Similar to this, you must make sure that all mandatory parameters are specified, either in the task context or directly in the service definition. If one or more mandatory parameters are missing at run-time, the system will have to ask the user for a value. As you can see, many of these parameters are of a technical nature, so they should be handled by the models, rather than by users.

Connecting Infrastructure Web Services to Tasks

Web services are connected using the same pattern as for portal services. Web services are distinguished from most portal services in two ways:

- The services are automatic, and seldom involve user interaction, at least no interaction with the user who is calling the service.
- The services can return parameter values that can be used by a task pattern as input to later services.

If you check the automatic property of a task that has a works on relationship to a Web service, the system will try to perform and complete the task automatically as soon as the preceding tasks have been completed. You can also chain multiple automatic tasks together into an automatic task pattern. The following model shows an example of this (Fig. 8.17).

Here, the two innermost subtasks (*Login to CURE* and *Copy template documents...*) are both automatic, and they invoke one Web service each. The surrounding task *Initialize new task...* is also marked as automatic, so if all the mandatory parameters are given values, the whole initialization task will run automatically, without users having to care about what goes

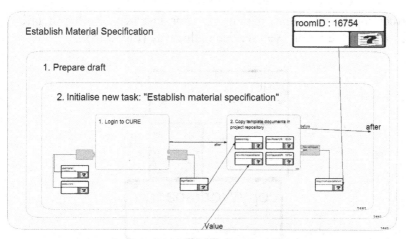

Fig. 8.17. Automated task pattern with Web service parameters

on. Because there is a before–after relationship going from the final *Copy...* task to its parent, the parent will complete automatically as well, as soon as the subtask is completed. The status and results of these tasks, however, may be inspected by the users later, and users may decide to manually redo a task, e.g., to change its parameter set.

This example shows two ways of modeling input parameters:

- Attached to the task input (cf. the log-in task)
- As children of the task (cf. the copy task)

These variants are equivalent, but the result parameters must always be linked to the task output interface (at the right).

The value relationship between the output parameter of the *Copy template documents...* task and the *roomId* parameter on the top-level material specification task defines where the result should be stored. The id of the new room created in the subtask is returned by the Web service. It will be stored as roomId for the process, and can be used by later services, such as the example shown earlier. You can also see a relationship between the output of the log-in task and the *sessionId* parameter of the copy task. Indeed, the whole purpose of having the log-in task here is to provide this parameter to the copy task, which does the actual work.

The Web services used are shown below. A useful hint when defining a new task that invokes a Web service is to copy the Web service object, and then change its type to task. In this way, you will automatically get the correct input and output parameters. For instance, the log-in task was copied from the log-in Web service in this way (Fig. 8.18).

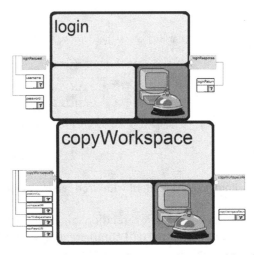

Fig. 8.18. Sample Web service operations, used in Fig. 8.15

8.4 Task Management

This section briefly describes the services and user interfaces for task management.

8.4.1 Creating and Starting a Task Pattern

A task pattern is created by copying an existing task pattern. You can do this from a list of available tasks or by opening the task you want to copy, and click the *Copy* button on the lower left bar. We have, however, configured some services that specifically help you create new instances of the most common task patterns. They are available from the navigation menu on the left, *Create new → Task → Your task pattern* (Fig. 8.19).

After you have called this service, the task definition form of the new task is opened up.

To add new task patterns to the menu, follow the procedure outlined in the following section.

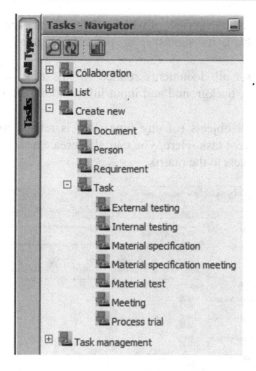

Fig. 8.19. Portal navigation menu

8.4.2 Task User Interfaces

The following task definition form contains a number of tabs (Fig. 8.20):

- *General*: contains the properties that describe this task.
- *Part: Task*: lists the subtasks of this task.
- *Part: Document*: lists the documents that are part of this task.
- *People*: gives you an overview of who is responsible, participant, owner, customer, manager, etc., of this task, its subtasks, and parent task. The overview is shown in a relationship matrix. The relationships shown here may be created through the Roles tab or directly in the People tab, as discussed later.
- *Roles*: gives you an overview of who fills the roles that have been defined on this task (see for e.g., *Allocating People to Roles* later) using a relationship matrix.

- *Tasks*: gives you an overview of which other tasks are related to this one (e.g., before/after), its subtasks, or parent task using a relationship matrix.
- *Documents*: lists all documents related to this task, its subtasks, or parent task, e.g., background and input information using a relationship matrix.
- *Objects*: lists all objects (of any type) that is related to this task, its subtasks, or parent task. Here, you can also create new relationships by adding new objects to the matrix.

Fig. 8.20. Task description form

After you have created a new task from a task pattern, we recommend changing its name, in order to be able to differentiate it from the pattern. You may also want to add a description, set deadlines, etc., using the earlier form. After you have made these changes, press *Save* to update the repository.

When you open a task that is in progress from the navigation menu, the task form will occupy the top half of the main portal frame. At the bottom, you will find the interface for the service that is used for performing the task. When the task is completed, you will also see a split screen, but the result of the service will be displayed, and you will find a button for redoing the service, so that you may open the service user interface again later.

8.4.3 Allocating Persons to Roles

Before one can start to perform a task pattern, people should be allocated to fill the roles defined in the process. This is done in the relationship matrix under the Roles tab of the top-level task in the pattern, as shown later.

Fig. 8.21 shows the interface used for allocating people to the material specification process modeled in Fig. 8.22. The roles on the horizontal axis of the matrix are the ones modeled as task resource (the gray elements in the lower left corner) in Fig. 8.22. The model as well shows the indirect resource allocation links from the high-level roles to more concrete responsibilities (roles) on each of the four subtasks.

In the relationship matrix, new relationships are created and existing ones removed through the right mouse button menu on the + icon. When you create a *fills role* relationship between a person and a task resource role, the following things happen behind the scenes:

- An additional direct relationship between this task and the person is created. This relationship is the one that will be used by the task management application. Depending on the value of the Responsible, Manager, and Customer attributes of the role, different relationships (has Participant, has Responsible, has Customer, has Business Owner) will be created. These relationships will be visible in the *Person* tab of the task form.
- Each subtask where a role is related to the one selected in the matrix also gets a fills role and direct relationship to the person, as do subtasks of subtasks (recursively).

When a fills role relationship is deleted, the reverse procedure is followed, and all secondary relationships are deleted alongside the original one. You can use this function on all levels in the task decomposition hierarchy, e.g., to define that *Johanna* fills the role of *Material specification responsible* on the whole process, except for in the *process trial* subtask, where *Lennart* takes over the role. Secondary fills role relationships will be available from the role allocation matrix for the subtask, and so they can be deleted (overridden) at any level.

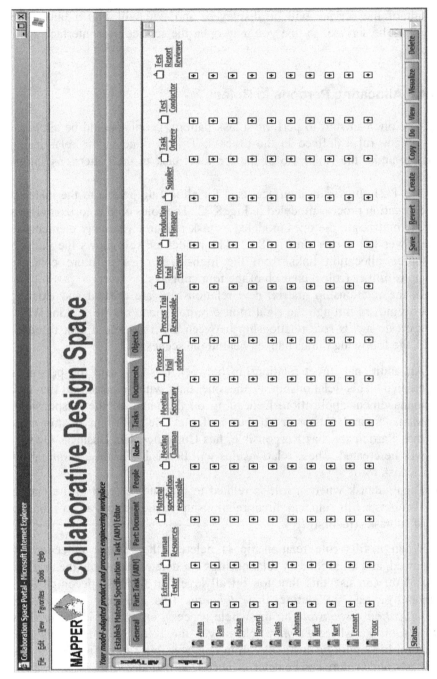

Fig. 8.21. Relationship matrix for allocating people to roles

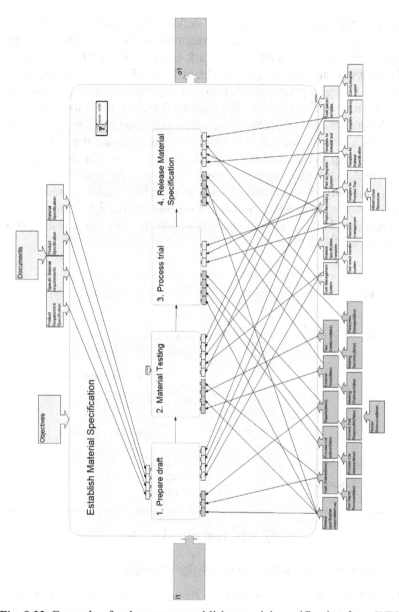

Fig. 8.22. Example of task pattern: establish material specification from WP3

8.4.4 Task Execution Rules

After you have created a new task, defined its properties, and allocated people, you are ready to start the execution of the task. This is done by changing the *Status* property of the task from *Undefined* to *Ready to start* or *In progress*, and pressing *Save*. The task will then appear in the *My new tasks* or *My ongoing tasks* work lists of the people allocated, as well as in any other user-defined list that has been model-configured for your pilot.

In general, the task execution engine is controlled by changing the status of the tasks. The engine reacts to these changes, updating the status of other tasks according to the execution rules. User can however manually override and complement the automatic execution rules by updating the status values manually. Some changes, such as reporting a task started (Status = In progress) or completed (Status = Completed), must be done manually for manual tasks. The typical state transition diagram for a task is shown here (Fig. 8.23).

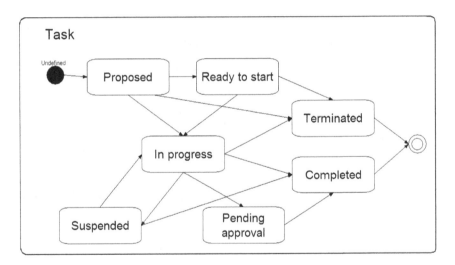

Fig. 8.23. Task execution rules

These rules are executed automatically by the engine:

- When the status of a task is set to Ready to start, all of its subtasks are set to *Proposed*.
- When a task is started, those of its subtasks that are not waiting for an input from another task are automatically set to Ready to start.

- When a task is completed, all its subtasks that are In progress, *Suspended*, or *Pending approval* are set to *Completed*, and all subtasks that have not yet started are *Terminated*.
- When a task is completed, all tasks that follow it (has a before/after relationship from it) are set to Ready to start. If the task that follows it is the parent of the newly completed task, complete the parent task as well.
- When a task is opened by a user who is responsible for it, it becomes *In progress* by default.

For automatic tasks, these additional rules apply:

- When the task becomes ready to start, start it.
- When the task is started, trigger its service (the one it has a works on relationship to).
- If the service has the needed parameters, and is performed without errors, complete the task automatically.

This implies that when everything works, the whole life cycle of an automatic task takes place behind the scenes, and users only need to care about its effects. This also works for composite automatic task patterns.

8.5 Summary

In this chapter, we have described in more detail a possible configuration of basic ICT and AKM services, using the infrastructure in the MAPPER project as an example. Referring back to Fig. 8.1, we have thus focused on the lowest three layers of the AKM infrastructure, with a particular focus on task patterns at level 3. In the next chapter, we will move upward in this figure, describing some of the methods in CPPD that are devices to build more solution-specific services utilizing the common platform.

9 Enterprise Design and Development

We will in this chapter present the different parts of CPPD as used in different parts of the C3S3P approach described in Chap. 7, indicating how it is using the different parts of the infrastructure described in Chaps. 5 and 8.

The AKM Platform extended with the CPPD methodology components and layers of services provide support for:

- Stakeholder involvement from day one, providing services for role-specific perspectives on and interpretations of the enterprise dimensions and model domains, managing their particular aspects, methods, data, and parameter values.
- Improved innovation by enabling idea externalization and conceptual design in distributed design environments. AKM model execution works through interaction, complementing automation with user control, enabling robust, dynamic solutions, and languages.
- Design knowledge externalization and sharing from idea to end of life. Team learning and collaboration require simultaneous modeling in *multiple knowledge dimensions*, organizing models into core knowledge domains and views, and maintaining work dependencies.
- Reduced change and version management by closing the gap between evolving business operations and facetted software support. AKM platforms, workplaces, views, and services are configured by business level *models*.
- Generating effective role-specific workplaces as well as services and views for portfolio management and agile collaborative work. AKM solutions are simplified by integrating object and *task* modeling. Task-specific user interfaces create easy-to-use and learn solutions and services.
- Configuring services for enterprise knowledge capture and architecting, building and adapting *modeling templates, workplaces, and services*, partly automating knowledge management and organizational learning.
- Runtime extensions and adaptations, effectively including also SMEs in design projects without demanding IT investments. AKM services clearly separate roles and responsibilities in a service-team organization.

- Flexible, interoperable, and reusable solutions, avoiding software changes. The model execution services are loosely coupled by *event notification*, making the platforms robust, extensible, and configurable.

The CPPD methodologies and services are anchored in pragmatic product logic, open data definitions, and practical work processes, capturing local innovations and packaging them for repetition and reuse. Actually most of the components, such as the configurable product components (CPC) and the configurable visual workplaces (CVW), are based on proven and documented industrial methodologies. CPPD mostly reimplements them, applying the principles, concepts, and services of the AKM Platform.

Industrial customers need freedom to develop and adapt their own methodologies, knowledge structures, and architectures, and to manage their own workplaces, services, and the meaning and use of data. The AKM approach and the CPPD methodology provide full support for these capabilities, *enabling collaborative product and process design and concurrent engineering.*

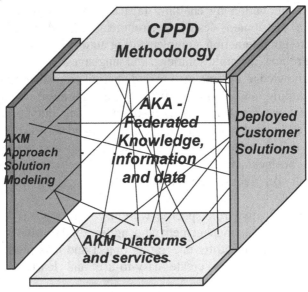

Fig. 9.1. Dimensions in delivering AKM business solutions

9.1 The CPPD Project Context

As illustrated in Fig. 9.1, the AKM approach, the CPPD methodology, the AKM platform and industrial customer solution platforms, integrated by the AKA, make up the mutually reflective knowledge dimensions of personal, customer innovative, business networking, and industrial community knowledge spaces. Customer solutions modeling extend the four AKM spaces, their dimensions, aspects and views by capturing enterprise business and customer knowledge, such as product structures and process perspective views.

In the following section, the knowledge to be considered for externalization, model-capture, view-sharing, model-cultivation, and management will be limited to the structures, views, and contents of the knowledge spaces of individual roles and innovative design teams.

9.1.1 Integrating Life-Cycles

Industrial disciplines engaged in different project phases, applying different methods and calculating separate parameter and value-sets, often refer to the same bulk of information, but use it for different aspects with different degrees of precision and/or detail. As a matter of fact, plain information does not record the status of a process (i.e., whether a process has been completed and with what results it has been completed), but it is the substrate product data that supports the evolving knowledge about the product. Collaborative design must support the sharing of data as knowledge rather than just the transfer of data as information in documents associated to business processes.

Product design has resulted in numerous models of the life-cycle product design process across industrial sectors. Common to most of them, if not all, is that the entire product life-cycle is conceived of and described as a business process flow, using either the procedural or the information flow as the integrator. This will never support collaborative design and the needs and requirements already defined. Design and innovation projects must discover and start building enterprise knowledge architectures, exploiting visual proactive knowledge. This is attempted and illustrated in Fig. 9.2, where the white line is indicating the current level of focus in the design process driven by information flows rather than by applying an operational enterprise knowledge architecture, capturing and sharing work-driving, and work-generating knowledge as individual and common views in real-time.

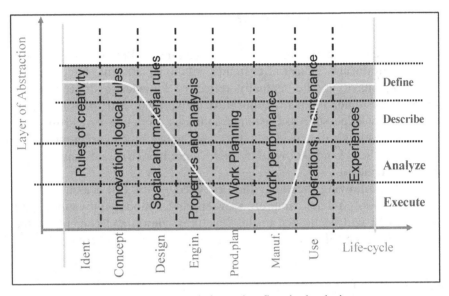

Fig. 9.2. Level of focus on information flow in the design process

Another consequence of the top-down business process integration of legacy systems is that we will never be able to capture situated or work-generating knowledge and use work-generated knowledge, but will forever be stuck with information carrier change and version management. In a visual proactive knowledge architecture, the services to update and align views dramatically simplifies these standardized procedures and document-driven work processes. Removing these costs and management barriers from design and engineering work can save up to 20% of total project costs. But, there are more savings and more than just savings due to old technology to be gathered from developing and applying visual operational enterprise knowledge architectures.

9.1.2 Nature of Work-Generative Knowledge

Work-generative or situated-knowledge has four intrinsic properties, which if exploited will radically change design and human perception of any artifact be it industrial products, IT systems, or artistic artifacts. These properties are *reflection, recursion, repetition, and replication.* Work-generative or situated-knowledge is intrinsically created in our minds as reflective views, recursive task-patterns, repetitive flows, and replicable templates.

Externalizing and capturing these structures of mutually dependent views allow us to build powerful AKAs.

All CPPD components take advantage of these properties, mainly as reflective views. Automotive industry consultants said, as early as 1989: "One man's floor is another man's roof!" implying that views of how you should perform is reflected in what you need in order to perform. This interplay between operational and descriptive views is tried illustrated in Fig. 9.3. Perhaps a better metaphor is simply recognizing the ladder of decomposition, specialization, concretization, and execution of knowledge views that automatically yield the four intrinsic properties of work-generative knowledge.

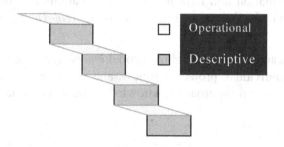

Fig. 9.3. Interrelating operational and descriptive views

The knowledge work spaces of designing and engineering, internalized in the heads of knowledge workers, may be externalized, captured, and reused as the EKA or the more organizational-specific AKA. This is one of the ambitions with the CPPD. With integrated role, task, and view structures at its core and with some powerful intrinsic properties, such as reflection, recursion, repetition, and replication of views, it holds a lot of promise for the future of holistic industrial artifact design and human learning. This core structure is built by designers performing task-structures for creating ideas, concepts, function-means views, architectural views, functional system-structure views, and so forth.

9.1.3 The Active Knowledge Architecture

Our customers and partners will eventually be able to build their own EKA using the AKM platform and the CPPD methodology. The customer adapted and extended EKA (AKA) integrates the products, organizations, processes, and systems of one or a network of enterprises:

- capturing all facets and views of knowledge needed to run a business
- handling layers of knowledge to support both common, company and discipline specifics in a secure, but integrated manner
- enabling enterprises to capture knowledge that is previously found only in the heads of key people, making the enterprises more resistant to human turnover, solving "the brain-drain" problem
- using dynamic visual languages to reflect knowledge evolution, and the transfer of core knowledge to other roles and working environments
- utilizing visual workplaces and visual scenes to support knowledge representation, communication, coordination, execution, and work management
- integrating information and data in legacy applications and databases with knowledge in the AKA, making the AKA *the Real-Time Enterprise Integrator*.

The AKA is organized into multidimensional *knowledge structures* that separate between individual, project, business, and community knowledge spaces, offering a systemic approach to knowledge and work management.

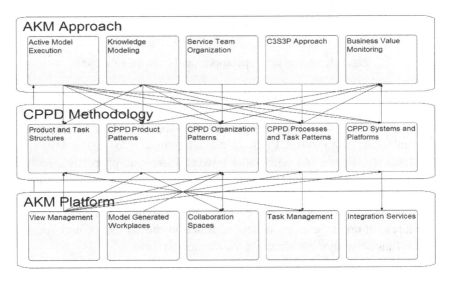

Fig. 9.4. Building-blocks for the AKA

As indicated in Fig. 9.4, the CPPD components will operate on the EKA with increasingly richer contents and intelligent services as the number of industrial delivery projects grow. The solutions modeling stage of the AKM approach has as its prime objective to extend and customize the EKA with enterprise role-specific views needed by the targeted solutions.

The EKA is composed of structures and contents of service-team role-views, data, information, and knowledge from the enterprise knowledge spaces, and knowledge dimensions and aspects involved. Building a customer-specific EKA not only implies capturing specific views of data and knowledge, but also implies extending the AKM platform capabilities and generic services into enhanced industrial platforms and services. These extended services enable model-configured and business-composed platforms and services for industry to build a variety of solution platforms for internal innovation, partnering, and customer delivery, possibly without developing or buying new software. Enterprise integration with the EKA is performed by capturing and managing customer business data, information, and knowledge as reflective views.

9.2 Addressing Industrial Demands

Initial or early design involves creating new products covering idea expression, conceptual design, and architectural compliance design, and focuses on creating a precise definition of the product family logic and logistics. This is innovating new products, by realizing new ideas and applying new principles and product materials, functions, and technologies to define agile configurable product platforms.

Product design to deliver to specific customer requirements is maybe better denoted product development. This implies taking an already validated design solution, designed in a holistic approach, such as the AKM approach using configurable product platform methods, delivered services to customize the product, making it ready for manufacturing, delivery, and life-cycle support.

9.2.1 Industrial Use of the CPPD Methodology

The CPPD methodology provides methods, languages, and workplaces for enterprise and product designers and other stakeholders to effectively and continuously perform collaborative business, design, and engineering. Before allowing designers, engineers and users access to the CPPD components that any project should identify certain service-teams with clearly defined roles and responsibilities. The *platform integration team* typically provides basic visual languages and methods for customer project delivery teams to effectively build customer solutions and services enabling holistic design and engineering of products. Service team competences and skills, business work processes, and business services must be extended with Web-services and adapted to the specific project.

Data and knowledge management, handling parameter structures and parameter value ranges, controlling influences on logical rules as well as single parameter values is rarely supported in current IT systems. Verifying that any parameter value calculated, accumulated, or estimated is within bounds, and validating its impact on the total solution is another capability in demand. Also with current PLM, systems data and the meaning and validity of data are defined by system developers, and there are no services to support designers and engineers in validating, managing, and reusing their own data. Controlling "design bandwidth," making sure all parameter values are within the correct value ranges, securing logical and numeric quality is not even possible with traditional IT system approaches.

9.2.2 Customer and CPPD Requirements

One of the main purposes of the CPPD methodology is to provide languages and methods for improved stakeholder involvement, design, engineering and business interactions, and knowledge and data sharing from day one of any new innovation or delivery project. Collaborative design for increased customization and life-cycle support are key industrial demands for improving and growing dynamic service-oriented industrial communities.

The key customer requirements for achieving collaborative product and process design include the following:

- Designers must be able to model and reuse their own ideas, concepts, and to create visual languages to describe their designs to fellow designers and engineers
- Designers must be relieved from having to learn how to use IT tools and manage information files and data transfer, so disjoint software tools and disrupting contexts must be hidden
- Designers and engineers, particularly in SMEs, must be able to join networked projects and perform their services with a minimum or zero investments in IT systems and competence
- Suppliers and service providers should be able to provide their offers and solutions through workplaces generated by models created and adapted in customer collaboration spaces

More specific requirements to CPPD components are:

- to provide an alternative approach to IT solutions design, development, and delivery
- to harness enterprise knowledge, information, and data for life-cycle sharing and reuse
- to allow business knowledge to drive IT integration, project collaboration, and operations
- to provide a persistent source of enterprise knowledge, information, data and role views
- to become the work-driving, innovating, and integrating knowledge source of any enterprise

9.2.3 Support for Early Design

The early phases of design are characterized by high degrees of uncertainty about most product aspects. This is also the phase where most important product design decisions are made. However, because of the lack of structure and reliable data, conventional IT systems poorly support early design.

The knowledge-intensive and human exploratory-learning nature of early design phases demand an EKA-based approach supporting holistic design. Moreover, such an approach should be

- Service-oriented and component-based, plugging in available IT tools in a need-driven manner
- User-controlled, with semiformal and interactive reasoning, because the key knowledge is the individual's technical design skills
- Collaborative, because most products are too large to be designed by a chief designer, and involve too many different engineering disciplines and other business roles
- Business-oriented, because business resources, constraints, and requirements constitute the basic framework within which design takes place
- Configurable in every aspect, allowing dynamic creation and adaptation of design languages, processes, systems, and services
- Configurable on every level, allowing, capturing, and learning from local deviations, exceptions, and innovations
- Extensible, allowing new organizational roles, working practices, system services, experiences, design issues, etc. to be brought into the joint design arena when needed

- Based on multiple views
  - Allowing each person to access the rich and complex product information structure through simplified role and task-oriented workplaces
  - Allowing heterogeneous and inconsistent views to coexist, enabling negotiation between perspectives and shared reality construction, not enforcing a global, shared model prematurely by only allowing consistent, already interoperable, views to be expressed
  - Multidimensional, combining multiple-type hierarchies, part structures, properties, and parameter aspects, for different disciplines
- Inter-organizational, because design increasingly requires core competence found outside of the company, among e.g., suppliers and consultants

In summary, we must recognize the nature of innovative enterprise knowledge: the multidisciplinary complexity of early design can only be effectively solved by developing an AKA.

9.2.4 CPPD Roles and Responsibilities

Continuous success in collaborative product and process design will depend on model-configured, user-composed platforms, and services, supporting the implementation of the CPPD components and services, eventually requiring a new form of organization, performing, adapting, and managing the CPPD and project services over project and product life-cycles.

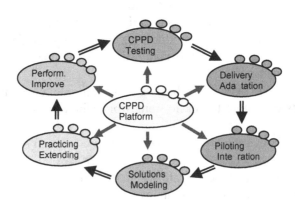

Fig. 9.5. The core teams of a service-team organization to support CPPD

We have named this new form for *the Service-team Organization*. It is driven by the needs to have clearly defined teams and team roles with competence and skill profiles for delivering and performing adapted sets of services, possibly to all other teams even across many projects. Figure 9.5 depicts the core teams. Each team has four key roles: managing, engineering, adapting, and controlling services for other project teams.

The key organizational roles for developing, delivering, adapting, applying, managing, and reusing the CPPD components and services are:

1. *The Business Development Manager* having the overall responsibility for new markets, market strategies, approaches, and business performance
2. *The Customer Project Manager* having the responsibility for that particular project, its performance, customer delivery, and resources
3. *The Product Manager* having the responsibility for product innovation, product platforms, product families, data, and life-cycle support
4. *The Engineering or Technology Manager* having the responsibility for engineering approaches and platforms, including the AKM approach and platform
5. *The Product and Process Designer* having the responsibility for the design and knowledge capture and reuse, satisfying all requirements
6. *The Knowledge Engineer* having the responsibility for building, adapting, and supporting the CPPD components, platform services, and templates, and for contents management
7. *The Infrastructure Manager* having the responsibility for interoperability, integrating all platforms, and systems, including legacy IT systems
8. *The Business Controller*, taking care of business governance for all other teams in the project, and possibly for the total product portfolio

These roles can also be filled by extending the responsibilities, competences, and skills of already existing roles. Any networked organization should, however, be aware of these organizational demands.

9.3 The AKM Approach to Product Design

Knowledge about product life-cycles, captured from performing work, is the key sources of knowledge for most companies. Current practices are that this knowledge is either tacit in the minds of workers or captured in databases, documents, or other information carriers. This information reflects three main forces that shape product design as previously described in Chap. 6:

- The voice of the customer (VoC), representing the needs and requirements of the market
- The voice of business (VoB), ensuring that the company is profitable, managing its resources and competences in the best way, following clear visions and strategies
- The voice of technology (VoT), representing the various disciplines who design and manufacture the products, technological trends, constraints, and opportunities

Different technologies have emerged to support each of these forces as repeated here as Fig. 9.6:

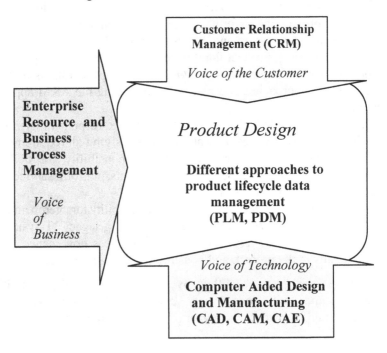

Fig. 9.6. Inroads toward enabling product lifecycle data management

9.3.1 CPPD Development

There are many global initiatives to define common product data formats, system frameworks, design rules, product structures, and norms and design rules, but only AKM technology offers a new holistic design approach backed by new methods of working and dynamic working environments. The CPPD methods are implemented as services on top of the EKA, and they create knowledge contents, functional and contextual views, visual language templates, workplace layout definitions, and role-specific services.

Building a solution that supports CPPD faces a series of major challenges. It requires that we are able to handle the following models in an integrated and interoperable manner:

- The product representations
  - There are several product structures that themselves must be supported in an integrated manner
- The process and task representations
  - The ability to plan and perform work on the basis of task patterns
  - The ability to capture the actual tasks, and why they were performed, is essential
- The view definitions and the views
  - Different users in different phases of the product lifecycle requires different views, i.e., a flexible view definition mechanism is necessary
- The user interface
  - The solution must support the user's way of thinking and his/her preferred way of working. This applies specifically to the user interface of the modeling environment, which often is quite complex

The basis for such work is a flexible modeling environment with the ability to dynamically develop the modeling language itself. This is evident if we think about supporting product design – a new product is the result of performing multiple design work processes and the language used to describe the product is also a result of a work process. When you start the design you do not know how to describe the product structure in detail, because you do not know what the result of the design should be, but repeatedly using and extending the EKA with increasing detail will narrow the design solutions space to a few alternatives.

9.3.2 The Voice of the Customers

Customers and partners need simple interfaces to input product requirements, problems, and issues with current product variants, etc. The Dynamic Requirement Definition System (DRDS) built and used by ATHENA B4 project supplies many functions and features needed for such an application, e.g.

- Configurable Web forms for registering problems, issues, requirements, and wishes
- Configurable visual interface (enterprise models) for classifying, organizing, managing, and prioritizing requirements
- Configurable language and metamodel, allowing different properties and classification schemes to be added to the requirement set when needed
- Multidimensional classification schemes, allowing different disciplines to structure the information in different ways suited to their needs, (in ATHENA B4, business oriented classifications based on industry sectors and main business processes was complemented by various technical classification schemes for grouping requirements, according to the solutions that may meet them).

In addition to an open, low overhead interface for collecting requirements, professional market analysis is of course also needed. The input from these sources should be merged into a collection of requirements and constraints that is available to product design projects. If the companies involved already possess special purpose requirements management applications, e.g., as part of their CRM solution, data from these systems should be imported into the overall product knowledge architecture of the company.

9.3.3 The Voice of Business

Business managers are concerned with maximizing the profitability of the company. They provided governance structures and frameworks to be applied in product design, such as

- Company visions, strategies, and tactics
- Product families, platforms, and portfolios
- Resource management, allocating people to maximize results
- Competence development and management

- Standard methods and procedures, e.g., captured in quality manuals consisting of business process models and descriptions
- Rules and standards for how the business is organized, managed, and conducted

In the CPPD methodology, enterprise modeling is used for capturing and applying these management structures. It is important that they are captured in a structured format, so that they may be easily enacted in individual product lifecycles. We are, however, not advocating that existing tools used for business management are thrown out. Instead, data from these systems should be imported as views into the integrating product knowledge architecture.

9.3.4 The Voice of Technology

The number and diversity of technological perspectives vary across industry sectors. The methodologies and views for representing and applying technological knowledge must thus be adapted to each industry, and indeed to the local ways of working within each company or business network. However, to enable a move from loosely coupled multidisciplinary design to interdisciplinary collaborative design, new mechanisms for integrating diverse technological models are needed. Interdisciplinary knowledge sharing, problem solving, and learning is needed to speed up early design phases, increase innovation, avoid suboptimization, and change management ripple effects throughout the design processes. Our CPPD methodology applies some generic kinds of technology views to facilitate this as depicted in Fig. 9.7:

- CPC defining the reusable elements of the companies' product platform, with their parameterization interfaces and composition structures
- Configurable properties and parameters (CPP), describing and characterizing the configurable components according aspects defined by and for the different engineering disciplines involved
- Products constraints, rules, and statements representing what is technologically feasible from the viewpoints of different engineering disciplines
- Configurable lifecycle services, bringing the concerns of support, maintenance, and other activities late in the lifecycle into the product design process
- Configurable manufacturing plants, enabling joint design of the product platforms and the manufacturing plants and processes that will produce them, enabling design for manufacturing

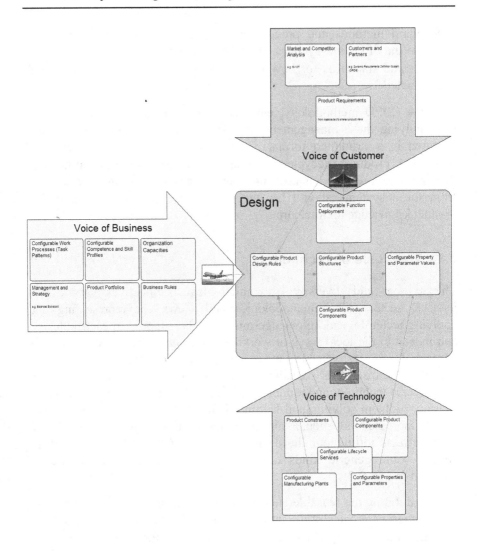

Fig. 9.7. CPPD components relative to product design

Of course, the technology stakeholders are also key actors in the design process. The VoT should thus represent the engineering concerns in such a way that they provide reusable components to practitioners, and sufficient insight to outsiders from other disciplines. Multiple views are needed.

9.3.5 Component Development

CPPD components are delivered to customer projects as a set of generic knowledge models and services, allowing and guiding cross-partner service-teams in developing generic and adapting project specific enterprise knowledge models, methods, and rules, thereby creating application platforms and services to meet customer specific demands.

CPPD Services

Industrial customers contribute the pragmatic logic, active business knowledge, and operational data that are captured and harnessed by applying CPPD methods to build operational enterprise knowledge architectures. A core set of CPPD component variants will emerge from each industry sector and the resulting customer platforms.

From a customer perspective, CPPD is a set of customizable visual language services, extending generic enterprise data, information structures and views with customer-specific operational data and knowledge to build and generate working solutions. In all industrial projects, we propose to follow the AKM approach (as described in Chap. 7). Modeling in the scaffolding phase is started by delivering the needed CPPD components and templates, and by making available required MUPS services for integration, coordination, and so on. MUPS and CPPD services represent layers 3 and 4 of the AKM Platform and Services architecture as described in Fig. 8.1 and explained in detail in Chap. 8.

CPPD components are delivered to customer projects as a set of generic knowledge models and services, allowing and guiding cross-partner service-teams in developing generic and adapting project-specific enterprise knowledge models, methods, and rules, creating application platforms and services to meet customer-specific demands.

Configurable CPPD components will be developed, improved, and validated in a growing number of commercial projects across various industries. This will gradually raise the quality and value of the methodology and its supporting components.

9.3.6 The CPPD Architecture

A critical challenge, then, is the design of an interoperable information infrastructure for this product knowledge architecture. The core in our approach is the enterprise knowledge architecture (EKA) as described in

Chap. 5. It is a revised version of the EKA core defined in ATHENA A1 (DA1.5.2). To realize CPPD we have defined a set of configurable solution components on top of this core.

9.4 The CPPD Components

This section will describe those of the 12 configurable components that are currently defined:

- CPC: Configurable product components, capturing parameterized variants, shapes, and materials
- CVW: Configurable visual workplaces, designing and generating user workplaces
- CWP: Configurable work processes, managing dependencies between tasks
- CPP: Configurable property and parameter-sets, making it possible to handle properties, and parameters separately by each engineering or business discipline
- CPS: Configurable product structure, an early design support language for generic model and services
- CFD: Configurable function deployment, to correlate requirements and constraints with product properties and features
- CDL: Configurable design language, linking conceptual EKA to sketches illustrating fundamental and innovative product concepts
- CIB: Configurable idea bank, capturing and relating design ideas, principles, requirements, sketches, constraints, and stakeholder views for more effective innovation
- CWI: Configurable Web service integration, interfacing legacy systems as Web services
- CWW: Configurable Web workplaces, designing and generating workplaces on the Web
- CCS: Configurable collaboration spaces, configuring roles, tasks, and views
- CCP: Configurable competence and skill profiles, for visual competency management

The 12 CPPD components, described herein, is developed, applied, and operated as a coherent, consistent, and compliant set of generic services and reference architectures for capturing, representing, and reusing enterprise knowledge to support holistic product design. The resulting customer enterprise architecture integrates the enterprise, providing involved stakeholders with shared tasks, views, and workplaces, enabling work performance, self-managing knowledge work, and extensive reuse of data and software.

- Design requires support for
  - Instance-driven modeling
  - Designer-managed metadata
  - Strong viewing and presentation capabilities
  - Model and view comparison, merging, alignment, and differentiation
  - Parameter-structure propagation and aggregation to manage values
  - Concurrently working on alternative solution models
- Concurrency requires support for
  - New ways of supporting work management
  - Task definition, monitoring, assignment, execution, and management
  - Service-team organizations
  - Managing multiple types and kinds of views

At its core, CPPD has a *product knowledge architecture*, which is created and maintained through model-configured services for CPC, product structures, function deployment, design languages, idea banks, and property and parameter-structures. The knowledge architecture and the collaborative design work that creates and uses it is further supported by platform services for model-configured workplaces (visual scenes and Web portals), task management, and Web service integration, all combined into a CCS for the networked manufacturing enterprises. This solution allows companies to exploit the Web as an agile knowledge sharing medium.

Each CPPD component will be realized by service-teams working in customer project teams.

CPPD is the configurable components modeling platform, representing layer 4 of the platforms and services architecture perspective, and used to develop customer-specific application platforms and services. The concepts and early prototypes of most of the components are developed in the ATHENA and MAPPER EU R&D projects. All components are dependent on services and knowledge from the platform layers below (Fig. 9.8).

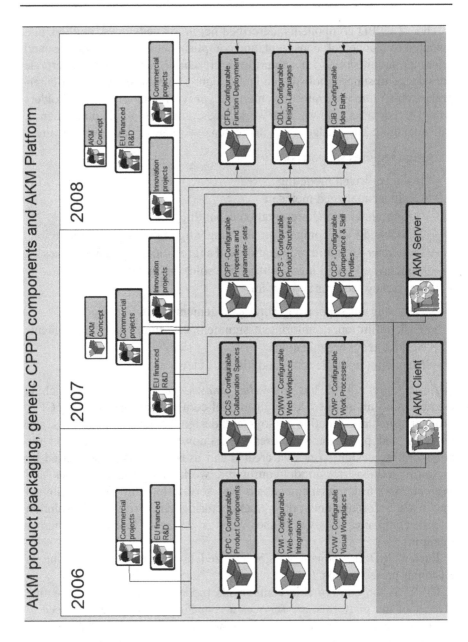

Fig. 9.8. The 12 configurable components of the CPPD methodology

In the following, selected CPPD components will be defined and described by its development background, purpose, enterprise services, EKA contents, and mutual dependencies.

9.4.1 Configurable Product Components (CPC)

Product models are used in most stages of the product lifecycle, and they play different roles dependent on the stage. We have focused on the design and development phases of our work in ATHENA, and one result is the CPC module that allows a designer to model and represent a configurable product structure with ultimate flexibility. The work has been performed as a cooperation between Chalmers University, Kongsberg Automotive (as part of MAPPER), Saab Automobile and AKM (ATHENA and MAPPER).

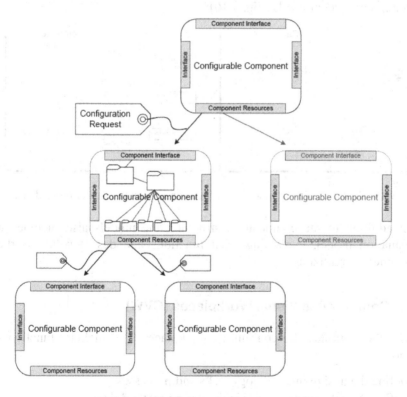

Fig. 9.9. Structure of configurable components

In this work, we differentiate between components and parts. The component represents a solution to a design problem, whereas the part is a representation of a physical part. This means that configurable components define configurable product structures that take care of the product logic without representations of instantiated physical parts. When a physical part is needed a part instance is created using the component as the generative parent of the part.

Figure 9.9 shows a conceptual view of configurable components where the message is that a component requests other components to build different variants. The variants are specified by variant parameters, and rules are used to control the variant configurations. It is important to notice that when a component requests another component, it means that it requests a component that itself may be configurable. Variant parameters in one component may control the values of the variant parameter in the components it uses. It is a dependency between variant parameters on different component levels (Fig. 9.10).

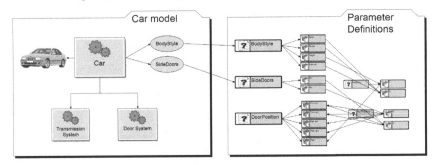

Fig. 9.10. Example of a car model with focus on variant parameter dependencies

In addition to the composition structure, the models also include an explanation model, explaining what functions and design solutions the component is realizing.

9.4.2 Configurable Visual Workplaces (CVW)

This is the workplace for configuring workplaces. This includes functionality to

- Define the design methodology tasks and processes
- Define the roles participating in the design methodology
- Define the product information structures
- Define the views on product information structures needed for each task

- Perform the work in role-specific workplaces
- Extend, adapt, and customize when needed

Figure 9.11 illustrates the core approach

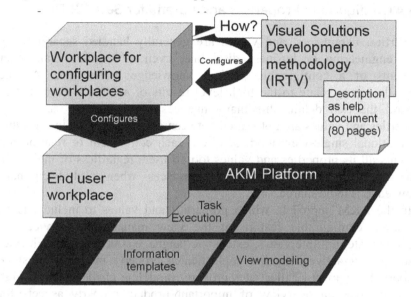

Fig. 9.11. Using the workplace for configuring workplaces

We provide a brief example of this approach in Sect. 9.5.

9.4.3 Configurable Work Processes (CWP)

Managing dependencies reflected by relationships is an important class of business processes that can be derived from the product structure. Other process classes include deciding among design alternatives, elaborating the design of a component, testing and verification, production design, etc. In current systems, this is reflected in generic business processes, e.g., change handling. At the same time, it is evident that the core knowledge that helps the enterprise roles solve problems and decide what to do, lie in the product structures, rather than the administrative procedures. During design, product structures are thus the core of the knowledge sharing architecture, while processes are invoked on a need driven basis, and must be adapted (as automatically as possible) to the holistic context where they take place. In this phase, we thus need "configurable process components" to plug-and-play, rather than top-down, logical process hierarchies. We call such configurable processes *"task patterns"* as described in Chap. 8, to distinguish them from conventional BPM processes.

9.4.4 Configurable Properties and Parameter Sets (CPP)

Properties, parameters, and values are generally handled separately by each engineering or business discipline, even more often than other elements of a configurable product knowledge architecture. A role typically has to relate to the high level results of another's work, but in general the rich details, the many nuances, versions, and variants of properties and values are not shared between disciplines. This implies that conventional single-view models, where each component or relationship presents all its properties and values too all users regardless of their role, ends up with too complex user interfaces when multidisciplinary knowledge is to be shared.

In the AKM approach, which properties and values to include, is an important configurable feature of the view management service. To accommodate multiple views, extensible language concepts and rich rule-based or interactive behavior, sophisticated property modeling must be supported. Figure 9.12 illustrates property modeling challenges at a high level. It gives an overview of important product property aspects for electronics design. In the left side of the model, electronics engineering disciplines are organized into five levels, ranging from system properties, via architecture, digital, and analogue design, down to the physical layout in silicon (geometry). Some engineers work on more than one of these levels, but there are also clear boundaries where the set of important properties and values change dramatically, e.g., between digital and analogue design. Nevertheless, there are of course dependencies between the digital and analogue design structures and properties, because the digital design specification is to be implemented by the analogue design, as one component in a larger structure.

In addition to these different engineering disciplines, Fig. 9.12 illustrates

- Cross-cutting technical aspects, such as electromagnetic interference, energy, heat, and power consumption
- Aspects relating to the manufacturing process (mechanic properties and packaging)
- Aspects relating to major technological platform alternatives (materials, transistors)
- Business aspects, exemplified by cost, further specialized into different kinds of costs

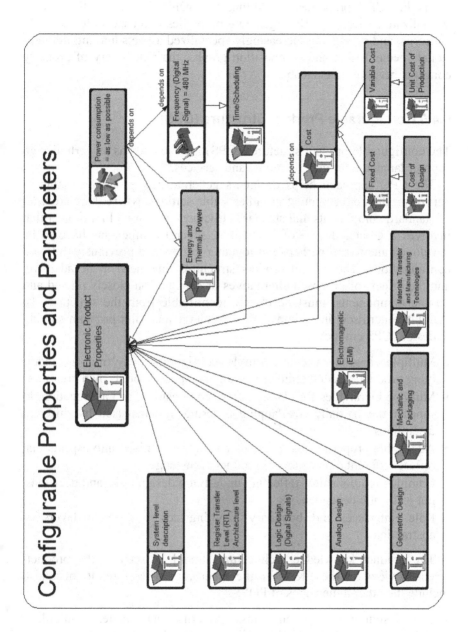

Fig. 9.12. Property aspects for electronics product design

Just like CPC, properties should thus be organized in a multidimensional specialization hierarchy. By organizing properties into aspects for separate concerns, and organizing increasingly specialized aspects into multidimensional specialization and composition graphs, the rich library of property concepts becomes manageable.

9.4.5 Configurable Product Structure (CPS)

The configurable product structures (CPS) is developed as an early design support language for generic model and services.

The CPC approach helps designers generate new product variants as part of product development in rather stable settings, where there are a lot of standard components and standard structures available. In a project that involves a greater degree of innovation, several components have to be developed anew, and perhaps put together in new and previously untested configurations. The overall product structures thus need to be adaptive, and the effects of proposed alternatives or changes, on closely related and remote components, must be clearly identifiable from the structure. To facilitate interdisciplinary knowledge exchange and joint problem solving in design, CPS embody

- Multiple views derived in a simple, configurable way from an underlying product model that integrates any perspective on its own premises
- Multiple hierarchies for classification, composition, and aggregation, to support the partially overlapping ordering systems used by different disciplines
- Attachable properties and parameter values, organized into aspects that reflect different dimensions of product knowledge
- Complex relationships, reflecting underlying design tasks and decisions, not just static dependencies
- Role, interface, and boundary handling across different layers of abstraction

The product knowledge architecture should be seen as the product-oriented view on the EKA for the enterprise. Therefore, it must also include the other dimensions of POPS:

- The design *processes* and task patterns that create, manipulate, elaborate, use, manage, and coordinate the product structures
- The roles and *organizations* that work on different parts and aspects of the product structures
- *Systems* and services they use for performing their work

9.4.6 Configurable Function Deployment (CFD)

A modular function deployment (MFD) component platform supporting methods to correlate requirements and constraints with product properties and features may be developed by setting up a partnership with Modular Management AB in Stockholm (Vinnex 2007). The method consists of five major steps. It starts with quality function deployment (QFD) (Zultner 1992) analysis to clarify customer requirements and to identify important design requirements with a special emphasis on modularity. The functional requirements on the product are analyzed and technical solutions are selected. This is followed by systematic generation and selection of modular concepts, in which the module indication matrix (MIM) is used to identify possible modules by examining the interrelationships between "module drivers" and technical solutions. The expected effects of the redesign can be estimated and an evaluation can be carried out for each modular concept. Their methodology is well tested in many industries, but support for it is only available as disjoint tools producing paper. With AKM platforms, the MFD matrices can become powerful set of business manager views to support, e.g., car platform collaboration, business governance, and decision making.

9.4.7 Configurable Design Language (CDL)

So far, we have discussed the structure of a *conceptual* product knowledge architecture. However, we are well aware that during the early phases of design, *engineering drawings* and sketches, not conceptual structures, are the visual representation preferred by most engineers. Therefore, it is important that the conceptual EKA can be directly linked to sketches illustrating fundamental and innovative product concepts. Richer visualization capabilities, with WYSIWYG user editing, are needed to fully support such configurable design languages (CDL). Sadly, existing design tools such as CAD-tools do not focus on supporting early phase concept development either, and pen-and-paper, Powerpoint, or simple sketching tools are still the most used technologies. Such drawings must therefore be imported, e.g., as pictures, into the conceptual modeling tools. Often the drawing should be split into elements, and the elements linked to elements of the conceptual product architecture. Using visualization macros, the concept sketch could then become an active, rich symbol, e.g. changing color of elements to reflect their degree of completion, of requirement fulfillment, or other status elements that it would makes sense to monitor. Making the concept sketch an integral part of the work environment might also tacitly influence the way engineers collaborate, by making it easy to always refer back to the initial concept visualization. As an ambiguous structure, the sketch could in this way act as an enabler for negotiation of meaning and learning across disciplines and roles. As shown in Fig. 9.10, it is much easier to read a model that includes meaningful symbols for the car and its doors, than if all the symbols are just simple boxes.

9.4.8 Configurable Idea Bank (CIB)

An Idea Bank for Product Concept Design, capturing and relating design ideas, principles, requirements, sketches, constraints and stakeholder views in an idea bank has been mentioned as the prime objective for more effective innovation among tier 1 and tier 2 suppliers to the car industry and also the construction industry.

As the CPC solution becomes established and used in a company, supply chain, or business network, organizations may build up a library of reusable components, managed as a central part of the Configurable Idea Bank (CIB). In addition to the product component representations, the idea bank may provide links to IT services, CWP as task patterns, and organizational role and competence structures that are relevant for the application of each reusable component. The idea bank thus provides a holistic context for reusing components, centered on product structures, but includes as well the other POPS-dimensions of the innovative knowledge space.

9.5 Example of CVW

As indicated in Chap. 1, the first industrial piloting of model-configured solutions applying the most recent AKM technology were started at Kongsberg Automotive (KA) in the Autumn of 2006 as one of the three industrial scenarios of the EU project MAPPER, IST 015 627. The goals at KA are improved seat heating design, better product quality, less data errors, and improved ways of working to interpret and fulfill customer requirements, producing improved product specifications and supplier requirements.

The CVW-example relates to material specifications that are the core knowledge of collaboration between the customer, represented by Kongsberg Automotive (KA) and the supplier, represented by Elektrisola (E). As illustrated in Fig. 9.13, the material specification is today managed as a document, typically created in MS-Word. The content in a specific version of the material specification is put together by one person in KA and approved by one person in E, and both companies are filing one copy of the approved material specification. Of course over time additional customer requirements needs to be communicated resulting in new parameter values in new versions of the document. The biggest disadvantages with the existing solution are:

- The content in the material specifications is not easily accessed and cannot contribute to the two companies' operational knowledge architecture
- The process and work logic to achieve a consistent specification is not captured, making integration with other processes impossible
- The involvement and commitment from the supplier is not encouraged, there is no support for mutual adjustments in supply and demand
- Keeping the material specifications updated in both companies is quite time consuming

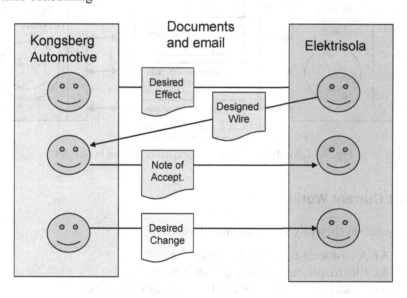

Fig. 9.13. Illustrating the current work logic with material specification document

The general approach as illustrated in Fig. 9.14 has been to replace the document with an operational knowledge architecture built by using the CVW module developed by AKM within MAPPER. A demo has been developed were two communicating workplaces, one at KA and one at E is modeled and configured. The biggest advantages with the model-based knowledge architected solution are:

- The content in the material specifications will be easy to access by both companies and can be part of the each company's complete knowledge architecture, provided that the model-based solution is replacing the document-based solution for other applications within the companies
- The involvement from the supplier will be encouraged and the supplier commitment will be more obvious
- The time for updating the material specifications is expected to be reduced in both companies. There is no real need of filed paper copies anymore

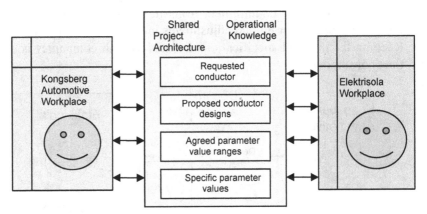

Fig. 9.14. Model-configured workplaces driven by AKAs

9.5.1 Current Workplaces

The solution currently supports these five CVWs:

1. AKA customer-responsible workplace
2. An Elektrisola customer-responsible workplace
3. An Elektrisola smart-wire family designer workplace
4. AKA material specification workplace
5. AKA heating conductor component designer workplace

All workplace model elements are stored in and share a common AKA. The AKA is used to communicate, configure, coordinate, context-preserve and perform work, acting as a "knowledge amplifying mirror." By extending the scope and methods of work more workplaces can be modeled and generated from the AKA. All workplaces have a similar appearance and behavior.

The content in the material specifications is continuously refined. The origin for the material specification is the conceptual design. The demonstrated workplaces shall be able to support the refinement of the material specification in the complete life cycle. The focus below is on the early conceptual design phase. In the specific use case, the component responsible at the customer, Kongsberg Automotive (KA), will request heating conductor proposals from the supplier, Elektrisola (E), with a targeted property value for the conductor resistivity.

The demonstrator is developed from both customer and supplier perspectives. The change in perspective is managed by switching workplaces, one customized for KA and one for E.

The logic of product variants, customer projects, families, specifications, and parameters of interest for describing heat conductor design requests are modeled and predefined in the shared seat heat model. All demonstration scenarios are adding to or editing these contents as an example of automating the reuse of knowledge.

The *product variants* built are sinus-wires and smart wires. The variants are defined by their product families and the families by their specific occurrences.

Customer projects may be defined independent of product variants. In the example, there is a design collaboration of KA customer heat conductor and Elektrisola smart-wire product responsible. This is the customer project collaborative work process to coordinate the heat conductor design based on smart-wires.

The start-page of the KA-customer responsible workplace is shown in Fig. 9.15. All functionality show in this and the following screen-shots are model-generated on top of METIS-models, although as we see here, one often combines pictures with the more classical modeling. When choosing "select component variant" in top of the menu, the welcoming Kongsberg workplace front-end is replaced with a dialog box for component variant. In this example, we select smart wires, and then choose "Select Customer project" in the left menu, define a new project KA 1002. The project name appears when you perform "New Specification" or "Select Component Family," reflecting requirements and life-cycle experiences. When choosing "New Specification," one give relevant name to Specification; e.g., 201015 and the screen in Fig. 9.16 appears.

Fig. 9.15. KA component responsible front-end

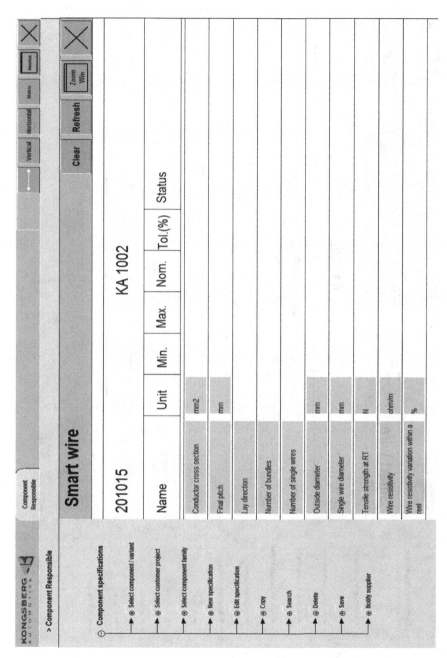

Fig. 9.16. Customer project KA 1002, specification 201015 when first defined

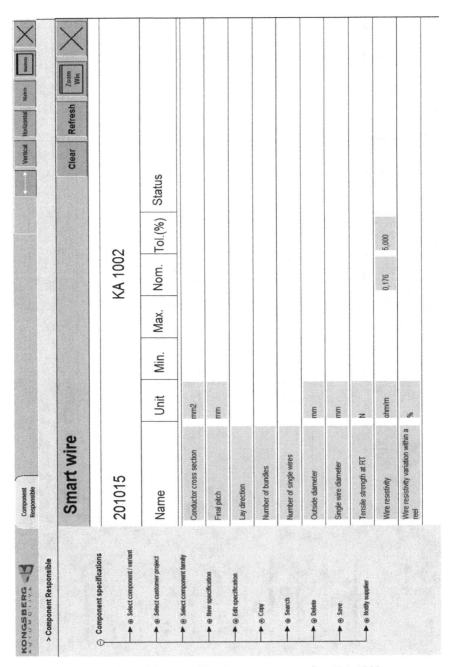

Fig. 9.17. Editing specification customer project KA 1002

Choosing "Edit Specification" one can give nominal value to resistivity; e.g., 0,176 Ohm/m. Wire resistivity appears as shown in Fig. 9.17.

The next step in the cooperation is to select "Notify Supplier" – to make the supplier aware of the new specification. An email is set up, ready for completion and sending. Alternative notifications are easily modeled.

Figure 9.18 illustrates the front end of the Elektrisola customer – responsible workplace. The role name appears also here in the top left of the screen.

Fig. 9.18. Elektrisola customer responsible workplace

Selecting "Component/Variant, in the top of the menu, one can choose Smart Wire, Select customer project, KA 1002 and select specification 201015 using the "Search" functionality bringing up the screen given in Fig. 9.19.

Now the request from the Kongsberg customer responsible must be responded to. In the example, we have chosen "Edit Specification," and deliberately given some out of range values to show up in later comparisons, including setting single wire cross-section to 0.08. Choosing "Calculate" one get the last two values of conductor cross section and outside diameter. Selecting "Edit Calculation Rules," one can open, e.g., an excel spreadsheet with formulae for calculating the outside diameter and the cross section is invoked. Figure 9.20 includes the results after the first requirements are given, indicating the status of different properties.

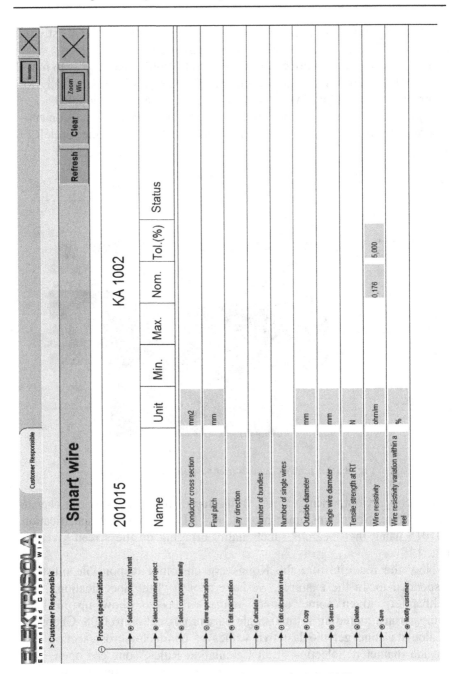

Fig. 9.19. Addressing requirements for KA 1002

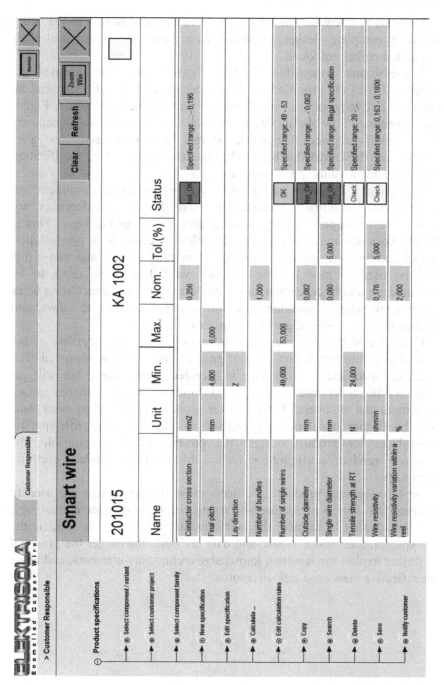

Fig. 9.20. First attempt to address requirements

Updating problematic parameters can give a picture as seen in Fig. 9.21, where a complete design proposals with parameter values and their calculated ranges are found.

The customer responsible can then choose "Save," which saves the specification of the proposed conductor design, and "Notify," to send an email to KA requestor, or sets a flag in the designer workplace. Figure 9.22 illustrates how the model looks like seen from the KA-customer-responsible workplace. The values stored for this concrete case goes directly into the knowledge base to be able to compare future specification with this and previous specifications.

The dynamic evolution and adaptation of work-generative content and context, the workplace composition, and the user preferences are impossible to support by programming and compiling the logic. This is simply because any extension or adaptation of contents in one solution model and its views need to be reflected in other models and views that will be used to model-configure other workplaces. The tasks to be executed are totally dependent on the context created by interrelating work solution, workplace behavior, and configuration models and views, and role-specific, model-configured workplaces.

Product and material requirements and supplier specifications of the Kongsberg Automotive seat comfort product line has been improved. The materials specification workplace is accepted by the users, but will get some additional services to manage and communicate design issues among customers and suppliers. The customer product specifications workplace will be further developed and related to three or more role-specific workplaces for product design: the product family responsible, the customer product configuration responsible, and the product portfolio responsible.

In the customer product specifications workplace, colors are used to indicate the degree of requirements satisfaction, parameter consistency, and the solution fit to meet the requirements. The more role-specific the workplaces, their tasks, views, and data are built, the bigger the potential to further exploit the resulting knowledge architecture elements, and reuse the reflective views and task-structures.

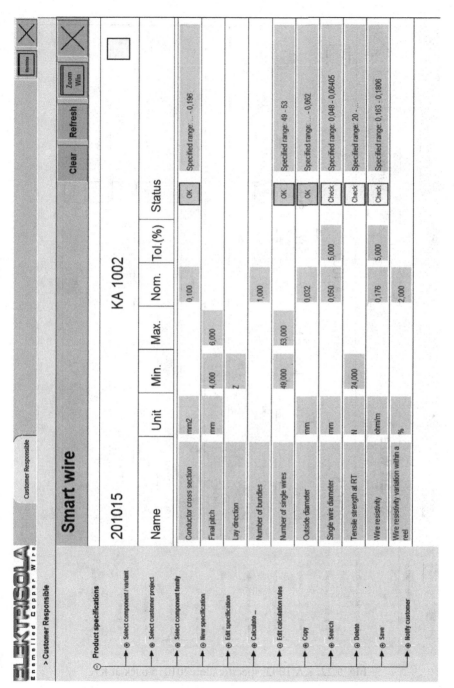

Fig. 9.21. KA 1002 after adapting some properties

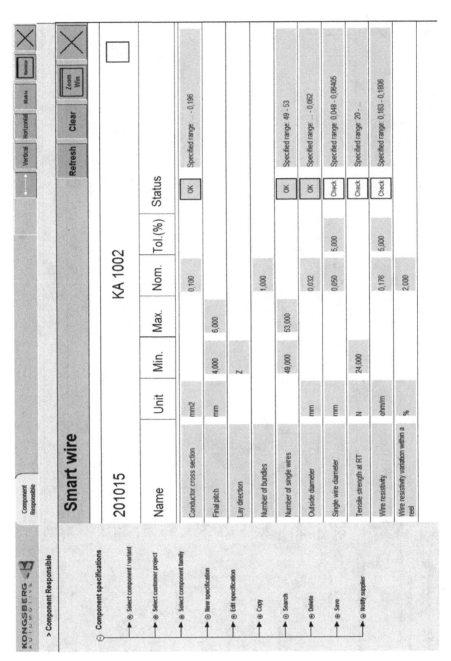

Fig. 9.22. KA 1002, specification 201015 back at KA

9.6 Summary

Product-based interoperability utilizes the structures that reflect the content of the work as a collaboration infrastructure. Models reflecting products, and the organizations, processes, and systems that take part in the product life-cycle are interpreted and activated in different ways to create purposeful, contextual, and holistic collaboration support. High-level models that reflect the realities of the users and their business puts control into the hand of the users, unlike low-level software-oriented representations, which puts control into the hands of programmers with a poor grasp of the complexities of product design and manufacturing business.

This lack of understanding is one reason why many IT interoperability solutions fail to support early design, creative and innovative processes. When you do not grasp all the complexity of a situation, it is much easier to resort to simple, formal, and well-defined IT solutions focusing on a single dimension, such as administrative procedures (BPM) or data exchange (semantic Web). By contrast, the CPPD methodology outlined here embraces the real complexities and uncertainties of design, seeking to generate a pragmatic web of shared understanding among the many companies, functions, and disciplines involved in a design project.

Many of the elements of products-based interoperability has been piloted and tested, e.g., in ATHENA and MAPPER, and also in following commercial projects. Still this work is in its early phases. The chapter thus presents ideas and directions for further work, on the level of concrete components in a CPPD offering. As shown, some of these components, including collaboration spaces, task management, model-generated workplaces, and Web service integration, have been designed, implemented, and tested in commercial projects.

These methodologies will be delivered and supported by AKM business partners. There are also a large number of internationally standardized methodologies that we, in due time, may consider as candidates for partners to implement to further enhance our approach.

On a longer term, the product and process design components must be considered as core components of an innovation project toward a given industry sector. Certain capabilities to apply CWP as multidimensional "intelligent relationships" must be tested and validated in a practical industrial setting.

The product information infrastructure of PLM systems thus often consist of a large number of general, poorly integrated product structures, ranging. from established engineering tools to ad-hoc solutions in spreadsheets, document tables, drawings, etc. Product design and lifecycle management becomes a poorly coordinated multidisciplinary endeavor, and interdisciplinary collaborative engineering remains a distant vision. An integrating *product knowledge architecture*, configurable working environments, and effective role-oriented workplaces are lacking. To support design interoperability, we must go way beyond hub-and-spoke integration, toward supporting dynamic service-team roles and knowledge configured role-specific workplaces.

10 Realizing the Knowledge Economy

This chapter discusses how the AKM approach and technology can help realizing the expectations of the knowledge or network economy, while simultaneously achieving improved innovation, stakeholder involvement and satisfaction, and competitive advantage. The AKM approach can turn business knowledge, innovative capabilities, and operational networking methods into shared manageable assets and decisive competitive instruments. Adopting the AKM approach also means building stronger competitive alliances, tighter business relations, and developing service-teams as a new organizational form. Extending operational networks on the fly to involve students, interest organizations, standardization bodies, and policy-makers is performed by configuring role-specific Web-workplaces.

The content of the chapter is:

- Describing the background for knowledge economy initiatives, starting with the EU policies and foundations for interoperable value networks and collaborative business arenas
- Describing knowledge economy approaches and their theoretical foundations, including value-chain analysis, Schumpeterian methods, network economics, and transaction cost economics
- Results from the EU research community for realizing the knowledge economy; such as analyzing competition, bridging education, research, interest organizations and industry
- Discuss how to transform industrial computing and networking from present day applications and peer-to-peer networks to agile services and networks configured by real-time business knowledge
- Describing AKM contributions; the active knowledge architecture (AKA), enabling early stakeholder involvement, interaction and sharing in visual collaboration arenas
- Discussing the impacts on industry, research, education, interest organizations and science, what are the short and long-term impacts on industry and on industrial communities

There is a growing body of relevant research work on enterprise frameworks, networked organizational forms and structures, impact assessment and benchmarking models, as well as on socio-economic aspects of ICT. However, there is a lack of research, focusing on knowledge technologies for realizing industry-configurable business and knowledge networks.

Most all EU research and industrial development is devoted to reengineering the legacy and to enable semantic tagging of information content, and management of documents and files. Few projects target new approaches that meet the many challenges described in Chap. 2. Most of these challenges can be resolved by applying a holistic design approach, designing for interoperability and agility. Industry demand is pushing for self-serviced innovation and product family manufacturing, and refining and integrating methodologies to appear as views in configured workplaces. This implies new approaches to Systems Engineering as will be demonstrated by the INCOSE Model-Based Systems Engineering (MBSE) initiative (INCOSE 2007).

10.1 Background

The subject of collaborating enterprises and organizational forms has been in the research agenda of the EU and worldwide institutions for more than two decades. The peak effort was probably reached in the early 1990s, when research programs were started in different disciplines, especially Computer Science, Manufacturing and Economics, under the "Holonic/ Virtual Enterprise" umbrella.

The "holon" concept and the "holarchy" organization were not recent discoveries, having been introduced by Koestler (1967) in his famous book "The Ghost in the Machine" The theory by itself, in spite of its undeniable appeal and innovation potential would have not been sufficient to trigger so much interest worldwide. The "Holonic/Virtual Enterprise" movement was favored by important transformations taking place in the same years:

- Computer networks acquired a central role in companies of size as support to basic but essential forms of information exchange and communication, first inside organizations then between organizations.
- Supporting SMEs became a priority. Supporting collaboration between SMEs appeared as the only way to ensure their long-term survival.
- Traditional enterprises started exploring new approaches like, e.g., lean/agile manufacturing, on the basis of outsourcing and cooperation between autonomous units.

Considering the interest raised in those years and the amount of resources spent, one would expect most of today's business to happen in networked organizations, formed by inter-operating systems and companies. However, as that is clearly not the case, let us analyze the efforts from the main players involved in an attempt to find answers:

- *Industry* has been investing significantly in networking and business process improvements, as testified by the amount of work produced by standardization consortia like the VICS initiatives (VICS 2004). Industry has focused more on concrete solutions, immediately applicable by individual companies, than on innovative organization models.
- *Research Communities* see collaborating enterprises as an undisputed IT systems architecture challenge with little regard for knowledge evolution and representation of pragmatic methods. Work logic is more important to work processes than any mathematical or physical methods. However, research has contributed many sophisticated models and solutions, such as intelligent agent research by FIPA (2008).
- *IT Vendors*, despite the marketing hype that has almost any software tagged as "Collaborative," only develop solutions that can be sold in great numbers to single enterprises. Business-to-business Integration platforms and on-line purchasing services are the main types of solutions currently found on the market.

The risk in taking a unilateral approach to multienterprise collaboration, as many researchers and interest organizations do, is that of overlooking business and knowledge work requirements and contexts, in particular:

- Creative work to design new enterprises, product families, organizational forms, rich work environments, work arenas, and services.
- Models based on advanced collaboration strategies might not take into account lower-level requirements, such as the impact on the individual company's internal processes, organization, and culture.

On the opposite side, point solutions to communication problems, although of limited impact and simpler implementation, might fail to achieve results on a proper scale due to lack of a strategic vision.

The gap between theory and practice is not simply a matter of maturity but rather testifies that a common, comprehensive view of networked organizations is not yet available. In our opinion the main reason is the complete absence of smart or intelligent infrastructures, exploiting the powers of work-centric and situated knowledge.

10.2 Networked Business Theories

A number of economic theories have been developed and applied to explain specific economic aspects to provide a theoretical baseline for the development of networked organizations and e-Business. The ATHENA project (ATHENA 2007; Meyer et al. 2006) categorized the theories by how well they respond to the following questions:

- What are the long-term effects on human and social factors?
- What are the effects on industrial competencies and skills?
- What is the impact on competitive advantage and profitability?
- What are the business drivers for determining the selection and the implementation of specific interoperability solutions?
- What are the drivers for determining and evaluating the success of an interoperability solution?
- What exactly is the value proposition of interoperability for individual businesses?

After an extensive review of the existing research results, it became obvious that there is not a closed theory of value-innovation, networked organization, integrated initiatives, and interoperable infrastructures. However, many theoretical streams contribute to explain specific aspects, whether based on reengineering the legacy or on a holistic design approach to designing future systems. For an initial set toward a "theory of knowledge economy," we decided to investigate the following theories:

- Value Chain Analysis is used for defining terms such as value model or value creation.
- Schumpeterian Innovation Theories are used to discuss the question of whether holistic design concepts and interoperability should be regarded as evolutionary or rather as revolutionary in terms of their long-term impacts.
- Network Economics contributes to explanations about the dissemination of standards and provides insights on how the openness and free availability of standards may affect business and social welfare.
- Applying insights from Transaction Cost Economics allow investigating how holistic design may change industry structures in terms of firm services, size, and vertical integration. Transaction Cost studies are often the basis for further analysis of the impact of various approaches on profitability and competitive advantage. In this context, the Resource-Based View provides significant arguments that any approach alone will hardly lead to improved profitability as efficiency

improvements could be bargained away by competition. However, insights from the Dynamic Resource-Based View and the Relational View of Transaction Cost Economics show a way to turn technology approaches into sustainable competitive advantages by developing dynamic capabilities to adapt the organization to the new conditions and possibilities provided. The necessity of developing these dynamic capabilities is corroborated by applying Porter's Competitive Analysis Framework, which in conclusion shows that there are good reasons to assume that holistic design approaches may increase competition, which means that single firms should try to find ways to sustain profitability and to develop competitive advantages.

Business interoperability covers interoperability between two or more business partners, and business services and products may have to be designed on the fly. Thus, we should be able to build methods and services to implement and efficiently run business operations, coping with business dynamics and not just evolving patterns of transactions and tasks. Business interoperability is defined to comprise the following aspects:

- Ability to share information views, and data and knowledge across firm boundaries
- Ability to collaborate across firm boundaries and to establish collaboration arenas cost-efficiently and within a short period of time
- Ability to seamlessly design, adapt, and integrate business collaboration across firm boundaries, handling real-time parameter values
- Ability to efficiently plan, assign, monitor, reassign, approve, and validate business tasks and work performed

In effect, Business Interoperability describes the ability to join and leave a business network, and to establish and remove links within a network at – in relation to the expected benefit – low costs. Most business networks must be designed for interoperability as for other properties.

10.2.1 Value Chain Analysis

Value Chain Analysis, developed by Porter (1985), provides an analytical framework to investigate value creation at firm level. According to Porter, there are two basic sources of competitive advantages: cost leadership and differentiation, the latter meaning that a product meets customer requirements better than competing products and thus sells at a higher price. Competitive strategies should aim to either gain cost leadership or differentiation for a given product. Adding a third strategy, which is orthogonal to the former ones, may yield the desired effects. In a given industrial environment, focusing on a narrower market segment can be more profitable than trying to serve the whole market.

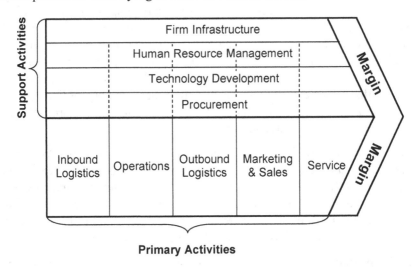

Primary Activities

Fig. 10.1. The generic value chain according to Porter (1985)

As illustrated in Fig. 10.1, there are nine generic value activities, which are distinguished by being primary or support activities. The primary activities such as Inbound Logistics, Operations, Outbound Logistics, Marketing and Sales, and Service represent the core of a firm's value creation process. The primary activities are complemented by four support activities.

The dotted lines indicate that Procurement, Technology Development, and Human Resource Management support distinctive primary activities as well as the whole value chain, whereas Firm Infrastructure exclusively supports the entire chain. All activities together contribute to create value as "the amount buyers are willing to pay for what a firm provides them." Margin is "the difference between total value and the collective cost of performing the value activities" (Porter 1985). Thus, total value can conceptually be seen as the sum of value activities and margin.

It is important to point out that primary as well as support activities do not necessarily correspond to any organizational forms. They group functional activities that can be distributed throughout the whole firm without having any organizational equivalent, even if in many cases firm's organization charts tend to correspond at least to some extent to the value chain framework. A firm's value chain is embedded in a value system, which consists of the value chains of surrounding business partners like suppliers, sales channels, or buyers. Value chain, supply chain, and value system are often taken as synonyms.

Different activities within the value chain can mutually influence each other. For example, the procurement of high-quality input factors can lower manufacturing costs. This circumstance is called linkage. Linkages exist between actions within the value chain but also across firm boundaries. The latter are called vertical linkages.

Clearly there are many limitations to the value-chain, most of them stem from the fact that it is a chain of tasks performed by rigid application systems and services, product adaptation or design is not supported, and knowledge cultivation across time and space is not even considered.

10.2.2 Schumpeterian Innovation

Schumpeter (1934, 1942) identified innovation as the primary source for value creation. Economic growth is driven by entrepreneurs, disturbing the economic equilibrium by introducing innovations such as:

- New goods and services
- New design and production methods
- New marketing and selling methods
- Creation of new markets
- Discovery of new supply sources
- Reorganization of industries and alliances
- New financial instruments

The ever-lasting cycle of the emergence of innovations, which are displaced after a period of time by new innovations, is called creative destruction. Entrepreneurs enter an industry with an innovation and possibly change the whole industry until they are displaced by a new innovative entrepreneur. Innovations allow extra profits that are not reachable by business as usual. These extra profits are called Schumpeterian Rents and are the driving force for entrepreneurs to strive for innovations.

The question for our customers is whether and how holistic design and the AKM approach can contribute to innovations and to achieving Schumpeterian rents. The first part of the question is simple as most new techniques can be seen as an innovation, but how can holistic design lead to Schumpeterian rents? How can AKM technology be applied to achieve solutions, yielding supra-normal profits?

Any firm should be able to build an Active Knowledge Architecture (AKA) that is particular to it, representing its core competitive advantage.

This means that no sustainable, long-term competitive advantage will be reachable by any firm in isolation. The long lasting competitive advantages lie in the inter-firm relations and alliances. Competitive advantages in e-Business and traditional networks can only be short-time, first-mover advantages, which will soon be obsolete when these techniques are widely adopted. Most networking techniques will fail to be a direct source of competitive advantage, and under the assumption of a perfect market, cost savings will be passed to the consumer because above-the-average profits cannot be sustained.

Holistic design is, however, not about making the same things as today, only better and smarter. When holistic design and the AKM technology are used to replace existing monolithic processes, this will yield many competitive advantages. Entrepreneurs will find new ways to make use of these techniques, for example to define new markets or develop innovative products and services. This in turn leads to real competitive advantages and some may even lead to creative destruction.

10.2.3 Network Economics

According to Varian, the economics of networks are one of the central differences between the old and the new economy: "The old industrial economy was driven by the economies of scale; the new information economy is driven by the economics of networks" (Shapiro and Varian 1999). Firms in the information economy often face highly competitive markets with volatile market shares and the threat of new or established entrants with superior technology, while firms in the old industrial economy dominated their markets with quite stable market shares.

The basic concept of network economics is positive feedback. Shapiro and Varian distinguish between real networks and virtual networks. The first one consists of physical linkages between nodes in the network such as railroad tracks. Linkages in the second type of networks are rather virtual in the sense that they are invisible to the user. Nevertheless, networks have a typical, yet crucial, economic characteristic. Their overall value as well as the value for the individual participant depends on the number of contributors in the same network. That is what Shapiro and Varian (1999) meant by positive feedback. The greater the number of people in the network the more likely it is that other participants will join, as a consequence, networks are dependent on the expectations of potential users.

Supply-side economies of scale are the basics of most industrial large scale enterprises with mass production. The idea is that the average costs of a product decrease with scale. Although such industries have high fixed costs and assets, the marginal costs decrease with the amount of output. In the case of demand-side economies of scale the average demand increases with scale. The demand curve for a network good usually shows the reverse parabolic shape as seen in Fig. 10.2. With an increasing number of adopters the willingness to pay for the good increases as well. After the network size has reached the point where the early adopters and technology friendly consumers have already purchased the good the willingness to pay decreases due to the falling willingness to pay by late adopters.

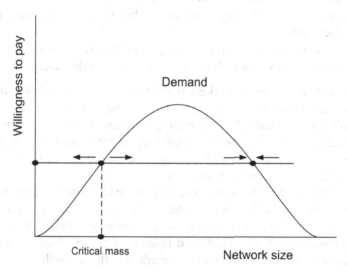

Fig. 10.2. Demand and supply for a network good. Adapted from Varian et al. (2004)

In the literature about network effects, authors distinguish between direct network effects and indirect network effects. Direct network effects are networks where the demand for a commodity or service depends on the number of people who already use it, i.e., the network size. Indirect network effects arise when the demand for a good or service depends on the availability of complementary goods or services. Industrial collaborative networking typically has many indirect networking effects.

Now this behavior may not be valid for the knowledge sharing, service proving value constellations that the AKM technology and holistic design will enable. It will therefore be necessary to involve market analysts, financial and business experts in performing new analysis of the future value constellations. In these constellations value creation and sharing is equally if not more important than costs.

Indirect network effects as opposed to direct network effects are trickier as the demand for the core service depends on the costs of both the basic service and the complementary service. Varian et al. (2004) show five possibilities to improve the situation for complementary service providers:

- Integrate: One of the vendors acquires the other to internalize the external effects
- Collaborate: The firms negotiate a revenue sharing arrangement so that one of them sets the price for the whole system
- Negotiate: Both firms can agree on cutting their prices, which could ensure rapid adoption of the complementary service
- Nurture: One firm cooperates with other firms outside their industry to reduce costs
- Commoditize: One firm attempts to motivate competition in the complementary vendor's market to push down the prices

If firms compete in markets with strong positive feedback quite often, only one competitor may emerge as the winner of the battle for establishing a standard or normative solution. Thus, those firms are well advised to select an appropriate strategy to get a head start in attracting a large number of buyers. Influencing the expectations of their customers is crucial in network services markets

Market systems in which positive feedbacks prevail tend to follow a certain pattern. In the start-up phase of a product, the number of users is still minor with a tendency to grow quickly when critical mass is reached. This phase is called Takeoff and leads to a phase of saturation when the majority of potential customers have adopted the technology (Fig. 10.3).

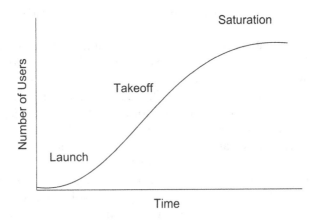

Fig. 10.3. Adoption Dynamics, from Shapiro and Varian (1999)

Instability

Network markets are often considered to be unstable meaning that multiple, incompatible technologies cannot coexist in the long term since a single standard is likely to emerge. Related to the instability of these markets is the relevance of expectations about the final size of the network. As mentioned earlier, expectations of potential consumers and suppliers about the network size and the possibly superior technology are crucial to the success of a technology.

Excess Inertia

Excess inertia is a start-up problem of new technologies that can occur when no actor is willing to adopt this technology due to the risk of high switching-costs if the technology fails to become accepted. Uncertainty about the other actor's preferences and behavior is a main reason for potential early adopters to refuse the new technology. Some economists call such an effect the penguin effect: "Penguins who must enter the water to find food often delay doing so because they fear the presence of predators. Each would prefer some other penguin to test the waters first."

Excess Momentum

Excess momentum is somewhat related to excess inertia. Just in this case the vendor or provider tries to push its technology to the market, which means that adopters are influenced by certain strategies to switch or get the new technology, although individually they would retain their old system. Farrell and Saloner (1986) identify two popular strategies by companies to push their products. First, they use low prices to reduce the switching costs, and second, firms also use predatory preannouncements to catch their customers.

Pareto-Inferior Market Results and Monopolies

Previous paragraphs showed that standardization processes in network economies may lead to a monopoly of one technology. The resulting equilibrium in these markets may be considered as Pareto-inferior to other available technologies. Moreover, Arthur (1996) states that in network economics under increasing returns there is no rule to stop market penetration like marginal costs equal marginal benefits.

Centralized vs. Decentralized Coordination

Buxmann et al. (1999) analyze the possibilities of using centralized or decentralized coordination. In centralized coordination, it is an institution that determines the best way of fulfilling the needs of all participants. So it tries to find the global optimum for the system. As users will know the individual costs of standardization as well as the costs of communication between the participants of the network, it is fairly easy to build a model to formalize this problem. The model may be formalized mathematics or model-configured by emerging methods and parameters. Considering that such a model has to include all the relevant data, it becomes obvious that such a solution might face a serious problem of complexity. So, decentralized decision-making will be helpful to solve standardization problems in networks.

In contrast to centralized coordination, in decentralized coordination, all actors in the network try to optimize their individual costs and gains. In this case the actors may have trouble in estimating the unstandardized communication and coordination costs between the other actors. It is assumed that one actor knows his own relevant costs and also knows all standardization costs of the other participants or can at least estimate them. Facing these problems it is more difficult for the individual actor to decide whether to standardize or not, because he does not know about the decisions of the others. Buxmann et al. (1999) propose a model in which one actor uses a probability function to determine the decisions of the other participants. Again an architecture-configured common view of relevant parameters may be more precise and participant friendly.

Holistic Design of Business Networks

The AKM approach has the potential to impact and change most of the principles and problems discussed. In particular, standardization plays an important role. If actors in a network intend to work together seamlessly without failures in data management or coordination, they need to establish dynamic data sharing. Although every actor should find its own interest in interoperable systems, certain questions do appear. First, which standards should be used? Which vendor is able to fulfill the needs of all participants? Second, how should the transformation be coordinated? Is there an authority within the network or an independent institution from outside which has the power to enforce the changes? These kinds of problems may appear within networks of independent firms or even between segments of large enterprises. If there is no authority, the complexity of the network exhibits prohibitive costs. Decentralized coordination adopting the service-team organizational form could be the way to go.

10.2.4 Transaction Cost Economics

Transaction Cost Economics goes back to the concept of labor division and specializing, which usually resulted in productivity boosts (Fleisch 2001). Labor division means that a task conducted by a single person is decomposed into several subtasks, each of which is assigned to a different person. Coordination is necessary to align the execution of the subtasks to produce the goods and services demanded by customers. This causes coordination costs, which is the basis for transaction cost economics. Little or no consideration is given to what could be gained in terms of concurrency and earlier delivery.

As transaction cost economics investigates the management of interactions among economic activities and the costs resulting from the related tasks, this theory is fundamental for analyzing ICT and interoperability in a cooperative context (Clemons and Row 1992). It is particularly important to note that transaction costs comprise the costs of information and communications (Picot et al. 1996).

In the theory of transaction cost economics, transaction efficiency is regarded as a major source of value, because of its capability of significant cost reductions by lowering uncertainty, complexity, information asymmetry, and small-numbers bargaining conditions. Reputation, trust, and transactional experience contribute to these cost reductions (Williamson 1975; Williamson 1979). The theory of transaction costs economics provides a framework to come to a decision on how tasks and resources should be coordinated. The two extremes are pure market coordination and hierarchical coordination. Between those extremes, there are many forms of hybrid coordination. Hybrid forms comprise all forms of coordination where hierarchy and market are mixed. Examples range from joint venture to virtual enterprises. Clemons and Row (1992) equate hybrid coordination with cooperation. The transaction costs within each of these coordination forms are a function of the degree of specificity. Specificity of a given input resource, necessary to fulfill a task, is a metric for the value loss when the resource is reallocated to another than the intended task (Picot et al. 1996).

Figure 10.4 illustrates the correlation between transaction costs and degree of specificity subject to a given coordination mechanism. All coordination forms feature a baseline of fixed transaction costs and variable costs that are a function of the degree of specificity. According to this diagram, for a given degree of specificity, there is a coordination form that minimizes transaction costs. S1 and S2 are marking the transition points from one coordination form to the other. In essence, Transaction Cost Economics suggests that specific tasks should be coordinated by vertical integration.

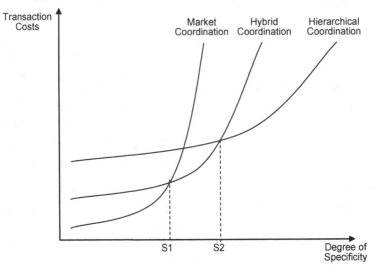

Fig. 10.4. Adoption Dynamics, from (Shapiro and Varian 1999)

This assumes that vertical integration avoids costly contractual safeguards to protect highly specific resources against opportunistic behavior.

10.3 Realization Approaches

After one year of AKM operations, we can synthesize and articulate the state of practice for industrial value networking in these two bullets:

- Networked Organizations are "Bridged Islands-of-Automation" and "Fuzzy Organizational Entities" – no ideal models exist to support coordination, collaboration, or holistic enterprise design.
- Networks are built and operated by several approaches, adapting organizational theories, management techniques, and IT infrastructures studied and implemented by industry and traditional IT vendors.

Some effort has been vested in defining the networked organization serving the "community space" in terms of organizational features, knowledge dimensions, services, and requirements. One approach may be to adopt any organizational model intended to fulfill specific requirements of a network of business entities. As shown in Fig. 10.5, the target business entities are represented by the stakeholders promoting the network services and infrastructures.

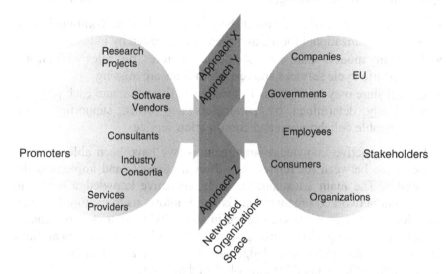

Fig. 10.5. Networked Organization approaches and influencers

Promotion of a specific approach happens through normal marketing and technology transfer channels, on the initiative of several types of organizations. Depending on the type of approach, the business entities interested in its promotion may include IT companies, for those models that strongly rely on commercial ICT platforms, service providers for models based on ASP or outsourcing, and consultants for models placing reorganization and change management requirements on the target users.

We only consider as relevant approaches that have created a significant impact on targeted user communities. Impact is testified by running businesses that actually implement the approach, either practicing it in their organization or offering it as part of their product and services.

As described in Chap. 2, a number of definitions exist for *Virtual Organization, Networked Enterprise, Extended Enterprise*, or any combination of these concepts. Most of them contain assumptions about the scope, objectives, or technical means of collaboration. We are interested in networked businesses with the following characteristics and capabilities:

- Not biased toward a certain organization model or solution
- Not dependent on any particular or proprietary IT infrastructure
- General enough to support an open active knowledge architecture

- Able to capture and share work-centric knowledge
- Able to support services composition and management

To achieve this we propose to apply a new and different holistic design approach toward networking, on the basis of the following principles:

- Networked organizations must be operational as a combination of several organizational forms, as already being tested by industry.
- The many models share a set of relevant features, but roles with clearly defined life-cycle services and responsibilities are missing.
- Each feature may be expressed as role-specific views, and each property as clearly determined by parameters and tasks, supporting open configurable collaboration and coordination services.

By using active knowledge architectures, we have been able to make associations between (or relate) the different concepts and implement the principles. The main advantage of using an active knowledge model to implement networked organizations is that it allows us to capture complex situations as work-centric knowledge in situ or with context. This renders complexity manageable through powerful visualization capabilities provided by the active knowledge architecture. It also facilitates quick visual analyses by using different colors and symbols.

The current version of the architecture is focused on visualizing the relationships among the concepts and qualitative analyses. Quantitative analyses can be supported by adding numerical values to the objects and relationships in the model, and finally adding rules to process these values. This will facilitate the configuration of networked organization workplace services. Similarly to the trust feature example, it is important to identify the requirements that have to be fulfilled to reach the desired business value. Examples of business value created by Networked Organization approaches are: increased customer satisfaction, increased sales, improved efficiency, reduced network setup and operation costs, and reduced risks in network operations.

10.4 EU Research

Much of the research being performed is based on these fragmented disciplines and activities:

- Business requirements for information technologies
- Assessment of networked organizations and value models
- Economic theories of interoperability

- Trust issues for interoperability
- SME issues for interoperability
- Business framework for interoperability
- Interoperability impact analysis model
- Future direction for business-economic aspects of enterprise interoperability

The two firsts themes are discussed in the following subsections. The other themes are discussed in ATHENA documentation. The ATHENA project adopted a holistic approach to interoperability, but chose to supply IT support by reengineering the legacy, and not by adopting a holistic approach to enterprise design and development. Three dimensions of business interoperability were considered: Policy, Business-Economic, and IT Technical. However, a fourth dimension of Knowledge Community should have been included to identify roles and responsibilities for configuring visual arenas, capturing work context, and supporting team-learning. Clarifying the relationships between these dimensions is important for setting future research directions in enterprise design and development for interoperability, reusability, and other purposes.

10.4.1 Business Requirements

Requirements distinguish between what relates to IT infrastructures and services, what relates to holistically designed enterprise knowledge architectures, and finally what related to business planning and operations.

Our analysis suggests that the need for holistic design is sector specific and closely linked to existing and future approaches to product design, future uses of IT, and future business processes. The degree of stability within a sector value-constellation is another vital factor. On this background, different sectors would have different objectives with respect to the choice of IT. This should result in different business process solutions and management, different enterprise services and different schematics (ontologies). Clearly, there is no single winning business model for the design and use of a particular product or service.

10.4.2 Assessment of Networked Organizations and Value Models

One of the results of ATHENA is a framework to assess networked organizational forms and approaches and their interoperability requirements from a business perspective. The Networked Organizations assessment framework was conceived to provide answers to a series of questions concerning network features. Now, we can state that most of them are obsolete as the active knowledge architecture inherently gives the answers to these as well as questions never discovered and articulated. Capturing and preserving work-centric contexts, enabling collaboration, coordination and consistency checking, have made all questions superfluous.

To exploit IT for the benefits of people and organizational needs means: hiding technology complexity and revealing functionality on demand; making technology very simple to use, available and affordable; providing new ICT-based applications, solutions, and services that are trusted, reliable, and adaptable to the users' context and preferences.

Within FP7, enterprise interoperability is expected to be part of the activity "ICT supporting businesses and industry," which is part of the "Applications Research" activities. Specifically, enterprise interoperability research is expected to be within the scope of the "bullet" on "new forms of dynamic networked cooperative business processes, digital ecosystems; optimized work organization and collaborative work environments."

Nowhere is there any mention of Enterprise Design and Development, or a more holistic multidimensional design approach, recognizing that the true Enterprise Integrator is work-centric knowledge and operational data.

Emphasis on Community Knowledge

The paradigm for doing business on the Internet is rapidly changing. Technologies are converging, so are markets. Markets are fluid structures. Such developments challenge the established research areas. Even more important, Europe has an unique opportunity to develop new business platforms that are not only sustainable in classic business-economic terms, but consistent with the European values that underpin our society. These business models and operational platforms will be based on increasingly interconnected and interdependent networks of enterprise roles.

Different forms of collaboration, coordination, and business control will be needed encompassing different types of innovation enabled by ICT. The current AKM platform developments can dramatically lower entry barriers and open up new markets for SMEs.

10.5 AKM Contributions

As described in Chap. 2, industrial IT exploration challenges persist, and the number of major challenges is growing. However, we now see that most of them can be solved by model-based approaches and Web-based methods, methods that consistently support holistic design and concurrent engineering. Excellent solutions for needs and demands, not worth attempting by traditional IT systems are now realizable, such as supporting holistic design and concurrent engineering of product families and eventually entire enterprise families.

Problems in handling information flows and data sharing in systems will never be solved by traditional IT thinking and software engineering. The required real-time knowledge simply cannot be captured and made part of the software system. Holistic design approaches with knowledge-growing and self-adapting services and open architectures are required, and suppliers, customers, and other stakeholders must be invited and involved on-demand by offering them tailored real-time configured Web-workplaces.

In the following, we will describe and discuss initiatives and concepts we believe should be pursued to improve on the situation.

10.5.1 Industrial Communities

Analysis of the automotive, the aerospace, and the offshore industries shows that the current usage of computing is quite often decided by community opinions and requirements to standards alone. Industrial computing can still be characterized by linking the "islands-of-automations," as illustrated in Fig. 10.6, and early phases of design projects still rely on Power-point, Visio and Excel for computing support.

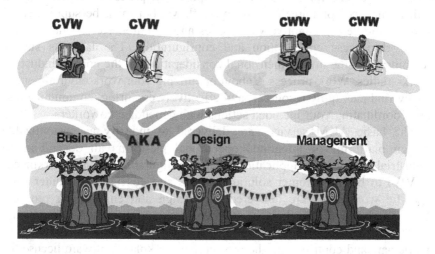

Fig. 10.6. Enterprises are integrated by Active Knowledge Architectures

Tools to capture design ideas, intent and build conceptual product models are rarely seen, and design methodologies that take a holistic knowledge approach are just being developed. A holistic design approach, an unified federated product model, and common active enterprise knowledge architectures are all dependent on a common approach to and language for visual solutions modeling. Holistic also means dynamic interaction of life-cycle roles and perspectives.

10.5.2 From Paper to Models and Knowledge Architectures

Most industrial companies that have started exploiting the AKM technology are middle size system-suppliers either to the automotive, the aerospace, or the new energy producers. Asked about what challenges they would give the highest priority they unanimously reply: "Moving from paper-based information and thinking to models and then to active knowledge architectures with configurable elements." The advantages and benefits they are looking to realize are data and knowledge sharing, proactive learning and behavior, and collaborative work execution, reducing changes, versions and errors in handling information carriers and data.

10.5.3 From Process Flows to Workspaces

The present need for top–down development of processes and flows will still be needed for logistics and object flows, but must be supplemented and by middle-out adaptive workspaces and common views, and bottom-up work-process composition and configuration. The latter is simply learning from the multidimensional considerations at the core of industrial work-studies. Work-process is about organizing your work environment to easily find and apply resources, and effectively capturing, communicating, and coordinating your intended actions with dependant coworkers.

The basic AKM services are delivered to industry as customizable design platforms or integrated operational platforms all depending on industrial sector and application area. Configurable Visual Workplaces (CVW) to build customer solution models and configure customer role-specific workplaces are delivered. As design and engineering progress Configurable Web-Workplaces (CWW) are configured on-demand and on-the-fly. This enables industrial projects to invite just anybody to participate and contribute to the project. No workplace software license fee and installation costs are paid for connecting SME's, consultants, or students.

10.5.4 One Integrated Product Model

Today most products are described by between 8 and 15 disjoint product structures created on paper or in IT application system data-models. The most familiar product structures are:

1. Arrangements or conceptual layouts to interpret requirements
2. Topological structure for defining geometric element structures
3. Functional system structures to determine properties and features
4. Geometric structures for calculating dimensions and tolerances, and defining shape
5. Material list or bills of materials (BoM), derived at stages
6. Technical product-structures to support the many engineering calculations, such as center of gravity, strength, vibrations, etc.
7. Module and part structures to plan for manufacturing and assembly variants
8. Assembly structures and part-lists
9. Maintenance and repair structures
10. Property and parameter structures to support concurrent engineering

To support market and technology variations and mass-customization, we must develop smart product family representations. These representations should exploit the capabilities and capacities of Web-based active knowledge architectures and visual techniques for proactive collaborative work, using the Web as a knowledge-sharing medium.

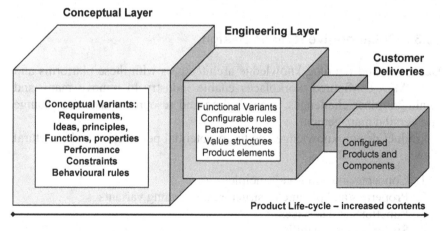

Fig. 10.7. Layers of product architecture knowledge contents

Figure 10.7 illustrates how using the AKM Approach and the CPPD Methodology, modeling adaptive product families is feasible. Different layers of knowledge representations are created. A family definition of any artifact is characterized by features and external properties such as usability, services offered, and values created with users, and the latter are often expressed as performance parameters. In contrast, industrial classes are defined by internal parameters and the design rules of the class. The leftmost representation may span community and network knowledge spaces, the middle representation spans projects with customer groups and suppliers, and the customized product is delivered in customer projects.

The conceptual product family layer, with parameters and rules for defining the product conceptual architecture, and the artifact language, concretize the AKA structures and elements of the product family. The parameters and rules for all layers of product family descriptions are represented as configurable elements in the active knowledge architecture. Conceptual and functional design and engineering should provide services to define these properties and parameter-trees, the methods to give values to them, methods to aggregate and propagate values, and to compose rules and clusters of pragmatic, empiric, and technical rules. Designing and engineering market variants, varying in services, functions, and properties, in parameter values, and variant and design rule composition, is possible. The challenges will be to manufacture and service these products. Finally on the far right we illustrate the possibility of fully automating customized design.

10.5.5 Collaborative Holistic Design

Designing and building knowledge architectures with these platforms and their AKA-configured workplaces enable industry to remove many and minimize other challenges, such as time and resource-consuming change and version management.

Product design knowledge has these potential perspective and structural views:

1. Concepts and solution principles
2. Properties and parameter structures, including variants
3. Functions and services
4. Systems and capabilities
5. Form and features
6. Materials and appearance
7. Location and spatial relations

8. Environmental aspects
9. Costs and economic concerns
10. Legislation and standards
11. Production and maintenance
12. Life-cycle and end-of-life considerations

Today this knowledge is dispersed and not easily and precisely expressed, shared, applied, and managed. Many stakeholders are spending huge amounts of money to maintain huge amounts of overlapping information added to documents and models just to create meaningful context.

10.5.6 Data and Knowledge Management

In present IT systems the same properties are redefined as disjoint parameters many times by different disciplines in each of many disjoint product structures. So there are no common shared parameter-structures, no role-specific parameters and value sets to support concurrency, value aggregation, and balancing of values across disciplines. To describe configurable product families, designers of CAD systems for tankers, as early as the 1970s, introduced different variant parameters for defining the longitudinal and transverse steel structures by their function, shape, and structural position. Now to meet current demands variants should be by performance parameters, constraints, functions, and system and structural features. Family variants depend on both metric and logical rules, and the rules must themselves be configurable, as rules do change with parameter values. Now let us better define the various types of design parameters:

- Performance Parameters are measures used to evaluate alternative design solutions that users notice, feel, and care for. They can express the value of a given property, defining a demand or a constraint, such as acceleration. The user may be any customer in the complete supply chain and even the configurable components developer.
- Functional and Structural Parameters express capabilities and services of the product in use, such as turning radius. These parameters are often derived from requirements and have values that through design rules change the functional composition and structures of products and their systems.
- System Design Parameters are both internal and external parameters of the product, calculated or determined by engineering methods and by aggregation. Designers and engineers can directly influence a business decision through the values of design parameters. Each engineering

discipline must have a separate set of parameters to support concurrency.

- Component Design Parameters are internal parameters of the product components, most often calculated or determined by technical methods. They express characteristics of a design directly influenced by design parameter value. Methods should have separate sets of parameters to support concurrent engineering.
- Variant Parameters are logical parameters used by pragmatic and logical rules and expressions defining configuration rules. They should all be defined in the conceptual layer, as they will influence the choice of systems, definition of product structures, and the working methods and maybe even empiric formulae for engineering and configuring systems.

10.5.7 Project Design

All projects we have studied and been invited into have enforced our conviction that projects just like product families must be designed and involve many more stakeholders before an entrepreneur is given the responsibility to build whatever makes most profit for him. Let us take an example from urban planning and construction, illustrated in Fig. 10.8, and remember that at the conceptual layer we have to take a holistic approach to the project, implying that we also have to consider the community knowledge space and the project's impact on society and the environment at large. Now how many stakeholders are involved, and how many should have been involved before solutions for the areas and sites are decided?

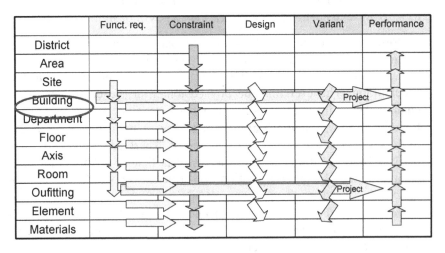

Fig. 10.8. Urban development projects embrace many layers of knowledge

The decision to develop an urban area into a housing complex, industrial estate, or a playground implies that we have to extend our concept of product to embrace more layers of knowledge and involve many more stakeholders. Clearly this is not achievable by today's approach to Systems Engineering and software development. Solutions to support such projects must progressively develop shared knowledge architectures and methodologies to support visual arenas of communication and consensus making. Agile knowledge architecture configured approaches will yield solutions with great flexibility, interoperability, predictability, and accountability

10.5.8 Changes in Management

Value chains, shops, and networking have been discussed since the turn of the millennium, but none of these organizational concepts have considered the ultimate business requirement that most all business services must be adaptable and be configured to the specific customer delivery project, and be managed for life-cycle repetition and support. The configuration and life-cycle management have to be performed by the industrial delivery team and not by IT providers to the delivery team. This situation requires the introduction of a new organizational form.

10.6 Building Industrial Platforms

To meet the challenges described in Chap. 2, and the needs expressed in the EU I2010 doctrine and by leading customers, AKM has developed a holistic design approach. In Sect. 10.1 of the doctrine, under the second pillar, it is stated: "a new era of e-business solutions is coming, based on integrated ICT solutions, secure web-services and collaboration tools to raise worker productivity."

Indeed, a new era is coming, but not just for e-Business, but for all interactive systems, and in particular for systems supporting design, problem-solving, and proactive team-learning. However, as one of the pioneers of Norwegian computing once said: "You can buy knowledge, but can't buy competence and skill, transforming personal assets to corporate values. You have to work hard to earn it"! In the context of AKM, this means that we have to model and experiment, reiterate and learn by doing before we are competent enough to get it right first time.

So, if we cannot buy ready-made knowledge-architected platforms for our core business the only alternative must be to engage in developing them. In Fig. 10.9, we illustrate the current state-of-practice and how we

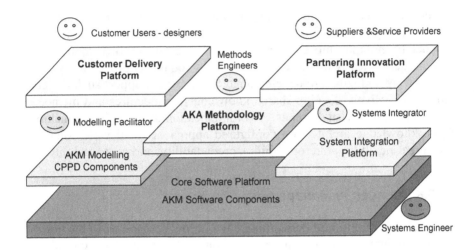

Fig. 10.9. Building layers of reflective methodic and operational knowledge

collaborate with customers and partners to adapt methodology platforms and develop operational platforms.

AKM delivers a core platform of generic workplaces and services. The generic CVW workplace is used to model, adapt, and extend existing methodology and use-case descriptions to form a customized AKA platform. This methodology and infrastructure-integrated platform, denoted as AKA methodology platform in Fig. 10.9, is further adapted and extended to serve specific market and customer platform solutions. As innovations and customer delivery projects are performed, best practices and best-business deliveries are gathered and analyzed to update the other platforms. This gathering, updating, and upgrading of methodology and innovation platforms is performed by workplaces configured from a platform as depicted in Fig. 10.10. The behavior of this platform is somehow related to performing analyses on a data-warehouse to support performance data driven continuous improvement.

The AKA, Partnering Innovation, and Customer Delivery Platforms must be developed in a teaming effort applying the IRTV language, capturing POPS, and other spaces and the relevant aspects and views. Enterprise design and knowledge architecting needs a visual language of higher granularity than any operational knowledge element it needs to capture from any aspect in any context. The language and its supporting models and templates, implementing and integrating methodologies, must evolve in detail with the product, system, and process design intent and

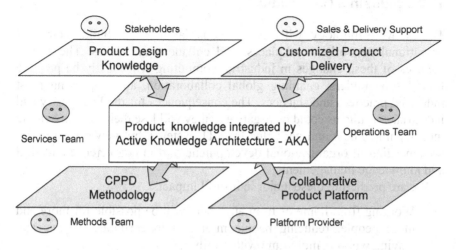

Fig. 10.10. Holistic approach to customer product family design

contents. The availability of knowledge content decides the amount of modeling work required and the time to generating prototype solutions.

The significance of the C3S3P and the CPPD methodologies, and of modeling these and other industrial methodologies using the IRTV language cannot be overemphasized, without them the AKA and its contents would be rubbish and simply would not work.

10.7 Impacts and Consequences

The impacts and consequences of fully implementing and deploying the AKM technology could have some "destructive effects," as defined by Schumpeter; an example would be the removal of costly off-the-shelf IT systems. However, we believe that the industry, the public and the sciences will harvest major benefits by exploiting knowledge technology and IT for improved human creativity and more pragmatic learning. Effects already validated include: enabling knowledge sharing, reducing IT costs, developing collaboration and proactive learning, and bringing scientists closer to industrial and public practices, thereby increasing their value contributions to society. We are turning the Web into a visual medium for improved human learning, creativity, communication, and collaboration.

10.7.1 Industrial Communities

The AKM technology will enable industrial users to build their own operational networks, workplaces, and collaboration arenas. The consequences of these changes in industrial computing will mostly be positive for all stakeholders, enabling global collaboration, and improving most industrial practices and sciences. The consequences for the IT industry and industrial consultants could be negative as they will lose their roles in helping industry implement and get value from IT systems, but new opportunities are emerging in organizational development, and in competence and skill and knowledge management.

We are predicting these major industrial impacts:

1. Working from home or from anywhere will be possible for more and more people, reducing people migration to corporate offices, and leaving workers more time with family
2. SMEs will be able to join communities and industry programs without heavy IT investments
3. Services enabling conceptual holistic design will lead to better quality products and services, and knowledge repositories that can be exploited by most stakeholders
4. The capabilities to share community knowledge will invite the 34–36 interest organizations such as SCOR and PMI to model and provide their methodologies as context sensitive work supporting views
5. Industrial postgraduate education
6. Systems Engineering
7. Organizational Learning

10.7.2 Business Economics

As explained in the section on Networked Economics, there are many theories available for how to invest and cut costs in IT investments, but little work has been performed on the economics on knowledge sharing communities. In all the theories mentioned earlier, the focus is on controlling costs, and very little support is given to measuring and validating values. The future direction of business-economic research needs to be established with reference to added values through sharing knowledge rather than by transaction costs incurred by rigid IT systems.

An active knowledge architecture covering the early design stages has the capabilities to implement all this and cut time and costs by factors.

10.7.3 Industrial Research

The ATHENA consortium concluded: *"Interoperability is the main ally of ICT in the coming years. Europe should invest in interoperability development and leverage the considerable research results expected from ATHENA and other initiatives to target the world market. However, interoperability is not an isolated discipline. ICT is an enabler and not an end in itself."* This is just an extract of a three page conclusion and roadmap.

We are not necessarily disagreeing with these statements, but to us interoperability is a property of any enterprise, and is first and foremost driven by shared knowledge of goals, methodologies, achieved results, and resources available to achieve expected results. This means collaborative business and innovative enterprises and networks must be designed by visual modeling of spaces and aspects, applying the IRTV language, and storing the knowledge elements in an AKA. It also means that more research should be performed on how to capture and represent pragmatic logic. Most best-practice work processes represent just one of the four workspace dimensions that must be captured as IRTV modeled elements.

10.7.4 Scientific Research

Many sciences got a boost when the computer was first introduced, and when microphotography and nanotechnology entered the scene. We believe that cross-fertilization among sciences is hindered today because a huge gap in and lack of common descriptions of problems, approaches to describe them, and potential solutions persist.

Visual modeling using the IRTV language and the C3S3P methodology has the potential to describe any role in industry, and we believe this is also true for the public as well as any field of science. Now, imagine what could happen if all these experts could share work-centric knowledge described in a common problem-solving visual language. Another general impact from the AKM technology would be convergence of scientific concepts and disciplines

10.7.5 Education and Training

College, high-school, and university education stand to benefit greatly by the foreseen development. Students are already the dominant user category on the Web, and searching for information is about to be replaced by searching for additional knowledge.

The many educational and professional training challenges described must be met and fulfilled within the next ten years, but with escalating innovation new challenges will always emerge. Most major industries are aware of the challenges described and emerging, such as the need for more industrially oriented graduate education, but currently many companies find themselves paralyzed by the complexity of the situation.

10.7.6 Future Directions

We are now in the broadband era, extending the communication bandwidths among individual workers, enterprises, and creating global communities. This is giving rise to new opportunities for collaborative development of harmonized services, product families, processes and systems, leading to rapid prototyping, wide experimentation, faster time-to-market, and new business constellations.

The scope of enterprise design is broadening. We are talking about new infrastructures, new platforms, new ways of procuring and provisioning services and utilities, and new ways of managing knowledge, and competences and skills. This is a green-garden for innovation, and for involving people and sciences that never earlier have been exposed to each other's active knowledge, so inventions are expected to flourish.

Scientific excellence alone is not sufficient for bringing about innovation. The potential impact of research needs to be clearly identified in business, economic and societal terms, which are critical for industry buy-in for enabling exploitation. The business benefits for inventing new techniques and approaches and the value proposition of such techniques and approaches for the intended users need to be clearly articulated.

To validate the possibilities with the AKM technology, we are working to launch at least one innovation project in each industrial sector. These innovation projects will have to be staffed by leading industrial practitioners to produce the expected quality results, such as best practice contents of active knowledge architectures. Through holistic design we are addressing enterprise interoperability in a way that is meaningful and understandable to the business world and individual enterprises. Enterprise interoperability in this sense is an intersection of business, economic and technology knowledge and innovation, embedded within a legal and regulatory environment.

State-of-the-art of markets, as opposed to state-of-the-art of technologies will be more important for innovation and business. Clear vision of how markets, sectors and firms develop with reference to societal and environmental goals will gain growing importance. Industry differences around the globe will diminish.

10.8 Outlook

An over-riding focus is the management of innovation and creation of value in the full cycle of Knowledge Architecture and ICT research, from ideas generation to operational product experience gathering to innovation of improved products and services reengineering and reuse.

The paradigm for doing collaborative business electronically is rapidly changing. New scientific concepts and disciplines, such as knowledge architectures, business-economic models, as well as societal models are redefining the context for doing business. Technologies are converging, so are markets. Markets are fluid structures of diversified customer-groups, where customer satisfaction is everything and changing. These developments challenge the established structures. Firms have an unique opportunity to develop new business models that are not only sustainable in classic business-economic terms, but by creating stronger relations and alliances. These business models are based on increasingly interconnected and interdependent networks of enterprises with different forms of collaboration and encompassing different types of innovation enabled by ICT.

Enterprise Interoperability has come a long way in European research. The key question is whether the research work in the area will move forward to embrace the broader developments that are breaking through in related and neighboring domains and disciplines.

11 Toward Enterprise Visual Scenes

Enterprise Visual Scenes (EVS) can provide users with modeling approaches, user environments, and solutions for knowledge creation, sharing, rendering, engineering and work management and for meeting most of the industrial challenges discussed in Chap. 2.

We will now look around the next bends to uncover the potential for further developments in how we envision modeling, using, and developing enterprise knowledge as visual scenes, exploring 3D and 4D model rendering, and visual navigation and interaction.

We will first recap some of the main principles of our thinking. We will next present some existing applications exploring 3D and 4D rendering and finally present visions for where and how to develop and apply improved modeling, navigation, visualization, and analyses techniques. We will end the chapter looking at extending the way of visualizing knowledge even further to three-dimensional immersive environments.

11.1 Main Principles for Enterprise Visual Scenes

As described in Sect. 1.6 and to be explained in more detail in Chap. 13, an enterprise has many knowledge spaces. Most of these spaces can be implemented as EVS by developing and applying the AKM technology. Visual scenes are ensembles of views to interrelated active knowledge models supporting archetypical work in an organization.

We see four major enterprise visual scenes required to continuously innovate, operate, evolve and transform, and govern and manage future enterprises. In addition, there will be a multitude of smaller, more project and task specific scenes to support situated project work. The four major scenes are illustrated in Fig. 11.1.

Each scene extends uses and manages different elements of an operational AKA. Each scene has a specific purpose, specific approach, has different methodology models associated, and has design models delivering different workspace solutions and results.

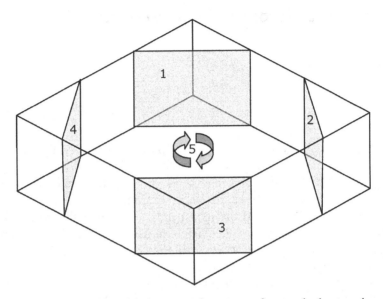

Fig. 11.1. The four visual scenes of any type of networked enterprise

As described in Chap. 1 the four main Visual Scenes for future enterprising are briefly defined as:

1. The Innovative scene where focus is to invent, update, reuse, design, configure, engineer, and learn
2. The Operations scene where focus is to plan, orchestrate, operate, generate, adapt, extend, manage, and terminate
3. The Governance scene where focus is to govern, monitor, decide, assign, measure, validate and strategize
4. The Evolutions scene where the focus is to analyze, reengineer, change, transform, align, and manifest

Each scene has specific roles with reflective views and recursive tasks and work processes, and the scenes are themselves mutually reflective and recursively interdependent. This assumes that they share the same AKA work environment descriptions. So models of work environments and workplace settings and behavior are important contributions to the AKA contents.

11.1.1 The Powers of Visual Scenes

There is a need to enhance the way people think about computing. A need to extend enterprise modeling from being a tool-based exercise for experts, isolated from operational business to enable visual environments for a new styles of computing supported by active knowledge architectures.

Visual patterns, scenes and languages, have at least six properties that natural language and current software methods will never acquire. We believe these properties are fundamental in driving a new approach to holistic enterprise design. The AKM approach and visual scenes technologies will enhance product and process design, and systems engineering, enabling solutions to the challenges facing industry and IT providers:

1. Being able to collapse life-cycles by removing the stow-piping, i.e., play with abstractions of the time-dimension, removing the phases of material and document flows
2. Providing work environments and methods for concurrently evolving concepts, content, context, and actions
3. Correlation of conceptual views (metaviews), several content and functional views, and finally contextual views, and their dependencies, becoming independent on predefined typed object templates
4. Defining and applying business and working services and rules that are valid in given contexts and for limited parameter value sets
5. Performing innovative work, and being able to create artifacts, concepts, and properties, and metamodels by executing tasks
6. Supporting work execution and proactive learning on workplaces and in visual scenes for role-playing, dry-runs, and experimentation

When we are able to support these properties then we are closer to truly supporting design, problem-solving, and organizational team learning.

11.2 Three-Dimensional Model Applications in Industry

Most industries have since years used 3D models for different spatial analysis and for communicating design solutions to customers and engineering In Scandinavia a research project entitled Geometric Product Models (GPM) was executed as early as 1978–1980 to investigate the suitability of geometric entities as object structures for representing and storing life-cycle product knowledge. The project included leading industrial expertise from maritime, aerospace, and outfitting industries.

The conclusions were unanimous; – *geometric object structures are not suitable for capturing and representing product or enterprise knowledge.*

Still many ongoing projects and entire communities are doing just that. The main reasons given were: Geometric structures and parameters, including topology, are outcomes from design and engineering, as any other product structure or model, and do not in any way support the conceptual and functional system layers, so important for early design. Now we can add; geometric product structures are just one knowledge dimension. However, geometric spatial rendering is great for visualization meeting needs for verification and validation and for communicating with nontechnical stakeholders.

11.2.1 Early Virtual Reality Experiments

The first virtual reality software was available around 1992, and the Metis company had a test project with MCI Inc. in Colorado, US, where the experiment was to test the usability of the Virtual Reality (VR) 3D space to navigate, execute, and manage traffic and maintenance of their telecom network. The test project gave some encouraging results, but an operational solution was to our knowledge never built.

The system was modeled as a series of knowledge dimensions captured in submodels and planar one-dimensional object views, which is the industrial standard. One model would typically describe customer locations supporting 3D VR navigation to locate the various MCI installations, while a related model would describe the MCI services installed, and a third model would typically capture the history of events calling for repair and maintenance. Clicking on the UK container in the customer model would open a more detailed virtual space of the UK. In this space all MCI UK customer where objects and clicking on one customer would allow you to fly-in to say its premises in Manchester.

This test project illustrated very well the interaction on the VR software and the knowledge models built to capture the logic and functionality of the desired solution. VR components were integrated as any other method or software component by modeling the components as properties of metamodels.

11.2.2 BIM Models

The international architecture, engineering, construction, and building societies started, around 1995, a major coordinated effort to standardize terminology, information and data formats, and the different building processes creating, using and managing the data formats and the information terms. The International Alliance for Interoperability (IAI 2007) has since grown to more than 600 member companies.

The IAI services are delivered as Building Information Models or Modeling (BIM). BIM is founded on three standards, governed by the IAI world organization. More standard approaches and methods are being worked on. To avoid getting lost in details IAI members have coined the term building SMART to brand their approaches, methods and standards (Fig. 11.2).

Fig. 11.2. Examples of input and output views from a BIM

The following sections describe the three cornerstones of BIM:

Information Framework

A framework for representing construction information, enabling information to be understood, extended and used as illustrated in Fig. 11.3. This expresses the key ideas of building SMART; an approach that takes building information modeling further into an active information environment through the application of dictionaries (via International Framework for Dictionaries – IFD, see later, process maps (via the Information Delivery Manual – IDM, see later) and knowledge (via business rules) over a standard global schema (in this case, the IFC model or information schema).

The Framework comprises a series of components that interact with each other including:

- A standard global schema
- A dictionary of terms for property definition
- Standard and user-defined property sets that extend the global schema and support product libraries
- Functional parts that define reusable units of information from the global schema
- Exchange requirements that provide subsets of the global schema to support business processes
- Business rules that control and validate the use of exchange requirements
- Process maps that enable identification of exchange requirements, describe how they operate together, and provide a basis for identifying reference processes in construction

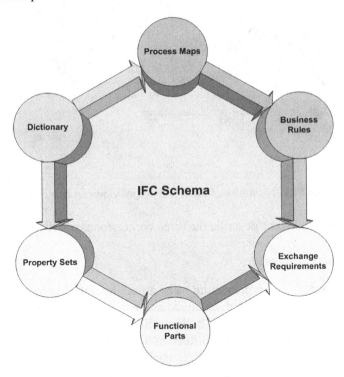

Fig. 11.3. Main components of the BIM information framework

In addition to the components, the framework proposes a layered structure that enables elaboration of the components to meet particular needs and to support concepts of validation and quality assurance.

Four information layers are proposed as illustrated in Fig. 11.4:

- A layer of standards in which global standards are defined and applied
- An enterprise layer supports extensions of the global standards. In this context, an enterprise may be a national, regional, local, project, or even organizational requirement
- A user layer that expresses how the framework components should be used in practice
- An assessment layer provides for checkable constraints and rules for validation of information

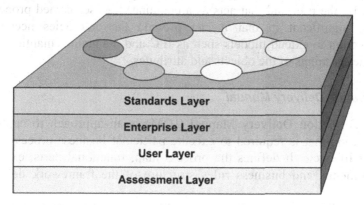

Fig. 11.4. Layers within the information framework

International Framework for Dictionaries

The International Framework for Dictionaries (IFD) is an international effort that is developing around the proposed ISO12006-3:2007 standard and encompasses major initiatives in Norway, Netherlands, The United States, and Canada. It provides the dictionary component of the framework described earlier.

IFD provides a flexible structure for managing multiple ontologies. It supports ontologies in multiple languages and multiple structures to coexist within the same library. By adding an ontology to IFD, the ontology becomes mapped to every other ontology within the library. That will in turn enable automatic translation of the concepts within the particular ontology as well as giving each of the terms a globally unique identifier (GUID). The GUID will not be visible for the end user of the ontologies, but will perform a vital role in any automatic processing of the information. While a term in a particular ontology is unique within that ontology, adding a GUID will assure that the term is understood also outside the given ontology. The IFD GUIDs will in other words perform a similar role in identifying terms or concepts as a social security number or passport number has in identifying people. The GUID allows a concept to be defined in multiple languages and using synonyms, while still being able to recognize as being the same concept.

The IFD repository provides a significant resource for standard information models such as IFC. The IFC model provides an ontological framework for information within the construction industry but intentionally does not try to explicitly model every type of object that may be used in construction. Instead, it enables user extension of the model through a "property set" metaschema. A property set is an object that is named by the user and that acts as a container for user named properties. IFD is significant in that it can provide the ontologies needed by construction to extend models such as IFC and maintain semantic control over the meanings of the objects and attributes.

Information Delivery Manual

The Information Delivery Manual (IDM) is an approach to capturing information that is required to execute particular business processes in a project lifecycle. It defines the process map, functional parts, exchange requirements, and business rules structure of the framework described earlier.

To use BIM effectively the quality of communication between different participants in the construction process needs significant improvement. If the information required is available when it is needed and the quality of information is satisfactory, the construction process will itself be significantly improved. For this to happen, there must be a common understanding of the building processes, and of the information needed for and produced by projects.

IDM aims to identify the discrete processes undertaken within building construction, the information required for their execution, and the results of that activity. For each of these "information exchange requirements" it will specify the following:

- Where a process fits and why it is relevant
- Who are the actors creating, consuming, and benefiting from the information
- What is the information created and consumed
- How the information should be supported by software solutions

Processes that are "exchange requirements" (Fig. 11.5) within IDM result from common specification as business process objects. IDM-based exchange requirements can operate within the OWL-based process ontology defined within Inteligrid (2007).

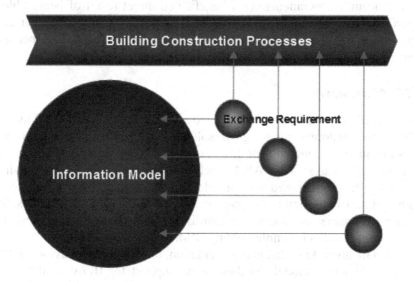

Fig. 11.5. The role of the IDM is exchanging the right information

The Changing Paradigm

BIM is a new approach to describing and displaying the information required for the design, construction, and operation of constructed facilities. It can bring together the numerous threads of different information used in construction into a single operating environment – reducing, and often eliminating, the need for the many types of paper document currently in use.

BIM is rapidly changing the way in which organizations are doing business. This is a worldwide phenomenon, based on anticipated benefits. In a recent article (Riskus 2007), it was reported that *"almost one-half (46 percent) of firms with over $5 million in gross billings had acquired BIM software."* In respect of international work, it was also reported that *"35 percent of firms with an international scope of practice have acquired BIM software, BIM may simplify overseas projects, as it allows for easy transmission of detailed information quickly over long distances."* This is as opposed to reports in previous years that indicated more than 90% of all work in this industry sector being 2D CAD based. Although these figures are reported from US practice, they are also considered to be applicable to European practice, which is generally held to be in advance.

However, for organizations that are using BIM, the biggest benefit being seen so far is in enhancing project quality through fewer change orders and more accurate documents. This benefit is a direct result of being able to perform multiple analyses and produce the various documents needed from the single BIM, and information will be more available through increased interoperability and process collaboration.

BIM Assessment

BIM implements shape variants, as extended object-oriented CAD models, these are customer predesigned solutions, and the IDM is extremely document flow oriented. The IFC model is a static structure lacking most of the capabilities of an AKA, such as context-sensitive work environments. The product structures modeled by ontologies and CAD do not support holistic design at the conceptual and functional system layers. Still many companies producing standardized houses and constructions may gain great benefits by implementing BIM.

IAI talk about knowledge representation, but we prefer to associate BIM with information models as there is no support for IRTV modeling. So there are no reflective views, recursive tasks, repetitive roles and workplaces, and replicable templates and environments.

The BIM is a very good specification and starting point for building an Active knowledge Architecture, truly buildingSMART.

11.2.3 NASA Concurrent Design

Developing rovers for Mars is by any stretch of the imagination a very complex and challenging task. NASA and Jet Propulsion Laboratory (JPL) realized this, and also realized that the traditional way of working with meetings and following office work would not cut it. They had to look for new ways of working together. The answer: Highly integrated and permanent design teams working in focused sessions in dedicated work arenas.

In 1996 a team at JPL counting some of the finest scientists and engineers started to refine and implement the Concurrent Design method.

The Concurrent Design approach is conducted in sessions. A session may last about 3.5 h, and a set of sessions will typically be planned and set up to solve a specific task, such as: the generation of a study. Given the short duration of a session, it becomes possible to include the "customer" (project manager), internal experts from design, planning, and operations; as well as external contractors in these sessions. The sessions are conducted in a dedicated work arena. Session participants may take part either through physically being present in the work arena or through video or telephone. Video has been used very successfully for involving operations experts from the off-shore oil and gas platforms.

In the work-arena, all participants have a desk and their own networked computer. Each participant will have access to the same tools on this computer as they have access in their office. The participants will, therefore, be able to perform near real-time analysis, and 3D design and simulations, while they are physically located in the work arena. The set of tools will depend on the problem to be solved. Each discipline will be encouraged to utilize sophisticated tools early on in the design/planning phases.

Six wall screens are located on three of four walls in the work arena. All computers in the work arena can be dynamically displayed on any of these screens. This makes it possible to see input from many people in the work arena at the same time and ensure that everybody in the work arena is on "the same page." Participants in a session will include the team members, the facilitator, external experts, and the customer "the decision maker." External experts may be physically present or participate through telephone or video. The dynamics between the facilitator and team will function very similar to that between a conductor and an orchestra. The decision maker "customer" will during the session make the required decisions and adjust requirements and directions to effectively help that team and facilitator home in on a preferred problem solution.

Concurrent Design Assessment

Concurrent Design implements and uses extended object-oriented CAD models and real world models in 3D and 4D spaces to primarily capture life-cycle knowledge from either outer space or from subsea environments.

This is a very interesting approach, but we think calling it Concurrent Design is stretching it quite a bit. This is using CAD models extended with data capture and visualization services in real and virtual spaces.

11.2.4 Maritime Applications

The oil and gas industry has created advanced 3D visualization related to building and operating offshore installations. Currently, a lot of the exploration is for underwater installations, and one could have virtual installations where you "drive" a ROV (remote operated vehicle) on the bottom of the ocean (Fig. 11.6).

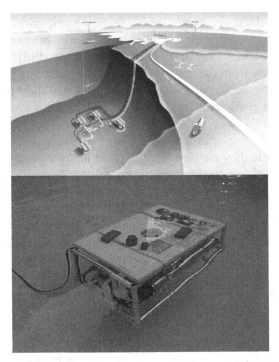

Fig. 11.6. *Above*: Underwater installations. *Below*: ROV

When constructing ships, in addition to the ships themselves, models of the actual ships could be combined with engineering models and potentially also conceptual models of ships. Below is illustrated one possible approach to this. Let us say that you choose the ship to the left. From this, one can get other depictions and models of the ship, e.g., information about stability or how the internal arrangements are made (Fig. 11.7).

11.3 Nonindustrial Applications

Computer games are virtual enterprises. Not very productive or ethical in their behavior, but nevertheless their use of spatial graphics is impressive, and is paving the way for other applications.

11.3.1 Virtual Environments

Environments being used for computer games are also being taken into use for more "serious" computing (also termed "serious gaming"). Although environments such as Second Life is getting increased focus, projects are using similar technologies for enhancing applications within the public sector e.g., Virtual Canada (2005), and lately, Virtual Trøndelag (John Krogstie's home county). Second Life is an Internet-based virtual world that came to international attention via mainstream news media in late 2006 and early 2007. Developed by Linden Lab, a downloadable client program enables its users, called "Residents," to interact with each other through motional avatars, providing an advanced level of a social network service combined with general aspects of a metaverse. Residents can explore, meet other Residents, socialize, participate in individual and group activities, create and trade items (virtual property) and services from one another.

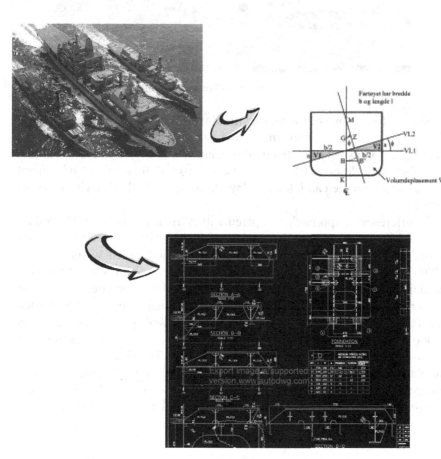

Fig. 11.7. Combination of different representational forms

Fig. 11.8. 3D-buildings (Toronto Royal York Hotel)

Second Life is one of the many virtual worlds that have been inspired by the cyberpunk literary movement, and particularly by Neal Stephenson's novel Snow Crash. The stated goal of Linden Lab is to create a world like the Metaverse described by Stephenson, a user-defined world of general use in which people can interact, play, do business, and otherwise communicate.

A difference in approach compared with Virtual Trøndelag is that rather than a Metaverse, we are in (variants of) the existing universe. Virtual Trøndelag is basing the approach on another project called Virtual Canada (2005). The project was launched in March 2005. With Virtual Canada, participants are meant to enter a 3D world in which one could choose an avatar and travel, explore, play, and learn. Virtual Canada distinguished itself by its rich content on diversity and the ability for users, such as schools, to contribute their own stories. Figure 11.8 indicates how an environment of this sort can look like. In Virtual Trøndelag, one looks at a similar concept combining two-dimensional maps with three-dimensional environments and landscapes (Fig. 11.9). It is also possible to combine the existing scenery with proposed new buildings and building contents.

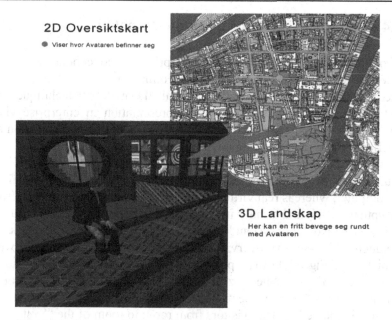

Fig. 11.9. Combined 2D and 3D representation in virtual Trøndelag

In addition to going around in these types of mixed virtual/real worlds, one can arrange meetings virtually, staging a scene for a potential role-play (or a real meeting as in Fig. 11.10).

Fig. 11.10. Virtual meetings in virtual Trøndelag

11.4 Real Virtuality and Augmented Reality

Although most modeling so far has been primarily conceptual, we see the modeling of enterprise visual scenes becoming more concrete. Abstract conceptualizations known from traditional 2D modeling techniques will most likely vanish. Thus linking the representation in enterprise visual scenes to more concrete virtual representations of e.g. the organization and its offices, plants, and working environments is a next natural step.

On one extreme, we have what we can term "real virtuality". In virtual reality we try to represent something real (a human say) virtually in the computer, whereas real virtuality means taking a virtual structure (say a conceptual model) and bring it into the real world. A very concrete example of this is called "the system" (Systemet) in Ringve botanic garden in Trondheim, Norway. An overview of the conceptual structure is shown in the picture of Fig. 11.11. The popular name for the systematic division of the Ringve gardens is "the maze"; and rightly so, as the collection consist of as many as 50 compartments walled by hedges of alpine currant. The openings in the hedges lead visitors from room to room of the "System," at the same time as the hedges prevent from seeing the plants hidden in the adjacent spaces.

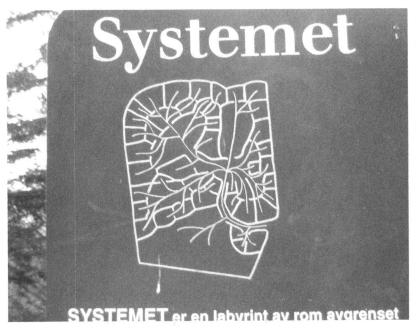

Fig. 11.11. Sign in Ringve botanic garden at the entrance to the System

The maze is organized by classification of higher plants; each of the 50 spaces is dedicated to an Order, embracing selected species from representative genera and families. The placement of the spaces and the links between them identify probable evolutionary lines and relationships. The first plants you meet on entering the maze are the pteridophytes, represented by ferns, club mosses, and horsetails. These plants reproduce by spores, and are the oldest group of surviving higher plants. Then comes a room with gymnosperms, which make seeds not enclosed by fruit, such as the conifers; the first gymnosperms arose about 270 million years ago. All the other spaces of the maze contain the angiosperms, which make seeds and fruit, and these include everything that laymen call "flowering plants." These outcompeted most of the older plant groups and have dominated the Earth for the last 60–70 million years. There are now more than 250,000 species of angiosperms, or about 95% of all higher plants. The plants classified as the most primitive are gathered in the center of the maze, from where you can follow different evolutionary lines to the more advanced families (Fig. 11.12).

Now, studying this botanic order of families may be useful for ordering product and enterprise families. These families are defined by their many diverse requirements, by design principles, and performance parameters, which is expected product or enterprise goals to be met.

Fig. 11.12. Picture from the middle of the System, looking upwards

In most cases, our models are not as well-defined as the one's made real in this example (Although our knowledge of this part of the world (botany) is developing, if this is why part of the system is currently undergoing major changes, we are not sure about). On the one hand, this kind of "creation in the world" also has severe limitations when it comes to create personalized views obviously. On the other hand, we find other examples for more efficient ways of making our models real. One such development is what is known as metal and plastic printing.

11.4.1 Metal and Plastic Printing

The metal printing process (MPP) is aimed at developing the equivalent of a high-speed photocopier that produces three-dimensional objects from powder material. This technique is based upon the commercially proven technology and patents of high-speed photocopiers that use photo-masking and electrostatic attraction. The MPP technique uses the same fundamental functions to build solid objects on a layer-by-layer basis. Layers of powder are generated by attracting the metal or ceramic powder to a charged photo-receptor (PR) under the influence of an electrostatic field. The attracted layer is deposited on a building table where it is consolidated. The process is repeated layer-by-layer until the three-dimensional object is formed and consolidated. Different powders (various building powders and support) in the same layer and a progressive change from one material to another (functional graded materials) will be offered with the MPP technology. The metal printing process will offer processing of entire layers with the final material of the object. When the model is used in this way (and you can create numerous copies in real life, based on the same model), there is an almost philosophical question: What is most "real?" The original model or one of the numerous physical copies?

11.4.2 Augmented Reality

One approach in what can be looked upon as a middle ground, and which is also often used in connection to virtual reality, is augmented reality (AR). In the Virtual Trøndelag case, this would be to have the virtual reality presentation (e.g., the future plan of the city of Trondheim) available as an overlay to what you see when walking around in Trondheim. AR is a field of computer research, which deals with the combination of real world and computer generated imagery. At present, most AR research is concerned with the use of live video, digitally processed and augmented by generative computer graphics. Advanced research includes the use of motion tracking data, fictitious marker recognition using machine vision, and the construction of environments containing any number of sensors and actuators. AR has clear connections with the ubiquitous computing (UC) and wearable computers domains. Weiser (1991) stated that "embodied virtuality," the original term he used before coining "ubiquitous computing," intended to express the exact opposite to the concept of virtual reality. Note that Weiser's concept is somewhat different from what we termed real virtuality. The most important distinction to make between AR and UC is that UC does not focus on the disappearance of conscious and intentional interaction with an information system as much as AR does. UC systems such as pervasive computing devices usually maintain the notion of explicit and intentional interaction, which often blurs in typical AR work such as Azuma (1997). When compared with UC, Azuma's definition is more focused and covers a subset of AR's original goal, but it has come to be understood as representing the whole domain of AR: AR is an environment that includes both virtual reality and real-world elements. For instance, an AR user might wear translucent goggles; through these, he could see the real world, as well as computer-generated images projected on top of that world. Azuma defines an AR system as one that

- combines real and virtual images
- is interactive in real time
- is represented in 3D

Examples for Current Applications of AR

- Support with complex tasks, in assembly, maintenance, surgery, etc.:
  - By inserting additional information into the field of view (for example, a mechanic getting labels displayed at parts of a system and getting operating instructions)
  - By visualization of hidden objects (during medical surgery as a virtual view, based on real time images from ultrasound or open NMR devices, e.g., a doctor could "see" the fetus inside the mother's womb)
- Navigation devices
  - In buildings, e.g., maintenance of industrial plants
  - Outdoors, e.g., military operations or disaster management
  - In cars (head-up displays or glasses showing traffic information)
  - In fighter jets (head-up displays were one of the first AR applications; later fully interactive approaches with eye-pointing were invented)
- Military and emergency services (wearable systems, showing instructions, maps, enemy locations, fire cells, etc.)
- Prospecting in hydrology, ecology, geology (display and interactive analysis of terrain characteristics, interactive three-dimensional maps that could be collaboratively modified and analyzed)

- Visualization of architecture (virtual resurrection of destroyed historic buildings as well as simulation of planned construction projects)
- Enhanced sightseeing: labels or any text related to the places seen, rebuilt ruins, building, or even landscape as seen in the past. Combined with a wireless network the amount of data displayed is limitless
- Simulation, e.g., flight and driving simulators
- Collaboration of distributed teams
  - Conferences with real and virtual participants
  - Joint work at simulated 3D models
- Entertainment and education
  - Virtual objects in museums and exhibitions
  - Theme park attractions
  - Computer games

Future Applications

- Expanding a PC screen into the real environment: program windows and icons appear as virtual devices in real space and are eye or gesture operated, by gazing or pointing. A single personal display (glasses) could concurrently simulate a hundred conventional PC screens or application windows all around a user.
- Virtual devices of all kinds, e.g. replacement of traditional screens, control panels, and entirely new applications impossible in "real" hardware, such as 3D objects interactively changing their shape and appearance on the basis of the current task or need.
- Enhanced media applications, like pseudo holographic virtual screens, virtual surround cinema, virtual "holodecks" (allowing computer-generated imagery to interact with live entertainers and audience).
- Virtual conferences in "holodeck" style.
- Replacement of cell phone and car navigator screens: eye-dialing, insertion of information directly into the environment, e.g., guiding lines directly on the road, as well as enhancements like "X-ray"-views.
- Virtual plants, wallpapers, panoramic views, artwork, decorations, illumination, etc., enhancing everyday life. For example, a virtual window could be displayed on a regular wall showing a live feed of a camera placed on the exterior of the building, thus allowing the user to effactually toggle a wall's transparency.
- With AR systems getting into mass market, we may see virtual window dressings, posters, traffic signs, Christmas decorations, advertisement towers, and more. These may be fully interactive even at a distance, by eye pointing for example.

- Virtual gadgetry becomes possible. Any physical device currently produced to assist in data-oriented tasks (such as the clock, radio, PC, arrival/departure board at an airport, stock ticker, PDA, PMP, informational posters/fliers/billboards, in-car navigation systems, etc. could be replaced by virtual devices that cost nothing to produce aside from the cost of writing the software. Examples might be a virtual wall clock, a to-do list for the day docked by your bed for you to look at first thing in the morning.
- Subscribable group-specific AR feeds. For example, a manager on a construction site could create and dock instructions including diagrams in specific locations on the site. The workers could refer to this feed of AR items as they work. Another example could be patrons at a public event subscribing to a feed of direction and information oriented AR items.

11.5 New Modeling and Visualization Techniques

As seen above visualization techniques in many fields have a long time ago moved from 2D to 3D or multidimensional representations, but this has not influenced enterprise and conceptual modeling much, at least not until lately. As standard computational equipment is getting cheaper, three-dimensional knowledge representations will also become more popular and widely used within this area. This is a large and fast growing area, and we will here only scratch the surface.

11.5.1 Three-Dimensional Modeling

On the basis of the ideas on structural object perception developed by Hummel and Biederman (1992), there are ideas for using three-dimension geometrical shapes (so-called geons) as modeling primitives rather than the two-dimensional forms that are normally used. The geon theory (Ware 2000) proposes a hierarchical set of processing stages leading to object recognition. Visual information is decomposed first into edged, then into component axes, oriented blobs, and vertices.

At the next layer, three-dimensional primitives such as cones, cylinders, and boxes (called geons) are identified. Next the structure is extracted that specifies how the geon components interconnect. Finally, object recognition is achieved.

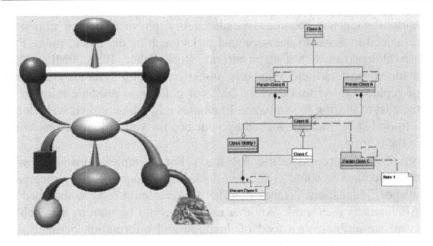

Fig. 11.13. Geons vs. traditional diagrammatical modeling (UML)

The geon theory can be applied directly to modeling. If cylinders and cones are perceptual primitives, it will make sense to have modeling languages using these kinds of primitives. The geon diagram concept is illustrated in Fig. 11.13. Geons are used to represent the major concepts of a compound data object, while the relationships are represented by the structural skeleton linking the geons. The size of the geon becomes a natural metaphor for the relative importance of the data entity, or some other important property. The strength of the relationships is given by the neck-like linking structure. Irani and Ware (1999) evaluated the geon diagram concept in a comparison with UML class diagrams. Equivalent diagrams were constructed by matching geon elements to UML elements (Fig. 11.13). They found that when the task involved rapid identification of substructures in a larger diagram, participants performed both faster and with only half the number of errors using the geon diagrams. Another experiment showed that geon diagrams were easier to remember.

Although we have not pursued geon-like languages, if anything, this can teach us that it can be beneficial to rise from two to three-dimensional views.

11.5.2 Annotated Maps

A number of approaches for presenting maps annotated with other information (or only links to other information) exist. One of the best known is Google Earth. Google Earth is a virtual globe program that was originally called Earth Viewer and was created by Keyhole, Inc. It maps the earth by the superimposition of images obtained from satellite imagery, aerial photography, and GIS 3D globe. The degree of resolution available is based somewhat on the points of interest, but most land (except for some islands) is covered in at least 15 m of resolution. Las Vegas, Nevada and Cambridge, Massachusetts include examples of the highest resolution, at 15 cm. Google Earth allows users to search for addresses, enter coordinates, or simply use the mouse to browse to a location.

Google Earth also has digital elevation model (DEM) data collected by NASA's Shuttle Radar Topography Mission. This means one can view e.g., Grand Canyon or Mount Everest in three dimensions, instead of 2D like other map programs/sites. In addition, Google has provided a layer allowing one to see 3D buildings for many major cities in US and Japan.

Many people using the applications are adding their own data and making them available through various sources, such as the BBS or blogs. Google Earth is able to show all kinds of images overlaid on the surface of the earth and is also Web Map Service client.

Google Earth supports managing three-dimensional geospatial data through Keyhole Markup Language (KML). It is available in a free version, and in licensed versions for commercial use.

Google Earth has the capability to show 3D buildings and structures (such as bridges), which consist of users' submissions using SketchUp, a 3D modeling program. In December 2006, Google Earth added a new layer called "Geographic Web" that includes integration with Wikipedia and Panoramio. In Wikipedia, entries are scraped for coordinates via the Coor dms series of templates. If the options to show Wikipedia or Panoramio entries are selected, users will be presented with clickable dots in their current Google Earth view. When any of these dots are selected, the user will be shown the Wikipedia or Panoramio entry right in Google Earth. There is also a community-layer from the project Wikipedia-World. More coordinates are used, different types are in the display and different languages are supported than the built-in Wikipedia layer.

There are also a number of similar approaches. In GeoDec (Geospatial Decision Making) (2007), one works at constructing an information-rich and realistic three-dimensional visualization and simulation of a geographical location, rapidly and accurately.

GeoDec is a collaborative project that allows navigation through a 3D model and enables users to ask queries and get information about the area in a convenient way. Recent growth of the geo-spatial information and their availability has motivated the effort to integrate them to support a comprehensive set of queries in different modalities.

By utilizing various information integration approaches such as orthoimagery and street maps conflation, vector data and satellite imagery conflation, and road network and map fusion, they strive to create intelligent, information-rich, and detailed models that incorporate the visual appeal and accuracy of imagery with detailed attribution information in diverse maps and realistic 3D visualization for geographic locations.

The proposed framework is composed of the following components:

- Rapid 3-D model Construction from Photographs
- Texture Mapping of Buildings and Video Fusion
- Model Enhancement with Data Integration
- Integrating Vector Data and Imagery
- Glove-Based User Interface
- Video Query

A usage somewhat closer to our ideas is the one found e.g., in nuclear power plants, where you can get a visualization of the radiation as it varies when you go within the plant. Taking it over into a more traditional modeling realm (than nuclear radiation) could be a system where you get immediate access to relevant modeling concepts as you enter an organization, meet a person, enter a project meeting, etc. In cases where you can manipulate the modeling objects in the same way as the physical objects in the AR, we enter into the field of tangible modeling, related to current work in HCI in tangible user interfaces (Ullmer and Ishii 2000), a techniques used more in relation to modeling of physical objects than modeling of concepts.

11.6 Future Solutions

With the growing emphasis on collaboration, global team-building, and holistic design, there is a need for intensified R&D work on how we can represent product and enterprise families. How we can better model multidimensional enterprise knowledge spaces, using 3D and 4D geometric spaces. How can we facilitate navigation and interaction in these spaces?

The important principle is to clearly separate knowledge and geometric spaces and dimensions, but pursuing the idea of being able to map knowledge dimensions and views to geometric spatial dimensions. Imagine traveling through an innovation space where:

- All initiatives, projects, and tasks were on one wall
- All teams from communities, to enterprises, to teams, individuals, and work-roles on another
- All requirements, experiences, information, and product structures on a third

- All system architectures, operational and design structures, and components on the fourth and last

This would be activating and animating the old-time war-room.

11.6.1 Croquet: An Example Environment

A number of approaches for creating the scenes exist, e.g., Croquet (2007). Croquet is an open source software development environment for the creation and large-scale distributed deployment of multiuser virtual 3D applications and metaverses that are (1) persistent, (2) deeply collaborative, (3) interconnected, and (4) interoperable.

Croquet features a peer-based network architecture that supports communication, collaboration, resource sharing, and synchronous computation between multiple users on multiple devices. Using Croquet, software developers can create and link powerful and highly collaborative cross-platform multiuser 2D and 3D applications and simulations – making possible the distributed deployment of very large scale, richly featured, and interlinked virtual environments.

Every part of the system is designed around enabling real-time, identical interactions between groups of users. The architecture of Croquet actually makes it quite easy to develop collaborative applications without having to spend a lot of effort and expertise in understanding how replicated applications work. There are a number of simple patterns and rules to remember, but otherwise, it is quite simple to quickly develop very powerful systems.

TeaTime and Islands are the basis for Croquet's replicated computation and synchronization. They are designed to support multiuser applications that can be scaled to massive numbers of concurrently interacting users in a shared virtual space. Croquet's treatment of distributed computation assumes a truly large scale distributed computing platform, consisting of heterogeneous computing devices distributed throughout a planet-scale communications network. Applications are expected to span machines and involve many users. In contrast with the more traditional architectures, Croquet incorporates replication of computation (both objects and activity), and the idea of active shared subspaces in its basic interpreter model.

11.7 Summary

We have in this chapter looked at some industrial efforts to take modeling and models into 3D and 4D geometrical space to ease navigation and communication and to extend usability. Assessing these solutions we have warned against using CAD models as sole knowledge carriers.

Some potential avenues to follow to provide the future enterprise visual scenes have been explored, but some application areas have simply been too much for us to absorb. We have given you some useful Web sites where you can follow many exiting research endeavors. This includes current work on three-dimensional modeling, virtual environments, real virtuality, AR, tangible modeling, map-solutions, and ubiquitous computing. We will not go into further details on the possibilities in this book, but leave this as inspirations for further research in connection to make it possible for actors to play on the enterprise visual scene.

12 Scientific Foundations of AKM Technology

In Chap. 3, we claimed the following:

"The variations in knowledge from one enterprise to another are mostly changes in semantics, complexity in structural layers, visual representations and type-hierarchies of the four main enterprise knowledge dimensions, in particular of process and product aspects. So in order to model for solutions with coherence, consistency and reuse in evolving extended enterprises we must be able to separate business, knowledge and IT architectures and solutions."

"Coherent and logically consistent representations of the enterprise core knowledge dimensions automatically yield reflective views, recursive processes, repetitive working solutions and replicable structures of meta-data. Knowledge from other layers and representations on other media does not have all these properties. Implementing the war-room concepts, the POPS methodologies, as visual languages, these intrinsic properties will give us powerful development, integration, management and reuse capabilities. Most other knowledge domains needed for business operations, such as abstracted process flows, or single views of any domain, do not exhibit these properties. Any aspect and view must be derived from the core, compliant with AKM technology and thinking."

Although we throughout have given references to supporting work in a number of disciplines, we will in this chapter present more of the scientific basis of the AKM-technology supporting our claims. Figure 12.1 shows the sciences influencing and inspiring the AKM technology. We will in this chapter go into the main areas depicted.

12.1 Epistemology

Organizational change may be viewed from different philosophical points of view. Two common sets of assumptions are the objectivistic belief system and the constructivistic belief system (Guba and Lincoln 1989). They may be distinguished through differences in ontology (what exists that can be known), epistemology (what relationship is there between the knower and the known), and methodology (what are the ways of achieving knowledge).

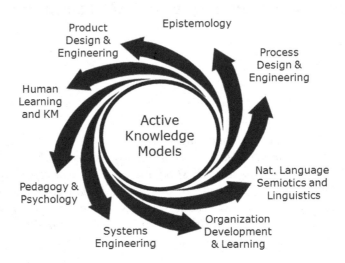

Fig. 12.1. Scientific methods and theories that provide explanations and principles for the AKM discoveries

Organizations are made up of individuals who perceive the world differently from each other. The constructivistic view is that an organization develops through a process of social construction, based on its individuals' constantly changing perception of the world. In the objectivistic view (Guba and Lincoln 1989), there exists only one reality, which is measurable and essentially the same for all. According to Guba and Lincoln, the objectivistic belief system can simplistically be said to have the following characteristics:

- The ontology is one of realism, asserting that there exists one single reality, which is independent of any observer's interest in it and which operates according to immutable natural laws. Truth is defined as that set of statements whose natural or intended model are isomorphic to reality.
- The epistemology is one of the dualistic objectivism, asserting that it is possible, indeed mandatory, for an observer to exteriorize the phenomenon studied, remaining detached and distant from it and excluding any value considerations from influencing it.
- The methodology is one of the interventionism, stripping context of its contaminating influences so that the inquiry can converge on truth and explain the things studied as they really are and really work, leading to the capability to predict and to control.

The constructivistic belief system has the following characteristics (according to (Guba and Lincoln 1989)):

- The ontology is one of the relativism, asserting that there exist multiple socially constructed realities ungoverned by any natural laws, causal or otherwise. "Truth" is defined as the best-informed and most sophisticated construction on which there is agreement.
- The epistemology is subjectivistic, asserting that the inquirer and the inquired-into are interlocked in such a way that the findings of an investigation are the literal creation of the inquiry process.
- The methodology is hermeneutical and involves a continuing dialectic of iteration, analysis, critique, reiteration, reanalysis, and so on, leading to the emergence of a joint construction and understanding among all the stakeholders.

Many features of the constructivistic world-view have in fact emerged from hard natural sciences such as physics and chemistry. The argument for this paradigm can be made even more persuasively when the phenomena being studied involve human beings, as in the social sciences. Much of the theoretical discussion in the social sciences is dedicated to analyzing constructivism and its consequences (Dahlbom 1991). The idea of reality construction has been a central topic for philosophical debate during the last three decades, and has been approached differently by French, American, and German philosophers. Many different approaches to constructivistic thinking have appeared, although probably the most influential one is that Berger and Luckmann (1966).

Their insights will be used as our starting point. Their view of the social construction of reality is based on Husserl's phenomenology. Husserl was primarily a philosopher, whereas Schutz (1962) took phenomenology into the social sciences. From there on it branched into two directions: ethnomethodology, primarily developed by Garfinkel (1967), and the social constructivism of Berger and Luckmann. Although ethnomethodology is focused on questioning what individuals take as given in different cultures, Berger and Luckmann developed their approach to investigate how these presumptions are constructed.

Organizations are realities constructed socially through the joint actions of the social actors in the organization (Gjersvik 1993), as illustrated in Fig. 12.2.

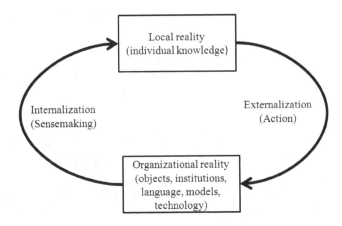

Fig. 12.2. Social construction in an organization

An organization consists of individuals who view the world in their own specific way, because each of them has different experiences arising from work and other arenas. The local reality refers to the way an individual perceives the world in which he or she acts. The local reality is the way the world is for the individual; it is the everyday perceived reality of the individual social actor. Some of this local reality may be made explicit and talked about. However, a lot of what we know is tacit. When the social actors of an organization act, they externalize their local reality. The most important ways in which social actors externalize their local reality are by speaking and constructing languages, artifacts, and institutions. What they do is to construct organizational reality by making something that other actors have to relate to by being part of the organization. This organizational reality may consist of different things, such as institutions, language, artifacts, and technology. Finally, internalization is the process of making sense out of the actions, institutions, artifacts, etc. in the organization, and making this organizational reality part of the individual local reality. This linear presentation does not mean that the processes of externalization and internalization occur in a strict sequence.

Externalization and internalization may be performed simultaneously. Also, it does not mean that only organizational reality is internalized. Other externalizations also influence the construction of the local reality of an individual.

12.2 Human Learning, Pedagogy and Psychology

An important area in these fields is Activity Theory, going back to Vygotski and Leontev. The following overview of the field is based on (Krogstie 2000). According to activity theory, human knowledge, learning, and activity in general are fundamentally related to collective systems engaging in goal-directed action on the basis of underlying motives shared among the activity participants (Leont'ev 1981). The instruments used to achieve activity goals influence, and are influenced by the activities in which they are employed.

Activity theory stresses that human activity has to be regarded in a holistic manner. Still, there are aspects or elements of activity that can be said to conceptually comprise a structure in which the relations between the elements play an essential part.

A basic tenet is that the elements subject–object–instrument/tool can be understood only in relation to each other and only in the context of activity.

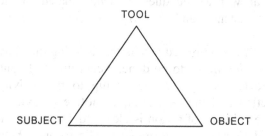

Fig. 12.3. The basic structure of human activity

Subjects change and develop themselves in fulfilling the activity, which means purposefully changing natural and social reality. The purpose is directed at an image of a foreseen result of a creative effort. This image is the activity's object.

Subject and object are connected by instruments (tools), or instrumental artifacts, that make the processes of work possible. An instrument cannot be described completely as an isolated tool, but must be seen as a "subject–object unity," a process unity formed by the relation between subjective activity and its object (Fichtner 1984).

The triangle model of Fig. 12.3 indicates Leont'ev's focus on the relation between the subject and the object and instruments of activity. In Fichtner's view, Leont'ev's main interest was in the single, active, and personal subject; in the mediation between internal, psychological processes and external, concrete processes of activity (Fichtner 1984). Still, the collective nature of activity is present in Leont'ev's accounting for the meaning of the hierarchy of activity, action, and operation, as shown in Table 12.1:

Table 12.1. The activity-action-operation hierarchy

Activity	*Motive/object*	*WHY*
Action	*Goal*	*WHAT*
Operation	*conditions*	*HOW*

The activity object is a *motive* and a driving force. As an image of a future state, it may not be fully attainable, but serves as a guiding light and something to strive for. There may be varying consciousness of the object among participants, and the object may or may not be explicitly formulated. There may also be a varying degree of overlap between individual motives for participating in one and the same activity, as will be discussed below in the section on various levels of collective activity. The activity object represents an answer to the question *why*, related to the rationale for the activity's existence and possibly the reason for the individual's participation.

Actions are the goal-directed means for realizing the activity, answering the question of *what* needs to be done. According to Leont'ev (1981), an action is characterized by its relationship to the activity motive. The "object" of action and the over-arching motive (activity object) are not coinciding. The "object" of action is clearly defined and attainable, and is hereby denoted as a *goal*. The apparent discrepancy between goal and motive in a short-term perspective is due to the fact that activity is complex and collective with many steps needed. There are many possible combinations of sets of actions that may together serve to realize the object of the activity.

Operations are automated ways of realizing actions, and represent the answer to the question *how*. There may be many different operations possible for realizing each action. Operations are subject to certain conditions for their execution.

There may be transformations between the three levels described. Under stable circumstances, the meaning-giving motive of an activity may gradually turn into a straightforward goal being instrumental to some over-arching activity. Likewise, on one hand, an action may turn into an operation if it becomes made into a routine (or automated) to the extent that it is perceived as a unity conducted as one single step. On the other hand, increased consciousness and questioning of the way operations or actions are performed may be required if their execution no longer lead to satisfactory results. An operation may need to be reexamined and recon-structed as a goal-directed action with several steps. Bardram (1998) refers to this process as *reflection on the means of work*. Also, the goal of an action can be questioned and reconceptualized, receiving increased attention to the extent that it becomes a meaning-defining motive to be realized through steps of subordinate, goal-directed actions. This process entails *reflection on the object of work* in Bardram's terms (Bardram 1998).

The complexity of collective activity is resolved through a division into *roles*, with associated *scripts* describing which actions should be applied and in what sequence in order to fulfill each role. These scripts may or may not be formalized, but there needs to be some degree of common recognition of the structure of roles and scripts among the participants of the activity. However, there may be various consciousness about the scripts actually followed.

Engeström (1987) has proposed a model of the *activity system* that includes the activity subject, instrument(s) and object/motive as well as rules pertaining to the activity performance, the performing community, and the division of labor in this community (Fig. 12.4). The object of the activity is related to an outcome, corresponding to the product of the activity. Activity systems are interrelated, providing each other with input and serving as instruments for each other. Engeström points to the contra-dictions inevitably occurring within and between activity systems and how such tensions initiate and fuel processes of transformation.

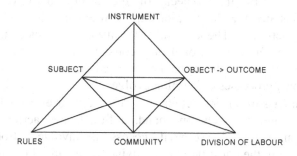

Fig. 12.4. An extended structure of human activity (Engeström 1987)

The activity motive and the *scripts*, sets of actions that may be applied in realizing the motive, can be more or less articulated and subject to participants' conscious attention. Different *levels of interaction* have been suggested in this respect (Engeström 1992; Bardram 1998). During a "normal" flow of interaction, scripts are followed without being questioned, in accordance with participants' roles. This state is denoted as the *level of coordination*. When the motive is articulated and participants experience that they work on a shared problem, activity takes place on a *level of cooperation*. Finally, there is the *level of coconstruction*, at which both scripts and motive are subject to participants' attention and reconstruction. Through their interaction, the actors reconceptualize their organization and interaction in relation to the shared motive

About the activity system as a basic unit, Engeström claims: "the model is actually the smallest and most simple unit that still preserves the essential unity and integral quality behind any human activity." (Engeström 1987)

In Engeström's view, *tensions* due to contradictions within and between activity systems are the source of change and thereby learning. He distinguishes between various forms of contradictions, of which the essential one is "the mutual exclusion and simultaneous mutual dependency of use value and exchange value in each commodity. This *double nature* and inner unrest is characteristic to all the corners of the triangular structure of activity" (Engeström 1987). The contradiction is the primary one in "capitalist socio-economic formations." The secondary contradiction appears between the corners of the model, exemplified by a hierarchically structured division of labor that does not match the possibilities of new and advanced instruments (Engeström 1987). Tertiary contradictions appear when the object of a "culturally more advanced form" of an activity is introduced into the activity in question (denoted the "central activity" by Engeström). This new form may be introduced from outside or it may be actively sought by the subjects of the central activity. Quaternary contradictions involve the relationship between the central activity and neighboring activities. The latter may, for instance, produce the instrument used in the central activity, or it may consume the output product of the central activity. From the dynamics created through the four types of contradictions, processes of learning evolve.

In the analysis of tensions/contradictions and their effects, the historical dimension is essential. On one hand, a full-fledged activity-theoretical analysis of an empirical case would necessarily involve a strong focus on history, enabling the construction of a dynamic picture of changing reality. On the other hand, the framework offers a structural perspective on reality that may give a useful "instant overview" of a situation. The universal nature of the model and theory makes it generally applicable, even if it is clearly inspired by Marxist theory. It is feasible as well as defendable to talk fruitfully of primary or inner tensions in an activity system without relating to the concepts of use and exchange values.

An activity system can be somewhat loosely and pragmatically as *a relatively stable community producing something over time in accordance with a largely shared and articulated motive.* According to Leont'ev, the object/motive is the defining characteristic of an activity system, but common motives may be difficult to identify in practice. Blackler (1993) suggests that common *routines* be activity-defining, which would imply looking for procedural or functional "clusters" when modeling an organization in terms of its activity systems. It should be stressed that the structuring of a given "world" into activity systems is not unambiguous.

A concept related to that of activity systems is that of communities of practice, elaborately described by Wenger (1998). At the heart of *practice* are the complementary processes of *participation* and *reification*. Participation refers to "the social experience of living in the world in terms of membership in social communities and active involvement in social enterprises" (Wenger 1998). Reification is "the process of giving form to our experience by producing objects that congeal the experience into 'thingness.'" Through this process, we create focal points around which meaning is negotiated. Wenger proposes three dimensions of "the relation by which practice is the source of coherence of a community" (Wenger 1998):

- *Mutual engagement* means that participants understand each other and experience mutual accountability that they interact in meaningful ways and negotiate their enterprise. Importantly, mutual engagement entails utilizing other's competence as well as one's own.
- *Joint enterprise* results from the negotiation of the enterprise through mutual engagement. The joint enterprise is "defined by the participants in the very process of pursuing it" (Wenger 1998), as a negotiated response to their situation.
- A *shared repertoire* of artifacts, concepts, historic events, etc. may be applied by participants in the constant meaning-making processes of the practice.

According to Wenger, belonging to any community may be accounted for in terms of engagement, imagination, and alignment, which all contribute to the identity-formation of the members. There is a strong relationship between participation and identity formation: "Participation goes beyond direct engagement in specific activities with specific people. It places the negotiation of membership in the context of our forms of membership in various communities. It is a constituent of our identities" (Wenger 1998). In interplay with participation, *identification* contributes to identity formation as a process "through which modes of belonging

become constitutive of our identities by creating bonds or distinctions in which we become invested" (Wenger 1998).
A final point made by Wenger is the thought of communities of practice as shared histories of learning. Participation and reification serve as forms of memory and "sources of continuity and discontinuity, and thus as channels by which one can influence the evolution of practice" (Wenger 1998). Knowledge is fundamentally related to practices: "Knowing is defined only in the context of specific practices, where it arises out of the combination of a regime of competence and an experience of meaning" (Wenger 1998).
The dynamic theory of organizational knowledge creation (Nonaka 1994) was important in focusing on the need to continually externalize tacit knowledge, and being able to reactivate knowledge. The distinction between explicit and tacit knowledge follows from Polanyi (1966): Explicit or codified knowledge is transmittable in a formal systematic language, while tacit knowledge has a personal quality, which makes it hard to formalize and communicate. Nonaka and Takeuchi (1995) identify four patterns of interaction between tacit and explicit knowledge commonly called *modes of knowledge conversion* as depicted in Fig. 12.5.

	Tacit knowledge **To**	*Explicit knowledge*
Tacit knowledge	**Socialization** creating tacit knowledge through shared experience	**Externalization** conversion from tacit to explicit knowledge
From		
Explicit knowledge	**Internalization** conversion of explicit knowledge to tacit knowledge	**Combination** creation of new explicit knowledge from explicit knowledge

Fig. 12.5. Modes of knowledge conversion

The internalization mode of knowledge creation is closely related to "learning by doing," hence action is deeply related to the internalization process. Nonaka and Takeuchi criticize traditional theories on organizational learning, like (Schön 1983; Argyris and Schön 1973), for not addressing the critical notion of externalization and having paid little attention to the importance of socialization. The authors also argue that a double-loop learning ability implicitly is built into the knowledge creation model, as organizations continuously make new knowledge by reconstructing existing perspectives, frameworks, or premises on a day-to-day basis. It is this dynamic view of knowledge as something continuously being created, refined, and reformed on the basis of available information that makes Nonaka and Takeuchi's theory special.

When tacit and explicit knowledge interacts, innovation emerges. Nonaka and Takeuchi propose that the interaction is shaped by shifts between modes of knowledge conversion, induced by several triggers as depicted in Fig. 12.5, we have the socialization mode starting with building a field of interaction facilitating the sharing of experience and mental models. This triggers the externalization mode by meaningful dialogue and collective reflection where the use of metaphor or analogy helps articulate tacit knowledge, which is otherwise hard to communicate. The combination mode is triggered by networking newly created knowledge with existing organizational knowledge, and finally learning by doing triggers internalization.

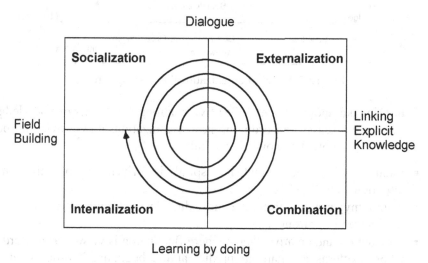

Fig. 12.6. Knowledge spiral

These contents of knowledge interact with each other as indicated in the spiral of Fig. 12.6, illustrating the epistemological dimension of knowledge. Adding Nonaka and Takeuchi's ontological dimension of knowledge creation, we end up with the *spiral of organizational knowledge creation* as depicted in Fig. 12.7, which shows how the organization mobilizes tacit knowledge created and accumulated at the individual level, organizationally amplified through the four modes of knowledge conversion and crysta-llized at higher ontological levels. Thus the authors propose that the interaction between tacit and explicit knowledge becomes larger in scale as the knowledge creation process proceeds up their ontological levels. The spiral process of knowledge creation starts at the individual level and potentially moves upwards through expanding interaction communities crossing sectional, departmental, divisional, and possibly organizational boundaries.

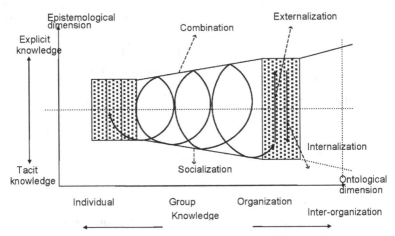

Fig. 12.7. Spiral of organizational knowledge creation

In (Nonaka and Takeuchi 1995) five enabling conditions of knowledge creation are discussed according to how organizations may provide proper context to promote the knowledge spiral:

- Intention; i.e., the knowledge spiral is driven by organizational intention.
- Autonomy; ranging from the individual level through team levels to sections and departments.
- Fluctuation and creative chaos; where fluctuation is viewed as an "order whose patterns are hard to predict at the beginning" (order without recursion), which fosters continuous self-assessment and creative chaos may be intentionally introduced to increase organizational tension and focus attention on problem definition and solving.
- Redundancy; i.e., the existence of information that goes beyond the immediate operational requirements of the organizational actors.
- Requisite variety; i.e., that an organization's internal diversity matches the variety and complexity of the environment with which it interacts.

In much knowledge management literature, inspired by Nonaka, a model of a business process – whether active or not – would be considered externalized knowledge about the organization. However, this "knowledge-as-object" view has been criticized by Walsham (2005), maintaining that *knowledge* is something within the human mind, so that the term should not be used for passive representations of information in writing or in computer systems. We will follow up on this in Sect. 12.3 below.

12.3 Natural Language, Linguistics and Semiotics

Natural language is important for industrial nomenclature and logistics. Nomenclature covers all from terminology to taxonomy and ontology as discussed in Chap. 6, and their practical uses for identity, identification, coding, categorization, and classification. The contingencies and short-comings of natural language as an encoding language for situated knowledge have been described by many and in particular by epistemologists. Words are the instruments by means of which men and women grasp the thoughts of others and with which they do much of their own thinking. They are the "tools of thought," and may not convey enough situated knowledge and context to be useful on their own.

Work on ontology using terms and taxonomies from natural language as systems and enterprise logic has received a lot of attention as also discussed in Chap. 6. Ontology is important, but only as mechanisms to dynamically update the logic and logistics of evolving enterprise models.

We are in this book focusing on the use of models rather than words as primary knowledge representation approach. What is a *good* model is obviously important to have a clear conception on. Early proposals for quality goals for conceptual models as summarized by Davis (Davis et al. 1993) have included many useful aspects, but unfortunately in the form of unsystematic lists (Lindland et al. 1994). They are also often restricted in the kind of models they regard (e.g., requirements specifications (Davis et al. 1993)) or the modeling language (e.g., ER-models (Moody and Shanks 1994)).

Looking for a basis to create a more comprehensive framework, we have looked at the field of semiotics, the science of *signs* and what they refer to. One of the authors have worked for many years on notions of quality of models, inspired by work from semiotics (Morris 1946) where the notions of syntax, semantics, and pragmatics were introduced, later being extended with physical, empirical, social, and organizational levels.

The way we apply semiotic theory is very similar to what was described in the FRISCO report (Falkenberg et al. 1996), which identifies that the means of communication and related areas can be examined in a semiotic framework. The below semiotic layers for communication are distinguished, forming what they term a *semiotic ladder*. Model denotations are signs, and thus they have considered the semiotics of models. The key concepts to be included in information systems models is regarded to be

- Physical: use of various media for modeling – documents, wall charts, computer-based CASE-tools, and so on; physical size and amount and effort to manipulate them.
- Empirical: variety of elements distinguished; error frequencies when being written and read by different users; coding (shapes of boxes); ergonomics of computer–human interaction (CHI) for documentation and CASE tools.
- Syntactic: languages, natural, constrained, or formal, logical and mathematical methods for modeling.
- Semantic: interpretation of the elements of the model in terms of the real world; ontological assumptions; operations for arriving at values of elements; justification of external validity.
- Pragmatic: roles played by models – hypothesis, directive, description, expectation; responsibility for making and using the model; conversations needed to develop and use the model.
- Social: communities of users; the norms governing use for different purposes; organizational framework for using the model.

These layers can be divided into two groups to reveal the technical vs. the social aspect. Physics, empirics, and syntactics comprise an area where technical and formal methods are adequate. However, semantics, pragmatics, and the social sphere cannot be explored using those methods unmodified. This indicates than one has to include human judgment when discussing quality in the higher semiotic layers. The problem when discussing a problem area is that people, when using multilayer-related terms, frequently fail to make clear the layer they are focusing on, which may result in severe misunderstandings.

Earlier, a generic quality framework, SEQUAL (Krogstie et al. 2006), has been developed on the basis of this thinking. The original framework was geared toward traditional information system models, which primarily acted as an intermediate representation, and not active models as we look upon here. Thus later version also takes the active parts into account. Other researchers are in line with this view, furthermore stressing that an essential quality of knowledge lies in its ability to support action (Braf

2004). Hence, knowledge is not only about action, but *for* action, or even *part of* action (Cook and Brown 1999). The same view pertains to information systems, which can be seen as (partial) automations of conceptual models of the problem domain. IS Actability Theory (Goldkuhl and Ågerfalk 2002; Ågerfalk 2003) stresses that information systems are action systems used in a social action context (Ågerfalk and Eriksson 2003).

We support the criticism of the "knowledge-as-object" view, hence here a model is not as such considered to *be* knowledge, but it may *contribute to knowledge* when interpreted (and acted upon) by a human or other intelligent agent. Since process models describe – or even prescribe – specific paths of action under specific circumstances, the road from interpretation of the model to action may be very short, especially for interactive models, where changes have immediate effect on system behavior. This also makes it especially important to understand and be able to evaluate the quality of such models. We will here present a specialization of SEQUAL for this purpose.

The main concepts of the framework and their relationships are shown in Fig. 12.8 and are explained later. Quality has been defined referring to the correspondence between statements belonging to the following sets:

- G, the goals of the modeling task.
- L, the language extension, i.e., the set of all statements that are possible to make according to the graphemes, vocabulary, and syntax of the modeling languages used.
- D, the domain, i.e., the set of all statements that can be stated about the situation at hand.
- M, the model itself.
- K_s, the relevant explicit knowledge of those being involved in modeling. A subset of these is actively involved in modeling, and their explicit knowledge is indicated by K_M.
- I, the social actor interpretation, i.e., the set of all statements that the audience thinks that an externalized model consists of.
- T, the technical actor interpretation, i.e., the statements in the model as "interpreted" by modeling tools.

The main quality types are indicated by solid lines between the sets, and are described briefly below:

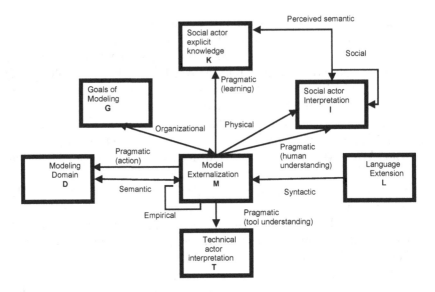

Fig. 12.8. SEQUAL: Framework for discussing the quality of models

- Physical quality: The basic quality goal is that the model M is available for the audience.
- Empirical quality deals with predictable error frequencies when a model is read or written by different users, coding (e.g., shapes of boxes), and HCI-ergonomics for documentation and modeling-tools. For instance, graph layout to avoid crossing lines in a model is a mean to address the empirical quality of a model.
- Syntactic quality is the correspondence between the model M and the language extension L.
- Semantic quality is the correspondence between the model M and the domain D. This includes validity and completeness.
- Perceived semantic quality is the similar correspondence between the audience interpretation I of a model M and his or hers current knowledge K of the domain D.
- Pragmatic quality is the correspondence between the model M and the audience's interpretation and application of it (I). We differentiate between social pragmatic quality (to what extent people understand and are able to use the models) and technical pragmatic quality (to what extent tools can be made that interpret the models). In addition, we include under pragmatic quality the extent that the participants after interpreting the model learn based on the model and that the audience after interpreting the model and learning from it is able to change the

domain (preferably in a positive direction relative to the goal of modeling).

- The goal defined for social quality is agreement among audience members' interpretations I.
- The organizational quality of the model relates to that all statements in the model contribute to fulfilling the goals of modeling (organizational goal validity), and that all the goals of modeling are addressed through the model (organizational goal completeness).

Language quality relates the modeling language used to the other sets. Six quality areas for language quality are identified, with aspects related to both the language metamodel and the notation as illustrated in Fig. 12.9.

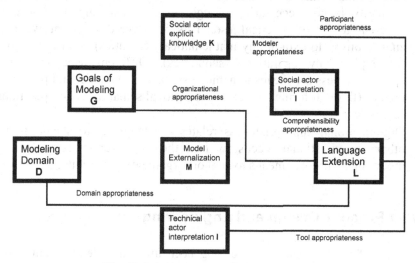

Fig. 12.9. Language quality in SEQUAL

- Domain appropriateness. This relates the language and the domain. Ideally, on one hand, the conceptual basis must be powerful enough to express anything in the domain, not having what (Wand and Weber 1993) terms construct deficit. On the other hand, you should not be able to express things that are not in the domain, i.e., what is termed construct excess (Wand and Weber 1993). Domain appropriateness is primarily a mean to achieve semantic quality.
- Participant appropriateness relates the social actors' explicit knowledge to the language. Participant appropriateness is primarily a mean to achieve pragmatic quality both for comprehension, learning, and action.
- Modeler appropriateness: This area relates the language extension to the participant knowledge. The goal is that there are no statements in the

explicit knowledge of the modeler that cannot be expressed in the language. Modeler appropriateness is primarily a mean to achieve semantic quality.

- Comprehensibility appropriateness relates the language to the social actor interpretation. The goal is that the participants in the modeling effort using the language understand all the possible statements of the language. Comprehensibility appropriateness is primarily a mean to achieve empirical and pragmatic quality.
- Tool appropriateness relates the language to the technical audience interpretations. For tool interpretation, it is especially important that the language lend itself to automatic reasoning. This requires formality (i.e., both formal syntax and semantics being operational and/or logical), but formality is not necessarily enough, as the reasoning must also be efficient to be of practical use. This is covered by what we term analyzability (to exploit any mathematical semantics) and executability (to exploit any operational semantics). Different aspects of tool appropriateness are means to achieve syntactic, semantic, and pragmatic quality (through formal syntax, mathematical semantics, and operational semantics).
- Organizational appropriateness relates the language to standards and other organizational needs within the organizational context of modeling. These are means to support organizational quality.

12.4 Process Design and Engineering

Models of work processes have long been utilized to learn about, guide and support practice. In software process improvement (Bandinelli et al. 1995; Dernami 1998), enterprise modeling (Fox and Gruninger 2000), and quality management, process models describe methods and standard working procedures. Simulation and quantitative analyses are also performed to improve efficiency (Abdel-Hamid and Madnick 1989; Kuntz et al. 1998). In process centric software engineering environments (Ambriola et al. 1997; Cugola 1998) and workflow systems (WfMC 2000), model execution is automated. This wide range of applications is reflected in current notations, which emphasize different aspects of work. Carlsen (1998) identifies five categories of process modeling languages (PMLs): transformational, conversational, role-oriented, constraint-based, and systemic. The increased interest in modeling processes with UML (Marshall 1999) requires that object-oriented process modeling also be discussed.

12.4.1 Transformational PMLs

Most PMLs take a transformational (input–process–output) approach. Processes are divided into activities, which may be divided further into subactivities. Each activity takes inputs, which it transforms to outputs. Input and output relations thus define the sequence of work. This perspective is chosen for the standards of the Workflow Management Coalition (WfMC 2000), the Internet Engineering Task Force (IETF) (Bolcer and Kaiser 1999), and the Object Management Group (OMG 2000) as well as most commercial systems (Abbot and Sarin 1994; Fisher 2000). IDEF (1993), Data Flow Diagram (Gane and Sarson 1979), Activity diagrams (OMG 2002), Event-driven Process Chains (Aalst 1999), and Petri nets (Aalst et al. 2000) are well-known transformational languages.

The transformational PML category has been subdivided into *task* and *state*-oriented approaches (Lei and Singh 1997), depending on which kind of element is represented as nodes in the flow graphs.

Given the extensive use of transformational languages, most PML analyses focus on this category (Conradi and Jaccheri 1998; Curtis et al. 1992; Green and Rosemann 2000; Lei and Singh 1997). The expressiveness of these languages typically includes decomposition, control, and data flow, while organizational modeling and roles often are integrated. Aspects like timing and quantification, products and communication, or commitments are better supported by other paradigms. User-orientedness is a major advantage of transformational languages. Partitioning the process into steps matches well the descriptions that people use elsewhere. Graphical input–process–output models are comprehensible given some training, but you can also build models by simply listing the tasks in plain text, or in a hierarchical work breakdown structure. Hence, the models can be quite simple, provided that incomplete ordering of steps is allowed.

12.4.2 Conversational Process Modeling

The language action perspective was brought into the workflow arena through the COORDINATOR prototype (Winograd and Flores 1986), later succeeded by the Action Workflow system (Medina-Mora et al. 1992). This perspective is informed by speech act theory (Searle 1969), which extends the notion that people use language to describe the world with a focus on how people use language for coordinating action and negotiating commitments. The main strength of this approach is that it facilitates analysis of the communicative aspects of the process. It highlights that each process is an interaction between a customer and a performer, represented as a cycle with four phases: preparation, negotiation, performance, and acceptance. The dual role constellation is a basis for work breakdown, e.g., the performer can delegate parts of the work to other people. Process models may thus spread out.

This explicit representation of communication and negotiation, and especially the structuring of the conversation into predefined speech act steps, has also been criticized (Button 1995; De Michelis and Grasso 1994; King 1995; Suchman 1994). On one hand, minimal support for situated conversations, the danger that explication leads to increased external control of the work, and a simplistic one-to-one mapping between utterances and actions are among the weaknesses. On the other hand, it has been reported that the Action Workflow approach is useful when people act pragmatically and do not always follow the encoded rules of behavior (De Michelis and Grasso 1994), i.e., when the communication models are interactively activated.

12.4.3 Declarative and Constraint-Based Process Modeling

Declarative workflow approaches have also been promoted. Constraint-based languages (Dourish et al. 1996; Glance et al. 1996) do not prescribe a course of events, rather they capture the boundaries within which the process must be performed, leaving the actors to control the internal details. Instead of telling people what to do, these systems warn about rule violations and enforce constraints. Thus, on one hand, common problems with over-serialization are avoided (Glance et al. 1996). On the other hand, the resulting models are not very comprehensible. A graphic depiction is difficult as it would correspond to a visualization of several possible solutions to the set of constraint equations constituting the model. The support for articulation of planned and ongoing tasks is limited. Consequently, constraints are often combined with transformational models (Bernstein 2000, Dourish et al. 1996). Constraints mainly capture outside control on the workflow, not articulation inside the process.

12.4.4 Roles and Their Interaction

Role-centric PMLs have been applied for workflow analysis and implementation. Role Interaction Nets (RIN) (Singh and Rein 1992) and Role Activity Diagrams (RAD) (Ould 1995) use roles as their main structuring concept. The activities performed by a role are grouped together in the diagram, either in swim-lanes (RIN) or inside boxes (RAD).

The use of roles as a structuring concept makes it very clear who is responsible for what. RAD has also been merged with speech acts for interaction between roles (Benson et al. 2000). The role-based approach also has limitations, e.g., making it difficult to change the organizational distribution of work. It primarily targets analysis of administrative procedures, where formal roles are important.

12.4.5 System Dynamics

Holistic systems thinking (Senge 1990) regards causal relations as mutual, circular, and nonlinear, hence the straightforward sequences in transformational process models is seen as an idealization that hides important facts. This perspective is also reflected in mathematical models of interaction (Wegner and Goldin 1999). System dynamics have been utilized for analysis of complex relationships in cooperative work arrangements (Abdel-Hamid and Madnick 1989). A simple example is depicted in Fig. 12.10. It shows one aspect of the interdependencies between design and implementation in a system development project. The more time you spend designing, the less time you have for coding and testing, hence you better get the design right the first time. This creates a positive feedback loop similar to "analysis paralysis" that must be balanced by some means, in our example iterative development.

System dynamic process models are used for analysis and simulation, but not for enactment. Most importantly, system dynamics shows the complex interdependencies that are so often ignored in conventional notations, illustrating the need for articulating more relations between tasks, beyond simple sequencing.

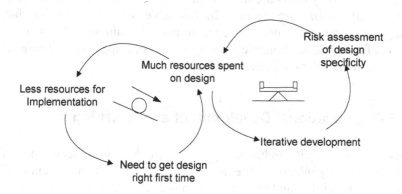

Fig. 12.10. A system dynamic process model

12.4.6 Object-Oriented Process Modeling

UML (Booch et al. 2005) has become the official and de facto standard for object-oriented analysis and design. Consequently, people also apply UML to model business processes. Object orientation offers a number of useful modeling techniques like encapsulation, polymorphism, subtyping, and inheritance (Loos and Allweyer 1998; Mühlen and Becker 1999). On one hand, UML integrates these capabilities with e.g., requirements capture in use case descriptions and behavior modeling in state, activity, and sequence diagrams. On the other hand, UML is designed for software developers, and not for end users. A core challenge thus remains in mapping system-oriented UML constructs to user and process-oriented concepts (Hommes and Reijswoud 1999). To this problem no general solution exists (Loos and Allweyer 1998; Störle 2001). UML process languages utilize associations, classes, operations, use cases, interaction sequence, or activity diagrams. The lack of a standardized approach reflects the wide range of process modeling approaches in business and software engineering.

12.4.7 Other Explicit Process Representations

Numerous other textual, informal, or semiformal process descriptions exist (Curtis et al. 1992). In project management, *temporal* considerations are important. This is evident in the frequent use of milestones and visualizations like Gantt diagrams. Ad-hoc *inscriptions on artifacts* also carry process information, e.g., for coordination and error recovery (Twidale and Marty 2000). There has even been some research on utilizing *programming languages* for process representation (Osterweil 1987; Yang 2003). Process support systems are not the only area where *evolving, incomplete operational models* are needed. In tailorable systems, user interfaces, groupware protocols, method engineering, domain-specific modeling, agent infrastructures, dynamic ontologies, multiperspective and reflective systems, and similar challenges are faced.

12.5 Organizational Development and Learning

Since the early 1960s, industrialists and researchers have seen a need for new forms of organization. The motivations for Argyris and Schøn (1973) were more flexibility and transparency in organizations, more effective use of resources, and improved competencies and skill management.

In the views of Argyris and Schön (1996), the prevalent models of reality in the organization influence learning. The substitution of "activity system" as discussed in Sect. 12.2 for "organization" in this context seems unproblematic, and we pursue the work of Argyris and Schön further with this in mind. There is significant similarity with Dewey's thinking in the authors' perspectives on learning. What deserves special attention is Argyris and Schön's recognition of different *theories of action* as well as that of *single- and double-loop learning* processes (although as indicated earlier, this is criticized by Nonaka et al.).

According to Argyris and Schön, the prevailing models influence how the organization acts upon itself and its environment in general. Models of reality exist as organizational knowledge that is "embedded in routines and practices which may be inspected and decoded even when the individuals who carry them out are unable to put them into words." The authors denote such knowledge as *theories of action*, which may have two different forms, the contents of which do not necessarily coincide. *Espoused theory* is the "official" theory used in explaining or justifying a way of performing some activity, whereas *theory-in-use* is the "real" theory governing activity, found implicit in the performance. The latter may be partly tacit and thus needs to be constructed from observation (Argyris and Schön 1996). We note that Argyris and Schön believe it is possible to gain an understanding of theory-in-use by observing a pattern of interactive behavior. Organizational inquiry implies uncovering the theories that govern activity.

If we relate the theories of action to the repertoire model of activity, we might regard such theories as artifacts and/or objects, the theories having an instrumental function as well as being subjects of reconstruction as the activity develops. It seems plausible to speak of both individual and shared aspects of theory of action, which may accordingly be related to both individual and shared components of activity objects. Espoused theory may be viewed as largely shared, being explicit and official. However, theory-in-use should also be considered as mainly shared even if not expressed. The reason is that theory-in-use as described by Argyris and Schön largely corresponds to what is usually denoted organizational culture, which is by definition shared among organizational members.

Argyris and Schön lend on Dewey in their theory of organizational learning, viewing inquiry as a basic feature of learning. There is a need for every member to be a researcher in the process of organizational inquiry (Argyris and Schön 1996). The authors note the constructive aspect of inquiry: *"the inquirer participates in constructing the situation to which he also responds."* There is a dialectic between inquirer and situation as new problematic features of a situation occur through the process of inquiry itself (Argyris and Schön 1996). The situation is interpreted in terms of a model that includes certain expectations related to the processes involved. Learning processes occur as a consequence of perceived error in the organization, a mismatch of outcome to expectations. Errors signal underlying mistakes, which need to be identified and understood. The notion of errors corresponds to the change-initiating tensions described by Engeström.

Organizational learning implies *organizational inquiry* into the models that govern practice within the organization. Argyris and Schön identify single-loop and double-loop learning as two conceptually different processes, distinguished by the extent to which existing models are changed as part of learning. Stated briefly, *single-loop learning* results in the learner solving the same problem in another way; a more effective or efficient one if the learning is productive. *Double-loop learning* implies that the problem is reframed in accordance with higher-order goals or strategy. The result of the learning process is the ability to solve new problems differently, preferably in a way serving the overall strategy in a more effective or efficient way than before. It can be argued that the limit between the two learning types is floating; it is not clearly defined how extensive the reframing or reconceptualization must be for learning to be double-looped as opposed to single-looped. *Deutero learning* is a third concept, pertaining to the process wherein consciousness of one's own learning is developed. Insight in one's own learning processes increases the ability to detect nonproductiveness or stagnation in learning and to determine and effectuate the most appropriate learning strategies.

The three forms of learning can be related to reconceptualization of activity repertoires. Single-loop learning involves a revision of scripts and possibly artifacts in accordance with a largely unchanged object. Double-loop learning implies a thorough object reconceptualization, followed by necessary change of the scripts and possibly artifacts. Deutero learning involves object and artifacts through its focus on meaning-making and learning-procedural capabilities. In the case of single and double-loop learning, scripts need to be explicitly focused and changed in accordance with an object at focus (being changed or nonchanged). In the case of deutero learning, the object, scripts and artifacts, and their relationships are all focused and reconceptualized. In other words, organizational learning requires interaction on a level of coconstruction.

Researchers and practitioners in the 1970s proposed and implemented many new forms of organization: the matrix organization, the network, cross-functional teams, and autonomous teams. These have all been tested without any great success. Networked learning organizations got a break-through with the work of Senge (1990), and his work on mental models and system dynamics (as discussed briefly earlier as a process modeling approach). More recently work on Intellectual Capital assessment and Systems Dynamics (Morecroft 1999) have influenced our research.

12.6 Product Design and Engineering

Most design and modeling projects start from quite abstract and general views, far out from the core knowledge of the targeted result. Core knowledge is the metaknowledge supporting and created by performing work. Modeling is about capturing, structuring, and evolving this knowledge. Industrial knowledge to be collected and captured is influenced by legacy thinking and sources such as paper, drawings, and natural language. Most enterprise flows and structures are paper diagrams and views, in these four evolving knowledge adapting dimensions, that have different names and terminology from sector-to-sector and from discipline-to-discipline:

- Business/project/activity/service
- Arena/plant/infrastructure/workplace
- Approach/methodology/script/control
- Delivery/production/result/value

Industry is still struggling to support product and process lifecycle design. The POPS methodologies will support a holistic design approach. The major contributors here are the German school of design shaped by Pahl and Beitz (1996), and later Ulrich and Eppinger, and the Scandinavian school shaped by Jacobsen, Olsson, and Myrup-Andreassen with their work on organic structures. These theories have been extended and applied in the car industry (Malmquist 1993) and also widely in German industry in the iVIP project.

Balancing Parameter Values

Parnas' theories about the industrial challenges of classes and decomposing properties into parameters, parameters into attributes, and managing attributes with multiple value-sets have inspired the development of a holistic approach to enterprise design and development. That is, we are always working in a space of at least four dimensions. His and other work reveals a deep understanding of the limitations of designing and engineering in static, isolated, and abstracted views of objects that are involved in many different structures. The holistic approach provided by AKM will enable much of what Parnas described, supporting sets of parameters for desired, max./min., actual and last agreed values, and value aggregation and propagation.

12.7 Systems Engineering

The ongoing work and discussions of INCOSE/IEWG (INCOSE 2007) on the past performance and the future of Systems Engineering (SE) matches closely the discoveries of the AKM technology. Systems engineering is not providing solutions that support design and evolutionary engineering approaches.

In modeling there has been a long-time trend on supporting the development of new modeling languages (so-called metamodeling) rather than the use of existing languages. The term "meta" indicates that something is after something, i.e., a metamodel is a model after (of) a model. It can be argued that the term metamodel is most correctly used when it is the data-model used for designing the database structure of a model repository (i.e., so that the instances in the model constitutes a model). Often, the term is also used for the related (but at times somewhat different) model that you get when describing the modeling concepts and relationships of a modeling language (below termed as language model). The metamodel for defining the storage of the model and the language model usually are quite similar, but the metamodel typically contains additional technically oriented aspects. We will use both terms below, and try to use them correctly vs. how we have defined the difference here.

In a sense, it is possible to apply an infinite number of metalevels. In practice, one normally looks at this at (maximum) four levels. Generally accepted conceptual framework for metamodeling explains the relationships between meta-meta-model, meta-model, model, and (not completely correctly named) "user data." Together they form four layers on top of each other, illustrated in metaobject facility (MOF) in OMG (which again is based on the work on CDIF in the 1980s):

- The user object layer is composed of the information that we wish to describe. This information is in a database-world typically referred to as "data," but this is just as much a model as any of the other levels. More precisely, it is a model on the instance level.
- The model layer is composed of the metadata that describes information. Metadata are informally aggregated as models.
- The metamodel layer is composed of the descriptions (i.e., meta-meta-data) that define the structure and semantics of meta-data. Meta-meta-data is

informally aggregated as meta-models. A meta-model can also be thought of as a "language" for describing different kinds of data.

- The meta-meta-model layer is composed of the description of the structure and semantics of meta-meta-data. In other words, it is the "language" for defining different kinds of meta-data.

In EXTERNAL (2003), another four level model was proposed, but which can be said to bifurcate the two lowest level (data and model) in the CDIF/MOF level as for the specific or general applicability of the model. Even if the terms below refer to process modeling in particular, these levels can be used for all sorts of modeling approaches.

The four levels identified in EXTERNAL are:

- Layer 1 – Describe process logic: At this layer, one identifies the constituent activities of generic, repetitive processes, and the logical dependencies between these activities. A process model at this layer should be transferable across time and space to a mixture of execution environments.
- Layer 2 – Engineer activities: Here process models are expanded and elaborated to facilitate business solutions. Elaboration includes concretization, decomposition, and specialization. Integration with local execution environment is achieved, e.g., by describing resources required for actual performance.
- Layer 3 – Manage work: The more abstract layers of process logic and of activity description provide constraints, but also useful resources (in the form of process templates) to the planning and performance of each process. At layer 3, more detailed decisions are taken regarding the performance of work in the *actual work environment* with its organizational, information, and tool resources; the scope is narrowed down to an actual process instance. *Concrete* resources increasingly are intertwined in the model, leading to the introduction of more dependencies. Management of activities may be said to consist of detailed planning, coordination and preparation for resource allocation.
- Layer 4 – Perform work: This lowest layer of the model covers the actual execution of tasks according to the determined granularity of work breakdown, which in practice is coupled to issues of empowerment and decentralization. When a group or person performs the task, whether to supply a further decomposition may be left to their discretion, or alternative candidate decompositions might be provided as advisory resources. At this layer resources are utilized or consumed, in an exclusive or shared manner.

Combining the CDIF/MOF and the EXTERNAL approach gives in principle a framework of 8 levels. The lower four is already described above, whereas we below describe and exemplify the higher four.

- Meta-meta model for all types of modeling approaches. Meta-meta modeling will generally be on this level. The meta-meta model in for instance OMG (MOF) is meant to be of this type.
- Meta-meta model for specific types of modeling approaches. At this level, you only take the specific possibilities of a certain environment into account.
- Meta-model meant for all modeling tasks. UML for instance is stated to be a language for specifying, visualizing, constructing, and document the artifacts of software systems, as well as for business modeling and other nonsoftware systems. In other words, UML is meant to be used in analysis of business and information, requirements specification and design. UML is meant to support the modeling of transaction systems, real-time, and safety critical systems. The meta-model of such a language thus easily get very large and complex.
- Meta-model for specific modeling task. For example, a language made in connection to one task (or a set of specific tasks, i.e., so-called domain-specific modeling (DSM (Kelly et al. 1996)) or Domain-Specific Languages (DSL).

Note that these levels are conceptual, and should not be enforced in a technical implementation, as previously discussed in Chap. 5.

12.8 Summary

We have in this chapter presented the core scientific basis of the AKM technology and thinking. The follow areas have been covered:

- Epistemology
- Human learning, pedagogy, and psychology
- Natural language, linguistics, and semiotics
- Process design and engineering
- Organizational development and learning
- Product design and engineering
- Systems engineering

13 Enterprise Knowledge Spaces

In Chaps. 1 and 2 we introduced the concept of enterprise knowledge spaces. We will describe here the different spaces in more detail.

13.1 Enterprise Knowledge Spaces Revisited

A knowledge space is a four-dimensional representation, where the dimensions are mutually reflective, capable of altering each others' meaning. AKM methodologies are built upon a common framework, called the Enterprise Knowledge Architecture (EKA) as described in Chap. 5. The EKA defines the dimensions of four nested knowledge spaces:

- The *personal workspace*, reflecting a user's work and knowledge so that the information system can adapt to it, as information content, roles, tasks, and views (IRTV).
- The *innovation space*, reflecting the products, organization, processes, and systems (POPS) of an interdisciplinary team collaborating, e.g., in product design.
- The *business networking space*, reflecting how companies come together in value networks and supply chains, their services, networks, projects, and platforms (SNPP).
- The *community space*, reflecting how larger industries, sectors, cultures, and societies function, their values, resources, initiatives, and infrastructures (VRII).

These knowledge spaces exist in all enterprises from two people collaborating to global value-chains. Main roles and goals of the different spaces are depicted in Fig. 13.1.

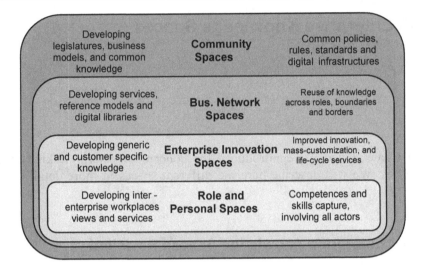

Fig. 13.1. Enterprise knowledge spaces

13.2 Modeling of Enterprise Knowledge Spaces

There are modeling methodologies associated with each of the four knowledge spaces. This book introduces the visual solution development methodology for personal workspaces, and the collaborative product design methodology for the innovation space. Later, we first introduce the basic dimensions of each space, and then we outline the principles for how the knowledge spaces are integrated into a holistic knowledge architecture.

13.2.1 Personal Workspace

A personal workspace should contain everything that someone needs for performing their work. To reflect this space, we need to model the four dimensions depicted in Fig. 13.2 below:

- Information (I), which information is needed to perform the work, which information is produced, etc.
- Roles (R), who are involved in the work, what is their responsibilities, which tasks do they perform, which information do they use, which views should their workplace consist of, etc.
- Tasks (T), which tasks are performed, which services are used to achieve the results.

- Views (V), which views should be available in the workplaces, which information and services should they give access to, what should it look like, etc.

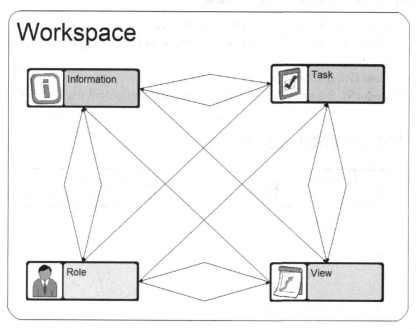

Fig. 13.2. Personal workspace components

As shown, the dimensions are mutually dependent. Tasks require and produce information, tasks are performed by roles, roles are defined by the tasks the role is· responsible for, roles need access to information, information is owned by roles, views are applied by roles performing tasks on some information, etc. Understanding and managing these dependencies are crucial for designing the right information, role, task, and view models. The four dimensions should thus be designed together. IRTV models typically contain several relationships between the elements in each dimension (information models, task patterns, etc.), and as well between the dimensions (e.g., roles and tasks such as a UML use case diagram). Large hierarchies of elements are, however, less common in this layer. Instead, task are often organized into process hierarchies, information by product structures, roles into organizational structures and views into application systems, in the surrounding innovation space discussed below.

13.2.2 Innovation Space

The innovation space defines the core structures of teamwork, especially in design projects. It contains these dimensions (Fig. 13.3):

- Product (P), the result and content of the work
- Organization (O), the personnel resources and skills required, available or applied
- Process (P), the structure of work tasks
- System (S), the underlying support tools and equipment used

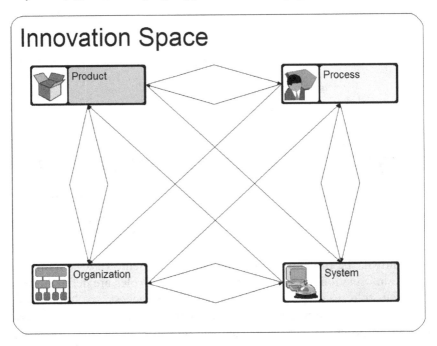

Fig. 13.3. Innovation space components

In a design project, a process is followed by an organization, using a system to develop a product. Again, the dimensions are mutually dependent on each other, and should be designed together, using the Collaborative Product Design methodology. The innovation space typically will contain hierarchical and aspect-oriented structures for each of the dimensions, such as work-breakdown structures for processes, component hierarchies for products, and of course organization hierarchies.

13.2.3 Business Networking Space

Behind the creative work performed in innovation spaces, we find strategic management and business transactions, establishing networks of groups and companies working together in value and supply networks, markets, and consortia. The dimensions of this space are (Fig. 13.4):

- Services (S) required and provided by the different companies and groups
- Network organization (N) structures of established collaborations
- Projects (P) where multiple partners cooperate to create new services
- Platforms (P) providing interoperable IT support for the networks

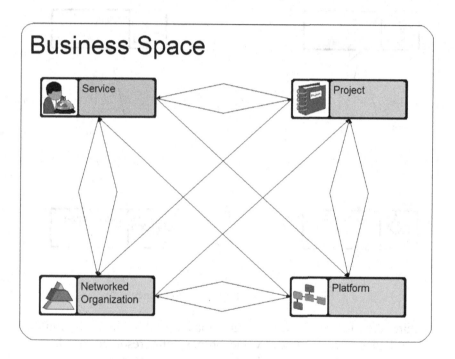

Fig. 13.4. Business space components

13.2.4 Community Space

Finally, the backbone of personal knowledge spaces, innovative teams, businesses and networks, is the society, culture, industrial setting, etc. where the businesses operate. Though not under the control of the business, they influence the operation of most businesses profoundly, in a number of dimensions (Fig. 13.5):

- Values (V) represent the worth of commodities, services, assets, or work, and the principles, standards, or quality that guides human actions
- Resources (R) are the personnel and material applied to create value
- Initiatives (I) to apply resources and infrastructure to create new values
- Infrastructure (I) is the overall set of tools and mechanisms for communication, logistics, and value creation in general

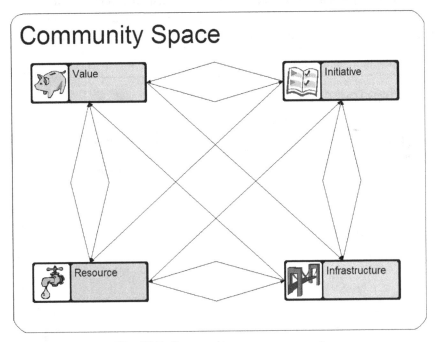

Fig. 13.5. Community space components

Future AKM-based corporate governance and community building methodologies need to assess value propositions, resource development and management, initiative portfolio management, infrastructure extension and maintenance (Fig. 13.5).

13.2.5 Overview

Table 13.1 summarizes the main knowledge spaces discussed earlier, illustrating as well how the dimensions reflect what to produce, who should do the work, how they should go about, and the tools applied. The last line refers back to the dimensions described in Fig. 5.2.

Table 13.1. Roles vs. knowledge spaces

	What/why	Who	How	Enabler
Community and network	Value	Resource	Initiative	Infrastructure
Business	Service	Network	Project	Platform
Team innovation	Product	Organization	Process	System
Individual	Information	Role	Task	View
Software	Data	User	Code	Programming

13.2.6 Knowledge Architectures

Knowledge architectures provide the structure that integrates the various knowledge spaces described earlier, and define the services for developing and customizing the knowledge spaces. Crucial challenges include the following:

- How the four dimensions of a knowledge space relate to each other and interact
- How different knowledge spaces interact, e.g., how elements are reflected across the knowledge spaces

Reflective Views

The dimensions of a knowledge space are interdependent. When you work on one dimension, you should take the others into account. For instance, in Fig. 13.6, we see how the products, organization, and system elements appear as input, output, and mechanism roles in IDEF process models.

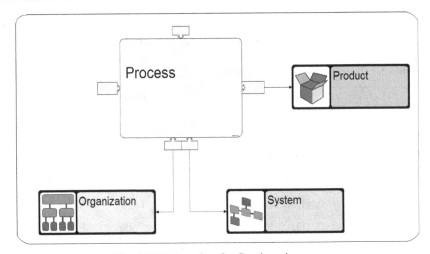

Fig. 13.6 Example of reflective views

Table 13.2 Reflections in the innovation space

Dimension→ Foreign ↓ element	Product	Organization	Process	System
Product	Design of production equipment	Organize by system, component, or discipline	Input/output roles, flows as product states	Identification and coding schemes across systems
Organization	Responsibility for product components; The effects of e.g., manufacturing org. on design	Management and organizational design units	Resource roles, control roles	Infrastructure provisioning organization
Process	Product lifecycle, multiple parameter value sets in different phases	Organize by phase, relationships (e.g., reporting) entail tasks	Planning processes and business process engineering and improvement methodologies	System usage processes
System	Engineering tools manage different product aspects	Deployment architecture	Mechanism roles	Systems for systems development

Table 13.2 gives more examples of the innovation space, showing that each of the dimensions may appear as "foreign" but integral elements (vertical) of models that primarily deal with another dimension (horizontal). As indicated, there is also inherent reflection within one dimension, e.g., planning processes that define other processes and production equipment being designed alongside the product they are to produce, etc. Examples from other spaces include data and metadata in the information dimension, and learning how to learn.

This mutual reflection between the dimensions in a space implies that all views and representations can be kept consistent. For instance, when someone adds a flow between two steps in a design process, that flow implicitly denotes a state in the product lifecycle as well, e.g., "as designed," "as built." When a new product component is added, the process model should immediately include steps for designing, testing, and producing the newly added component as well and the organizational roles that are responsible for these tasks should be defined alongside the information system elements needed for managing the information about the component and services for performing the tasks.

13.2.7 Reflection Across Knowledge Spaces

Perhaps even more important than the reflection inherent in a knowledge space is reflection between the knowledge spaces, e.g.:

- How the IRTV models are reflected into software services to create customized IT solutions, with parameterized services and information content available through role-specific workplaces
- How innovation space models, such as the collaborative product design methodology, map to IRTV models for configurable IT support
- How IRTV models capture bottom-up tasks, information content and targeted roles that need to be managed through the hierarchical process, product, organization, and system structures

As depicted below (Fig. 13.7), the dominant relationships for managing lower layer structures typically follow the main dimensions. For instance, tasks are aggregated into processes, roles into organizations, views into systems, and the primary information elements reflect product structures.

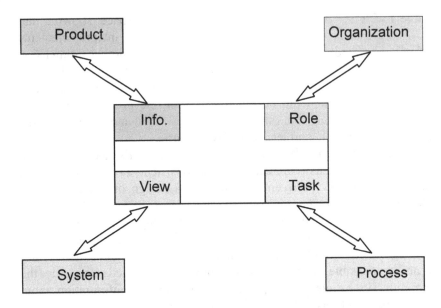

Fig. 13.7. Dominant reflections across knowledge spaces

This simplistic view is held by most modeling methodologies, such a business process management, information and data modeling, organization hierarchy charts, etc. It does, however, violate one of the core principles of knowledge spaces that the dimensional views are all mutually reflective and interdependent. Its single-dimensional, top–down perspective also violates common sense: Of course, processes, organizations, and systems are described as information as well, not just products. In the design, the product structures capture the critical dependencies between tasks, and the product structures are also used for managing and coordinating tasks, e.g., monitoring the progress of product component design rather than the progress of subprocesses and subtasks. Similarly, administrative tasks such as reporting emerge from relationships in the organization structure, and low level tasks are associated to the usage of information systems. Likewise, roles deal with responsibilities toward processes, products, and systems, not just the simple organizational structures. Figure 13.8 thus gives a more accurate, albeit complex representation of how the innovation space is reflected into personal workspaces, and vice versa.

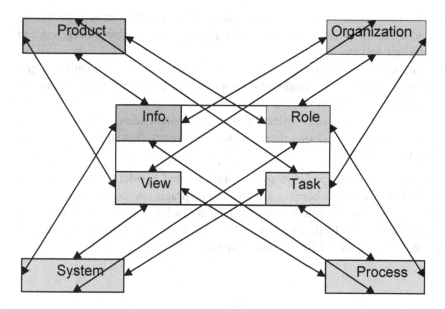

Fig. 13.8. Totality of reflections across knowledge spaces

The figure above also shows that each of the POPS elements can be seen from four different workspace perspectives (sides), as information, role/responsibility, task, and view, respectively. When these spaces are brought together, we thus define derived concepts illustrated by the above relationships, such as

- Product role, process role, organization role, and system roles
- Product, organization, process, and system information
- Product lifecycle, organizational, process, and system tasks
- Product, organization role, process phase, and system (aspect) view

Similar arguments can be made for the surrounding business and community knowledge spaces.

13.3 Summary

We have in this chapter described of four nested knowledge spaces in more detail:

- The *personal workspace*, reflecting a user's work and knowledge so that the information system can adapt to it, as information content, roles, tasks, and views (IRTV).

- The *innovation space*, reflecting the products, organization, processes and systems (POPS) of an interdisciplinary team collaborating, e.g., in product design.
- The *business networking space*, reflecting how companies come together in value networks and supply chains, their services, networks, projects and platforms (SNPP).
- The *community space*, reflecting how larger industries, sectors, cultures, and societies function, their values, resources, initiatives and infrastructures (VRII).

The enterprise knowledge spaces are bounded by identifiable but fuzzy borders. Whether the borders are a result of pragmatic boundaries, such as gateways between project phases and the isolated roles of engineering disciplines and so forth, or whether they are caused by limitations inherent in the mental models of our brains remains a research issue.

14 Summary and Directions

On one hand, some might point to a certain irony in presenting a *book* (using primarily one-dimensional alphabetic linear writing) on a topic touting the use of two and many-dimensional knowledge representations. On the other hand, even if traditional knowledge representation is not the best in all situations as we have argued for in the book, it does have some merit to present a linearization of the knowledge e.g., for making it easier for others to understand certain aspects. Although an Active Knowledge Modeling (AKM) tells many stories with precise meanings, thanks to the context, a written book tells one story, but leaves many interpretations, depending on the mental models of the readers. Therefore, we have tried to create as much context as possible from the first chapter. So what has been presented in this book is just one possible path through the AKM landscape.

Mankind has used different types of knowledge representations for thousands of years. The earliest examples of a conventional use of written symbols are on clay tables discovered in various parts of the Middle East and south-east Europe from around 3500 BC (Crystal 1987). This involves both informal natural language, and the start of the more formal language known as mathematics. Note that the matter of origin of these symbol systems are complicated by the fact that in early times, it is by no means easy to decide whether a piece of graphic should be counted as an artistic image or as a symbol of primitive writing. In principle, the difference is clear: the former conveys personal and subjective meanings, and does not combine into a system of recurring symbols with widely accepted values; by contrast, the latter is conventional and institutionalized, apparently capable of being understood in the same way by all who use the system. When the product is a rock carving or a painting, there is little doubt that its purpose is nonlinguistic (though it might have aesthetic, religious, or other functions). However, when the product is a series of apparent geometrical shapes or tiny characters, the distinction between art and writing become less obvious. As an example in early Greek and in Egyptian, the same word was used for "write" and "draw." Although alphabetic languages rule today (with some competition from logographic languages such as Chinese), many early languages were pictographic. On one hand, Egyptian hieroglyphs, for instance, are primarily pictographic interspersed with more traditional letters.

On the other hand, semiformal nonlinearized graphic representations have a much shorter history, and have only come very short in its evolution as a way of representing and creating knowledge.

14.1 Core Principles and Solutions

The AKM technology is reforming and extending the roles for enterprise modeling to address important issues, such as:

- Modeling specific roles, tasks, information, and views to capture context, improve coordination, and configure role-specific workplaces
- Modeling products, organizational resources, processes, and systems to support core industrial design and engineering knowledge
- Modeling properties and parameter-trees and their values and value-ranges as separate structures, independent of objects
- Managing corporate modeling elements and workplace contents in families of active knowledge architectures
- Managing contextual descriptions of work, and workplace configurations to support extensive reuse of knowledge and data
- Enabling industrial users to build and manage their own working environments, workplaces, and services
- Enabling life-cycle data and knowledge management, capturing and sharing experiences, unresolved issues and lessons learned
- Expressing knowledge and experiences readily reflected as updated menus and views in model-configured workplaces
- Building one integrated product structure model of a family of products variants, covering the entire product life-cycle
- Building knowledge models and architectures of methodologies, information libraries, and reference models, currently only available on paper
- Building collaboration spaces and visual scenes for design, engineering, work process experimentation, validation, and proactive learning.

To be an *active model* a visual model must first and foremost be available to the users of the operational information system at execution time. Second, the model must automatically influence the behavior of the computerized work support system or workplace. Third, the model must be dynamically extended and adapted, and users must be supported in changing the model to fit their local needs, enabling tailoring of the work environment's behavior. Industrial users should therefore be able to manipulate and use active knowledge models as part of their day-to-day work (Jørgensen 2001; Jørgensen 2004). AKM regards business and work-centric pragmatic knowledge to be the main innovative and integrating force. For IT to facilitate expressing, harvesting, and cultivation of business knowledge, it must be driven by pragmatic representations of people's knowledge. The only way to achieve this is to enable end-users to define, manage, and own their active knowledge models and model-views. This requires a new way of representing knowledge as visual structures, where complex, rigid, software-oriented languages are replaced by simple and agile concepts.

We have as discussed in Chap. 5 introduced more than 30 principles for AKM.

1. A model is a constellation of multiple views
2. Related views are mutually reflective
3. Views capture different dimensions of reality (as aspects)
4. Views from different perspectives may seem to be inconsistent
5. Different perspectives will define different model structures and hierarchies (types and parts)
6. Metamodeling is modeling, and all elements are inherently reflective
7. Any model element can have a multitude of types, (including basic types such as object, relationship, and property in different views)
8. Explicit classification should be complemented by implicit and derived classes
9. "Property" is a fundamental modeling construct
10. Properties anchor evolving parameter trees and value sets
11. "Relationship" is a fundamental modeling construct
12. Relationships represent complex task patterns
13. "Value" is a fundamental modeling construct. Values can be related to other elements, have properties, etc.
14. Identification of individual elements happen through many nontrivial identification schemes, utilizing any model hierarchy or relationship
15. Reuse is better supported by templates (prototype and stereotype instances) than by class instantiation
16. The essence of an element is its context, not the element by itself. The meaning of any model element may depend on the meaning of any other element (semantic holism)
17. Every model/view is an open system, and the meaning of any model fragment may depend on factors yet unknown, implicit, or tacit
18. During design, all dependencies are bidirectional

19. A model/view is always in flux. Evolution must be managed as versions, variants, and configurations
20. Access rights should be explicitly managed through modeled privileges. Role restrictions should not be hard-wired into the modeling services
21. Models represent reality with different and evolving degrees of formality and ambiguity
22. Models should be interpreted pragmatically
23. Models should be executed interactively
24. Inheritance is meaningful through any model structure, so detailed inheritance semantics must be model-configured
25. Parameters and values are propagated according to modeled inheritance and execution rules
26. Models can be viewed through multiple presentation formats
27. Models can be edited through multiple media interfaces
28. Modeling user interfaces should be customized to role, task, and user preferences
29. Model and view translation and transformation is best facilitated through interaction, identification, and propagation
30. Any modeled relationship can be viewed as an annotation, adding semantic content to the elements it connects
31. Like stories, templates should be connotations, conveying meaning by describing parallel realities that users can identify as overlapping their own in some way

These principles are all build into the Enterprise Knowledge Architecture (EKA), as described in Chap. 5. The EKA is the most abstract and general enterprise model of the entire family of enterprise models, acting as a family reference model for all other kinds and variants of enterprise models. An Active Knowledge Architecture (AKA), built using the EKA template, integrates all other enterprise architectures, such as product architectures and system architectures. An enterprise-specific AKA will support simultaneous modeling, metamodeling, model management and work execution, using the Configured Visual Workplace (CVW). Relationships between AKA, EKA, and ICT infrastructure was originally depicted in Fig. 1.3, and is reiterated here as Fig. 14.1.

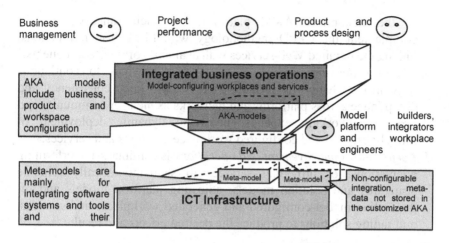

Fig. 14.1. Active Knowledge Architectures integrate enterprises

A more detailed account of these layers were provided in Fig. 8.1 including a possible layering of the ICT, whereas Chap. 7 provided the overall methodological approach C3S3P:

1. *Concept testing* is about creating customer interest and motivation for applying the AKM technology. This is done by demonstrating existing pilots and by assessing value propositions and potential benefits.
2. *Scaffolding* is about expressing stakeholder information structures and views, and relating them to roles, activities, and systems, to raise the customer's understanding for modeling and inspire motivation and belief in the benefits and values of the AKM approach.
3. *Scenario modeling* is about modeling "best-practice" work processes. Modeling the tasks, views, and routines that should be adhered to when performing work in an open extendable knowledge architecture is key to support local adaptations, experience capture, and agility.
4. *Solutions modeling* is about cross-disciplinary and cross-functional teams working together to proactively learn and improve quality in most enterprise life-cycle aspects. The purpose is creating a coherent and consistent holistic model or rather structures of models and submodels meeting a well-articulated purpose. Solutions modeling involves top–down, bottom–up, and middle-out multidimensional modeling for reflective behavior and execution.
5. *Platform configuration* is about integrating other systems and tools by modeling other systems data models and other aspects often found as UML, ER, or STEP models. These are created as integral submodels

of the customized AKM platform, and their functionality will complement the CPPD methodology with PLM system functions, linking the required Web-services with available software components.

6. *Platform delivery and practicing* adapts services to continuous growth and change by providing services to keep consistency and compliance across platforms and networks as the user community and project networking expands, involving dynamic deployment of model-designed and configured workplace solutions and services.

7. *Performance improvement and operations* is continuously performing adaptations, or providing services to semiautomatically reiterate structures and solution models, adjusting platform models and re-generating model-configured and generated workplaces and services, and tuning solutions to produce the desired effects and results.

The high-level C3S3P process will, depending on the particular use-cases, be further refined for different solutions by adapting and configuring tasks and views of any of the CPPD-components provided, as described in Chap. 9:

- CPC: Configurable Product Components, capturing parameterized variants, shapes, and materials
- CVW: Configurable Visual Workplaces, designing and generating user workplaces
- CWP: Configurable Work Processes, managing dependencies between tasks
- CPP: Configurable Property and Parameter-sets, making it possible to handle properties, parameters separately by each engineering or business discipline
- CPS: Configurable Product Structure, an early design support language for generic model and services
- CFD: Configurable Function Deployment, to correlate requirements and constraints with product properties and features
- CDL: Configurable Design Language, linking conceptual EKA to sketches illustrating fundamental and innovative product concepts
- CIB: Configurable Idea Bank, capturing and relating design ideas, principles, requirements, sketches, constraints, and stakeholder views for more effective innovation
- CWI: Configurable Web Service Integration, interfacing legacy systems as Web services
- CWW: Configurable Web Workplaces, designing and generating workplaces on the Web

- CCS: Configurable Collaboration Spaces, configuring roles, tasks, and views
- CCP: Configurable Competence and skill Profiles, for visual competency management

This list reflects components that would be adapted and built for partners and customers who require the capabilities to build their own methodology, innovation, or customer product delivery platform.

14.2 Addressing the Main Challenges

In Chap. 2, the main industrial challenges and demands was summarized, by focusing on problems within the four different enterprise knowledge spaces (Fig. 2.1). We here reiterate these points, indicating how AKM can partly address the different challenges. Although the main focus on the examples used in the book is on enterprise systems, we have also indicated the use of the approach in other areas. The challenges include the following:

1. Building searchable digital information libraries of present common information sources, to improve data and knowledge sharing and use
2. Developing consistent reference models, which are easily integrated with Web-platforms, to allow more effective community and project extensions and adaptations
3. Developing knowledge engineering platforms and services, which can add value to and integrate present IT application systems, "the islands of automation"
4. Developing operational enterprise knowledge architectures and platforms to concretize and make operational current blueprint architectural frameworks
5. Develop methodologies as descriptive templates to support the building of industry platforms, for example the CPPD methods to build collaborative design platforms
6. To model reference models that can be reused and drive knowledge standardization initiatives across projects and sectors
7. To support holistic design implying that multidimensional modeling capabilities to express mental models of designers and engineers must be supported

8. To provide modeling team services and role-specific workplaces and views to support concurrent knowledge engineering for collaborative product design

9. To provide model or knowledge architecture configured workplaces to enable new approaches to model-based systems engineering and solutions deployment

10. To provide services enabling data definition and sharing without being dependent on IT-defined data-models, thus supporting idea capture and conceptual design

In addition to these mostly technical challenges, there are educational, organizational, and managerial challenges that must also be dealt with.

The definition of what is an IT-system may have to be rethought and systems engineering will need to align with product design and engineering to cover holistic conceptual and system design. Business and industry will take advantage of active knowledge architectures and configured workplaces and collaboration spaces.

In Chap. 10 we described the following impacts of AKM Technology relative to these challenges:

- The AKM technology will enable industrial users to build their own operational networks, workplaces, and collaboration arenas. This will be instrumental in addressing challenges 7–10 in particular.
- The future direction of business-economic research needs to be established with reference to added values through sharing knowledge rather than by transaction costs incurred by rigid IT systems. An active knowledge architecture covering the early design stages has the capabilities to implement all this and cut time and costs by factors. This will be instrumental in addressing challenges 3–6.
- Visual modeling using the IRTV language and the C3S3P methodology has the potential to describe any role in industry, and we believe this is also true for the public as well as any field of science. Now, imagine what could happen if all these experts could share work-centric knowledge describe in a common problem-solving visual language. Another general impact from the AKM technology would be convergence of scientific concepts and disciplines. This will be instrumental in addressing challenges 1–2.
- Finally, the many educational and professional training challenges described must be met and fulfilled, but with escalating innovation new challenges will always emerge.

14.3 Industrial Exploitation

Although AKM technology is applicable in a large number of industries and markets AKM AS has decided to target these industrial markets, starting in the Scandinavian area:

- Aerospace – focusing on architectures for systems design
- Automotive – targeting configurable components for integrated product models
- Construction – enabling product development and portfolio management
- Offshore – Oil and Gas – moving from document flows to knowledge model sharing

Other market segments will be explored if there is a partner that can take charge of developing and selling targeted service platforms.

AKM and partners can fill many roles, and thus have many ways of collaborating and generating values, exemplified by:

1. Being a service provider, developing solutions for e.g., a supplier or community network
2. Selling licenses of the AKM components to other design service providers, who develop, sell and host their own platforms, as found in some industries
3. Selling the AKM components and suites of the CPPD components directly to industrial projects and customers, including significant training and consulting services
4. Selling the AKM components and suites of the CPPD components to value-adding partners, platform providers and consultants, creating long term relations
5. Support network sales, where the customers of AKM's customers experience the value of AKM in projects, and then build new platforms to cover other parts of their business

The technology development plan of AKM facilitates all of these business model alternatives. For instance, the configurable collaboration space with Web portal, Web services integration, and task patterns, is important for all network sales. Configurable visual workplaces, available over the Web, will further promote customer-site networked sales.

Building, delivering, and operating these new value constellations and the supporting platforms is not without technical and organizational challenges. The most resource demanding challenges are:

1. Making business and technical managers understand the opportunities
2. Involving leading engineers to work with AKM in industrial innovation projects
3. Finding partners and suppliers to build platforms and sustain innovation and growth
4. Making IT people understand the core AKM concepts, such as knowledge spaces
5. Promoting Communities of Excellence, sharing knowledge for competitive advantages
6. Supporting new Standards and Methods for concurrent holistic design and engineering
7. Involving educators and interest organizations in applying the AKM technology

Selling and delivering operational knowledge platforms from scratch can be very hard sales, demanding services for customer personnel to:

1. Deploy, customize, and manage workplaces and collaboration spaces
2. Introduce new roles, build workplaces, methods, components, and services
3. On-demand involve remote partner contributions and competences
4. Extend, adapt, and manage the knowledge architectures and contents
5. Train and coach users, customers, suppliers, and partners
6. Operate, update, and manage the platform components and services
7. Integrate and configure the existing applications and databases
8. Continuously improve workplaces and solutions

As we deploy more and more solutions, covering a rapidly growing number of application domains, we expect to find solid reasons for building strong local as well as global communities. Global communities will typically need services in categories 1–4 above, while local communities will be more using service categories 5–8 from the list above.

The AKM technology have tremendous market and business potential, but its success relies on people's willingness to learn new ways of applying and exploiting, changing from off-the-shelf IT systems to plug-and-play components configured by business knowledge.

AKM's secret for success lies in four major discoveries:

1. An enterprise is integrated and run by pragmatic logic, providing work context through reflective views, recursive task-structures, repetitive flows, and replicable templates
2. A holistic design approach, creating layers of reflective knowledge, is needed by enterprises to create an integrating *Active Knowledge Architecture (AKA)*

3. Data-models should be defined, designed, and engineered in the AKA, communicated as knowledge views in workplaces, and engineered for persistent storage in databases
4. Real-world knowledge is not entirely Object-Oriented (classes of types), so we also need to understand Design-Orientation (managing families), Environment-Orientation (bottom-up or emergent work processes), and Role-Orientation (adaptive contexts for use).

There will be different approaches to systems engineering, but the key is discovering that we need to totally rethink enterprise design and engineering; taking a holistic approach to engineer integrated product families and self-configuring solutions. This will allow lean, generic quality software components to be produced and IT solutions to be configured by modeling business and work logic, captured in an active knowledge architectures. AKM technology represents the first steps toward true c-Business:

- Jump-starting the *knowledge economy*, value networking, and service-teams development
- Enabling new approaches to *holistic design* of products, work processes, and IT systems, establishing interoperable concepts and functional system architectures
- Improving industrial *innovation and creativity,* turning experiences and lessons learned into improved tasks and views in contextual work environments
- Fostering *industry driven research*, education and industrial reference model development by creating collaborative communities

14.4 The Way Ahead

We will end the book with a short set of core questions related to AKM:

1. What is AKM? AKM is an approach for adding visual workplaces, collaboration spaces, and knowledge arenas to existing industrial IT platforms.
2. Why use AKM? Get more values from your human, computer and IT system assets, support visual communication, coordination and holistic design and learning.
3. How to use AKM? Apply AKM to build visual models for improved insight to solve problems and support continuous evolutions and improvements.

4. Who uses AKM? Build project teams including AKM enterprise expertise and a visual modeling facilitator involved to become effective from day one.
5. When to use AKM? When your company is mature enough to let core knowledge add a competitive edge to your business platforms.
6. Where to use AKM? AKM investments pay the best longer term dividends when applied in the early stages of technology development and innovation projects, providing capabilities prohibited by traditional IT application systems.
7. What is AKM giving you? Ways of harnessing and using your own core business knowledge to configure and drive computing solutions.
8. How to get started? Engage AKM people as knowledge modeling experts and facilitators in project teams to perform a concept study or problem solutions test scenario.

We have in the book illustrated why we need to move toward model-designed service-configurable enterprises, and value communities, and shown how AKM technology can get us at least part of the way.

The future will be model-designed and model-managed. IT and knowledge engineering will move from object-orientation toward view-orientation, where industrial users will develop their own model-configured, user-composed services, and platforms.

Goals to strive toward:

1. Turning the Web into a visual medium, enhancing our use of the left part of the human mind.
2. Providing generic software tools/components that can be a common platform for AKM driven higher level customer and networking platforms.
3. Providing a platform to integrate the increasingly more isolated communities of modern societies.
4. Providing increased citizen involvement in democratic activities to shape our future nations and global societies.
5. Giving the ownership of data back to the users, providing services for people to define data, calculate and share values, and control data availability.
6. Combining design, learning and problem-solving to make closed environments and industrial and other workspaces accessible by trainees.

Thus even if this is the end of this book, it is only the end of the beginning of the use of AKM-technology.

References

Aalst, W. M. P. v. d.: Formalization and verification of event-driven process chains, Information and Software Technology, 41(10) (1999)

Aalst, W. M. P. v. d., Desel, J., Oberweis, A. (eds): *Business Process Management.* Lecture Notes in Computer Science 1806 (Springer, Berlin Heidelberg New York 2000)

Abbot, K. R., Sarin, S. K.: Experiences with workflow management: Issues for the next generation, In: *ACM CSCW Conference*, Chapel Hill, North Carolina, United States (1994)

Abdel-Hamid, T. K., Madnick, S. E.: Lessons learned from modeling the dynamics of software development, Communications of the ACM, 32(12) (1989)

Akmodeling: http://www.akmodeling.com (2007) Cited Dec 2007

Alonso, G., Fiedler, U., Hagen, C., Lazcano, A., Schuldt, H., Weiler, N.: WISE: Business to business eCommerce, In: *International Workshop on Research Issues on Data Engineering*, Sydney, Australia (1999)

Alonso, G., Casati, F., Kuno, H., Machiraju, V.: *Web Services: Concepts, Architecture and Applications* (Springer, Berlin Heidelberg New York 2004)

Ambler, S. W.: *Agile Modeling: Effective Practices for Extreme Programming and the Unified Process* (Wiley, New York 2002)

Ambriola, V., Conradi, R., Fuggetta, A.: Assessing process-centered software engineering environments, ACM Transactions on Software Engineering and Methodology, 6(3) (1997)

Ankolekar, A., Martin, D., McGuinness, D., McIlraith, S., Paolucci, M., Parsia, B.: OWL-S' Relationship to Selected Other Technologies, Technical report, W3C Member Submission 22. http://www.w3.org/Submission/OWL-S-related/ November (2004) Cited 1 Feb, 2006

Antoniou, G., van Harmelen, F.: Web ontology language: OWL. *In: Handbook on Ontologies* ed by Staab, S., Studer, R. (Springer, Berlin Heidelberg New York 2004)

Argyris, C., Schön, D.: *Organisational Learning: A Theory of Action Perspective.* (Addison-Wesley, Reading MA 1973)

Argyris, C., Schön, D.: *Organizational Learning: A Theory of Action Perspective* (Addison-Wesley, Reading MA 1978)

Argyris, C., Schön, D. A.: *Organizational Learning II. Theory, Method, and Practice.* (Addison-Wesley, Reading MA 1996)

Arkin, A., Askary, S., Bloch, B., Curbera, F., Goland, Y., Kartha, N., et al.: Web services business process execution language version 2.0, Technical report, OASIS Open, Inc., Committee. From http://www.oasis-open.org/committees/download.php/16024/wsbpel-specification-draft-Dec-22-2005.htm (Draft, 21 Dec, 2005) Cited Dec 2007

Arthur, W. B.: Increasing returns and the new world of business, Harvard Business Review, **74** (July–August) 100–109 (1996)

ATHENA: First version of state of the art in enterprise modeling techniques and technologies to support enterprise interoperability (EU IP- Project – No. 507849). http://www.athena-ip.org/. (2004) Cited Dec 2007

ATHENA Integrated Project, IST –2002- 50678: http://www.athena-ip.org. (2007) Cited Dec 2007

Azuma, R. T.: A survey of augmented reality, Presence: Teleoperators and Virtual Environments **6**(4) 355–385 (1997)

Bandinelli, S., Fuggetta, A., Lavazza, L., Loi, M., Picco, G. P.: Modeling and improving an industrial software process, IEEE Transactions on Software Engineering, **21**(5) (1995)

Bardram, J. E.: *Collaboration, Coordination, and Computer Support. An Activity Theoretical Approach to the Design of Computer Supported Cooperative Work.* Ph.D. thesis, Aarhus University, Computer Science Department, DAIMI PB – 553 May (1998)

Barros, A., Dumas, M., Oaks, P.: A critical overview of the web services choreography description language, BPTrends (http://www.bptrends.com), March 1–24 (2005)

Batzarov, Z.: Orbis latinus: Linguistic terms. http://www.orbilat.com/General_References/Linguistic_Terms.html (2004) Cited Dec 2007 http://www.businesscentricmethodology.com/navigation/workspace.html (2007) Cited Dec 2007

Benson, I., Everhard, S., McKernan, A., Galewsky, B., Partridge, C.: Mathematical structures for reasoning about emergent organization, In: *ACM CSCW Workshop: Beyond Workflow Management*, Philadelphia, USA (2000)

Berardi, D., Cabral, L., Cimpian, E., Domingue, J., Mecella, M., Stollberg, M., Sycara, K.: ESWC Semantic web services tutorial. http://stadium.open.ac.uk/dip/ (2005) Cited Dec 2007

Berger, P., Luckmann, T.: *The Social Construction of Reality: A Treatise in the Sociology of Knowledge* (Penguin, London 1966)

Berners-Lee, T., Hendler, J., Lassila, O.: The semantic web, Scientific American, **284**(5), 34–43 (2001)

Bernstein, A.: How can cooperative work tools support dynamic group processes?: Bridging the specificity frontier, In: *ACM CSCW Conference*, Philadelphia, USA (2000)

Bernus, P., Nemes, L.: A framework to define a generic enterprise reference architecture and methodology, Computer Integrated Manufacturing Systems, **9**(3), 179–191 (1996)

Blackler, F.: Knowledge and the theory of organizations: Organizations as activity systems and the reframing of management, Journal of Management Studies **30**(6) (1993)

Bolcer, G., Kaiser, G.: SWAP: Leveraging the web to manage workflow, IEEE Internet Computing, **3**(1) (1999)

Booch, G., Rumbaugh, J., Jacobson, I.: *The Unified Modeling Language: User Guide Second Edition* (Addison-Wesley, Reading MA 2005)

Borgida, A., Brachman, R.: Conceptual modeling with description logics. In: *The Description Logic Handbook: Theory, Implementation and Applications* ed by Baader, F., Calvanese, D., McGuinness, D., Nardi, D., Patel-Schneider, P. (Cambridge University Press, UK 2003)

Business Process Management Institute (BPMI): http://www.bpmi.org/ (2007) Cited Dec 2007

Braf, E.: *Knowledge Demanded for Action: Studies on Knowledge Mediation in Organizations.* Ph.D. thesis, Department of Computer and Information Science, Linköping University, Sweden (Linköping Studies in Information Science, Dissertation no.10) (2004)

Brickley, D.: RDF: Understanding the striped RDF/XML syntax, from http://www.w3.org/2001/10/stripes/ (2001) Cited Dec 2007

Broekstra, J., Kampman, A., van Harmelen, F.: Sesame: An architecture for storing and querying RDF data and schema information. In: *Spinning the Semantic Web: Bringing the World Wide Web to Its Full Potential* ed by Fensel, D., Hendler, J. A., Lieberman, H., Wahlster, W. pp. 197–222 (MIT Press Cambridge, MA 2003)

Butler, H.: Barriers to *real world adoption of semantic web technologies* (Hewlett-Packard, USA 2002)

Button, G.: What's wrong with speach act theory? Computer Supported Cooperative Work, **3**(1) (1995)

Buxmann, P., Weizel, T., König, W.: Auswirkung alternativer koordinationsmechanismen auf die auswahl von kommunikationsstandards. In: Zeitschrift für Betriebswirtschaft, Ergänzungsheft 02 133–151 Innovation und Absatz (1999)

Carlsen, S.: Action port model: A mixed paradigm conceptual workflow modeling language. In: *Third IFCIS Conference on Cooperative Information Systems (CoopIS'98)*, New York (1998)

Cavantzas, N., Burdett, D., Ritzinger, G., Fletcher, T., Lafon, Y., Barreto, C. (eds): Web services choreography description language version 1.0. Technical report, W3C Candidate Recommendation, from http://www.w3.org/TR/2005/CR-ws-cdl-10-20051109/ (2005). Cited Dec 2007

Chen, P. P.: The Entity-relationship model – Toward a unified view of data, ACM Transactions on Database Systems **1**(1), 9–36 (1976)

Chen, D., Doumeingts, G.: The GRAI-GIM reference model, architecture, and methodology. In: *Architectures for Enterprise Integration* ed by Bernus, P. (Chapman & Hall, London 1996)

Chen, D., Vernadat, F.: Enterprise interoperability: A standards view. In: *Enterprise Inter- and Intra-Organizational Integration* ed by Kosanke, K., Jochem, R., Nell, B. (Kluwer, Boston 2003)

Chrysostalis, M., Hildrum, J., Krogstie, J., Scagno, G., Strømseng, K.: Use Case Evaluation Report, Deliverable 9-93-S-2003-01-2, The EXTERNAL Project (2003)

Clemons, E. K., Row, M. C.: Information technology and industrial cooperation: The changing economics of coordination and ownership, Journal of Management Information Systems, 9(2) 9–28 (1992)

Cockburn, A.: *People and Methodologies in Software Development*, Ph.D. dissertation, University of Oslo Press (2003)

Conradi, R., Jaccheri, M. L.: Process modelling languages, In: *Software Process: Principles, Methodology and Technology*. Lecture Notes in Computer Science 1500 (Springer, Berlin Heidelberg New York 1998)

Cook, S. D. N., Brown, J. S.: Bridging epistemologies: The generic dance between knowledge and knowing, Organization Science 10(4), 381–400 (1990)

CoSpaces project: http://www.cospaces.org/ (2007) Cited Dec 2007

Croquet: http://www.opencroquet.org (2007) Cited Dec 2007

Crystal, D.: *The Cambridge Encyclopedia of Language* (Cambridge University Press, New York 1987)

Cugola, G.: Tolerating deviations in process support systems via flexible enactment of process models, IEEE Transactions on Software Engineering, 24(11) (1998)

Curtis, B., Kellner, M. I., Over, J.: Process modeling, Communications of the ACM, 35(9) (1992)

Daconta, M., Orbst, L., Smith, K.: *The Semantic Web: A Guide to the Future of XML, Web Services and Knowledge Management.* (Wiley, London 2003)

Dahlbom, B.: The idea that reality is socialy constructed. In: *Software Development and Reality Construction* ed by Floyd, Zullighoven, C., Budde, R., Keil-Slawik, R. (Springer, Berlin Heidelberg New York 1991)

Davenport, T. H., Prusak, L.: *Working Knowledge* (Harvard Business School Press, Boston, MA 1993)

Davis, A. M., Overmeyer, S., Jordan, K., Caruso, J., Dandashi, F., Dinh, A., Kincaid, G., Ledeboer, G., Reynolds, P., Sitaram, P., Ta, A., Theofanos, M.: Identifying and measuring quality in a software requirements specification. In: *Proceedings of the First International Software Metrics Symposium* pp. 141–152

DelaHostria, E.: Interoperability of standards to support application integration. In *ICEIMT 2002* pp. 283–294 (Kluwer, Dordrecht 2002)

DeMarco, T.: *Structured Analysis and System Specification* (Prentice Hall, Englewood Cliffs NJ 1979)

(De Michelis and Grasso 1994) De Michelis, G., Grasso, M. A.: Situating conversations within the language/action perspective: The Milan conversation model, In: *ACM CSCW Conference*, Chapel Hill, North Carolina, USA 1994

Derniame, J. C. (ed): *Software Process: Principles, Methodology and Technology.* Lecture Notes in Computer Science 1500 (Springer, Berlin Heidelberg New York 1998)

Dijkman, R., Dumas, M.: Service-oriented design: A multi-viewpoint approach, International Journal of Cooperative Information Systems, **13**(4), 337–368 (2004)

Department of Defence (DoD): DoD architecture framework. Version 1.0. Volume I: Definitions and guidelines. Washington, DC: Office of the DoD Chief Information Officer, Department of Defense. (2003)

Department of Defence (DoD): DoD architecture framework. Version 1.0. Volume II: Product descriptions. Washington, DC: Office of the DoD Chief Information Officer, Department of Defense. (2003)

Doumeingts, G., Vallespir, B., Chen, D.: Decisional modelling using the GRAI grid. In: *Handbook on Architectures of Information Systems* ed by Bernus, P., Mertins, K., Schmidt, G. pp. 313–338 (Springer, Berlin Heidelberg New York 1998)

Dourish, P., Holmes, J., MacLean, A., Marqvardsen, P., Zbyslaw, A.: Freeflow: Mediating between representation and action in workflow systems, In: *ACM CSCW Conference*, Boston, USA (1996)

ebXML http://www.unece.org/cefact/index.htm (2007) Cited Dec 2007

Elvekrok, D. R., Lillehagen, F., Solheim, H. G.: Use case driven Active Knowledge Models (AKM) in extended enterprises. In: *CE 2003*, ed by Jardim-Goncalves, R., Cha, H., Steiger-Garcao, A. Proceedings of the 10th International Conference on Concurrent Engineering, Madeira, Portugal. July 2003 (A.A. Balkema Publishers, Netherlands 2003)

Engeström, Y.: *Learning by expanding.* Ph.D. thesis, Orienta-Konsultit Oy, Helsinki (1987)

Engeström, Y.: Interactive Extpertise: Studies in distributed working intelligence. Helsinki: Research Bulletin, Department. of Education, University of Helsinki (1992)

ESPRIT Consortium AMICE: CIMOSA: Open system architecture for CIM. Volume 1 (Research report ESPRIT, Project 688/5288) (2nd revised and extended edition). (Springer, Berlin Heidelberg New York 1993)

Estublier, J.: Software configuration management: A roadmap. In: *Proceedings of 22nd International Conference on Software Engineering, The Future of Software Engineering*, pp. 279–289 (ACM Press, New York 2000)

EXTERNAL IST 1999-10091; duration 2000–2003, http://www.external-ist.org/ (2003) Cited Dec 2007

Falkenberg, E. D., Hesse, W., Lindgreen, P., Nilsson, B. E., Oei, J. L. H., Rolland, C., Stamper, R. K., Assche, F. J. M. V., Verrijn-Stuart, A. A., Voss, K.: A Framework of information system concepts – The FRISCO Report, IFIP WG 8.1 Task Group FRISCO http://home.dei.polimi.it/pernici/ifip81/publications. html (1996) Cited Dec 2007

Farrell, J., Saloner, G.: Installed base and compatibility: Innovation, product preannouncements, and predation, The American Economic Review, **76**(5) (1986)

Fichtner, B.: Co-ordination, co-operation and communication in the formation of theoretical concepts in instruction. In: *Learning and Teaching on a Scientific Basis: Methodological and Epistemological Aspects of the Activity Theory of Learning and Teaching* ed by Hedegard, M., Hakkarainen, P., Engeström, Y. (Aarhus Universitet, Psykologisk Institut, Aarhus 1984)

FIPA http://www.fipa.org/ (2008) Cited Feb 2008

Fischer, L.: *Excellence in Practice IV - Innovation and excellence in workflow and knowledge management* (Workflow Management Coalition, Future Strategies Inc., Florida, USA 2000)

Fleisch, E.: *Das Netzwerkunternehmen* (Springer, Berlin Heidelberg New York 2001)

Fox, M. S., Gruninger, M.: Enterprise modelling, AI Magazine (2000)

Gane, C., Sarson, T.: *Structured Systems Analysis: Tools and Techniques* (Prentice Hall, Englewood Cliffs NJ 1979)

Garfinkel, H.: *Studies in Ethnomethodology* (Prentice Hall, Englewood Cliffs NJ 1967)

Geodec: http://infolab.usc.edu/projects/geodec/ Cited Dec 2007

GERAM, IFIP-IFAC Task Force on Architectures for Enterprise Integration. GERAM: Generalised enterprise reference architecture and methodology. Technical Report Version 1.6.3 http://www.cit.gu.edu.au/~bernus/taskforce/geram/versions/geram1-6-3/v1.6.3.html (1999) Cited Dec 2007

Giotopoulos, K., Vassiliadis, B., Scagno, G.: WP6 Worktop specification, Deliverable 6-63-W-2001-01-1, The EXTERNAL Project (2001)

Gjersvik, R.: *The Construction of Information Systems in Organization: An Action Research Project on Technology, Organizational Closure, Reflection, and Change.* Ph.D. thesis, ORAL, NTH, Trondheim, Norway (1993)

Glance, N. S., Pagani, D. S., Pareschi, R.: Generalized process structure grammars (GPSG) for flexible representation of work, In: *ACM CSCW Conference*, Boston, USA (1996)

Goldkuhl, G., Ågerfalk, P. J.: Actability: A way to understand information system pragmatics, In: *Coordination and Communication Using Signs* ed by Liu K. et al. pp. 85–114 (Kluwer, Dordrecht 2002)

Government of Canada: http://www.tbs-sct.gc.ca/fap-paf/documents/iteration/iterationtb_e.asp (2001) Cited Dec 2007

Green, P., Rosemann, M.: Integrated process modeling: An ontolocial evaluation, Information Systems, **25**(3) (2000)

Guba, E. G., Lincoln, Y. S.: *Fourth Generation Evaluation* (Sage, Newbury Park, CA 1989)

Haake, J., Ohren, O., Krogstie, J.: WP4 – D13. Prototype: Use case – External Project, Deliverable 4-00-D-2002-01-0, The EXTERNAL Project (2002)

Haake, J. M., Wang, W.: Flexible support for business processes: Extending cooperative hypermedia with process support. In: *ACM GROUP Conference*, Phoenix, Arizona, USA (ACM Press, New York 1997)

Havey, M.: *Essential Business Process Modelling* (O'Reillys, Sebastopol CA 2005)

Hayes, P.: RDF semantics. Technical report, W3C. http://www.w3.org/TR/rdf-mt/ (2004) Cited Dec 2007

Hommes, B.-J., Reijswoud, V. v.: The quality of business process modelling techniques, In: *Conference on Information Systems Concepts (ISCO)*, Leiden, Nertherlands (Kluwer, Dordrecht 1999)

Hummel, J. E., Biederman, I.: Dynamic binding in a neural network for shape recognition, Psychological Review **99**(3), 480–517 (1992)

IDEF-3x Process Modeling Language Specification, Standard NA-94-1422B, Rockwell International (1993)

IEEE P1516.1: D5. Standard for Modeling and Simulation (M&S) High Level Architecture (HLA) – Federate Interface Specification (2000)

IEEE: 1471-2000, Recommended Practice for Architectural Description of Software-Intensive Systems. http://standards.ieee.org/reading/ieee/std_public/ description/se/ 1471–2000_desc.html (2000). Cited Dec 2007

Intalio http://www.intalio.com (2007) Cited Dec 2007

Inteligrid: http://www.inteligrid.com Cited Dec 2007

International Alliance for Interoperability (IAI): http://www.iai-international.org/ Cited Dec 2007

International Council on Systems Engineering (INCOSE): http://www.incose.org/ Cited Dec 2007

INTEROP http://www.interop-noe.org (2007) Cited Dec 2007

Irani, P., Ware, C.: The geon diagram. *Graphics Interface '99* Poster Abstracts. Kingston, Ontario, June (1999)

ISO: 15704:2000, Industrial automation systems – Requirements for enterprise-reference architectures and methodologies. http://www.iso.org/iso/iso_catalogue/ catalogue_tc/ catalogue_detail.htm?csnumber=28777 (2000) Cited Dec 2007

International Organization for Standardization (ISO): ISO 15745-1 Industrial automation systems and integration – Open systems application integration framework – Part 1: Generic reference description. Geneva, Switzerland (2003)

Jørgensen, H. D.: Interaction as a framework for flexible workflow modeling, In: *Proceedings of GROUP '01*, Boulder, USA, (ACM Press, New York 2001).

Jørgensen, H. D.: *Interactive Process Models*, Ph.D. thesis, NTNU, Trondheim, Norway (2004)

Jørgensen, H. D., Carlsen, S.: Emergent workflow: Integrated planning and performance of process instances, In: *Workflow Management Conference*, Münster, Germany (1999)

Jørgensen, H. D., Karlsen, D., Lillehagen, F.: Product based interoperability – Approaches and requirements. In: *Proceedings of Challenges in Collaborative Engineering (CCE '2007)*, Krakow, Poland (2007)

Jørgensen, H., Krogstie, J.: Interactive models for virtual enterprises. In: *Virtual Enterprise Integration: Technological and Organizational Perspective* ed by Putnik, G., Cunha, M. M. (IDEA Group Publishing 2005)

Kallåk, B. H., Pettersen, T. B., Ressem, J. E.: Object-oriented workflow management: Intelligence, flexibility, and real support for business processes,

In: *OOPSLA Workshop on Implementation and Application of Object-Oriented Workflow Management Systems*, Vancouver, Canada (1998)

Karlsen, D., Lillehagen, F., Tinella, S.: The EXTERNAL intelligent infrastructure. In: *CE 2003*, ed by Jardim-Goncalves, R., Cha, H., Steiger-Garcao, A. Proceedings of the 10th International Conference on Concurrent Engineering, Madeira, Portugal, July 2003 (A.A. Balkema Publishers, 2003)

Karlsen, D., Lillehagen, F., Tinella, S., Krogstie, J., Jørgensen, H. D., Johnsen, S. G., Wang, W., Rubart, J., Lie, F. T.: D3 – EE infrastructure, Deliverable from the EXTERNAL Project – IST 1999-10091, Lysaker, Norway (2001)

Kelly, K.: Twelve principles of the networked economy, Wired 1997, see also http://valuebasedmanagement.net/methods_kelly_twelve_principles_network_economy.html Cited Dec 2007

Kelly, S., Lyytinen, K., Rossi, M.: MetaEdit+: A fully configurable multi-user and multi-tool CASE and CAME environment. In: *CAiSE'96*, ed by Constantopoulos, P., Mylopoulos, J., Vassiliou, Y. Lecture Notes in Computer Science 1080 (Springer, Berlin Heidelberg New York 1996)

King, J. L.: SimLanguage, Computer Supported Cooperative Work, 3(1) (1995)

Klein, M., Broekstra, J., Fensel, F., van Harmelen, F., Horrocks, I.: Ontologies and schema languages on the web. In: *Spinning the Semantic Web: Bringing the World Wide Web to Its Full Potential* ed by Fensel, D., Hendler, J.A. Lieberman, H., Wahlster, W. pp. 95–139 (MIT Press, Cambridge, MA 2003)

Koestler, A.: The Ghost in the Machine (Arkana, UK 1967)

Krogstie, B.: *Applying Activity Theory in Knowledge Management*. Master thesis, Department of Educational Research, University of Oslo (2000)

Krogstie, J., Elvekrok, D. R., Lillehagen, F., Ohren, O., Strømseng, K., Wang, W.: D6 – EE methodology, Deliverable from the EXTERNAL Project – IST 1999-10091, Oslo, Norway (2002)

Krogstie, J., Hildrum, J., Chrysostalis, M., Hestvik, R.: Enterprise methodology evaluation report, Deliverable D19, the EXTERNAL project (2002)

Krogstie, J., Jørgensen, H.: Interactive models for supporting networked organisations. In: *16th Conference on advanced Information Systems Engineering*. Riga, Latvia (Springer, Berlin Heidelberg New York 2004)

Krogstie, J., Sindre, G., Jørgensen, H.: Process models representing knowledge for action: A revised quality framework, European Journal of Information Systems 15, 91–102 (2006)

Krogstie, J., Veres, C., Sindre, G.: Integrating semantic web technology, web services, and workflow modelling: Achieving system and business interoperability. International Journal of Enterprise Information Systems 3(1) 22–41 (2007)

Kuntz, J. C., Christiansen, T. R., Cohen, G. P., Jin, Y., Levitt, R. E.: The virtual design team: A computational simulation model of project organizations, Communications of the ACM 41(11) (1998)

Lawton, G.: Knowledge management: Ready for prime time?, IEEE Computer, 34(2), 12–14 (2001)

Lei, Y., Singh, M. P.: A comparison of workflow metamodels, In: *ER Workshop on Behavioral Modeling*. Lecture Notes in Computer Science 1565 (Springer, Berlin Heidelberg New York 1997)

Leontyev, A. N.: Problems of the development of the mind. (Union of Soviet Socialist Republics, Progress Publishers 1981)

Li, M-S. et al.: ATHENA DB5.3 ATHENA contribution to interoperability policy action plan Version 1 http://www.athena-ip.org/ Public documents (2006) Cited Dec 2007

Lillehagen, F.: Visual extended enterprise engineering embedding knowledge management, systems engineering and work execution, In: *IFIP International Enterprise Modelling Conference, IEMC '99,* Verdal, Norway (1999)

Lillehagen, F.: The foundation of the AKM Technology. In: *CE 2003,* ed by Jardim-Goncalves, R., Cha, H., Steiger-Garcao, A.: *Proceedings of the 10th International Conference on Concurrent Engineering,* Madeira, Portugal, July 2003 (A.A. Balkema Publishers, Netherlands 2003)

Lillehagen, F., Dehli, E., Fjeld, L., Krogstie, J., Jørgensen, H. D.: Active knowledge models as a basis for an infrastructure for virtual enterprises, In: *IFIP Conference on Infrastructures for Virtual Enterprises (PRO-VE),* Sesimbra, Portugal (Kluwer, Dordrecht 2002)

Lillehagen, F., Krogstie, J., Jørgensen, H. D., Hildrum, J.: Active knowledge models for supporting eWork and eBusiness, In: *International Conference on Concurrent Enterprising (ICE),* Rome, Italy (2002)

Lindland, O. I., Sindre, G., Sølvberg, A.: Understanding quality in conceptual modeling, IEEE Software 11(2), 42–49 (1994)

Loos, P., Allweyer, T.: *Process Orientation and Object-Orientation – An Approach for Integrating UML with Event-Driven Process Chains (EPC)* (University of Saarland, Germany 1998)

Malan, R., Bredemeyer, D.: Software architecture: Central concerns, key decisions, *Software Architecture* (Bredemeyer Consulting 2002)

Malmqvist, J.: *Towards Computational Design Methods for Conceptual and Parametric Design.* Ph.D. thesis, Chalmers University of Technology, Göteborg, Sweden (1993)

Manola, F., Miller, E.: RDF primer. http://www.w3.org/TR/rdf-primer/ (2004) Cited Dec 2007

Marshall, C.: *Enterprise Modeling with UML* (Addison-Wesley, Reading MA 1999)

McGuinness, D. L.: Ontologies come of age. In: *Spinning the Semantic Web: Bringing the World Wide Web to Its Full Potential* ed by Fensel, D., Hendler, J.A., Lieberman, H., Wahlster, W. pp. 171–195 (MIT Press, Cambridge, MA 2003)

Medina-Mora, R., Winograd, T., Flores, R., Flores, F.: The action workflow approach to workflow management technology, In: *ACM CSCW Conference,* Toronto, Ontario, Canada (1992)

Mertins, K., Rabe, M., Jäkel, F.-W.: Neutral template libraries for efficient distributed simulation within a manufacturing system engineering platform, In: *Winter Simulation Conference,* pp. 1549–1557 Orlando, USA (2000)

Meyer, P. et al.: ATHENA B3 Working Document Economic Theories of Interoperability (2006)

MISSION http://www.ims-mission.de/ (2003) Cited Dec 2007

Moody, D. L., Shanks, G. G.: What makes a good data model? Evaluating the quality of entity relationship models, In: *Proceedings of the 13th International Conference on the Entity-Relationship Approach (ER'94)*, pp. 94–111, Manchester, England (1994)

Morecroft, J.: Visualising and rehearsing Strategy, Business Strategy Review, 10(3), 17–32 (1999)

Morris, C.: *Signs, Language and Behavior* (Prentice Hall, New York 1946)

Mühlen, M. Z., Becker, J.: Workflow management and object-orientation – A matter of perspectives or why perspectives matter, In: *OOPSLA Workshop on Object-Oriented Workflow Management*, Denver, USA (1999)

NOAA Observing Systems Architecture (NOSA). http://www.nosa.noaa.gov/ (2007) Cited Dec 2007

Nonaka, I.: A dynamic theory of organizational knowledge creation, Organization Science 5(1) 14–37 (1994)

Nonaka, I., Takeuchi, H.: *The Knowledge-Creating Company* (Oxford University Press, New York 1995)

Nysetvold, A. G., Krogstie, J.: Assessing business process modeling languages using a generic quality framework. *Advanced Topics in Database Research* (Idea Group 2006)

OAGIS http://www.openapplications.org (2007) Cited Dec 2007

Object Management Group (OMG) http://www.omg.org (2007) Cited Dec 2007

OMG Workflow Management Facility v. 1.2, Object Management Group (2000)

Österle, H., Fleisch, E., Alt, R.: *Business Networking – Shaping Collaboration between Enterprises*, Second Revised and Extended Edition, (Springer, Berlin Heidelberg New York 2001)

Osterweil, L. J. Software processes are software too, In: *ICSE Conference*, Monterey, California, USA (1987) Ould, M. A.: *Business Processes – Modeling and Analysis for Re-engineering and Improvement* (Wiley, Beverly Hills 1995)

OWL-S 1.1 Release http://www.daml.org/services/owl-s/ (2004) Cited Dec 2007

Pahl, G., Beitz, W.: *Engineering Design: A systematic approach* (Springer, Berlin Heidelberg New York 1996)

Picot, A., Rippberger, T., Wolff, B.: The fading boundaries of the firm: The role of information and communication technology, Journal of Institutional and Theoretical Economics, 152, 65–84

Polanyi, M.: *The Tacit Dimension* (Routledge, London 1966)

Porter, M. E.: *Competitive Advantage: Creating and Sustaining Superior Performance* (Free Press, New York 1985)

Powers: *Practical RDF* (O'Reilly, Sebastopol, CA 2003)

PRR: Production Rule Representation – Request for Proposal http://www.omg.org/ cgi-bin/doc?br/2003-9-3 (2003) Cited Dec 2007

Rabe, M., Jäkel, F.-W.: Simulation for globally distributed enterprises, In: *12th European Simulation Symposium (ESS)*, pp. 322–327 Hamburg (2000)

RIF – Rule Interchange Format http://www.w3.org/2005/rules/ (2003) Cited Dec 2007

Riskus, J.: Which architecture firms are using BIM? why?, AIArchitect, **14**(27) (April 2007)

Rosettanet http://www.rosettanet.org (2007) Cited Dec 2007

SBVR: Semantics of Business Vocabulary and Rules Interim Specification. http://www.omg.org/cgi-bin/doc?dtc/2006-08-05 (2006) Cited Dec 2007

Scagno, G.: Evaluation of the EXTERNAL tools applied to EXTERNAL use case, Deliverable from the EXTERNAL Project, Patras, Greece (2002)

Scheer, A. W.: *ARIS- Business Process Framework* (3rd ed.) (Springer, Berlin Heidelberg New York 1999)

Schön, D. A.: *The Reflective Practitioner* (Ashgate, Aldershot, UK 1983)

Schumpeter, J. A.: *Business Cycles: A Theoretical and Statistical Analysis of the Capitalist Process* (McGraw-Hill, New York 1939)

Schumpeter, J. A.: *Capitalism, Socialism, and Democracy* (Harper, New York 1942) Schutz, A.: *Collected Papers* (Njihoff, Netherlands 1962)

Searle, J.: *Speech Acts* (Cambridge University Press, UK 1969)

Senge, P.: *The Fifth Discipline: The Art and Practice of the Learning Organization* (Century Business Publishers, London 1990)

Shapiro, C., Varian, H.: *Information Rules: A Strategic Guide to the Network Economy* (Harvard Business School Press, Boston, MA 1999)

Singh, B., Rein, G. L.: Role Interaction Nets (RINs); A Process Description Formalism, Technical Report CT-083-92, MCC, Austin, Texas (1992)

Smith, M., Welty, C., McGuinness, D. L. (eds): OWL Web Ontology Language Guide. from http://www.w3.org/TR/owl-guide/ (2004) Cited Dec 2007

Sowa, J. F., Zachman, J. A.: Extending and formalizing the framework for information systems architecture, IBM Systems Journal, **31**(3) (1992)

Staab, S., Studer, R. (eds): *Handbook on Ontologies.* (Springer, Berlin Heidelberg New York 2004)

Stahl, T., Völter, M.: *Model-Driven Software Development: Technology, Engineering, Management* (Wiley, Chichester, UK 2006)

Strømseng, K., Olsson, N., Haake, J., Scagno, G.: EE Requirements, Deliverable 3-31-D-2000-01-1, The EXTERNAL Project, Oslo, Norway (2000)

Störle, H.: Describing process patterns with UML, In: *EWSPT 2001.* Lecture Notes in Computer Science 2077 (Springer, Berlin Heidelberg New York 2001)

Suchman, L.: Do categories have politics?, Computer Supported Cooperative Work, **2**(3) (1994)

SysML http://www.sysml.org/ (2007) Cited Dec 2007

TEAF http://www.eaframeworks.com/TEAF/index.html (2007), Cited Dec 2007

The Open Group architectural framework (TOGAF), http://www.opengroup.org/togaf/ (2000). Cited Dec 2007

Tinella, S., Karlsen, D., Lillehagen, F., Smith, M. W.: Model driven operational solution: The user environment portal server. In: *CE 2003*, ed by Jardim-Goncalves, R., Cha, H., Steiger-Garcao, A. Proceedings of the 10th

International Conference on Concurrent Engineering, Madeira, Portugal. July 2003 (A.A. Balkema Publishers, 2003)

Tølle, M., Bernus, P., Vesterager, J.: Reference models for virtual enterprises, In: *IFIP Conference on Infrastructures for Virtual Enterprises (PRO-VE)*, Sesimbra, Portugal (Kluwer, Dordrecht 2002)

Twidale, M. B., Marty, P. F.: Coping with errors: The importance of process data in robust sociotechnical systems, In: *ACM CSCW Conference*, Philadelphia, USA (2000)

Ullmer, B., Ishii, H.: Emerging frameworks for tangible user interfaces, IBM Systems Journal **39**(3/4) 2000

UML Specification v. 1.5, Object Management Group (2002)

Varian, H. R., Farrell, J., Shapiro, C.: *The Economics of Information Technology – An Introduction* (Cambridge University Press, UK 2004)

Vernadat, F. B.: *Enterprise Modelling and Integration: Principles and Applications* (Chapman & Hall, UK 1996)

Vernadat, F. B.: The CIMOSA languages. In: *Handbook of Architectures of Information Systems* ed by Bernus, P., Mertins, K., Schmidt, G. (Springer, Berlin Heidelberg New York 1998)

Vinnex: http://www.fy.chalmers.se/m/wingquist/vinnex/ (2007) Cited Dec 2007(Virtual Canada 2005)

Virtual Canada http://www.i-mmersion.com/sim_virtualcanada.shtml (2005) Cited Dec 2007

Voluntary Interindustry Commerce Solution VICS Collaborative Planning, Forecasting and Replenishment (CPFR) http://www.vics.org/committees/cpfr/CPFR_Overview_US-A4.pdf (2004) Cited Feb 2008

W3C http://www.w3.org Cited Dec 2007

Walsham, G.: Knowledge management systems: Representation and communication in context, Systems, Signs and Actions **1**(1), 6–18 (2005)

Wand, Y., Weber, R.: On the ontological expressiveness of information systems analysis and design grammars, Journal of Information Systems **3**(4), 217–237 (1993)

Ware, C.: *Information Visualization* (Morgan Kaufmann, San Francisco, CA 2000)

Wegner, P., Goldin, D.: Interaction as a framework for modeling, In: *Conceptual Modeling*, ed by Chen, P.P., Akoka, J., Kangassalo, H., Thalheim, B. Lecture Notes in Computer Science 1565 (Springer, Berlin Heidelberg New York 1999)

Weiser, M.: The computer for the twenty-first century, Scientific American **264**(3) 94–104 (1991)

Weitzel, T.: *Economics of Standards in Information Networks*. Information Age Economy Series (Physica, Heidelberg, Germany 2004)

Wenger, E.: *Communities of Practice: Learning Meaning and Identity*. (Cambridge University Press, UK 1998)

Wigand, R., Picot, A., Reichwald, R.: *Information, Organization and Management* (Wiley, New Jersey 1997)

Williamson, O. E.: *Markets and Hierarchies, Analysis and Antitrust Implications: A Study in the Economics of Internal Organization* (Free Press, New York 1975)

Williamson, O. E.: Transaction cost economics: The governance of contractual relations, Journal of Law and Economics, **22**, 233–261 (1979)

Winograd, T., Flores, F.: *Understanding Computers and Cognition.* (Addison-Wesley, Reading MA 1986)

Workflow Management Coalition (WfMC): *Workflow Handbook 2001* (Future Strategies Inc., Florida, USA 2000)

Workflow Management Coalition (WfMC): http://www.wfmc.org (2007) Cited Dec 2007

WSMO Working Group. The web service modeling language WSML. http://www.wsmo.org/wsml/wsml-syntax (2005) Cited Dec 2007

Yang, G.: Towards a Library for Process Programming, In: *Business Process Management.* Lecture Notes in Computer Science 2678 (Springer, Berlin Heidelberg New York 2003)

Young, J. W., Kent, H. K.: Abstract formulation of data processing problems. Journal of Industrial Engineering, (Nov. Dec.), 471–479 (1958)

Zachman, J. A.: A framework for information systems architecture, IBM Systems Journal, **26**(3), 276–291 (1987)

Zachman framework website http://www.zifa.com (2007) Cited Dec 2007

Zakis http://www.zaxis.com/services-onsite.htm (2007) Cited Dec 2007

Zelm, M. (ed): CIMOSA: A primer on key concepts, purpose, and business value (Technical Report). Stuttgart, Germany (1995)

Ziemann, J., Ohren, O., Jaekel, F. W., Kahl, T., Knothe, T.: Achieving enterprise model interoperability applying a common enterprise metamodel, In: *INTEROP-ESA 2005*, Bordeaux, France (Springer, Berlin Heidelberg New York 2006)

Zultner, R. E.: Quality function deployment (QFD) for software, American Programmer (1992)

Ågerfalk, P. J.: *Information Systems Actability: Understanding Information Technology as a Tool for Business Action and Communication.* Ph.D. thesis, Department of Computer and Information Science, University of Linköping, Sweden (2003)

Ågerfalk, P. J., Eriksson, O.: Usability in social action: Reinterpreting effectiveness, efficiency, and satisfaction, In: *Proceedings of European Conference on Information Systems (ECIS'03)*, Naples, Italy, 19–21 June (2003)

Terminology and Abbreviations

To communicate Enterprise Knowledge Spaces (EKSs), their design principles, implementations as visual models using the AKM technology, enabling model-driven solution design, and model-generated workplaces, we need to describe core concepts and terms using words that are already in use and having different meanings to different people. People are using the same terms in many different ways, and some new terms and expressions are constructed. Thus, it is important to have a common understanding and agreement on how we apply and use terms within our projects.

- **AIF** – Application Integration Framework
- **AIP** – Application Interoperability Profiles
- **AKA** – Active Knowledge Architecture
- **AKM** – Active Knowledge Models. AKM is defined as knowledge models that drive solutions and workplace generation, and work execution driving modeling. Thus closing the loop between describing, generating, performing, and improving work-generative knowledge
- **AMIS** – Approach, Methodology, Infrastructure (and platforms) and Solutions. The AMIS principle is the most important principle of knowledge acquisition, architecting, and representation that lays the foundations for the AKM technology. It rests on the cognitive neuro-scientific evidence that the motoric as well as the mental centers of the human brain have four dependent knowledge dimensions. The motoric center is denoted by SSFT – Selection, Sequencing, Force, and Timing, and the mental by PDCC – Pattern, Discrimination, Coordination, and Communication
- **APM** – Action Port Model, process modeling notation developed by Steinar Carlsen
- **AR** – Augmented Reality
- **ARIS** – Architecture of Integrated Information Systems
- **ATHENA** – Advanced Technologies for interoperability of Heterogeneous Enterprise Networks and their Applications
- **BCF** – Business Collaboration Framework
- **BIM** – Business Information Model

- **BIP** (ATHENA) – Business Interoperability Profiles
- **BPEL** – Business Process Execution Language
- **BPM** – Business Process Modeling/Business Process Management
- **BPMI** – Business Process Modeling Initiative
- **BPML** – Business Process Modeling Language
- **BPMN** – Business Process Modeling Notation
- **BPQL** – Business Process Query Language
- **C3S3P** – Concept Testing, Scaffolding, Scenario modeling, Solutions modeling, Platform configuration, Platform delivery and practicing, Performance improvement and operations
- **C4ISR** – Command, Control, Communications, Computers, Intelligence, Surveillance, and Reconnaissance
- **CAD** – Computer-Aided Design
- **CADSE** – Computer-Aided Domain Specific Engineering Environment
- **CAE** – Computer-Aided Engineering
- **CAM** – Computer-Aided Manufacturing
- **CBS** – Collaborative Business Solution
- **CBM** – Collaborative Business Management
- **CCP** (CPPD) – Configurable Competence and Skill Profile
- **CCS** (CPPD) – Configurable Collaboration Spaces
- **CDIF** – CASE Definition Interchange Facility
- **CDL** (CPPD) – Configurable Design Language
- **CDM** (Grai) – Conceptual Decision Model
- **CFD** (CPPD) – Configurable Function Deployment
- **CIB** (CPPD) – Configurable Idea Bank
- **CIM** (OMG MDA) – Computational Independent Model
- **CIM** (GRAI) – Conceptual Information Model
- **CIMOSA** – Engineering Change Management
- **Concert Chat** (MAPPER)
- **CPD** – Collaborative Product design
- **CPC** (CPPD) – Configurable Product Components
- **CPI** – Continuous Process Improvement
- **CPM** (Grai) – Conceptual Physical Model
- **CPP** (CPPD) – Configurable Property and Parameter Set
- **CPPD** – Collaborative Product and Process Design
- **CPS** (CPPD) – Configurable Product Structure
- **CRM** – Customer Relationship Management
- **CRUD** – Create, Read, Update, Delete. Basic database operations
- **CURE** (MAPPER) – Collaborative Universal Remote Education

- **CVW** (CPPD) – Configurable Visual Workspaces
- **CWI** (CPPD) – Configurable Web Service Integration
- **CWP** (CPPD) – Configurable Work Processes
- **CWW** (CPPD) – Configurable Web Workspaces
- **DODAF** – Department of Defense Architecture Framework
- **DRDS** (ATHENA) – Dynamic Requirements. Definition System
- **DSL** – Domain-Specific Languages
- **DSM** – Domain-Specific Modeling
- **EA** – Enterprise Architecture. Enterprise Architecture is used today to denote frameworks of views, types, and kinds, which describe enterprises, examples are the Zachman framework, DoDAF, TOGAF, and TEAF
- **EAI** – Enterprise Application Integration
- **ebXML** – Electronic Business using eXtensible Markup Language
- **EEM** (GERAM) – Enterprise Engineering Methodology
- **EET** (GERAM) – Enterprise Engineering Tools
- **EEML** (EXTERNAL) – Extended Enterprise Modeling Language
- **EKA** – Enterprise Knowledge Architecture. The Enterprise Knowledge Architecture of an enterprise is a set of structures and constructs developing an integrated but still decoupled representation of templates from these metamodel constructs: types and kinds of views, models and metamodel and submodels (objects), metamodel structures, language constructs, structures of metadata, and type-hierarchies.
- **EKS** – Enterprise Knowledge Spaces. The Enterprise Knowledge Spaces are externalized knowledge spaces of four or more knowledge dimensions that contain mutually and complex dependencies of domains. The dimensions have many layers and aspects with partly overlapping views. This knowledge spaces are formed according to the AMIS principle.
- **EM** – Enterprise Modeling. The process of externalizing and expressing enterprise knowledge related to work execution and learning, capturing situated knowledge for intelligent reactivation, and generation of solutions and workplaces.
- **Emergent Workflow** – Workflow solutions where modeling and metamodeling is viewed as an integral part of the work execution and management, performed by the process participants, as they are the only actors who have sufficient knowledge of the process
- **EML** (GERAM) – Enterprise Modeling Language
- **EMOs** (GERAM) – Enterprise Modules
- **EMs** (GERAM) – Enterprise Models

- **EOS** (GERAM) – Enterprise Operational Systems
- **EPC** – Event driven Process Chains
- **ER** – Entity Relationship
- **ERP** – Enterprise Resource Planning
- **eTOM** – Enhanced Telecom Operations Map
- **EVS** – Enterprise Visual Scenes. An Enterprise Visual Scene (EVS) is a visual team-working environment for designing enterprise knowledge architectures, work solutions, and intelligent services. The four major scenes of enterprises are: The Innovation Scene, the Business Scene, the Governance Scene, and the Evolution Scene
- **EXTERNAL** – Extended Enterprise Engineering, Resources, Networks and Learning
- **FEAF** – Federal Enterprise Architecture Framework
- **FIPA** – The Foundation of Intelligent Physical Agents
- **FRISCO** – Framework for Information Systems Concepts
- **GEMC** (GERAM) – Generic Enterprise Modeling Concepts
- **GERA** (GERAM) – Generalized Enterprise Reference Architecture
- **GERAM** – Generalized Enterprise Reference Architecture and Methodology
- **GIM** (GRAI) – Grai Integrated Methodology
- **GTLS** (MAPPER) – Global Tool Lookup Service
- **HLA** – High Level Architecture
- **IAI** – International Association of Interoperability
- **IDEF** – Integrated Definition methods
- **IEWG** (INCOSE) – Intelligent Enterprise Working Group
- **IFD** – Information Framework for Dictionaries
- **INCOSE** – International Council in Systems Engineering
- **ITIL** – IT Infrastructure Library, a series of documents that are used to aid the implementation of a lifecycle framework for IT Service Management
- **IDEAS** – EU Roadmap project in sixth framework program
- **IDM** – Information Delivery Manual
- **IFD** – International Framework for Dictionaries
- **INTEROP** – Interoperability Research for Networked Enterprise Applications and Software, FP6 508011
- **IRTV** – Information, Role, Task, View
- **KBE** – Knowledge-Based Engineering
- **KM** – Knowledge Management. Performing tasks such as to acquire, capture, structure, validate, associate and store information, to represent

knowledge to facilitate and enable reuse; i.e., recognition, recomposition, reactivation, and restructuring

- **KML** – Keyhole Markup Language
- **MAPPER** – Model-based Adaptive Product and Process Engineering: EU project in sixth framework program
- **MBSE** – Model-Based Systems Engineering/Model-Based Software Engineering
- **MDA** (OMG) – Model Driven Architecture
- **MEAF** – Metis Enterprise Architecture Framework, a METIS template (language) for enterprise modeling
- **MER** – Metis Enterprise Repository
- **METIS** – A general purpose enterprise modeling and visualization tool, allowing model builders to define tailored metamodels and views
- **MFD** – Modular Function Deployment
- **MGWP** – Model Generated Work Places
- **MIM** – Module Interaction Matrix
- **MISSION** – Research project
- **MOF** (OMG) – Metaobject Facility
- **MOOGO** (ATHENA) – Method for Object Oriented Business Process Optimization
- **MPCE** (ATHENA) – Modeling Platform for Collaborative Enterprises
- **MPP** – Metal Printing Process
- **MUPS** – Model-configured and user-composable services
- **NCPD** – Network Collaborative Product Development
- **OAGIS** – Open Applications Group Integration Specification
- **OCL** (OMG) – Object Constraint Language
- **OEM** – Original Equipment Manufacturer
- **OMG** – Object Management Group
- **OOAD** – Object-Oriented Analysis and Design
- **OWL** – Ontology Web Language
- **OWL DL** – OWL Description Logic
- **OWL-S** – Semantic Markup for Web Services
- **PDA** –Personal Digital Assistant
- **PDM** – Product Data Management. PDM refers to the management of all data flowing through an organization that is required for use in the development of new products or in the updating of current products. A PDM includes four components: the repository, the Process capture, the Workflow, the Data capture and management
- **PEMs** (GERAM) – Partial Enterprise Models
- **PERA** – Purdue Enterprise Reference Model

- **PIM** (OMG) – Platform Independent Model
- **PLM** – Product Lifecycle Management
- **POPS** – Product, Organization, Process, and System
- **POP*** (ATHENA) – Product, Organization, Process, etc., result of the ATHENA project for enterprise model interchange
- **PPM** (ATHENA) – Product Portfolio Management
- **PRR** (OMG) – Production Rule Representation
- **PSM** (OMG MDA) – Platform-Specific Model
- **QFD** – Quality Function Deployment
- **RAD** – Role Activity Diagram
- **RDF** – Resource Description Framework
- **RDF/S** – RDF Schema
- **RIF** – Rule Interchange Format
- **RIN** – Role Interaction Net
- **RM-ODP** – Open Distributed Processing Reference Model
- **RosettaNet**
- **SBVR** (OMG) – Semantics of Business Vocabularies and Rules
- **SCM** – System Configuration Management
- **SCOR** – Supply-Chain Organization
- **SDM** (Grai) – Structural Decision Model
- **SE** – Systems Engineering
- **SIM** (Grai) – Structural Information Model
- **SimVision** (EXTERNAL) – Process simulation tool http://www.epm.cc/ solutions/simvision.htm
- **SME** – Small and Medium-sized Enterprise
- **SNPP** – Services, Networking assets, Projects, and Platforms
- **SOA** – Service Oriented Architecture
- **SOAP** – Simple Object Access Protocol
- **SPM** (Grai) – Structural Physical Model
- **SSFT** – Selection, Sequence, Force, Timing
- **STEP** – Standard for the Exchange of Product data
- **Task pattern** – A self-contained model template with well-defined connectors to application environments capturing knowledge about best practices for a clearly defined task
- **TEAF** – Treasury Enterprise Architecture Framework
- **Template** (METIS) – A set of *domains* that are available for modeling. UML is in this sense a template. A template may also include other parts that aid modeling, like rules and constraints for types, predefined searches, *methods* that the user can invoke, styles, and symbols for each object and relationship type, etc.

- **TIP** (ATHENA) – Troux Information Portal
- **TISAF** – Treasury Information Systems Architecture Framework
- **TOGAF** – The Open Group Architecture Framework
- **TRMS** (MAPPER) – Tool Registration and Management System
- **UC** – Ubiquitous Computing
- **UEML** – Unified Enterprise Modeling Language
- **UML** (OMG) – Unified Modeling Language
- **VE** – Virtual Enterprise. A customer solution delivery system created by a temporary and IT enabled integration of core competencies
- **VICS** – Voluntary Interindustry Commerce Solution
- **VoB** – Voice of Business
- **VoC** – Voice of the Customer
- **VoT** – Voice of Technology
- **VRII** – Values, Resources, Initiatives, and Infrastructures
- **VSD** – Visual Solutions Development
- **W3C** – World Wide Web Consortium
- **Web 2.0**
- **WfMC** – Workflow Management Coalition
- **WSDL** – Web Service Description Language
- **WSMO** – Web Service Modeling Ontology
- **WS-CDL** – Web Services Choreography Description Language
- **WORKWARE** (EXTERNAL) – A Web-based emergent workflow management system with to-do-lists, document sharing, process enactment, and awareness mechanisms
- **WP** – Work Package
- **XCHIPS** (EXTERNAL) – A cooperative hypermedia tool integrated with process support and synchronous collaboration
- **XML** – Extensible Markup Language
- **XML/S** – XML Schema
- **ZIFA** – Zachman Institute for Framework Advancement

Index